THE BACK FORTY

"In *The Back Forty*, Darrell Gurney has laid down an effective and inspiring roadmap for getting deep and insightful with oneself at the midpoint—or any point—of life. Disassembling, recontextualizing and causing one's purposeful life going forward, guided by these seven Embraces, ensures anyone a future of possibilities that weren't going to 'happen anyway.' This is indeed radical thinking."

—Marshall Goldsmith, *Thinkers50's only two-time winner of #1 Leadership Thinker in the World, the World's #1 Executive Coach and Top Ten Business Thinker*

"Yes, your first half of life was simply research and development. This outlines what to do with the second half. Inspiring wisdom for any age, don't enter or leave midlife without *The Back Forty*."

—Chip Conley, New York Times *best-selling author of* Wisdom @ Work *and founder of Modern Elder Academy*

"*The Back Forty* is a testament to the unstoppable spirit in each of us. Darrell Gurney intimately shares his own midlife quest for purpose, stepping beyond fear and doubt to pave the way for himself and each of us to have our second half of life be the best half. This is required reading if you want the next phase of your life to be the best part ever."

—Cynthia Kersey, *best-selling author of* Unstoppable *and founder of The Unstoppable Foundation*

"Through his spiritual daring, Gurney sheds light upon the vital subject of discovering one's inner wholeness at any age and stage on life's journey. He moves his readers into a revolution in consciousness: loving ourselves for who we are, for the innate capacities of the heart and soul."

—Michael Bernard Beckwith, *author of* Life Visioning *and* Spiritual Liberation, *and founder/spiritual director of The Agape International Spiritual Center*

"*The Back Forty* is an honest, authentic take on how the most challenging moments lead to powerful truths. It provides an opportunity to examine the past like a scientist and experiment with creating mindsets which will set you up for a joyful present and enriching future. As Darrell points out: 'The only start that matters is the one you make now.' So true."

—Barbara Waxman, MS, MPA, PCC, *coach, gerontologist, speaker,*
author of Middlescence Manifesto: Igniting the Passion of Midlife

"Darrell Gurney tilled the soil of his personal experience and harvested an inspiring process for embracing challenges and living life to the fullest. In *The Back Forty*, Gurney offers a crucial counter to the prevailing pessimism about midlife and shows his readers the best is yet to come!"

—Margit Cox Henderson, PhD, *author of* Optimistic Aging:
from Midlife to the Good Life, an Action Plan

"Ever run into someone you felt like hitting when you turned forty and they said, "The best is yet to come"? Well, if they ducked when you took a swipe at them and then gave you a copy of *The Back Forty*, you'd not only thank them but you'd apologize profusely for taking the swing."

—Mark Goulston, M.D., *founding member Newsweek Expert Forum*
and author of Just Listen, *the top book in the world on listening*

"*The Back Forty* is a profound and engaging inquiry into what it takes to expand when society is betting you'll contract. For anyone seeking to clear their path of self-imposed obstacles, habits, behaviors and attitudes so they can build a rich and fulfilling second half of life, *The Back Forty* serves as a bible of empowerment."

—Sally Helgesen, *author of* How Women Rise,
The Web of Inclusion, *and* The Female Advantage

THE BACK FORTY

THE BACK FORTY

7 Essential Embraces to Launch Life's Radical Second Half

Darrell W. Gurney

Hunter Arts Publishing

The Back Forty: 7 Essential Embraces to Launch Life's Radical Second Half

The Back Forty® is a registered trademark of Darrell W. Gurney.

Hunter Arts Publishing books may be purchased in bulk at special discounts for sales promotion, corporate gifts, ministry, fund-raising, or educational purposes. Special editions can also be created to specifications. For details, contact Special Sales Dept., Hunter Arts Publishing, P.O. Box 14622, Long Beach, CA 90853 or info@hunterarts.com. Visit our website at www.HunterArts.com.

Library of Congress Control Number: 2021941967

Publisher's Cataloging-in-Publication Data
provided by Five Rainbows Cataloging Services

Names: Gurney, Darrell W., author.
Title: The back forty : 7 essential embraces to launch life's radical second half / Darrell W. Gurney.
Description: Long Beach, CA : Hunter Arts Publishing, 2022. | Series: Back forty tour, bk. 1. |
    Includes index. | Also available in audiobook format.
Identifiers: LCCN 2021941967 (print) | 978-1-9674229-2-3 (ebook)
Subjects: LCSH: Midlife crisis. | Middle-aged people. | Self-actualization (Psychology) | Conduct
    of life. | Self-help techniques. | BISAC: SELF-HELP / Personal Growth / Happiness. | BODY,
    MIND & SPIRIT / New Thought. | BODY, MIND & SPIRIT / Inspiration & Personal Growth. |
    PHILOSOPHY / Free Will & Determinism.
Classification: LCC BV4579.5 .G87 2022 (print) | LCC BV4579.5 (ebook) | DDC 248.8/4--dc23.

ISBN 978-0-9674229-1-6   paperback
ISBN 978-0-9674229-4-7   hard cover
ISBN: 978-1-9674229-2-3   eBook

10 9 8 7 6 5 4 3 2 1
First Edition

Published in the United States of America

Edited by Kay Derochie
Cover Design by Liana Moisescu
Interior design by Marisa Jackson for TLC Book Design, TLCBookDesign.com

DEDICATION

*To my second-half/best-half, embracing-of-the-beloved partner
in The Back Forty prime of life, Alexandra Levin.
The workshop continues.
And to all those who subscribe to ever-Becoming
as a way of life: let's play!*

Life really does begin at forty.
Up until then, you're just doing research.
CARL JUNG

❦

Life should not be a journey to the grave
with the intention of arriving safely in a pretty
and well preserved body, but rather to skid in broadside
in a cloud of smoke, thoroughly used up, totally worn out,
and loudly proclaiming "Wow! What a Ride!"
HUNTER S. THOMPSON

TABLE OF CONTENTS

PART I

THE
BACK
FORTY
TERRAIN

MY LAND GRANT

The Back Forty entered my life when a forty-year-old, broke and struggling man sat in his meditation chair at 11:43 p.m. watching his eight-year-old son sleeping in his father's bed because this man's parents were downstairs sleeping in his son's bed, having come into town to lend him more money so, hopefully, he could win a two-year, half-million-dollar custody suit and maintain half-custody of his son.

At that particular moment, experiencing the shame of needing his parents' help at age forty, along with feeling beat up by the family court system, this man was absolutely convinced that his life up to that point amounted to little. He was broke, in debt and pursuing a massive career change, all while struggling to maintain an involved, fatherly role in his son's life. He felt as if he had a big neon sign above his head that read, "Loser!"

This man was me—at my lowest point ever.

I had lived the way I thought I was supposed to: college, excellent grades and numerous activities, then a career, marriage, a kid, an entrepreneurial business, a nice home and multiple cars. With divorce, my focus narrowed, and I simply concentrated on being an involved, co-parenting, single dad.

But, on that night at 11:43 p.m., it seemed like I hadn't done *anything* right. I had nothing to show for myself except a huge debt, an uncertain career future and a fragile relationship with my son. Yet, what occurred at that lowest point I now consider to be a miracle. Because of it, I now better understand how in the darkest of times an answer comes.

What I can only describe as a voice suddenly popped into my head and said, "You are right where you are supposed to be right now to do what you came here to do. It's the second half of life, the Back Forty, that matters. The first half is simply R & D, research and development."

In a flash, I was in tears. Call it a sense of hope, a spiritual wake-up call or the seemingly insane possibility of the perfection of the moment, but a great release of pain and anguish gushed out of me uncontrollably.

I was also immediately uplifted by the idea that, perhaps, as the voice said, I was exactly where I was supposed to be. It's weird but, if I'm experiencing hell, somehow knowing that I'm there for a legitimate and perfectly designed reason makes it more bearable.

Beginning with that night, in that moment, I had a new mindset with which to embrace my own particular version of midlife hell and within seconds the title of a book came through, *The Back Forty: 7 Essential Embraces to Launch Life's Radical Second Half*. I had no idea what those "embraces" were. But, again within seconds, I heard "Your Past, Your Present, Your Gifts, Your Values, Your Initiation, Your Purpose, and A Presence."

Thus, my Back Forty began. That moment launched a long period of discovery, a new contextualization of my life with a new regard for it and a freedom to invent my future. This personal transformation has taken place over many years and continues to this day. Apparently, this Back Forty cultivation project has no end.

Thankfully, the custody suit wrapped up with me retaining half-custody of my son. Yet, I was still saddled with an enormous legal debt. My immediate focus was to recover financially while, at the same time, making a career change. I had no time to write a book. Some years later, in the loving space of a new relationship and having accomplished a newly designed career path, I found enough peace of mind to sit and begin writing down my experience. However, I had no intention of writing anything for others, only for myself to, ideally, undergo a personal healing from a book that I sorely needed to read but which had not yet been written.

If there is a book that you want to read and it hasn't been written yet, then you must write it. —*Toni Morrison*

What amazed me when I did begin to write was that I only needed to take dictation—the book wrote itself. I would begin with the title of each chapter at the top of a new page and then ask, "So, what is this 'embrace' about?" Words would then flow naturally without my thinking. And I wrote them down.

Granted, some assessments and exercises were later added from my own professional experience and knowledge and from my experience with the Embraces. And, over many years and through multiple edits of the manuscript, real-time life "experiments" provided new material that begged to be included. However, in the end, The Back Forty philosophy and *The Back Forty* book are comprised of a unique line of thinking and a bevy of revealing processes beyond even my own ability to comprehend.

Once I saw the book was being written for me, I dove into it, following its direction and accepting its invitation to inquire. I pondered the innovative ideas it offered and engaged in its prescribed exercises. Upon completion, I was inspired to begin.

Yes, to *begin*.

Just as the term "commencement" is used for graduation ceremonies, which mark the end of a course of education and the *beginning* of a next stage, I was at my own commencement in midlife. It was time for me to begin. Not to start over. Not to be renewed or revitalized. Not to be re-invented. It was clear to me that I wasn't to be re-anything-ed. I started to clearly see that everything that had come before had perfectly prepared me for this commencement and that I was entering my own "Back Forty" to be who I came here to be and to do what I came here to do. Now.

As I began to sense a new possibility for myself, I considered whether others might benefit from application of this philosophy as well. So, I started a reading group to review the initial manuscript. Many early readers reported that the message gave them hope. One particular individual experienced a total life transformation in the first Embrace alone. Her name is Alexandra. She had a breakthrough insight into what had kept her stuck in a fourteen-year marriage that had gone bad a few years earlier. Upon thoughtful engagement in the exercises, she distinguished the perfect, experimental, research-and-development nature of that relationship, which, in turn, gave her the freedom to immediately (and amicably) leave the marriage and initiate her own second half/best half of life.

What if that is the case in your life, too? What if your own particular circumstances, such as an unplanned career change or unfortunate business failure, were only research and development, a laboratory experiment, necessary for your bigger game to come? Not to be insensitive or morbid; but what if even losing a loved one or experiencing an unexpected health issue is only the precursor to a life of more play, passion and purpose ahead? What might be possible inside that mindset? What gifts, pointers and formulas for the future might be hidden in that experiment?

To wrap up my own Back Forty "initiation" story, through what I can only attribute to the good fortune that comes from using the Back Forty process and playing rigorously in applying the concepts to myself, Alexandra (my early reader) and I eventually connected in a deeper way, and I was blessed to have her become my wife and life partner.

As Alexandra and I began offering talks and programs about The Back Forty exploration and its Embraces, we were amazed as bold individuals flipped on its head society's generally accepted belief that at age forty, fifty, sixty or seventy the best of life/career/creativity/ingenuity/adventure/health/sex is behind them. They're saying "No! That's not so!"

Are *you* also ready to *begin* being who you really came to be and *begin* doing what you really came to do—at whatever your age? *Are you ready to play?*

You may have come to this book with plenty first-half-of-life accomplishments to feel proud of, or you may have arrived with a sense of having missed the boat during the first half of your life with a failure to launch on your fullest Self-expression. You may be experiencing midlife chaos, or you may just feel called to discover more possibility in life than what you now see. Whatever the reason, consider that the only start that matters is the one you make now. (Now is the moment, always the moment.) Consider that life has actually been designed to work this way and that your midlife opportunity is to awaken to and discover all that you've learned from your first half of R & D and to capitalize on it, now, to realize your own uniquely playful, passionate and purposeful second half of life.

No matter what has come before, be it perceived major successes or miserable failures, as Tony Bennett and Frank Sinatra sing, "The best is yet to come, and, babe, won't it be fine."

THE LAY OF THE LAND

To help you decide if you would like to take this journey with us and, similarly, create your own second half of life as your best half, it's only fair that you first get a look at the lay of the land—The Back Forty terrain.

The Back Forty: 7 Essential Embraces to Launch Life's Radical Second Half is a compilation of several powerful ideas, some of which are referenced in the book's title itself. The Back Forty, the name of the philosophy and movement, is a metaphor with a double meaning. It is a creative allusion to the second half of life, whether that second half will actually span thirty, forty, fifty, or even sixty years to come. It is also a reference to the farming term that means an uncultivated forty-acre patch of land with infinite growth potential that lies in a remote, back area of the farm.

Regardless of your particular age, you might call your first half of life The Front Forty. In that first half, you've experienced uniquely individual events and circumstances that may have fostered a mindset of limitation, shaping the way you see your life moving forward.

The Back Forty proposes that your Front Forty, first half of life, is all about research and development (R & D) and that you don't, and can't even, *begin* your true purpose until you've completed that R & D.

Further, The Back Forty asks you to embrace the concept that nothing that has ever happened to you could limit you in any way from being who you came to be or doing what you came to do in this lifetime. It asserts that your Front Forty has been absolutely perfect and exactly what you needed to have happen to put you on the path of your own unique, individual and radical second half.

This bold attitude—that absolutely nothing that has ever occurred in your life has any negative bearing on what is to come—is, indeed, a radical way to live. It's in direct opposition to society's cultural conversation about victimhood as well as aging and defies our conscious and subconscious belief systems, which have been shaped by a subtle, societal depiction of a bell-curve model of life. Society asserts that we gradually rise and supposedly peak at some point of "the best life has to offer us" (and that we have to offer life), and then we begin a slow decline. This viewpoint I call the "Down and Out Model."

As we age, this "Down and Out" belief system forecasts that we become less creative, less vibrant, less bold, less risk-taking, less vital, less energetic, less entrepreneurial, less playful and all around less (not more) of who we truly are.

Problems abound with that picture. Inside that anti-climactic model, we are left disappointed and depressed when we realize, only after the fact, that our prime came and went without notice or celebration because we weren't even aware of when we had supposedly "peaked." A second problem is that the assertion is actually not true, but simply a bunch of BS (belief system) that covertly shuts down the greater Self-expression still available within us.

In contrast, The Back Forty says life is *not* an eventual decline but rather a shooting out the top in a radical, contrary "Up and Out Model." The Back Forty asserts that all the creativity, vibrancy, boldness, risk-taking, vitality, energy and playfulness of your past was only the warm-up and precursor to your future. . .with no final peaks assumed.

What if, truly, your biggest game is still ahead of you, no matter what your age or what you've been through? That is exactly what The Back Forty way of thinking proposes and what many are beginning to align with. The Back Forty says no matter what you have or have not accomplished, your growing number of years on the planet serve a function of *staging* rather than aging.

In the world of theatre, staging is the carefully planned preparation for a production. The Back Forty proposes that, just as in theatre, everything in your life is constructed and laid out for the big "play" yet to be performed. This dynamic is occurring *continuously* with yesterday supporting today and tomorrow. Using another metaphor, in the field of rocketry staging refers to the in-flight separation of sequential stages (pieces) from a multi-stage rocket. Each stage does its job to propel the rocket. Similarly, the more the previous stages of your life do their job and drop away, the higher you'll fly. This Back Forty adventure will reveal that the past has done its job, and now you can shoot upwards without any previously perceived weight.

What would staging gracefully versus aging gracefully be like for you? I don't know specifically, but I do know that it would definitely include your stepping up and into greater possibility.

For those of us coming into the second half of life with perhaps few victories or not much of a foundation under our feet (those of us *truly* beginning right now), the idea that literally anything is possible from here on out is hugely exhilarating. And, even if you've already amassed so many accomplishments and such abundance of wealth and satisfaction in your life that you don't *need* to do a damn thing in your remaining years, what might be possible if you actually believed that the first half was simply a prelude to your truest Self-expression yet to come? Could you envision an even bigger game still to be played?

Radical thoughts! Thus, the idea of a "Radical Second Half."

Inside this possibly new-to-you mindset, you can begin to sow a yet uncultivated, limitlessly potential-laden patch of second-half years. This patch, your Back Forty, if given all the attention and nurturing it deserves, will become even more bountiful and fruitful than that Front Forty patch of research and development. It will produce a harvest of more play, passion and purpose than you'd have ever thought possible out of what could have easily become a neglected, overlooked and unpromising backside of life.

Interested?

CULTIVATING THE
BACK FORTY

Great, you *are* interested! Okay, let's plow ahead!

Here's what's necessary to cultivate the ground of your coming years. You must actively engage in and grow your Back Forty fields which, for the most part, have been given little thought other than perhaps saving money so that you would have the means to keep your body functioning in "retirement."

The word "retire" comes from French roots meaning "to draw back." God bless you if you have the wherewithal to draw back at this point in life . . .or want to. Yet, even with financial security in place, what might you accomplish for your Self and the world if you were to choose to play forward versus draw back?

For those of us in no financial position to consider retiring, playing forward inside of a model that says our best is still to come frees us up from the weight of guilt, shame and blame connected to a seemingly "failed" or "under-achieved" first half.

Note the quotation marks because failure or under-achievement don't actually exist in a staging model. Each sequential stage is appreciated for the perfect and necessary power it provides to elevate us to our next stage and even higher expression of Self—that capitalized Self, that bigger possibility of Being we all have within us that's connected to all of life and possesses supernatural powers and intelligence. Intuition, compassion, love, joy, unity and wisdom beyond our learnings are some elements of that higher Self.

Contrast this Big S Self with the small s self, which is more isolated, self-concerned and smaller-minded. Judgment, survival, ego, separation and a me-first attitude are some aspects of the small s self, which also resides within us. In cultivating your unique and individual expression of an unlimited and, therefore, radical second half through the Back Forty Embraces, you'll bring about more of the bigger Self into your experience and thereby contribute more of that bigger Self and its accompanying possibility to the world. More about this later. Just know that no matter what your experience of life thus far, if recontextualized in a transformative Back Forty way, it will contain the perfect and necessary power to propel you into your Big S Self.

I invite you, personally, to express your own greatest yet-to-be Self.

THE SEVEN EMBRACES

The invitation is to dive into this Back Forty exploratory adventure, where you will discover more play, passion and purpose by not just considering but *embracing* seven elements—some from the life you've lived so far (your Front Forty) and some from the second "half" of life that lies ahead (your Back Forty). These Seven Embraces are

Your Past
Your Present
Your Gifts
Your Values

Your Initiation

Your Purpose

A Presence

The word "embrace" means to grasp in one's arms, to hug, to take or receive gladly or eagerly, to accept willingly. Some of the elements in the list above are not aspects of your life that you've considered hugging gladly. Some have been colored by seemingly negative events or circumstances that happened to you in the past. Others include unwanted things happening now, making an embrace seem all but impossible. Still others are elements that you simply haven't recognized or thought about yet.

I propose that you take time to engage in not just a friendly side hug or superficial squeeze of these seven elements, but a full-bodied, full-Being *Embrace*. Doing so can and will have what comes next for you be a life that wasn't just "going to happen anyway." It won't be common or expected. *It will be radical.*

The Back Forty: 7 Essential Embraces to Launch Life's Radical Second Half will give you all the tools and detailed guidance you need to execute each Embrace; but for now, here's a little overview of how you'll harvest from the Front Forty of your life and cultivate your Back Forty terrain.

Embrace 1 will give you an opportunity to **embrace your past** like you never have before. I don't mean you'll gain closure on it or you'll be complete with it, or you'll even find the room to forgive yourself or others for what has occurred. Any of that may happen, but getting *only* those results would be getting the booby prize for this adventure.

You may have already pursued all of those standard goals, which are often involved in resolving one's past. Nonetheless, the pervasive limiting beliefs and subconscious shaping influences of your past may still wreak havoc on your life in both subtle and substantial ways.

Embrace 1 gives you a new understanding of how your past came to be and what purposes it served. It affords you the choice—maybe for the first time in life—to actually *own* your past. Through a systematic, logical and yet creative permutation of the scientific method, along with an investigative approach, you will come to see *yourself* as the designer of your *chosen* past and, thus, the capable designer of a *chosen* future not dictated by that past. If you make the choice to embrace your past through that lens, you will find no one—you or anyone else—was to blame for your history. You will be free to move forward informed and empowered by your findings and following certain directives you'll uncover through your investigation.

Embrace 2 will, similarly, give you the opportunity to **embrace your present** exactly as it is. To the degree that you own being right where you are as the perfect preparation for who you ultimately came here to be, you'll remove all the weight of victimhood that holds you down. Whatever seeming hell you may be currently facing will lose all its scary monster teeth when you assume the power of being "at cause" versus "at effect" of what's going on, and even more empowering findings and directives for moving forward will be placed into your hands.

Embrace 3 will help you discover and **embrace your gifts,** which you (yes, you) bestowed upon yourself through the life design you created. You will find that your greatest gifts and talents are not those areas you studied in your youth but rather the heretofore unnoticed or unrealized aptitudes and expertise that you developed in your "school of hard knocks" and/or "school of life." You'll conduct self-surveys and outside research in such a way as to clearly see how your first half of life built within you the capacities to fulfill the second half you always had in mind—though, perhaps in a Higher Mind than the one you usually turn to.

Embrace 4, the last embrace of your Front Forty, will help you assess and **embrace your values.** You'll see how many of the values you held years ago have changed. The underlying values that define a life worth living (or dying) for only arise through trial and more trial. Using Back Forty tools and exercises, you'll determine what matters most to you now—a now that begins a radical Back Forty of play, passion and purpose.

Embrace 5 invites you into **your Back Forty initiation** party, where any supposed midlife crisis is requalified into midlife opportunity. In

Embrace 5, you reach a necessary line of demarcation and a gateway. It's here where you'll both draw that line and step through the gate into your own Back Forty of infinite possibilities. You will at this point have in hand a detailed, retrospective flight plan showing how you got to where you are now as well as a sky's-the-limit invitation into your radical second half.

Embrace 6 will guide you into exploring where **your purpose** lies. You'll discover that the ideas we were all trained to believe—that it's all about what you've achieved, accomplished or amassed in your Front Forty—is a joke. I claim it's a joke because, if you subscribe to the Back Forty philosophy, what lies ahead of you will actually unfold to be the fullest and most satisfying part of your life.

The idea of finding one's "purpose" has enticed and eluded mankind for ages. In a humble contribution to that eternal quest, The Back Forty offers not easy answers but powerful questions. Your purpose, most likely, will never be a simple answer. Rather, it will arise in ongoing inquiry and continual engagement, which, if earnestly pursued, will have ripple effects you may never actually know of in your lifetime.

Embrace 7, finally and yet infinitely, will help you wrap your arms around the idea of **A Presence**. Your arms, of course, are not big enough to actually embrace the un-embraceable. However, when you're actively inquiring and engaging in a practice of purpose, courting an Energy greater than yourself can support you to play bigger, beyond what one seemingly separate individual could achieve on his or her own.

In a non-religious and yet admittedly spiritual exploration of tools and techniques by which to open yourself up for something greater to use you, you'll entertain the possibility that a Back Forty liberated from ego can have you playing the game you actually came to play.

If you already subscribe to the idea of something greater than yourself as a wind beneath your wings, you'll learn new ways to access that power. If you don't consider relevant anything beyond what the eyes can see and yet you'll humor me, Embrace 7 will at least give you some simple practices by which life can be lightened up. And who couldn't use a lighter Back Forty?

You should know, as you begin this exciting exploration, that engaging in these seven Embraces and cultivating these Back Forty fields is not something to be accomplished overnight. First, you must till the soil of your mind at the source of your life, then plant new seeds of consciousness and water, fertilize and repeatedly weed the garden to get the harvest.

I truly wish I had a magic pill to give you so that you could simply complete these seven Embraces in a day and walk out tomorrow into your all-things-possible second half of life. But you didn't get to where you are overnight, did you? So, it's not fair that either of us would expect instantaneous results. No, a deep and lasting Back Forty transformation, just like cultivating new acreage for growth, requires TLC (tender loving care). That will come in the form of your relaxed time and attention to this exploration.

So, rather than promise you another quick-fix "7 Easy Steps," so popular in the world today, I'm offering a thorough guidebook, program and practice to engage in *over time,* so that an authentic and sustainable new start, or rather, true start, can begin for you.

I suggest that you allow three to four months to immerse yourself in the seven-part process and that you cover each part sequentially. Set aside a certain time each week and actually schedule blocks of focused attention into your calendar to read each section and engage in the Homeplay assignments, processes and mindsets. Consider scheduling goal dates for completing one Embrace and beginning another. Perhaps ask a friend or group of individuals to join you in the exploration so you can support one another with accountability in moving forward.

"Wait," you say, "did you say 'Homeplay'?"

Yes, I said, "Homeplay."

Home*play* is much more fun than home*work*, and the Back Forty is all about bringing increasing amounts of play into your life. In so many ways, our first half taught us to work, work, work. "Play" became only that which was not "work," comprising very little if any of our existence. So, I will be asking you throughout our journey to re-awaken and even expand your relationship with play. What if play became your all-encompassing approach to life, such that it became impossible to recall your old concept of work?

Your Homeplay will not be about finding an "answer" or getting anything "right," a generally ingrained approach to work, but rather, playing around with ideas, exercises and games like a kid with a paintbrush. A powerful, awakened relationship with your Self will come about when you play your way through The Back Forty ideas, draw outside the lines, paint beyond the numbers and learn how each of the discoveries and directives from your Embraces shows up on your canvas of life and guides you toward your purpose. The Homeplay assignments are truly the only way the transformative concepts and new awarenesses can reach personally into your life and do their magic. Never think you'll come back and do the Homeplay later. Do it now. Later never comes, especially in The Back Forty.

Don't worry that this will take too long. This will be a fun and joyous experiment with increasing amounts of lightness coming into your life as you drop old baggage, worn-out ideas and limiting perspectives of your Self and life.

The 7 Embraces aren't necessarily milestones to be mastered, checked off a list and then moved on from. You're not being graded, and you'll never "graduate" from your Back Forty. Rather, staying engaged with these concepts will have you growing more into a Back Forty Freedom Flier every day, soaring ever higher because you've untethered yourself and your life from old concepts and limitations.

Neither will you be all alone in an isolated and solitary discovery process. The Back Forty is an ongoing and expansive territory that keeps widening. Growing live and online Back Forty communities are available to support you as you expand your own radical opportunities for play, passion and purpose. Alexandra and I, as well as an inspired and growing community of Back Forty Freedom Fliers, are here with you. We're all growing and expanding into this never-ending possibility. Plug in, participate, and prove to your Self that a mutually supportive Back Forty is far more powerful than any Lone Ranger, make-it-on-my-own Front Forty could have ever been. Yes, your Back Forty is personal to you; but it requires all of us playing together, side by side, to fulfill its most radical possibility.

To summarize: *The Back Forty: 7 Essential Embraces to Launch Life's Radical Second Half,* offers you an invitation into

- a philosophy that not only reframes any supposed mistakes of your past but beautifies and adorns them with honor;
- an approach to perceiving and holding your past in a way that removes any sense of victimhood, placing you at the head of your first-half-of-life design team;
- a method by which to take charge of the situations, circumstances and conditions of your present-day life so as to create your desired future;
- a toolkit for inventorying your first-half gifts, talents and values to empower you in who you are now versus being limited to who you used to be;
- a contrarian attitude toward midlife crisis which flips that worn-out cliché on its head, having you claim midlife opportunity instead, while gratefully accepting your initiation into a radical second half of life;
- a sense of true purpose from which to live out your remaining time on the planet, intent on being who you really came here to be and doing what you really came here to do;
- a mature, freeing and even mystical relationship with A Presence—whatever you choose to call it—that is bigger than you and is at the source of the infinitely intelligent and guiding Universe where you'll play out your next, best half; and

- an online and live community of Back Forty Freedom Fliers[1]
  dedicated to overturning a social belief system (BS) that claims
  that your greatest creativity, ingenuity, career, relationships,
  health and fitness and even hot sex is relegated to your first
  half of life.

Welcome into a playground in which you engage with others also
inspired by a philosophy that says your best is yet to come. Your Back Forty
begins now.

---

1 https://TheBackForty.com/book.

THE BACK FORTY FREEDOM FLIERS JOURNAL

Some type of notebook—paper or digital—is needed to serve as a regular home where you'll record your thoughts and insights, do your Back Forty Homeplay activities and journal on the various inquiries that will arise throughout the series of embraces. You'll also want to keep track of unexpected revelations that will occur regularly, even outside of Homeplay. These insights, inquiries, exercises and epiphanies will enable you to fly!

I recommend a clean, special journal, something indicative of your high regard for your Self and the lofty intentions you hold for your Back Forty Freedom. That doesn't mean you have to spend hours at the office supply store finding some picture-perfect binder. No, just get something new and clean that you feel good about and label it "Back Forty Freedom

Fliers Journal." (An optional workbook companion, *The Back Forty Freedom Fliers Playbook*,[2] is in the works.)

Next, engage in the following ritual with your Self by writing out and signing the following on the first full page of your journal.

1. "I, _____, declare that there is something greater within me that has yet to express itself fully in the world.

2. I release any idea that I've missed my chance at living the life of my dreams and accept that what lies in front of me is the life I've always been destined to live.

3. I reject any notion that my past or current circumstances and conditions are more powerful than my will to transform them.

4. I allow my Self the opportunity to explore, engage and inquire into both basic and profound questions of who I am, why I'm here and what my unique place and purpose on the planet truly is.

5. I surrender to the process with the intention and commitment to find nuggets of insight as well as full mother-lode veins of life-transforming gold by way of exploration and engagement in Homeplay.

6. I give my Self a chance to authentically seek, examine, and discover truths about my Self from both planned and unplanned intuitive exercises and inquiry.

7. I promise my Self to stay open to realizing the perfection of my life, my relationships, my history, my circumstances, my possibilities and my opportunities for greater Self-expression.

---

2 Find out more about The Back Forty Freedom Fliers Playbook *at https://thebackforty.com/ book. The* Playbook *will provide not only sections for you to complete each of the inquiries, exercises and surveys offered in this book but also bonus information, features and additional journaling opportunities to support your understanding of and "play" with* The Back Forty's *innovative ideas.*

8. I fully expect and allow my Self to experience the next half of life, my Back Forty, as distinctly enlivened and transformed through a new, empowering interpretation of my first half, my Front Forty. I expect to enjoy a radical second half of life fashioned in play, passion, and purpose, unlimited by anything that has come before.

9. This is an agreement I make with my Self, and I can be counted on to keep it."

_____   _____

My Signature   Today's Date

I suggest making a photocopy of your signed agreement and folding it in half to serve as your bookmark as you move through your discoveries. Unfold it and read it to yourself every now and then to reaffirm why you're here and what you intend to accomplish.

If you'd like to expand beyond this agreement made with only your Self, consider forging the agreement with others. Back Forty strength—and greater insight—lie in numbers. Find buddies to play with and to be accountable to at https://TheBackForty.com/book.

PART II

EMBRACING
YOUR
FRONT
FORTY

YOUR PAST

**Until you make the unconscious conscious, it
will direct your life and you will call it fate.**

CARL JUNG

NO VICTIM ZONE

The past and its perceived limiting effect on us is the single greatest obstacle to a vibrant Back Forty life, a radical second half of play, passion and purpose. So, the past must be embraced right off the bat.

We often explain circumstances and conditions by citing something from the past. We say "this is so *because* that happened" or "I am that way *because* so-and-so did or was such and such to me." Implicit in this belief is the judgment that aspects of our past are wrong and, thus, we are *victims* of the past, at effect, on the receiving end of what did or did not happen.

"Victim" is a strong word and not something we all readily admit to sometimes feeling. Even if you're pretty sure that you don't ever see yourself as a victim, just in case, take the following short quiz: Regardless of all the personal, psychological, emotional or spiritual development you may have achieved throughout your life, honestly do you sometimes

- believe that, if certain events and circumstances hadn't happened the way they did, your life would be better?
- think there are certain conditions or influences that would have benefited you better in your past than the experiences you actually had?
- entertain thoughts that the family, friends, people, places, organizations, structures, or even belief systems of your life were or are wrong in any way?
- see yourself as a survivor or an overcomer of any negative aspects of your past?

If you answered "yes" to any of the above, consider that there are traces of victimhood remaining in your consciousness, meaning to some extent you're simply a normal, default-view human being. Often, we can't help but feel ourselves at the effect of (meaning having no control over) influences, circumstances, events and people shaping our lives. We are conditioned by the prevalent, cultural mindset in which we live—a mindset that points to separation-based dualities such as me and them, good and bad, right and wrong, true and false as well as victim and perpetrator. So, it's easy to fall into the victim trap. The majority consciousness of the human race supports it.

But, here's the problem: if you had no say over bringing "lemons" into your first half of life—if you are the way you are "because" of what happened —then you will have no say over what is to come in your Back Forty, potentially your best half of life.

At this point, if you're feeling challenged, maybe even a bit defensive, and are beginning to wonder whether this Back Forty philosophy will support you to achieve what you want in the remainder of your life, the answer depends on which part of "you" you ask.

If you ask the small s self, chances are that the answer will be no. The small s self is that part of you that is attached to your complaints about what has happened to you or the hand you've been dealt in life. It's the part that slides really easily into victimhood. The small s self is committed to keeping you "safe" and "right" about how things have been and the way life is. But, that kind of safe isn't really safe; it's just being afraid and stuck in playing small. And, that kind of right isn't truly right or correct; it's just self-protection. So, most likely, your small "s" self will run from this proposal of responsibility.

If, however, you ask the Big S Self—the aspect of you that is tapped into a greater sense of possibility and inclusivity of all life—that Big S Self is likely to see a fit with this message. The Big S part of you wants to witness both your Self and the Self of others rising above seemingly adverse stories, situations, conditions and circumstances to become inspiring demonstrations of what's possible for humanity. That greater aspect of you gets *turned on* by the idea of a radical second half of life, where all past-based bets are off and anything's possible.

Your Big S Self understands that everyone is simply doing the best they possibly can, and it believes that the Universe is absolutely perfect in its makeup. The Big S Self may even take a quantum or existential view on life that it's all somehow wrapped up together inside a unified Whole with nothing and nobody left out of that perfect makeup. That view sees only One Life going on here, even in the midst of so much illusion and seduction into separation and division between people, places, things, countries, religions, belief systems, etc.

Your Big S Self may even have a hint of an idea, a glimpse that things could be different for you. Either way, fear not; you don't need to become an existential philosopher to benefit from the transformative goodies of The Back Forty. If you are simply willing to ask your bigger Self the "what if" and other similar questions posed throughout these pages and are willing to engage in thinking beyond the "I'm separate," "I'm different," "I'm a victim" paradigms, you'll thrive in The Back Forty playground.

If you're willing to explore and find some sounds-true-for-you answers to the questions raised in Embrace 1, you can release every age-old story of limitation by which you've held your Self hostage. Does that interest you?

LIFE DESIGN: TRANSFORMING BECAUSES

Ask most people why they are the way they are, how they ended up being the person they consider themselves to be, and you'll hear a lot of "becauses." This or that happened to them, which shaped or influenced (i.e., limited) how they evolved to be themselves.

Many of us have lived our lives either complying with our past (not deviating much from our influences and going along with them) or countering our past (going in completely opposite directions from our influences). It's important to notice that either direction is a *reaction* to the past and, therefore, a "because" response to life. To *react* to life is not to **Be Cause** life, that is, to influence, shape, create or *be the cause* of our own lives.

So, how do we Be Cause life? We start with viewing everything in our pasts differently. Just as the shape, size and characteristics of a bowl (context) create varied experiences of the fruit in it (content), the context in which you hold your past determines how that past (content) is interpreted and experienced by you. As the context of the bowl called your life—the frame of reference from which you view your past—changes, it is very likely your perception of the fruitfulness of the events in it will shift.

For example, consider this shift: What if, just *what if*, nothing from your past posed any limitation on your future, on who you are here to be and what you are here to do? What if anything and everything from your past were absolutely *perfect* and *exactly what needed to happen* for you to fulfill on a radical second half of play, passion and purpose? Think about it: *anything* and *everything* from your past—exactly *perfect*. In that context, the value judgments of having had a bad personal history become doubtful.

And let's toss in another idea. What if you actually had a hand in designing your past experiences? If your response is, "Oh no, how could I have done that to myself? How could I have screwed up my life so much?" hold onto this idea: there may have been a method to your madness! We will soon explore that possibility; but in the meantime, it's important to point out that No Victim Zone doesn't mean No Compassion Zone. Judging yourself wrong is no more useful than judging your past or other people or circumstances as wrong.

The alternative Back Forty lens gives you a chance to recontextualize your past, to choose a new reality that actually *empowers* you versus, by default, sticking with your old, worn-out, tried-and-true, disempowering story. Of course, sticking with the default is always easier; but think about it—what good has that old, easy, victim story done you lately? Change your story, change your life.

I don't claim this alternative Back Forty perspective to be True, just as I accept no Truth in the old, default, victim-based mindset. The way "it was" (or "is") may not actually be True, but only what you choose to hold as *true for you*. For the most part, "truth" and "reality" are what we each make of them. However, what you gain from being willing to explore and engage in The Back Forty's unique perspective is an opportunity you can't get by viewing the past as something that happened to you or was done to you from a force outside yourself.

If you live in any way "at the effect of" (shaped by, limited by, weighed down by) the past, **Embrace 1** offers you freedom through *owning your past*. As a matter of fact, until such time as you choose to completely *own* all that has come before this moment in a *causal* way—the word is *causal*, not in any way *casual*—you will stay stuck.

"*Own*," like "victim," is a strong word, but The Back Forty doesn't pussyfoot around; it bucks generally accepted wisdom. To conceive that you can fully *own* your past, present, and future—meaning that you called and continue to call the shots over all of it—is a big shout-out for the possibility of midlife transformation and for a powerful Back Forty second half of life.

Consider a related radical idea:

Your entire life has been a uniquely powerful laboratory for the discovery and expression of something.

Please read that again—and let it sink in.

That's a bold claim. How does that statement sit with you? Does it give you a sense of hope and possibility? Or does it sound like a bunch of positive-thinking nonsense? Remember, I don't purport to possess "the truth" within these pages. Rather, I'll simply offer you a twist of thinking, a model that—if you embrace it and *use* it—may offer you freedom from any shackles of the past.

I encourage you to play with this idea. Try it on like a coat to see how it fits and consider how your life appears when viewing it from this different perspective. Treat it like some gadget you're inspecting fully before purchase. Poke at it. Kick the tires. Check its teeth. Turn it inside and out. But, let's get real with each other. For you to accept that "your entire life has been a uniquely powerful laboratory for the discovery and expression of something," you'll need some fairly convincing evidence, yes?

> *Your entire life has been a uniquely powerful laboratory for the discovery and expression of something.*

I understand that. Until you and I meet up personally one day and can explore together how all the pieces fall into place in your own unique story, I can only use evidence of a personal, anecdotal nature, my story and the stories of others, to show you how this reframing and ownership come about.

Once you have some real-life examples of how the Back Forty approach works, you'll use Homeplay assignments to map onto your own life the model demonstrated in my and other Back Forty Freedom Fliers' stories.

Note I again said "Home*play*." We've all already "worked" very hard, so let go of the idea of having to do home*work*. Don't try to do the Back Forty activities "right," to get the "correct" answer. No! *Play* with these exercises and concepts! Like a kid with Play-Doh®, grab them in your hands and mold them; shape them; see what forms emerge. But, for sure, don't do a drive-by of the personal transformation available to you by only reading the book and not engaging in the Homeplay. Yes, my stories and the stories of others may present convincing evidence to you, but that evidence will *not* shift your own life. You'll only get that shift from the personal evidence that will be revealed to you by doing the Homeplay exercises and surveys yourself.

As you engage in the upcoming behind-the-scenes, constructivist investigation of how your life came together to form the you that you know yourself to be, you'll discover that you've already been playing in ways you didn't know. We call that play "experiments." And, given that you played yourself into these past experiments, you'll want to play yourself out of them while benefiting from the findings they reveal.

So, let's play personal investigators together, shall we?

You can either be a victim of the world or an adventurer in search of treasure. It all depends on how you view your life. —*Paulo Coelho*

The key to owning and consciously benefiting from your past versus being a victim of it and the way to Back Forty Freedom can be summed up as "**because to Be Cause**." That phrase and the transformative twist of thinking behind it—seeing yourself as the *cause* of everything in your life and not simply at the effect of it—gives you the ability, as Paulo Coelho states, to become a treasure-hunting adventurer for the rest of your life, seeking the gold in anything that has or could ever happen to you.

> *To react to life is not to BE CAUSE life.*

Only a shift of consciousness into the new paradigm of Be Cause can open the path to becoming a Back Forty Freedom Flier. That shift is achieved only by accepting that you've *always* had a say over the way life has gone, even though you may not have been aware of it.

So, what does choosing to Be Cause your life look like versus the standard victim fare of "because"? It's fully embracing your role as designer of your life. You either accept that you played and continue to play a causal role or you don't; there's no halfway. You can't "kind of" or partially "Be Cause." Like being pregnant, you either are or you're not, all or nothing. And, soberingly, your choice creates your world.

> *Only a shift of consciousness into a new paradigm of Be Cause can open the path to becoming a Back Forty Freedom Flier.*

Are *you* willing to explore the choice to Be Cause your life: past, present and future? If so, fanfares of trumpets should be blaring. Taking this bold step offers no peaceful return to victimhood. Sure, you may sometimes forget to take responsibility for your life and go slumming again in your old victim stomping grounds with a bunch of becauses, but you won't quite be able to settle in there like before. No, you'll have seen the promised land of Be Cause, and it will continue to inspire you with possibilities beyond the old, familiar, default ways of Front Forty life.

THE DISCOVERY & EXPRESSION METHOD (PSEUDO-SCIENCE AT ITS BEST)

Here's where I introduce you to the step-by-step process that will allow you to put yourself in the driver's seat of all that has happened to you in your life. The goal of the process is to show you how to transform your "becauses"—your sense of being at the effect of your past—into a Be Cause consciousness in which you're in charge of your past, which is the first step in fashioning your future. The primary tool we Back Forty Freedom Fliers use to turn our becauses into Be Causes and to become conscious designers of our own lives is the **7-Step Discovery & Expression (D & E) Method**, which we apply to circumstances in which we have experienced ourselves to be victims, or at least at effect, of an event or influence.

We will look closely at and repeatedly use each step of the process; but for now, here's an overview.

1. Choose and name a serious and significant event or influence in your life.
2. Tell the story (as it occurred then) in full victim form.
3. Identify the phenomena (blessings) from the event or influence.
4. Determine the possible hypothetical research questions you were experimenting for in the laboratory.
5. Own the laboratory and its design: how you picked the perfect lab assistants and ideal lab environments.
6. Determine the possible findings from your experimentation by answering your hypothetical research questions.
7. Determine, or simply postulate, the Self-Expression Directives that have arisen for you from the event or influence (from the experiment).

Discovery & Expression Step 1
Identify and Name Your Serious and
Significant Events or Influences

To implement the first D & E step, we identify and name some of our Serious and Significant Events or Influences. To do so, we consider in which events or circumstances we've seen ourselves as victims and from which we'd like to unlock treasures. The first such treasure may be no longer feeling hamstrung or trapped by the event or influence. We all have some Serious and Significant Events and Influences. And, honestly, unless you are the proverbial exception to the rule, some events and influences from your past still have some degree of hold over you, no matter how much therapy, personal growth and development or even spiritual release you may have accomplished in life.

The types of events we want to reflect on are those held by us as negative: unresolved, unsupportive, unappealing, unwanted, disempowering, disturbing, damaging, harmful, hateful, sad things that happened. Or, maybe we have had similarly negative influences in our past that to this day we believe had some adverse impact on our lives or the directions our lives went afterward. They may have come from childhood or last year; they may involve parents, relatives, friends, strangers, forces of nature, acts of God. Their one common denominator is we perceive something was done *to* us, we were at the effect of someone or something.

We focus on events or influences that left us with something to reconcile. If you sense any limitations on who you can be and what you can do right now and for the rest of your life because of your past, then you obviously have issues to resolve and reconcile. Those "becauses" are candidates for transformation through Discovery & Expression analysis.

When we identify these events and influences, we are on our way to first seeing, and then owning, that we had a very real and definitive hand in creating these events or influences—causing them to happen—and that we chose to have everything occur exactly as it did.

"Why would I do that?" you ask.

The answer is that Your Big S Self wanted those exact experiences so that your small s self could grow to express more as your Big S Self. You came here to be and do something special and particular and unique and you laid out your experiences, perfectly designed, to prepare you to be and do that.

> *Your Big S Self wanted those exact experiences so that your small s self could grow to express more as your Big S Self.*

Believe it or not, that's good news! It means you have no need to seek completion or closure or even express forgiveness for anything or anyone—even yourself. That leaves you with only one element left to resolve: what were you trying to reveal of your Self through those events and influences? That question will be addressed by steps three through seven of the Discovery & Expression Method.

Now, after covering the big-picture lay of the land in which we'll be traveling, let's get into the weeds with a real-life example so you can understand how and why this may all be worthy of your "true-for-me" consideration.

For your life-laboratory-design viewing pleasure, I will share with you one of the first dissections I made of one of my own Serious and Significant Events or Influences, which I have later, inside this philosophy, come to regard as and call my own personal "experiments." Then, you will have an opportunity to dissect Serious and Significant life events of your own.

I realize that the particular personal example I'll share with you may not rank as serious and significant compared to whatever you've been through. What occurs as serious and significant to one may seem inconsequential to another. However, we all process the world and our experiences in life differently. Every untoward personal event, big or small, is ripe for re-contextualization, no matter how it compares in severity to someone else's experience. As you begin this process, whatever comes up for you personally when you consider "serious and significant" will often simply be the lowest hanging fruit in your formative life design, the things that you can access easily in your consciousness from right where you are. Begin with that. Use it. Don't compare it in severity to another's experience or another one of your own experiences, just play with it as part of your own story.

Darrell's Experiment: Overly Critical Dad
Discovery & Expression Step 1: Identify and Name Event or Influence

Engaging in Step 1 of the Back Forty Discovery & Expression process, several years ago when I was first playing with the Back Forty philosophy, I chose the following Serious and Significant event from my childhood and named it "Overly Critical Dad."

Discovery & Expression Step 2
Tell Your Story (as it occurred then) in Full Victim Mode

Here's where you tell the story of your serious and significant event in full victim mode as I do in the example that follows.

Darrell's Experiment: Overly Critical Dad
Discovery & Expression Step 2: Victim Story

My telling of my story is from a present-tense point of view, even though it occurred many years ago, and it's also from a victim point-of-view I held for a huge chunk of my life. This one particular incident was one of many of a similar nature, which, blended together, formed the influential impact of an overly critical father.

I am five years old. It is a cold, overcast March morning on a beach in Virginia. My family is on a pier fishing, having woken up early to drive there and get our lines in the water. My mom and dad are fishing on one side of the pier and my older brother and I are fishing a good distance apart on the other side.

My mother comes over to me and puts two quarters in my hand, fifty cents, and tells me to go down to the little store at the end of the pier to get something to eat for breakfast.

I lean my pole against the wooden railing and walk down to the store. I'm greeted by a large, jovial woman standing behind the counter. She begins talking to me, asking if I am enjoying fishing and makes general, happy conversation with me. I am enjoying the conversation so much that I forget why I came to the store and, after a while, she asks "Do you want to get something?"

I see a display of peanuts on the counter in front of her and, being a big fan of peanuts, I give her the fifty cents and take a large bag of nuts. I'm eating them as I get back to the end of the pier where my family is fishing. When my mom sees me, she becomes livid and says, "Why did you get peanuts! That's not breakfast! I can't believe you wasted fifty cents on peanuts! That's silly. Didn't you see the donuts or honey buns?"

It's not my mother's being upset that is so significant in this moment, but rather my father, who is always very irritable and cranky and becomes scary when he gets upset. He has been raging a bit this morning already, but when he hears my mom, he gets even more angry, yelling, "Peanuts! How stupid!"

I begin to cry, which gets him even more angry, saying "And if you want to cry, I'll give you something to cry about," which means he will take off his belt and whip me. He then says, "You better eat every last one of those peanuts, or you'll be sorry you bought them."

So, I suppress my crying as best I can and walk back over to my side of the pier, pick up my pole and pretend to fish again. I can't concentrate, though, and a huge lump forms in my throat. Even if I still wanted to eat the peanuts, I can't force them down.

Sniffling and holding back my emotions, I decide that the best way to get rid of the peanuts is to pour them into the water, so I secretly tip the bag over and dump them out slowly, so as to not be noticed. The only problem is that, as a five-year-old, I think that peanuts will sink like rocks. But they float! I'm petrified as they bob up and down on top of the waves, and I watch as the current carries them under the pier toward the other side. . .where my dad is fishing.

Did he see them? No, thank God! And yet, I felt for most of my life that this event, occurring when I was five years old, shaped me in multiple ways: lump in my throat when fearful, afraid of making bad decisions, anxiety around having to make any choice in general, worthiness in relation to money and more.

That was how I felt before I chose to Be Cause my story using the Discovery & Expression Method, which I will share with you in a minute, to recontextualize my experience.

But, first, did you get caught up in my story? Did emotions come up for you? Perhaps this story triggered some related stories from your own past, though with different players, situations and circumstances. Maybe your stories were way more serious than this one? Maybe you dismissed this as just some whining babble from the past that should have been gotten over by now? Regardless of any judgment, reactions or resurfacing of your own stories, can we agree that the event sounds pretty serious and significant to a five-year old? Yes? Great. That's all I want to establish for now. Let's keep moving.

I Was Working in the Lab Late One Night

Moving from "it happened to me" to "I chose it," from because to Be Cause, and viewing the events and influences themselves in light of another basic Back Forty premise, "your entire life has been a perfect and uniquely powerful laboratory for the discovery and expression of something," requires looking at our Serious and Significant Events and Influences through a different paradigm, effectively recontextualizing the reality in which they occurred.

Recontextualizing the origin and the purpose of your Serious and Significant Events and Influences is actively and deliberately choosing a new context through which to view and understand your life. That choice is unusual and stands in stark contrast to living in the context of generally accepted default views of how life works. A radical and best second half is not usual, it *requires* this re-contextualizing.

Before I show you how I reframed, recontextualized and thus transformed my "Overly Critical Dad" Serious and Significant Event and Influence—how I Be Caused a new story out of it—and before getting started on the steps of the Discovery & Expression (D & E) method yourself, I need you to participate with me in a critical practice upon which the success of this entire method rests. Are you ready?

MuuuuuuuAAAAAAAAHaaaaHaaaaHaaaa!

Now, follow along with me, right where you are, seated or standing. Join me in sounding this out. It's a crucial piece which will, quite frankly, make or break your efforts. Loudly now. . .

MuuuuuuuAAAAAAAAHaaaaHaaaaHaaaa!

again. . .

MuuuuuuuAAAAAAAAHaaaaHaaaaHaaaa!

get a bit louder and more animated each time. . .

MuuuuuuuAAAAAAAAAHaaaaHaaaaHaaaa!
MuuuuuuuAAAAAAAAAHaaaaHaaaaHaaaa!

Look, let's come to terms with each other, for the sake of your freedom, okay? If you're not actually sounding it out with me, then you may want to look at how much you're really ready to drop victimhood. This D & E ana-lytical process and all the other activities we engage in with The Back Forty happen inside a context of play, not serious work. They require lightening up and being playful versus being attached to and invested in old stories. The best way to create that lightness is to let go, play full out and have fun! We're not going in the direction of darkness. We are headed for the light, so I encourage you to lighten up and play along. If you're not in a place to really let go right now, then I suggest you stop reading for the moment until you can get somewhere else where you can let loose and then join along with me.

Ready? One more time. . . .

MuuuuuuuAAAAAAAAAHaaaaHaaaaHaaaa!
MuuuuuuuAAAAAAAAAHaaaaHaaaaHaaaa!
MuuuuuuuAAAAAAAAAHaaaaHaaaaHaaaa!

Listen to yourself. Who do you sound like? A Mad Scientist, yes?

Let's suppose, for the sake of your Homeplay, that a Mad Scientist is and always has been inside of you conducting laboratory experiments to bring about the Discovery & Expression of something and that all your Serious and Significant Events and Influences were *those experiments* conducted to do just that.

The Mad Scientist motif has been around for centuries as a caricature of a scientist with unusual and even unsettling personality traits and ambitions. Though often portrayed as villainous, evil geniuses, they can also be benev-olent with good-spirited intentions, even if their actions may be eccentric and clumsy. Most relevant is their shared attribute of going against standard human protocol.

In Mad Scientist fashion, consider that *every one* of your Serious and Significant Events or Influences *was a laboratory experiment*. The Mad Scientist within you set it up! You were actually the Be Cause of it all, and you designed it specifically for the discovery and expression of *something*.

Our goal, with help from the 7-Step Discovery & Expression Method, is to begin diving into exactly what can be Discovered from those life experiments and what can be deduced from them as yours to Express. In effect, our intention is to tap into the mind of that Inner Mad Scientist, take ownership of our Be Cause of those events, and glean the gifts they have to give us. Doing so short-circuits any remaining victim-colored interpretations the memories have had up until now.

> *The Mad Scientist within you set it up! You were actually the Be Cause of it all, and you designed it specifically for the discovery and expression of something.*

Given that we are going to enter into the world of a scientist, albeit a mad one, let's take a moment to recall the Scientific Method. If you remember from early school days, we were taught that scientists are ever curious, always seeking to learn. Constantly observing life, they notice some particular phenomenon and create hypothetical research questions based on their observations. Then, they construct a hypothesis (a theoretical idea) in the form of a statement, which is something they want to either prove or disprove. Next, they design and run laboratory experiments to test their hypothesis, producing results from which they determine findings. Finally, they compare their findings to the hypothesis, thereby forming conclusions.

I propose, at a certain level of consciousness, we have been Mad Scientists for our entire lives and have executed this scientific method over and over, time and time again, in pursuit of certain guidance for how we are to self-express in fulfilling our lives—who we came to be and what we came to do. I call that guidance **Self Expression Directives**. Of course, given we're only waking up to this idea now, we didn't run these experiments consciously. Nonetheless, we've all been hard at work in the lab—in many labs, over many, many years, perhaps, even many, many lifetimes.

Of course, this is simply a model, a theory, a particular lens through which to view life, so stay playful with it. If models work and empower us, we use them. If they don't, we don't.

OK, let's hear it. . .

MuuuuuuuAAAAAAAAHaaaaHaaaaHaaaa!

Growing louder and more eccentric each time, you might roll
your hands mischievously over one another.

MuuuuuuuAAAAAAAAHaaaaHaaaaHaaaa!
MuuuuuuuAAAAAAAAHaaaaHaaaaHaaaa!

The most creative and fun part of this model is the Cause Scene Investigator (CSI) Homeplay we will conduct to decipher our laboratory experiments *after the fact* to extract their blessings, findings, and guidance. We will achieve this by working backwards from the experiment itself. First by acknowledging the phenomena we can readily observe, that is, the blessings that arose from our Serious and Significant Events and Influences, we can then postulate the findings and guidance for which the whole experiment was designed and which we are likely realizing only for the first time now. Through this reverse-engineering, we decipher the Self Expression Directives produced by the experiments that were run by our Inner Mad Scientist to support our greater-yet-to-be Self.

> **We've all been hard at work in the lab—in many labs, over many, many years, perhaps, even many, many lifetimes.**

MuuuuuuuAAAAAAAAAHaaaaHaaaaHaaaa!

Discovery & Expression Step 3
Identify the Blessings

The third step in analyzing a Serious and Significant Event or Influence is to ask, "What are the blessings of having had exactly THIS person/thing/event in exactly THIS situation with exactly THESE circumstances inside of exactly THIS environment happen to me?"

To accomplish this next step, we need to remember the power of context. Only from a particular context will we be able to grasp the idea of blessings coming from formerly held "bad" things that happened. That context is treasure and ourselves, "adventurers" in search of it.

Getting into the spirit. . .please join me:

MuuuuuuuAAAAAAAAAHaaaaHaaaaHaaaa!

You may say, "Darrell, now you've gone too far. Do you realize how horrible [this or that] Serious and Significant Event or Influence that happened to me was? Do you have any idea of how it marred and shaped me? You're asking me to look for blessings in it? That's ludicrous!"

If that's you, I'll ask you to continue poking at this idea and inspecting the teeth in this method because you already know how well holding onto [this or that] serious and significant event or influence has been working for you. You may still be white-knuckle gripping it tightly! It's time to let it go, and The Back Forty Discovery & Expression analysis is a way for you to do so.

Just turn your attention, in any possible way, toward what *could* have been a blessing coming out of this or that serious and significant event or influence and away from "that terrible thing that happened to me." By doing so, you'll begin a different flow of brain activity: adventuring for treasure.

Whatever comes into your imagination may be your subconscious talking to you, so pretend whatever comes to mind is a blessing. You may even have to start by totally making up some blessings, regardless of whether you believe them right now or not. When you begin to shift your focus toward finding even the smallest nuggets of sounds-true gold, it will increase your enthusiasm to dig further to find more.

> *Just turn your attention, in any possible way, toward what could have been a blessing coming out of this or that serious and significant event or influence and away from "that terrible thing that happened to me."*

Darrell's Experiment: Overly Critical Dad
Discovery & Expression Step 3: Blessings Derived

Here are some possible blessings I can come up with from my Overly Critical Dad experiment (story). None of these can be classified as "true"; yet, they're *my* newly cultivated Discovery & Expression-based, in-search-of-treasure interpretations. So, I'm not worried about being right, and nobody can debate me. My life, my creative interpretations.

I'm playfully giving myself the right to entertain new ideas for the sake of turning my eye toward the perfection of everything as it has been, which is the direction I'm choosing to go. Change my story, change my life.

1. I developed a critical nature similar to my father's, so I'm able to quickly analyze and see what's missing in situations. Some people notice what's good and right, and then there are those of us who notice what's missing. Sometimes that can be a huge talent of great benefit.
2. It made me a sensitive person, aware of the self-esteem challenges of others, given my own dearth of self-esteem from childhood.
3. It strengthened me in that it created a feeling of intimidation for me around powerful men and authority figures, forcing

me to forge my own, independent path since the prospect of mentorship from strong men was scary.

4. It turned me into a "seeker," because I looked for uplifting environments beyond the world I was born into.

5. As a seeker, I was propelled to experience a bigger world, outside of my small hometown in Texas (e.g., Austin for college; Europe for working overseas; Los Angeles for career, etc.).

6. What I then perceived as a lack of positive, fatherly attention led me to cultivate positive attention in other ways, leading to various forms of success such as being a nearly straight-A student, exhibiting a quick wit, stepping into leadership roles, becoming an actor, public speaker, author, coach and trainer.

7. It gave me an insatiable drive to succeed and prove myself, resulting in almost straight As through high school and college, awards on academic and leadership fronts and public recognition of various kinds.

8. Driven by my resistance to these early, critical, guilt and shame-inducing influences, I sought education and awareness in esoteric and spiritual realms that were light years beyond the culture of my upbringing.

9. It made me open and "coachable," as I sought missing fatherly wisdom from philosophers, teachers, and trainers of various sorts, though always in group formats.

10. The doubt and self-esteem issues gave me a private side, a basic Lone Ranger-ness and underlying shyness, which is probably the only way I could ever accomplish such a solitary activity as writing this or any book!

How's that for analyzing blessings from something I formerly held as a "bad thing" that happened to me? Much of this could be seen as favorable impacts and the development of admirable personal qualities! Those are blessings I wrangled myself into gleaning from a supposedly negative event or influence.

Now, you might say I'm rationalizing or "turning lemons into lemonade." You may believe it was, in reality, a truly negative event or influence that I'm just trying to somehow put a positive spin on. I understand that argument, but any negativity of the event or influence depends on my perceiving myself as being a victim to it. The blessings derived from the fishing pier event and overly critical father influence *change the picture entirely* so that the event and influence can easily be perceived as

> *I'm playfully giving myself the right to entertain new ideas for the sake of turning my eye toward the perfection of everything as it has been, which is the direction I'm choosing to go. Change my story, change my life.*

being hugely positive and perfect for me (i.e., there never were any lemons.)

> I saw grief drinking a cup of sorrow and called out, "It tastes sweet, does it not?" "You've caught me," grief answered, "and you've ruined my business. How can I sell sorrow when you know it's a blessing?" —*Rumi*

See how we are now getting into the alternative perception of the past that I mentioned earlier? Let's keep exploring. Had I actually been the Be Cause of this experiment so as to reap those exact blessings? If so, what other findings might have come out of the experiment? The remainder of the Discovery & Expression steps will reveal the answers.

> *Any negativity of the event or influence depends on my perceiving myself as being a victim to it.*

Discovery & Expression Step 4
Hypothetical Research Questions

While setting up an experiment, a scientist proposes certain research questions that may be answered in the laboratory experiment. To enable me to, in effect, walk backwards through this laboratory experiment, "Overly Critical Dad," I want to figure out what my Mad Scientist might have been researching for that produced these results (the blessings). What questions might he have had in mind?

Think of all the experiments you've heard of being conducted out in the world: clinical trials; psychological and behavioral studies; academic, social and cultural investigations and laboratory tests of small or massive proportions. All of them are initiated by some basic research questions from which the hypotheses are formed. A couple examples will demonstrate.

First, let's take a look at Harry Harlow's research on the needs of infant monkeys.[3]

- Possible Hypothesis: The psychological needs of an infant will prevail over physiological needs.
- Possible Research Question: What will be the effect of taking a group of newborn monkeys away from their mothers and giving them a choice between hard-wire and terrycloth surrogates for touch purposes when one surrogate has food and the other doesn't, or even isolating a group of these monkeys away from any touch whatsoever for several months?
- By testing baby monkeys in various controlled settings, Harlow proved that the terrycloth mother surrogate was chosen more often than the hard-wire surrogate, even though the latter provided necessary sustenance: milk. Therefore, the findings proved the hypothesis true.

In our second illustrative experiment, The Stanford Prison Experiment,[4] these were the hypothesis, research questions and findings:

---

3 See Harry F. Harlow's "Monkey Love Experiments" at https://www.verywellmind.com/ harry-harlow-and-the-nature-of-love-2795255.
4 See the Stanford Prison Experiment at https://www.prisonexp.org/.

- Possible Hypothesis: Prisoners and prison guards have inherent traits which cause abusive behavior in prisons.
- Possible Research Question: What will happen if an environment is constructed in which normal, everyday people are given the perception of power over others, such as being a guard over a prison inmate, and to what degree will those people utilize that power, even to the point of abuse?
- Through testing with normal, psychologically healthy students over six days in the basement of Stanford's psychology building, it was clearly demonstrated that people—regardless of their normal, individual personalities—would somehow change and adapt to the situation in which they found themselves. Power and subservience were shown to be elements induced by a particular environment and not inherent traits. Therefore, the findings proved the hypothesis false.

We're going to use this same hypothesis and research-question process in a more playful, creative and broad way to continue our discovery into the mind of the Mad Scientist within us, who has been creating lab experiments for us throughout the first half of our lives. We aren't so much interested in proving a hypothesis true or false as in the research questions themselves. Again, the difference between our endeavor and the strict scientific model is that we have no idea what our subconscious Scientist might have been trying to get at. For us, it's the *answers* (*the findings*) to the questions behind the lab experiments (the serious and significant events or influences) that we want to discover. Those findings, when informed by the blessings we've already determined, then reveal the ultimate goal and direction of our experiments, giving us directives for living. To do this, we put on our Mad Scientist wig and

> *It's the answers (the findings) to the questions behind the lab experiments (the serious and significant events or influences) that we want to discover.*

become creative again, setting aside the need for any "right" answers and simply playing with ideas on the imaginative side of the brain.

Darrell's Experiment: Overly Critical Dad
Discovery & Expression Step 4: Hypothetical Research Questions

Considering the blessings I've identified as coming from my Mad Scientist's experiment, Overly Critical Dad, and drawing from certain knowledge of myself and my life, I can creatively speculate that the following may have been some of the research questions my Mad Scientist was experimenting for in the laboratory of "Experiment: Overly Critical Dad." Working backwards from the blessings, I formulated these hypothetical questions:

A. Can a self-critical guy who has been taught to question himself, to drive himself hard to prove himself worthy, ever actually learn to love himself?

B. Can a person influenced early toward low self-esteem build a solid foundation of authentic, high Self-esteem later in life, rather than just a veneer of self-confidence overlying a chasm of insecurity?

C. Can someone afraid of strong male authority develop an empowered relationship with it? Or, can he benefit from this apparent insecurity by actually learning to trust himself more while relying less on the good opinion of others?

D. Can an individual driven to run from his roots and root influences come to terms with those roots in a way that empowers himself and others?

E. Can Self-acceptance be learned after self-rejection has been ingrained?

Okay, that was an admittedly deep dive. Notice how I formulated the questions impersonally from the objective point of view of a scientist. But, get this: though initiated so many years ago, this experiment had me as a test subject on some rather broad research questions that could only be answered through the later evolvement of my life.

The questions I proposed, we could say, formed the basis of my Mad Scientist's experiment. You can see that I'm drawing from a lot of historical self-knowledge and certain lifetime insecurities, which no doubt played a big role in my first half of life, influencing my actions, choices and directions. You, too, may have similar, early-adopted self-doubts that have colored your past and the paths you've taken.

As you begin to play with these ideas when you investigate your own Serious and Significant Events and Influences, know that there's no "right" way to do this process. Your own postulated questions may be lighter or deeper than mine are for this particular experiment (story). Either way, it's a creative endeavor, like painting on a blank canvas. Just tap into your intuition along with your knowledge of yourself and your life, and trust what comes to you, as I did.

MuuuuuuuAAAAAAAAAHaaaaHaaaaHaaaa!

Discovery & Expression Step 5
Laboratory Design

All viable scientific experiments must be controlled. So, as we reverse-engineer the steps of our Mad Scientist in action, we want to now look at how he or she set up this experiment in *exactly* the way it needed to be put together to legitimately test for answers to those hypothetical research questions. We want to discover how the experiment was organized with exactly the right Lab Assistants and the perfect Lab Environment to get the most controlled and accurate findings out of the research questions.

This is highly creative work, so let's get a big dose of Madness to move us forward.

MuuuuuuuAAAAAAAAAHaaaaHaaaaHaaaa!

Putting ourselves into the Mad Scientist's role, we ask:

- Why would I create the experiment that way?
- What was and is my responsibility in setting up this lab just as I did?
- In what ways were the Lab Assistants chosen perfectly for their roles?
- Exactly how was this the best Lab Environment in which to test?

Again, wrangling our creative selves to come up with viable, sounds-true answers to these questions begins to put us in a place of ownership of all that occurred; a more powerful place to stand than victim.

Here's what I came up with for "Overly Critical Dad:"

Darrell's Experiment: Overly Critical Dad
Discovery & Expression Step 5: Owning the Lab Design
My Lab Assistants

Of course, the main Lab Assistant chosen for this particular experiment was my father. I hired him well for the role! This man was from the Old South, raised in a farmland setting outside of Baton Rouge, Louisiana. He dealt with cattle and horses while growing up and went straight into the Navy after high school to learn a trade. These settings and these influences didn't foster much appreciation for what we now call "self-esteem needs."

> **Why would I create the experiment that way? What was and is my responsibility in setting up this lab just as I did?**

My father was born in 1940 and Maslow's Hierarchy of Needs came out in 1943, but the two never met up. Southern, male-dominated society worked like this: you did what you were supposed to do—and you did it right or you heard from "the man." You dealt with emotions privately, if at all, and kept your inner feelings hidden deep inside of you.

Add to this personality-shaping environ- ment the fact that my father married at age nineteen (common in the rural South) to experience the love and attention of a wife only to have two kids show up within two years. Deprived of a wife's attention with two babies now in the mix, you now have a twenty-year-old man with a family to provide for and the understandably perfect makings of a grumpy father! This wonderful man filled the job perfectly for the hypothetical questions I apparently wanted to test.

My Lab Environment

If you simply consider the tenor of not only the Old South but also a rural, blue-collar upbringing, the environment had a lot of general toughness to it, akin to a John Wayne swagger. Therefore, again, self-esteem and self-awareness were foreign concepts.

My own sensibilities were more artistic and creative, as opposed to the Texan "Friday Night Lights" emphasis on football, football. . .and, oh yes, football. No doubt, I enlisted the assistance of a typical Texan/Southern dad who had played football in high school and a brother who followed suit. I remember being asked as a six-year-old WHY, just WHY, didn't I want to play Little League Football like my brother and everyone else? The implication was that something must be wrong with me if I didn't.

Football just didn't call to me. Yet my first toy trumpet, picked up at a local fair, inspired me to get into music in fifth grade. I then played trumpet for eight years in the marching, concert and jazz bands.

My interests in drawing and art had me take art classes and enter art contests throughout my schooldays. My interest in creative expression had me acting in school plays and participating in district poetry, prose and one-act play competitions. I won awards in all these areas of interest. In my household, however, these interests were more of a nuisance. "Can you practice softer back there?" was shouted from the living room as I practiced my trumpet in the back, back, waaaaay back bedroom.

Sometimes these artistic activities gave rise to jokes. "How come there are no eyes or noses on the people?" was asked regarding my papier-mâché nativity scene.

Granted, my parents did come to my concerts and plays, initiated by my mom's forceful wrangling of my dad. Yet, recognition and appreciation for my unique interests and talents were not standard in my household.

So, there you have it. The PERFECT Lab Assistant and Lab Environment in which to initiate "Experiment: Overly Critical Dad." No better design could have existed! My Inner Mad Scientist was INCREDIBLY AMAZING in how he put all of this together!

MuuuuuuuAAAAAAAAAHaaaaHaaaaHaaaa!

Though I may have used triggering or emotion-laden words or phrases in describing the lab assistants and environment as I experienced them at the time, the point of this assessment is not to gather yet more reasons to believe in victimhood. Rather, I want to observe and realize with complete and utter fascination what my inner Mad Scientist was able to accomplish in his design of the experiment! The whole point of this process is to pivot from our past path of victimhood to begin viewing our past as much as possible from an unbiased, non-judgmental and disinterested observer's stance, in short, from the point of view of an experiment—an experiment that we ourselves set up.

As you continue to remove yourself from the emotional ties and triggers in your own stories of the past, you, too, will be able to observe events and influences from a disinterested observer's point of view. Note that disinterested doesn't mean uninterested. It simply means unattached to the heaps of meaning you've formerly placed on what happened. An unbiased observer's perspective will birth the freedom to fly that you're looking for.

But, we still have further to go.

MuuuuuuuAAAAAAAAAHaaaaHaaaaHaaaa!

(Remember to roll your hands over each other.)

Discovery & Expression Step 6
Determine the Findings

After all those well-thought-out research questions and laboratory designs were put into place, the inner Mad Scientist ran the experiments! Some of these experiments in the form of Serious and Significant Events or Influences may have lasted long periods of time. Some may have been accomplished within days. You may not even be finished with some of them yet! However, for the sake of introducing you to this Discovery & Expression method, I'll invite you to consider that you've been unconsciously running experiments until the present moment: the NOW point at which you are finally being clued in that they were all simply experiments!

Therefore, because some laboratory experiments may be complete while others are still in process, your experimental **Findings** may vary. Some may reflect concrete conclusions. Others may have inconclusive findings at this point with more experimentation still necessary in order for you to arrive at accurate answers to your hypothetical research questions. So, in some cases, you may need to pull only conditional findings from the currently available data.

> *Disinterested doesn't mean uninterested. It simply means unattached to the heaps of meaning you've formerly placed on what happened.*

Remember you don't have to do this perfectly. You have wiggle room in determining accurate findings based on your NOW best possible assessments.

Though we're playing with a scientific model, let's remember we are *playing* and this is a *creative* process. You won't be graded on what you observe in this analysis. This is simply a method meant to serve as an awakening tool, helping you gain openings, perspectives and insights into Serious and Significant Events and Influences that have previously left you limited, constricted or inhibited in any way.

You're doing great [Mad Scientist] play!

MuuuuuuuAAAAAAAAHaaaaHaaaaHaaaa!

Here are the answers, the findings, I conceived from my hypothetical research questions.

Darrell's Experiment: Overly Critical Dad
Discovery & Expression Step 6: Findings

A. *Question:* Can a self-critical guy who has been taught to question himself, to drive himself hard to prove himself worthy, ever actually learn to love himself?

Findings: Yes, I believe so. The jury is not completely out, but the possibility for progress is promising if I look at how far I've come. Focusing on "progress, not perfection" can, for sure, keep me moving in this direction.

B. *Question:* Can a person influenced early toward low self-esteem build a solid foundation of authentic, high Self-esteem later in life, rather than just a veneer of self-confidence overlying a chasm of insecurity?

Findings: Again, I sense that the answer is yes, as long as I stay on the path of the findings in A above. Guided by learned feel-good tools and principles, this means loving myself and taking actions every day to feel good about me. Self-care is a critical first step for any acts of service, empowerment of others or giving of myself to better others' lives to make any difference.

C. *Question:* Can someone afraid of strong male authority develop an empowered relationship with it? Or, can he benefit from this apparent insecurity by actually learning to trust himself more while relying less on the good opinion of others?

Findings: Maybe both. As I continue along the path of the first findings, I don't project onto "great" men the critical voice of the past and can, therefore, relax and reveal my true Self in their presence. I no longer experience a sense of losing my Self.

Also, I benefit massively from securing approval from within myself. Even if I had received esteem externally from male authority, it would not have filled the need I have, and I believe everyone has, inside of my heart/soul.

D. *Question:* Can an individual driven to run from his roots and root influences come to terms with those roots in a way that empowers himself and others?

Findings: Hopefully. The only chance of this is more and more authenticity. Early trauma in a person's life can have them locked down into personality traits and patterns developed to compensate for that trauma. Running from the "bad" stuff and influences creates a fractured individual. Coming to terms with it, whatever we each consider as trauma, allows a more authentic being to emerge. My path and continued experiment is in discovering this authenticity showing up even more when I own, Be Cause, the traumatic events as necessary for my pre-planned personal development.

E. *Question:* Can Self-acceptance be learned after self-rejection has been ingrained?

Findings: Likely so, as I combine greater authenticity with the findings of B above (loving myself).

MuuuuuuuAAAAAAAAHaaaaHaaaaHaaaa!

These findings are simply my current, best-guess attempt at answering my Overly Critical Dad hypothetical research questions. Yes, there's lots of wiggle room here. But, remember, we're simply looking for insights, awareness and movement towards being responsible for our lives versus being victims of them. We are constructing a viable, creative, alternative view— a different story—not some perfect and final answer.

> *This is simply
> a method meant
> to serve as an
> awakening tool,
> helping you
> gain openings,
> perspectives and
> insights into Serious
> and Significant
> Events and Influences
> that have previously
> left you limited,
> constricted or
> inhibited in any way.*

Your own experimental findings will be what they will, but I guarantee one thing: if you continue to expand your willingness to consider that you had complete say over all those big events or influences in your life, you'll grow into an awareness of your own power, which will transfer into a radical second half of life.

Discovery & Expression Step 7
Self-Expression Directives

Here's where we depart from our pseudo-scientific method and take ownership of the paths that our experiments have shown us.

Most worldly, scientific experiments are cut and dried with the hypothetical questions being answered or not and the related hypothetical statements being proven or not: true or false. Well, for our own Back Forty analytical purposes, we want more than that. If we've put all this time and energy into running these experiments for the biggest part of our lives, we not only want possible findings but also overall direction out of it! We'd like some payoff from all that time spent in the lab, yes?

What else do scientists create in laboratories?

Formulas!

In The Back Forty, we are empowered by the idea that our entire first half of life was comprised of a bunch of experiments which, if analyzed as we've done here, can help point the way toward our own **Formula of Unique Self Expression (FUSE).** Our second half of life, ignited and directed by that **FUSE**, becomes an adventurous and playful array of second-half experiments where we get to Be Cause in the same way we always have—but now *consciously.* The ability to consciously Be Cause our next half/best half is at the heart of the freedom we're here to claim.

Our individual FUSE is made up of all the possible **Self-Expression Directives** each of us can glean from all the experiments we've run along with some other elements we'll add later. To arrive at the Self-Expression Directives from any particular experiment, turn on the creativity again and simply look to see—from the blessings derived, the research questions asked and the findings determined—what direction does it all point to for you? What are the marching orders to be discerned from all of it? What is your go-forth charge, the spark for your FUSE?

In preparation for the big, Mad-Scientist finale. . .

MuuuuuuuAAAAAAAAHaaaaHaaaaHaaaa!

Darrell's Experiment: Overly Critical Dad
Discovery & Expression Step 7: Self Expression Directives

Here is what I found from this experiment to ignite me as I move into and through my second half:

- Self-love
- Self-acceptance
- Self-compassion
- Self-trust
- Authenticity

MuuuuuuuAAAAAAAAHaaaaHaaaaHaaaa!

Yes, a collection of one-word directives—yet each a very powerful and singular word pointing my way forward. For me to live my second half of life from a foundation/stand to embody and express each of these qualities is a profound path to take and completely contrary to how this very same event or influence might have shaped my future from the point of view of being a victim to it. In summary:

- This Method pulls out of you the powerful Self that you are, an aspect of the larger Self that came here to be and do something unique, specific and meaningful.

- This is the key to the gate of your own Back Forty.
- This is the Homeplay.
- This is the direction toward ownership of your entire life as it has played out thus far.
- This begins the road to freedom from all the "becauses" that you've ever held onto, consciously or subconsciously.
- This is the path to cultivating the Be Cause of your own life.

> *The ability to consciously Be Cause our next half/best half is at the heart of the freedom we're here to claim.*

So, at this point, let's put my experimental analysis aside and give you an opportunity to get vividly in touch with, and freed up around, one of your own serious and significant events or influences.

Really belt it out now, because you'll want this energy behind you. . .

MuuuuuuuAAAAAAAAAHaaaaHaaaaHaaaa!
MuuuuuuuAAAAAAAAAHaaaaHaaaaHaaaa!
MuuuuuuuAAAAAAAAAHaaaaHaaaaHaaaa!

Ready? One more time,

MuuuuuuuAAAAAAAAAHaaaaHaaaaHaaaa!

(Be sure to exhibit a slyly proud grin.)

Don't worry if this process is in a bit of a swim in your mind at this point. It's a contrarian way of thinking and, therefore, requires carving new neural pathways in the brain to even grasp it. Comprehending it more fully will happen over time, rest assured. This Discovery & Expression method will only seem like hard work until it doesn't, and you'll be taking it all one step at a time. What will have it become *play* is practice!

Additionally, the benefits of discovering your hidden power and the awesome directions in which your life can now go will create a Pavlov's dog effect. Just as in Russian scientist Ivan Pavlov's experiment in which he trained dogs to salivate at the ringing of a bell, you'll begin to notice that every "because to Be Cause" Discovery & Expression analysis gives you such a sense of freedom and direction that you'll start salivating at any opportunity to do the next one! Not only have I put many major events and influences from my past through this process, I continue to "because to Be Cause" the most challenging, victim-smelling situations in my ongoing, everyday life—getting freed up every time.

> *This method pulls out of you the powerful Self that you are, an aspect of the larger Self that came here to be and do something unique, specific and meaningful.*

YOUR TURN!

This is where you start to treat this book more like a course than a casual read. If you take the time to truly engage, this transformational Back Forty path will begin to requalify anything and everything that lies behind you. That in turn will free you up and bring new possibility to what you'll create in front of you. I wholeheartedly encourage you to let this book be an actual turning point for you, not just a bunch of good ideas.

Please Note: the upcoming Homeplay is the first of many exercises and surveys to come in this chapter and throughout the remainder of the book. I want you to notice and heed the stop signs I'll post along the way. I'll place these reminders after exercises and surveys to alert and encourage you to complete the task just given before proceeding further. That means stop and do the Homeplay if you haven't done it already. Doing so will ensure that you get the value out of this book that you came for.

The gold is in the Self exploration. And, only you can do that in your own Homeplay. Please don't short your Self. Truly engage in and complete the Homeplay exercises, even if the book takes longer to complete. Consider the journey as important, integral and necessary as the end game, which is your Back Forty Freedom.

Embrace 1—Homeplay 1
because to Be Cause: Your Past

Skip ahead to Appendix A on page 431 and read it in its entirety to get a really good feel for how the Discovery & Expression Method works. In the appendix you'll find additional personal Serious and Significant Events and Influences stories—some mine, some my wife Alexandra's, and (with permission, of course) some belonging to participants in our 3-Day Back Forty **INFUSE** (**I**gniting a **N**ew **F**ormula of **U**nique **S**elf **E**xpression) programs. Each event/influence has been taken through all seven steps of the Discovery & Expression—because to Be Cause—process. As such, reading them should give you a strong grasp on how to apply these steps to recontextualize your own Serious and Significant Events and Influences and of the benefits that can flow from the process.

A bit of advice, though: never get caught up mentally or emotionally in my personal stories or the stories of others offered as examples. Just use them to help you realize that it's possible for you to recontextualize everything from your own past to gain power and purposeful direction for your future.

Don't skip Homeplay 1.

Embrace 1—Homeplay 2
because to Be Cause: Your Past (Continued)

Open up your Back Forty Freedom Fliers Journal. Put on your favorite soft, relaxing music. Shield yourself from any possible interruptions for the next hour or two, so that you can focus on waking up your Inner Mad Scientist. You're going to answer some questions, with his or her help.

Close your eyes for a moment and do whatever it takes to become centered and relaxed in your mind. Let go of the idea that you have to do this right or that you need to get a perfect result. You can never do this or anything else right or wrong. You just do it the way you do it! Trust whatever comes up for you as perfect. Assume that what you discover here in practicing this method is *exactly* what you are meant to discover and that it is *exactly* the experience you are meant to have to realize your personal intention in reading this book.

Think of learning to ride a bike: you just climbed on and tried, again and again, until you somehow incorporated the experience of balance into your physiology. That's what you are going to do now: give yourself the opportunity to engage in a new thought process and model.

Notice that the first word in three of the seven Homeplay steps is "determine." Offering a word play, know that it only requires "determination" to view your past differently. Eventually, if you truly learn to *play* with this model, through brand new brain pathways, you'll find a sense of balance and will see how your entire life has been designed for your highest and greatest good and for the radical, playful, passionate and purposeful Back Forty you're here to live.

Now's the time for you to take the Discovery & Expression steps we Back Forty Freedom Fliers have used. Work your way through each one, following the instructions.

Step 1: Choose and name a serious and significant event or influence.

Write down something from your past that you would consider a significant event or influence, a serious happening that you still remember and still think about at times and you still believe has some effect on you. Then write down another and another, perhaps at least five. These are your "Top 5 Serious and Significant 'becauses'" from your past—events or influences that you consider still shape you or impact you today.

Now, *pick one* for you to Homeplay with first.

In your Back Forty Freedom Fliers Journal, write "Experiment 1" at the top of a new page. Then, write a name for your first chosen Serious and Significant Event or Influence. Just make up a short title for it.

Now, Mad yourself up!

MuuuuuuuAAAAAAAAHaaaaHaaaaHaaaa!

I encourage you to play with the Mad Scientist's voice throughout the exercise. It makes a difference and keeps you fun-loving. So, again. . .

MuuuuuuuAAAAAAAAHaaaaHaaaaHaaaa!

Step 2: Tell your story in full, as it occurred then, victim form.

I suggest you write it out long-hand, as if beginning a great, tragic novel. In telling the story, if possible, try to tell it from a present tense perspective as if it were happening now. This isn't required, but it may support your analysis. Be sure to demonstrate the dark, profound and indelible impact that this event or influence has had on you. Give it full meat and make it as clear as possible that you were wronged. Build it up massively. I don't mean to invent anything, but leave no sense of victimhood untapped.

Don't hold back here. Please don't pretend to possess any healing that's not real for you yet. Be as victim-mouthed and woe-is-me as possible. Have both yourself and me, were I personally hearing you describe it, left with no doubt whatsoever that you were completely and totally marred by that event or influence. Tell it like it really is or was for you, underneath any veneer of its being already resolved. Sell me, the one who says victimhood is fiction, on the idea that you are the one exception to this whole model. Prove to me that there *should be* quarter for victims in The Back Forty through the compelling evidence of your unique and special story.

Okay now, stay scientifically Mad. . .

MuuuuuuuAAAAAAAAHaaaaHaaaaHaaaa!

Step 3: Blessings Derived

Switching now to a different lens, look to see what benefits, in the end, actually came out of this event. Find some ways you can acknowledge that this Serious and Significant Event or Influence impacted your life in a favorable, even if contrary, reactive way. What are the blessings of having had exactly THIS person/thing/ event, in exactly THIS situation, with exactly THESE circum-stances, inside of exactly THIS environment happen to you? Come up with at least 10 blessings you received from the experience and write them in your journal. Yes, really. . .10!

Now, revel in your insane genius.

MuuuuuuuAAAAAAAAHaaaaHaaaaHaaaa!

Step 4: Determine or propose the possible hypothetical research questions your inner Mad Scientist may have been experimenting for in the laboratory.

What experimental questions could you possibly have been exploring that you weren't aware of consciously? Get playful with it! Based on the blessings that came out of the experiment, what were the research questions you were testing for and were apparently seeking to answer? Take some time to come up with several possible hypothetical research questions.

How magnificently insightful and exploratory you are!

MuuuuuuuAAAAAAAAAHaaaaHaaaaHaaaa!

Step 5: Claim your ownership of the laboratory and its design. Describe how you picked the perfect lab assistants and ideal lab environments.

Why would you create it this way? What is your responsibility? How smart were you to pick exactly those Lab Assistants and that Lab Environment? Describe how this experiment could have not taken place with more perfect assistance nor in a more perfect laboratory environment.

Amazing! How *did* you come up with all that!?
No Hollywood director could have done better!

MuuuuuuuAAAAAAAAAHaaaaHaaaaHaaaa!

Step 6: Determine the possible findings from your experimentation.

What are the findings from your hypothetical research questions? In assessing the overall experiment as it has played out in your life and what you can ascertain from it, what can you now claim to have realized or discovered as answers to your questions? For each research question, include all possible answers, whether conclusive, inconclusive or even conditional.

Astute! Observant! Creative! You are a most brilliant Mad Scientist!

MuuuuuuuuAAAAAAAAAHaaaaHaaaaHaaaa!

Step 7: Determine or simply postulate your Self-Expression Directives from the event or influence.

What can you now Discover and Express from this event or influence? What can you see as being your Self-Expression Directives? What are your marching orders? How are you to go forth? What was it all for? How will you now become who you came here to be and do what you came here to do? Write out your thoughts in short directives, likely of one or two words. This is the big payoff!

> [NOTE: If your Self Expression Directives point in any direction that limits life, I suggest you read Appendix A again. The goodies you worked for here should be life affirming and expansive of your bigger Self, not aiding and abetting your small self.]

You are Creator! Life, energy and possibility now come into what was a bleak, dark and dead experience! It's alive! It's alive!

MuuuuuuuAAAAAAAAHaaaaHaaaaHaaaa!

FIRST SEPTENARY ACKNOWLEDGMENT

All done? Here's to you. . .and a big whew! I want to acknowledge you for completing that initial piece of Homeplay for Embrace 1 of your Back Forty Freedom path by taking your first significant event or influence through all seven Discovery & Expression steps. These initial steps may begin a complete recontextualization of your past.

Early on, I proposed that, if you began to embrace this new point of view, something would begin to open up for you. And here you are! Ideally, some old, weighty stories are beginning to be dismantled or are, at least, becoming a bit wobbly. Your own continued deconstruction of the becauses of your past is where your freedom lies.

"Your entire life has been a uniquely powerful laboratory for the discovery and expression of something." The Homeplay you just completed is the beginning of the discovery of that *something*.

PRACTICE MAKES PLAY

Embrace 1—Homeplay 3

because to Be Cause: Your Past (Expanded)

Go back *right now* or *as soon as possible* in the next time slot you can dedicate to your Back Forty and use the same 7-Step Discovery & Expression Method around *each* of the other four serious and significant events or influences you uncovered in your first step of Homeplay 2. When you are finished, come right back here. I'll be waiting for you.

If you haven't done this assignment with a degree of thoroughness, spend more time with it. Identify more events or influences and completely run them through the Discovery & Expression process before moving on. Let this adventure be transformative for you, not just some random but intriguing conjecture.

> *Let this adventure be transformative for you, not just some random but intriguing conjecture.*

Keep persisting with this. Practice and play with the CSI (Cause Scene Investigation) process, and you'll get a big bonus from assuming this alternative view: a realization that nobody is to blame in your past, including yourself! You may even actually arrive at a place of gratitude for all of it happening exactly as it did, and for everyone involved, including yourself!

MORE KUDOS AND THE NEXT STEP

I'm so glad you've taken this journey! You've finished your Embrace 1 Homeplay, completing your own "because to Be Cause" analyses on your Top 5 Serious and Significant Events or Influences (or as many as you were able to identify at this time). You've set forth solid evidence against those people and events that wronged you, followed by proving convincing cases for your complete and total Be Cause of it all including the Blessings and Self Expression Directives that they provided.

Congratulations! You are extraordinary. I truly don't say that lightly. Most people avoid the past like the plague: Most people never come close to examining their lives. Extraordinary is someone who would take on this type of deep reflection and heady analysis of the past, all inside of a playful and light mood of exploration. It's no small matter that you're willing to go beyond the majority consciousness that makes up our world. Again, you are extraordinary.

Now, I invite you to proceed through the remainder of this book, *The Back Forty*, because if you can see *but a shred* of value in the Self-Expression Directives that came from the experiments your inner Self set up, you'll find a new life waiting for you, to be lived through you. It is The Back Forty life you came for, and you've done everything you were supposed to do to get here now, approaching its gate.

YOUR PRESENT

If you will let your dominant intention be to revise and improve the content of the story you tell every day of your life, it is our absolute promise to you that your life will become that ever-improving story. For by the powerful Law of Attraction—the essence of that which is like unto itself is drawn—it must be!

ABRAHAM

YOUR MESSY LAB

Viewing your life in the context of laboratories that offer you Self Expression Directives, which in turn help create *formulas for living*, and asserting that you've had a say in your unique life path, that you designed it all for the reason of becoming who you came here to be and of doing what you came here to do frees you up to live a radical second half of play, passion and purpose.

But, you may ask, is this idea that we create our life experiences true?

Remember, there is no "true"—only *true-for-you* or not. If our initial exploration in Embrace 1 has awakened in you any possibility of owning the direction your life has gone and if weighty events of the past—seemingly outside of your control—are assuming or beginning to assume a new, perfectly designed value, then I encourage you to keep playing with this method. We've only scratched the surface of the lightness of being available here.

Prior to this book, aspects of your Front Forty life may have seemed at a minimum messy, if not unwanted, traumatic or even tragic. A short story conveys the healing and directive forces that can arise out of such messiness.

Scientist Alexander Fleming was looking for ways to destroy bacteria. In 1928, he was growing lots of bacteria known as staphylococci on agar plates. Alexander Fleming could be a bit slapdash. His lab was rather untidy, and he sometimes left the lids off his plates for a long time, letting the air in. Before going on holiday, Alexander made two mistakes. He didn't put all of his plates in bleach to sterilize them, and he left the lab windows open. When he came back, he noticed that lots of his culture plates were moldy. A common mold that might have grown happily on a slice of bread had landed on Alexander Fleming's plates. Fleming's sloppiness turned out to form the basis of the discovery of penicillin—a stroke of luck which has saved millions of lives.[5]

Though unverified, an anecdote in circulation says that, years later, when being escorted through a laboratory cleanroom, someone confidently said to Dr. Fleming, "Just think what you could have done if you had had this kind of facility!" Fleming responded wisely, "Well, I sure wouldn't have invented penicillin!"

What's the point of the story? First, everything happens for a reason; second, laboratories can be messy; and third, sometimes the messiest give rise to the greatest discoveries. Your entire life, however messy, has been a uniquely powerful laboratory for the discovery and expression of something.

---

5 *Alexander Fleming and the discovery of penicillin,"* STEM Learning, *https://6637.stem.org.uk/ timeline6.html*

A closer look at the Alexander Fleming story offers some rich, metaphorical implications for pursuing your Back Forty Freedom. First, as you discovered with Embrace 1: Your Past, it's possible to take your perceived "messy" past and reverse-engineer it to find your own "penicillin." Now, you'll discover with Embrace 2: Your Present, that the same process can be applied to your *current*, challenging situations—those seemingly negative events and influences limiting your experience of the present. Freedom from your past and freedom in your present come from "opening the windows" to this Back Forty way of recontextualizing life. You are letting in fresh air and recognizing that the seeming mistakes or harm committed by others (or yourself) created or are creating the "mold" necessary to render a life-saving discovery: your Self Expression Directives.

Second, the ultimate result of your CSI exploration is to leave you not only owning what you created and why you created it, but also very proud of yourself for literally having saved your own life from being at the effect of circumstances, events, and influences and for having directed that life toward what it was *actually designed* to fulfill. A life with the possibility of fulfillment is a saved life. The CSI also saves the lives around you that are affected by the results of your research. Just modeling your newfound freedom for others makes one of the major differences you were meant to make in the world.

> *Your entire life, however messy, has been a uniquely powerful laboratory for the discovery and expression of something.*

You may be thinking, I'm not finished looking at all my past events and influences. No worries if you've found more than an initial five and are still CSIing them. Many of us have scores of past serious and significant events or influences to eventually run through the "because to Be Cause" Discovery & Expression CSI process. This is because we've never stopped creating our laboratories of experimentation. We are designing new experiments and running old ones even at this very moment!

Yes, your present is replete with multiple, simultaneously operating laboratories, all with the same design principles we've already uncovered and all pointing toward the continued Discovery & Expression of who and what you came here to be and do.

> *Your present is replete with multiple, simultaneously operating laboratories, all with the same design principles we've already uncovered and all pointing toward the continued Discovery & Expression of who and what you came here to be and do.*

So, let's explore *The Present*.

Analyzing the apparent limitations of your present will have you discover exactly how and why you designed these particular, real-time laboratories. And, once you own your hand in the matter—the amazing brilliance of the Mad Scientist behind it all—you can take the Self Expression Directives gained from recontextualizing these lab experiments and run with them also, igniting your Formula of Unique Self Expression, your **FUSE**, even more to transform your present.

PAST-PRETENDING-TO-BE-PRESENT

To begin, let's get logical for a moment on the subject of time. When exactly is "the present"?

We could say that it is now. . .and now. . .and now. . .and now. . .Right? So, if we're really in "the present," then we are living, being in action and dealing with what is occurring literally *in the moment*, not a moment before (past) and not a moment after (future).

Yet, try to capture "the present." Have you ever had a present-based thought? Have you ever taken a present-based action? The answer is yes, if, and only if, you are recognizing what you're thinking or doing while you're in the midst of actually thinking or doing it. To be in "the present" means simultaneous awareness, not recollection from memory of the moment before.

Such awareness, *in-the-moment* awareness, is a great level of consciousness to aspire to. You might describe it as being the Observer of yourself. For many of us, such a state is a long way off in our development. If available at all, it comes at best intermittently and fleetingly, not to be maintained throughout a typical day.

Instead, the past seems to reside in our present; and, for the most part, what we call "the present" is actually the past. Unless we are in a highly meditative observer state, we are generally experiencing the past in most of our life. When we realize that we are having a particular thought, the thought already came microseconds ago. When we're in action, the action already began and, therefore, is also in the past. Even our emotions are recognized only after they express, so sharing our emotional state is most often a reporting of the past.

Additionally, we often re-create the past, calling it the present. We marry or date the same kind of person with whom we're not compatible or experience the same kind of financial crisis over and over again. In so doing, we extend the duration of a bunch of unfinished laboratory experiments.

> **We often re-create the past, calling it the present. In so doing, we extend the duration of a bunch of unfinished laboratory experiments.**

So, the whole idea of "the present" is a smokescreen. Given the smokescreen-nature of the present, you might more accurately re-name your present as your "past-pretending-to-be-present."

BECAUSE TO BE CAUSE "THE PRESENT"

By flicking on the lights in the laboratories you're currently running, you'll see how you've organized your present-day experiments to deliver what you obviously want to Discover & Express here and now. If you want to know what you're committed to discovering, name, examine and own the lab experiments that you're in right now! And remember, power comes from owning that you put your Self where you are for a reason—for something.

You'll notice that often you're not only designing completely new experiments but at times you're also running re-iterations of past laboratories. When we do this, we are creating or maintaining patterns. You re-run those old experiments because when you ran them the first time, you weren't awake, aware and recognizing the results. You're not wrong for missing your Self Expression Directives on those first runs because you just didn't know then how all this experimentation stuff works!

If you want to cultivate the Back Forty model as a way of gaining a voice over not only your past but also your past-pretending-to-be-present, then you'll want to recognize both the new research you're conducting as well as those do-over projects you keep repeating and run them through a Discovery & Expression analysis. Then you can finally—once and for all—get the Self Expression Directives you need to move beyond those original and formative lab experiments. When you do so, you're performing pattern-busting at its best!

Wanting to stay positive, you may find it more difficult to admit victimhood around events and influences in the present than the past. However, this is where we pour out the real darkness of the situations we're facing. It's only perceived darkness, mind you; but, as with the past, we tell it like it is, meaning as if what we perceive in the present is real. We leave no stone unturned as to justifying the absolute victimhood into which certain present situations have placed us.

Some of us who have explored personal development or spirituality will often side-step this part. On the intellectual level, we do what can be called a "spiritual bypass," saying things like, "It's all good" or "I'm too blessed to be stressed" or some other throw-away, regurgitated, surface-fix line. Underneath it, oftentimes we're seething. That's not to say that maintaining a true and constant experience of nirvana throughout your day isn't a great accomplishment; it's just not a real possibility for most of us. Generally, undesirable stuff will get churned up in our everyday lives. Glibly glossing over these seemingly screwed-up situations won't create power and freedom. Examining and addressing them authentically will.

Therefore, if you really want to take full ownership of your past and present and thereby open the door to designing a radical and unlimited future, for the sake of playful exploration, please drop any spiritual bypasses and look seriously into the events and influences that nibble at you or that are even still apparently eating your lunch. To some degree, we always feel powerless in some situations.

That's a big word, *powerless*. Many of us are repulsed by it. The very idea of being powerless can trigger a strong, ego-driven reaction such as, "Hey, nothing can beat me! I can always take on whatever life throws at me!"

> *Glibly glossing over these seemingly screwed-up situations won't create power and freedom. Examining and addressing them authentically will.*

Yet, if we look deeper than that first haughty stance, we can all admit that—fight as we might—some areas in each of our lives are just not the way we'd like them to be. . .and we don't know how to change them. *Career. Family. Relationships. Finances. Health. Home.* If you look, there's a never-ending list of areas where circumstances aren't fitting your pictures right now, even though you may have rationalized them or simply learned to tolerate them.

A popular devotion "The Serenity Prayer" reads, "God, grant me the serenity to accept the things I cannot change; courage to change the things I can; and the wisdom to know the difference." The rub is the wisdom to know the difference. Freedom comes from being willing to identify and admit when and where we feel a lack of power and then point our "because to Be Cause" process directly at it. As we continue mustering the courage to play with the Embraces, we can increase the number of things we *can* change, giving us more power in certain assumed-to-be-unmanageable situations and events.

To start, we scan our current life for areas where we feel powerless in any way. The first Serious and Significant Event or Influence from our current life to analyze would be the one eliciting the most seeming powerlessness in the moment. We are likely to feel ourselves to be a victim of the situation.

To illustrate, let's walk through one of my own, past-pretending-to-be-present, current-as-of-this-writing situations that has had me utterly convinced that I'm a victim. (We almost always have that first reaction to seemingly adverse situations in life.)

Here, as a refresher, is the 7-Step Discovery & Expression Method with a twist to address the present.

1. Choose and name a serious and significant *current* event or influence.
2. Tell the story (as it is occurring now) in full victim form.
3. Identify the phenomena (blessings) from the event or influence.
4. Determine the possible research questions being experimented for in the laboratory.
5. Claim ownership of the laboratory and its design: how you picked the perfect lab assistants and ideal lab environments.
6. Determine the possible findings from the experimentation.
7. Postulate or determine the Self Expression Directives arising from the event or influence.

> *Gaining a say over all that has been and all that is now will support you in having a say over what is to come in your next half.*

The process of gaining a say over all that has been and all that is now will support you in having a say over what is to come in your next half. So, let's get into the weeds again with me sharing one of my more gnarly current-day Serious and Significant Events. Then it will be your turn to discover the freedom-producing Self Expression Directives arising from Your Present.

As you follow my story, use it as a template to begin analyzing one of your own Past-Pretending-to-be-Present Serious and Significant Events/Situations or Influences. As I expose my own imperfection and humanness alongside the empowerment available through utilizing the Discovery & Expression system, ideally you'll similarly allow your own vulnerability and transformation to unfold in any unbelievable and incredible situations that are currently "befalling" you.

The definition of "befallen" is quite interesting in light of our continued discovery. The modern definition is "to happen to, especially by chance or fate" (i.e., victim, because), whereas the archaic definition is "to come, as by right" (i.e., responsibility, Be Cause). Given that, choose which "befallen" you ascribe to!

So here we go.

MuuuuuuuAAAAAAAAHaaaaHaaaaHaaaa!

Darrell's Current-Day Experiment: Gym Bully
Discovery & Expression Step 1: Serious and Significant
Current Event or Influence

In reflecting upon the many and various situations in my own life where I could claim a current lack of joy, satisfaction or power (i.e., I'm a victim), I'm going to pick one that I'll call "Experiment: Gym Bully."

Darrell's Current-Day Experiment: Gym Bully
Discovery & Expression Step 2: Victim Story

At the time of this writing, I am in the midst of a seemingly completely bad and wrong situation at a gym where my wife, Alexandra, and I hold memberships. She is included in this story because we were both experiencing victimhood. It's a multi-city gym where we participate in classes a few times a week at different locations within the same metropolitan area. We've both been members of the chain for nearly twenty years and neither of us has ever had any experience or issue warranting a complaint, either by us or about us.

This overwhelmingly convincing victim situation surrounds one particular instructor of one particular class at one particular gym location. The gist of the issue is that there appears to be nobody watching the store in terms of customer experience. This instructor keeps harassing Alexandra and sometimes me, having us feel uncomfortable and even picked on. Yes, grown adults feeling picked on!

I could wax eloquent about how tough we are, not only in terms of strength—with regular workout regimens for years and strong commitments to health and fitness—but also in terms of willingness to be coached and receive constructive input. Also, Alexandra has been practicing the particular workout in question for over fifteen years, has been exposed to fifteen to twenty instructors and has rarely, if ever, elicited any necessary "instruction" from a teacher. In rare cases where instruction has been offered to Alexandra in a healthy and supportive manner, she generally incorporates it immediately.

However, this particular instructor is, to our sensibilities, more badgering us than coaching. She seems to have an issue, for some reason, with Alexandra. Her negative and judgmental attitude was clear the moment we started taking her particular class after moving our home to a new location in Southern California. Sure, we could have stopped taking her class and found others. Yet, as customers, we felt that we should be able to take any class that best fits our schedule without having to worry about being, in effect, bullied by an instructor over a period of nine months.

Even with perhaps forty to fifty people in class, this instructor seems to only ever watch Alexandra like a hawk, making snide comments from the front of the room about Alexandra's workout or getting a few feet in front of her glaring at her while demonstrating a move as if she is isolating out Alexandra for doing something wrong! It would seem less of a victim situation if this instructor would go about the room and impose the same intrusive and unasked for "coaching" upon others, but she doesn't. Alexandra gets all of her focus and badgering.

Alexandra has a genial personality and generally chooses to accommodate and not make waves, and she's ready and willing to grow if she can benefit from good instruction in any area of life.

In this case, Alexandra believed the instruction given by this particular teacher would be harmful to her body were she to follow it. So, being the generally polite and amicable person she is, Alexandra simply thanked the instructor the first time she came over to tell her how she "should" be doing the exercise, saying, "Thanks. I appreciate your opinion. I'd like to do the exercise in the way that works best for my body." She thought this was a perfectly respectful way to ask to be honored as a person.

Our joint opinion of the situation is that, if we had hired a personal, one-on-one trainer, then our role would be to simply listen and take the coaching or get another trainer. However, in a group situation such as this, with many people in worse condition than us in terms of form, stamina and fitness, we feel it completely inappropriate for this instructor to keep harping on Alexandra, especially after she has already politely requested to be left alone. We are there for a class, not for this particular instructor's isolating, demeaning, bullying, militaristic boot camp.

The badgering continued.

To Alexandra and me—both familiar with cutting-edge operations in today's companies—it seemed that this fitness chain *should* be putting attention on customer experience. We weren't having a good one.

> [NOTE: Here's a tip to help you find current events and influences for your own "because to Be Cause" process. Look for situations where your ego is telling you very LOUDLY that the situation is not the way it "should" be (as if there could ever be any definitive "shoulds" in life) and where you know way better than any other person/business/group/party how they "should" be doing things (grin).]

Admittedly, Alexandra's overall amicable disposition, even in the face of conflict, contrasts starkly with my own general stand-up-for-my-rights wiring. I'm sure mine stems from my personal, early childhood influences of feeling like the one downhill upon whom the shit rolled. So, I felt compelled to stand up for Alexandra when this seemingly inappropriate singling out and needling of her was taking place. My knight-in-shining-armor-on-a-white-horse thing.

The pressure had been building for about a month when one day the instructor was down on the floor in Alexandra's face during a bench-press exercise. In a firm but quiet voice—Alexandra was right beside me—I told the instructor to lay the fuck off. I spoke so quietly that she asked me, "What did you say?" I repeated, "Lay the fuck off," in a volume only she could hear. Alexandra didn't even hear what I had said.

Okay, no, I'm not spotlessly clean! I used an under-my-breath expletive! And, of course, it felt completely warranted! The instructor responded by stopping the class and leaving for a minute to bring in management, who asked us to step outside. Alexandra did, but I refused. Only then did Alexandra even learn that I had used an expletive in defending her from the instructor.

Alexandra came back, we finished the class, and we then sat down with gym management to share our side of the situation. They assured us that we should let them know in the future if we have any issues with the instructor and said they would email the chief instructor to let her know of our situation. We were assured they would follow up with us.

A week went by. Then another week. We kept attempting to get the contact info of the chief instructor, but to no avail. Finally, a few weeks later, we got a call and learned she had already spoken to our class instructor and seemed to already have a fixed opinion of what happened. After hearing our account, she eventually assured us that she would have another conversation with our instructor and follow up with us to let us know we could expect peaceful workouts in the future.

Many months went by and we never heard from the chief instructor again. Nor did we get responses from any other management figures to whom we sent numerous emails to notify them, as they had requested, of ongoing issues we continued to experience with the instructor. She hadn't backed off one bit and continued to single out, force-feed "coach" and humiliate Alexandra in class and even began to point some of it towards me.

Several months later, I chose to lodge a complaint with management about not getting in our full routine because of the instructor regularly starting the class late. When I went to the front desk to get the manager's name, unsure of whether it was the same non-responsive manager from months before, the instructor actually came up to the front desk and confronted me verbally in front of other staff and members, saying "Don't give him anything. He just wants to complain." It was a hugely uncomfortable moment with everyone watching. I chose to not engage or interact with her but simply got the manager's card.

We received no response to our emails to that location's management and decided to go higher. We couldn't believe that this complete lack of customer service was happening or that bullying was allowed to take place in a business supposedly committed to health and well-being. We figured we must have not gotten high enough to reach someone with a true customer-service mindset. We became intent on doing so.

[NOTE: Another intermission in my elongated, victim-laced monologue to acknowledge the fact that I was personally driving this whole charade more than Alexandra. She allowed me the freedom to take the lead on "standing up for our rights" and went along with me. Yet, left to her own devices, this would have never blown up to the level it did. So, I am clear that this was a Be Cause laboratory workout uniquely designed by and for me!]

About eight months into this apparently impossible situation, Alexandra decided to begin recording audios of the class on her phone to document the harassment taking place because not one manager had even responded to our emails or complaints nor observed any classes to investigate. She recorded not only particular classes but even the conversations she had in the parking lot afterwards when other members came to express their upset with what they were observing, saying things like, "How could you let her treat you like that?"

We thought this recorded evidence might finally get us some support. We again emailed the string of managers we had been unilaterally emailing for months, saying, "we have evidence!" At that point, the very low-level location manager responded that we could meet with him. However, by then we had lost faith that he had any clout in the situation whatsoever and did not attend.

Another meeting was proposed at a slightly higher level, but—my bad—I was so completely disgusted with that level's heretofore non-responsiveness that I passed on that meeting, too, in hopes of reaching someone even higher. We had only intimated that we had "evidence" (the audio recordings) but hadn't shared it yet. So, with recordings in hand, I sought to reach the highest corporate levels.

[NOTE: Ever happy to make an example out of myself, here's another tip. A way to smell good victimhood brewing in the lab is to watch for potential resolutions to your gripes and bitches being met with resistance—by you! Ever hear of folks who choose (perhaps unconsciously) being right over being happy? Perhaps you know a person like that? This is the point in the game of Charades where you touch your nose.]

The shit hit the fan when, about a month ago, the instructor again got right in Alexandra's face, staring her down as if she wasn't doing the exercise right, mocking her, and then laughing as she walked back to the front of the class. I couldn't bear to see this belittling continue and said, "Stay away from us." In nine months of emails and communications through management, we had only ever asked that she simply not interact with us. Yet, it seems her ego wouldn't settle for that. . .and mine wouldn't settle with hers not settling for that.

[NOTE: Further signposts along the road of treasure-produc-ing victimhood are phrases like "I couldn't bear to see" and instances when you're crystal clear that it's the other person's ego that needs to be put in check, not your own.]

The class was again stopped as she went out. Three managers came in, and after ten minutes of attempting to share with them our plight—of which they were completely unaware—the class ended because the instructor refused to finish teaching. Of course, though Alexandra and I were completely aware of the background of this ongoing issue, these three junior managers and many of the other forty participants in class were not. So, we felt the barbs of everyone's discontent.

One week later, a manager-in-training showed up to observe from the back of the class. Though the instructor continued the pointed and snide remarks, she didn't actually get in Alexandra's face. Afterward, this manager-in-training acknowledged the snide remarks, but only offered a comment that Alexandra might want to drop a little weight off her bar. I recorded our conversation with him, and I told him I'd be sending the recording on to higher management, which I did.

To put a bow on this most incredible experience, one week later, upon going into class one morning, I was informed that my twenty-year membership had been revoked. Just mine, not Alexandra's. The short reason offered was "due to issues with the instructor" and the club's policy of no audio or video recordings taking place in the gym.

Wow! That was a long story! It illustrates what many of us do as typical human beings: build up extensive, seemingly inconceivable and irrefutable cases that cast us as the victim at the effect of other people, circumstances or situations. In this serious and significant current event, I'm obviously a shining example of that tendency of humanity!

Even though this D & E step of full-out, victim wailing is necessary, it's important to quickly drop the negative vibrations that come with these deep dives into our stories. It's murky down here, full of hypnotic and seductive evidence of separation, division, good guys/bad guys, right/wrong, and perpetrator/victim! So, it's critical after a dive like this in which we've channeled our massively righteous, inner victim that we come to the surface, clean and clear. Rise above! Shake it off! Put on our Mad Scientist mojo and get to analyzing!

Remember, no person is *ever* bad or wrong inside this realm of life-creation analysis. Other people are simply spear carriers in our perfectly directed opera! As a matter of fact, initially even *we* are spear carriers in our own opera, having received no hint from any director beforehand that Act One has already begun. We can only discover and assent to our own directorial role in an after-the-fact way through Discovery & Expression analysis. As we learn to assert and own our powerful, creative Be Cause posture, we continue to affirm this critical mantra:

> *Other people are simply spear carriers in our perfectly directed opera!*

MuuuuuuuAAAAAAAAAHaaaaHaaaaHaaaa!

remembering the Inner Mad Scientist is always in control.

Darrell's Current-Day Experiment: Gym Bully
Discovery & Expression Step 3: Blessings Derived

Back Forty Alchemy

Alchemy, in short, is the age-old philosopher's pursuit of turning lead into gold. The "because to Be Cause" method supports a similar kind of alchemy.

You change the past when you change the way you see it. —*Alan Cohen*

Watch closely as I transform this apparently hellish situation into the best thing that could have ever happened to me.

Before I begin that alchemical process, here's a helpful tip that will help you when you're struggling to find the perfect design inside of your own incredible and often hellish situations: *judgment-free awareness* is key in the ensuing analysis of our victim-laced guts, which we spilled in Step 2 of the Discovery & Expression process.

Judgment as to who is right or wrong in a story can detract from your objective analysis. For instance, if you feel my pain and see my plight in this story as honorable or righteous, perceiving it that way may reveal your own tendency to fall into similar, self-justified victim traps. On the other hand, perhaps you see the errors of my ways in this story and think I got what I deserved. If so, you may want to watch for the need to quickly determine right from wrong in each in every situation you face in life. Why? Because, if the Universe is *for* me (and you) as we propose in this Back Forty philosophy, then none of us can ever be wrong in any situation. You and I are simply on task for conducting the experiments we've chosen to engage in, where right or wrong never come into play.

Even judging yourself is basically another victim stance, albeit, you're now victimized by yourself rather than others. Self-judgment will divert you from discovering the experimental goodies (Self Expression Directives) that are available for you in any and all situations that you face in life, including those going on right now.

Look, I could feel terribly embarrassed in sharing the story above. Believe me, I'm aware of the irony of this situation befalling me personally—someone supposedly consciously aware and law-of-attraction astute—a trained and certified licensed spiritual counselor, a high-level certified coach, an inspirational writer, a former assistant scoutmaster (can you say character?), and an overall good guy.

> *Judging yourself is basically another victim stance, albeit, you're now victimized by yourself rather than others.*

Yet, with all of my track record of personal development, I have yet to get beyond all the triggers of my ego and my default wiring arising from years of Front Forty research and development. Perhaps you know someone like me?

One thing I'm absolutely clear about: my Inner Mad Scientist is committed to my highest and greatest good! So, rather than go the traditional route of beating up myself, or others, for this soap opera of events, I'll use the Back Forty tools to discover what this experiment was designed and conducted for.

Crank it up now!

MuuuuuuuAAAAAAAAHaaaaHaaaaHaaaa!

My Blessings

1. I've recently been watching my ego pull smokescreens before my eyes to distract me from the good life I now have. Whether it be barking at LA traffic or having customer service or billing issues with service providers, I've noticed a recent tendency to find little things to gripe about as all of the bigger things in my life are going so well. Sounds crazy, I know. Silly humans we are. And, this huge issue playing out had me notice my apparent resistance to simply being happy!

2. Through inquiring into smokescreens such as this one of the past-pretending-to-be-present, I've discovered an old pattern of the ego pulling me towards the struggle and anxious ways of former times. My gripes and bitches will always keep me safe and comfortable in being who I've always been versus who I choose to be. This particular series of events revealed for me a great lesson: happiness is something I can own and operate from regardless of whether the situations in my life fit my pictures. If every day is simply about choosing which team to play on, I can begin choosing to side with The Great Life Team versus The Safe in the Comfort Zone of Gripes and Bitches Team.

3. Through this situation, I gained valuable insight as to the value of my time and attention and have begun to let go of the "small stuff" that I formerly allowed to hijack my attention. Perhaps every apparent wrong or injustice in the world isn't worthy of my time, dime, attention or emotional energy to fix. Maybe, as is the true heart of martial arts, the possibility of walking away from any fight is always the smarter way to go.

4. Alexandra and I have now had an experience of forming a united front on something of importance to us. In comrades-in-arms fashion, we've discovered that we can align and be "for" each other, no matter what. Sure, this wasn't a life-altering situation that impacted the world, but it was definitely an opportunity to test our joint alliance-for-truth muscles.

5. I got to be distracted from the peaceful state of mind I would have preferred to have while writing this book! But how is that a blessing? At first, the ever-present thoughts and negativity surrounding these events kidnapped my mind and destroyed my focus. Wanting to finish the book, I didn't like having this nuisance of a situation throwing my energy off. However, I now realize that the very reason it's all been happening in the midst of completing the book is to give me lots of current, relevant fodder for the book to support conveying the Discovery & Expression method! I had previously analyzed and documented a different "current" event in an earlier version of the manuscript. But that one was now years old. This one is ripe, real-time and victim-fresh!

6. In having my workout routine of the last three years taken away with my twenty-year membership (three to four classes with Alexandra each week), I got to experience the feelings of discombobulation and disorientation that many folks feel when they lose their routine of a job or business or have a

totally unexpected curve-ball hit them in life. This makes for more experienced compassion on my part for what anxious, routine-shattered living feels like and will likely result in my becoming a better coach.

7. I've had more time to write because I have yet to sort out a new gym in which to get back into my twenty-year fitness regimen!

8. I've resumed my prior emphasis on running from my pre-Alexandra lifestyle, when I ran three to four miles a day three to four times per week while listening to inspirational authors and audiobooks on my phone. In the group workout classes depicted in this story, I'd been missing the fill of inspirational messages I used to get while running.

9. I'm present to the amazing benefits of my tax dollars at work. Having incorporated regular running back into my life, I discovered a nearby park with cutting-edge workout equipment simply sitting there for anyone to use!

10. I was gifted a huge right-sizing of my ego. How is that a blessing? Perhaps, it's only a blessing if you enjoy personal development as I do. Yet, in attempting to live by certain principles along my own course of spiritual evolution, the more I can distinguish and quiet my ego, the better life is for me and others.

Whoa! Whoa! Whoa!

MuuuuuuuuAAAAAAAAAHaaaaHaaaaHaaaa!

As mentioned in "Embrace 1: Your Past," you can see this blessings list as me simply making lemons out of lemonade. Yet, I'll ask you to seriously consider the two paths I have to choose from:

Path 1: I can feel beaten, mistreated, unjustifiably stripped of my rights as a customer, as a twenty-year member of an establishment. Then, after beating myself up for having not seen how to deal with the situation better/sooner/smarter from the outset, thereby making myself wrong, also beating them up in my head for being so atrociously ignorant of their impact on customers, thereby making them wrong, I could become even more solidified in my position and file a lawsuit for Intent to Inflict Emotional Injury (IIEI) and, perhaps, even go on a crusade harkening back to Tom Peters' *In Search of Excellence*, creating a blog and book to re-awaken big companies that are obviously too big to care these days and maybe even create a whole new consulting business out of that?

> *Likely Destination:* WHEW! I'm tired just from writing that! Are you, from reading it? Separation. Division. Sides against sides. Right and wrong. Good and bad. Honor versus evil. Fighting. Anger. No peace.

Path 2: I can, as I have, look for the blessings this situation has provided. I can become interested and explorative about how and why I created this and the other circumstances and events of my life from a Self-awareness perspective. I can look for the positive aspects, the unexpected and unforeseen marvels, the absolute miracles stemming from this event or influence. I can use this unique opportunity to uncover some powerful insights as to how to direct or redirect my life and attention to become more of who I came to be and do more of what I came to do.

> *Likely Destination: ENERGIZED,* yes? Oneness. Responsibility. Fascinated investigation. Playful exploration. Awareness. Growth. Peace.

You, too, have forks in the roads of your own current-day serious and significant events or influences. Sure, it takes creative Homeplay to journey the road less travelled and pursue responsibility, blessings, and Oneness. But, strangely enough, once you get the horse going in that direction, it's amazing how a begrudging initial trot turns into a full gallop of possibilities.

I've been around long enough (as probably have you) to realize that I can only point my energy, time and focus in one general direction or another. I can point it toward more separation and belief in victimhood around both myself and others. (Remember, Alexandra was my supposed damsel in distress and I was attempting to rescue her!) Or, I can point it toward Oneness, responsibility and trust in my inner, life-designing laboratories, which keep directing me toward my highest Self-expression.

Separation or Oneness: Choose!

Victim or Mad Scientist: Choose!

because or Be Cause: Choose!

MuuuuuuuAAAAAAAAAHaaaaHaaaaHaaaa!

Darrell's Current-Day Experiment: Gym Bully

Discovery & Expression Step 4: Research Questions

What might I have been experimenting for in this prolonged, uncomfortable experience? What are the hypothetical research questions I must have had in the deep recesses of my Mad Scientist mind that I wanted answers to?

Stepping into the immense creative juices I must have been drawing from in designing this drama, I can postulate several interesting inquiries.

A.   Can something so seemingly justified as another person's "wrong" behavior ever warrant an individual moving away from his or her own peace?

B.   Is it any person's role to take care of the supposed injustices inflicted upon others? Does it help or hurt a situation in doing so? Are there really any "injustices" or is the Universe giving opportunities for everyone to grow through their own laboratories?

C. If committed to a world view of Oneness, what situations, circumstances or conditions could be strong enough to distract someone from that commitment?

D. What does it take for a person with a history of fighting-for-right combativeness to drop that old pattern and start being happy?

E. Is it valuable to shake up old routines, associations and patterns in life even while fearing change?

Such a very, very Mad Scientist I am!

MuuuuuuuAAAAAAAAAHaaaaHaaaaHaaaa!

Darrell's Current-Day Experiment: Gym Bully
Discovery & Expression Step 5: Owning the Lab Design

How did I set this whole drama up? How did I pick the perfect lab assistants, perfectly disposed for such an experiment, and put them in a perfect laboratory environment such that I could conduct a controlled study?

MuuuuuuuAAAAAAAAAHaaaaHaaaaHaaaa!

My Lab Assistants

The first critical lab assistant in this series of events is Alexandra, my life partner at the time and now my wife. Her general disposition is quite different from mine, being far more patient, tolerant, accepting and accommodating with life and circumstances than I. I'm growing in those areas, but she's got it down. Though generally flexible, she voices her gripes in private to those closest to her and can definitely be influenced onto a bandwagon of injustice if someone else wants to drive.

Juxtapose that way of being to my fairness-focused, Southern-gentleman, damsel-in-distress-rescuing and justice-crusader tendencies and you have the perfect assistant for the experiments conducted in this lab.

Another critical lab assistant was the class instructor. One must be careful when pointing a finger at another person claiming that they have a big ego because of the number of fingers pointing back at yourself. Nonetheless, I did feel she had an oversized ego and was operating as if she was the only instructor on the planet who knew how these exercises "should" be done. This instructor considered her opinion to be fact, even though other instructors did many of the moves she specifically claimed as wrong. Also, she was a fighter in the sense that, rather than question herself, her attitude or her idea of what customer service looks like, she was bulldog-pressed to make a case to management.

I couldn't have picked better lab assistants to test these questions! Add to this the other assistants in the form of management, who were absent and/ or slow, if ever, to respond to the situation, and you have an appropriately vetted group with which to jump into this social experiment!

MuuuuuuuAAAAAAAAAHaaaaHaaaaHaaaa!

My Lab Environment

Of course, the perfect laboratory environment came in the form of a nationwide gym chain which was—from the perspective of the "victim"— non-responsive to customer complaints and lacking any sense of customer experience at the grassroots touchpoints of the organization. When researching the company online after this "experiment" began, we saw hundreds, if not thousands, of complaints from members all over the country. Add to that a person like me, who feels privileged to expect a certain experience and you have a ripe and ready environment in which to enact seeming injustice.

Another ideal aspect to this environmental design is that the apparent injustices took place in the middle of a nearly fifty-person workout class. Experiencing interrupted classes and seeing only that we seemed to be in conflict with the instructor, it was easy for fellow class members to jump on her bandwagon of portraying us as the bad guys, creating immense social pressure and a further feeling of being singled out in the situation.

MuuuuuuuAAAAAAAAAHaaaaHaaaaHaaaa!

Darrell's Current-Day Experiment: Gym Bully
Discovery & Expression Step 6: Findings

Anyone who's ever been involved in any type of event design—all the way from organizing a child's birthday party to creating an epic, Oscar-winning film—has an appreciation for all the pieces that go into a well-executed production. It's not easy! With lots of moving parts, it requires an immense amount of dedication and perseverance to see a big production all the way to the end.

Therefore, given all the incredible design and operations effort our Mad Scientist put into this grand experiment, I don't want to leave without the goodies! I want answers to my hypothetical questions and I want the Self Expression Directives *to which the whole experiment points!*

Word to the wise: don't ever try to get your Findings or Self Expression Directives "right." Just take what comes from reflecting back on the event or influence as a general gist.

MuuuuuuuAAAAAAAAAHaaaaHaaaaHaaaa!

A. *Question:* Can something so seemingly justified as another person's "wrong" behavior ever warrant an individual moving away from their own peace?

Findings: For me, before analyzing this experiment, the findings were obviously yes. Yet, this experiment, which is likely a repeat of many earlier experiments based on exactly the same question (i.e., a pattern), has served as a true wake-up-call to drop my old habit of going into soldier-for-justice mode and simply choose the route of more peace.

In discussing these events with a trusted friend for many months while the victim story was playing out, my friend had me continue to look at the price I was willing to put on peace and whether in just walking away from a supposed injustice I could get to peace faster. Some options were to take other classes, drop my twenty-year membership and join another gym, etc. These conversations challenged my internal sense of responsibility for righting the "wrongs" in the world. I was operating as if I were on a mission, thinking that if I didn't hold the line on bad behavior and have management realize the inappropriateness of this instructor, nobody else would. I felt morally obligated to stand firm in my "right"ness.

In the end, a whole new commitment to "Peace First" arose from this experiment. I realized that every opportunity to ensure "justice" is not worth fighting for. Therefore, my answer to this research question is yes, but only *if* that moving away from peace creates an awareness that leads someone to commit to even more peace, which is what happened to me.

B. *Question:* Is it any person's role to take care of the supposed injustices inflicted upon others? Does it help or hurt a situation in doing so? Are there really any "injustices" or is the Universe simply giving opportunities for everyone to grow through their own laboratories?

Findings: I won't extrapolate to the grander, social-justice dimensions of this question considering, one-by-one, all of the "evils" that exist in the world, as that would be beyond the scope of my personal learnings here. In this situation specifically, I now realize that my standing up for the rights and proper treatment of my partner, Alexandra, perhaps diminished her own learning opportunity. Perhaps she was running her own lab experiment around the development of her voice, which I interfered with.

It's interesting to think that, at the same time I am running my own experiments, others are also running theirs. Is it possible to actually interfere with the experiments of someone else and in so doing deprive them of their own Findings and Self Expression Directives? An interesting question to ponder.

My awareness of the Law of Attraction also has me consider the idea that, if I'm not attracting experiences of injustice to myself because life is generally going pretty well, I might attract experiences of injustice to those I love, which can pull me into a Grand Defender mode. If you, too, have justice-bandwagon tendencies, perhaps you can relate: exactly where and in what ways do we attract situations that bring out our Grand Defender? Is every little "wrong" really worth the effort to correct?

The answer to these questions, as the experiment demonstrated here, are undetermined; but I have suspicions that everyone deserves the right to their own undisturbed laboratory experiments unless, of course, a higher-level, joint lab experiment is being conducted.

C. *Question:* If committed to a world view of Oneness, what situations, circumstances or conditions could be strong enough to distract someone from that commitment?

Findings: Obviously, what seemed to be clear bullying and harassment of Alexandra had me abandon any sense of Oneness with this instructor and even the gym as a whole. I operated from a being "right" mode, which never supports Oneness.

Plus, let's say I actually was right and had somehow effectively communicated the situation to management. Perhaps they could have taken some corrective action regarding the instructor. Yet, my stance of *being right* established an entrenched energy that simply called for opposition. This is a delicate distinction; someone might actually be right in a situation but *their way of being right* is what calls up resistance because nobody enjoys admitting that they are wrong.

So, in answer to my research question, it appears that situations in which I am *being right*, whether actually "right" or not, are those that will distract me from my commitment to fostering Oneness on the planet.

D. *Question:* What does it take for a person with a history of fight-for-right combativeness to drop that old pattern and simply start being happy?

Findings: This incident had me look deeper into the roots of my fight-for-right, combative pattern. It's probably at the source of my being such an emphatic professional coach, standing up for possibilities in people that they may not see for themselves.

The pattern likely began early in my life when I was struggling to make my way in a family/home situation where I felt myself to be the low man on the totem pole with shit rolling downhill. Add to that, as I described in my "Brother's Psychological Abuse" experiment (Appendix A) the feeling of being very different from my environment ("Why don't you want to play football?") and you have the makings of a soldier-for-justice taking root.

This, then, points me to another past influence in which I was bullied and which I could take through the whole "because to Be Cause" process by itself. It also proves the point made earlier in the chapter: often our past-pretending-to-be-present situations have us conducting do-over experiments so that we may finally take ownership of patterns stemming from unfinished, initial lab experiments in our past.

If we haven't Be Caused what happened back then, owned our creation of it, and reaped the Self Expression Directives from those events or influences, we can do so now based on the do-over "heads up" that our inner Self is giving us in our past-pretending-to-be-present, current life situations.

In final answer to this hypothetical question of "What does it take. . .," for me it apparently took a knock on the head to see that combativeness doesn't work, no matter how "right" I may be. That dog don't hunt anymore. . .and I only hope the knock sticks.

E. *Question:* Is it valuable to shake up old routines, associations and patterns in life even while fearing change?

Findings: I never expected a change in my twenty-year routine of going to my home gym for workouts. I would have never imagined that a one-time customer service issue would result in my being released, freed up and on-the-market following the loss of my longtime gym relationship.

I suppose this could be a metaphor for lots of other relationships we take for granted (marriages, jobs, businesses, communities), which when unexpectedly taken away cause discombobulation and stress. As creatures of habit, being uprooted from old relationships—be they good, bad or ugly—is not an opportunity we excitedly crave. We fear the unknown, having no sense of who we are outside of that relationship, and we question what will happen to fill the void if we leave.

Though I may be taking a simple, twenty-year gym membership loss to metaphorical heights, it nonetheless points to a new awareness I've gained. This awareness may enable me to be of greater support for others who have experienced similar losses of longtime relationships. I now better understand the voids they experience and the potential growth and development that may exist for them on the other side.

For the time being, I'll say this research question is unanswered at this point—undetermined—yet with a strong leaning toward probably. As mentioned in the blessings above, I'm enjoying the new possibility of getting back into my inspirational audios that has come with my reintegration with running.

MuuuuuuuAAAAAAAAAHaaaaHaaaaHaaaa!

Darrell's Current-Day Experiment: Gym Bully
Discovery & Expression Step 7: Self Expression Directives

I don't think too much on this last step. The Self Expression Directives are only slightly, if at all, hidden. As with the famous puzzle series Where's Waldo?®, if I just relax and take in the fabric of the experiment, the Blessings and the Findings, the Self Expression Directives will pop out at me. Here's what I drew from the Gym Bully Experiment.

> *Separation or Oneness: Choose! Victim or Mad Scientist: Choose! because or Be Cause: Choose!*

- BE Happy (special emphasis on the BE)
- BE Peace (versus right)
- Centered Allowance for the Labs of Others
- Empowered Non-attachment (to things and ego)
- Don't "Sweat" That Small Stuff
- Spiritualizing ALL of Life

Was it worth it to analyze in so much detail such a seemingly inconsequential-for-the-world gripe? You bet! Just look at the directions I now have to explore in life from here on out!

I could literally live the rest of my life with only these Self Expression Directives as my guiding standards and never reach the top of that mountain. Add to these so many more Self Expression Directives I've derived from my other Discovery & Expression analyses and I get a compilation of very strong life-design principles to take into the second half/best half of life: my radical Back Forty.

MuuuuuuuAAAAAAAAHaaaaHaaaaHaaaa!

YOUR TURN!

Enough about my petty bitches, gripes, moans and groans. Let's get into yours!

Embrace 2—Homeplay 1
because to Be Cause: Your Present

Get out your Back Forty Freedom Fliers Journal. Put on some soft, relaxing music and once again shield yourself from any and all possible interruptions for the next half hour.

Close your eyes and relax. Remember that this is a playful and creative experience. There are no right or perfect answers here. Though we will walk through a paint-by-numbers approach, your interpretations as to the colors you'll paint in each section is up to you. The more relaxed and open you are to simply allowing your insights and awareness to expand without editing your answers or trying to get it "right," the more you'll re-picture this unwanted situation into a masterpiece, a beautiful and golden opportunity for your life ahead!

Now identify five thorns in the side of your *current* life—Serious and Significant (to you) situations or influences that are having you feel powerless or in which you are sure you are right and someone/something else is wrong. To help, consider the seemingly inconsequential issues you currently have with this person or that, the problems you've been having with some group or organization or the nattering things you're tolerating in whatever area of life that's important to you. As mentioned before, mine areas where you feel powerless, situations you can't figure out how to change. Write each in your Back Forty Freedom Fliers Journal.

The five you select are your Top 5 Serious and Significant "becauses" from *Your Present*.

Embrace 2—Homeplay 2
because to Be Cause: Your Present (Continued)

Here's your Homeplay assignment followed by some helpful tips. The tips focus on the special challenges re-contextualizing the present can pose. Review the tips before proceeding.

1. Write "Experiment" at the top of a clean page.
2. Pick one of the five serious and significant situations/persons/events you have identified.
3. Name the situation you have chosen and write its name in your journal beside "Experiment."
4. Write out your story in full victim form.
5. Take the situation you have chosen through the remaining five steps of the Discovery & Expression analysis: Benefits Derived, Hypothetical Research Questions, Owning the Experiment, Findings, Self Expression Directives.

Tip for Step 2: Victim Story

When you write your Step 2 Victim Story, let yourself drop any and all spiritual bypasses you may have been using to get through the day (e.g., "It's all good" or "I'm too blessed to be stressed") and really tell it from your basest, most raw point of view. Make it a bitchfest.

Accentuate the negative, horrible and unjust. And, to support this creative act, remember the Mad Scientist that you are!

MuuuuuuuAAAAAAAAHaaaaHaaaaHaaaa!

Tip for Step 3: Blessings Derived

What are the blessings of having exactly THIS person/thing/event in exactly THIS situation with exactly THESE circumstances inside of THIS environment happening to you right now? Come up with at least 10. Finding blessings in uncomfortable to miserable current circumstances may require you to stretch your mind. Consider what blessings may be on the way even if they have not manifested yet. Turning the ship around to recontextualize our victim stories always requires willpower and patience, especially when the event or influence is currently in process. It's not instantaneous, but allow your mind to entertain the idea that this particular issue that's been disturbing you, keeping you up at night, causing you pain and robbing you of peace will one day be over and, in the meantime, actually has some benefits for you. If the serious and significant current event or influence continues to appear like a "bad" thing happening to you, you simply haven't come up with enough rich and savory real and potential blessings to change your opinion!

Tip for Step 4: Hypothetical Research Questions

Whatever blessings you come up with, simply KNOW that there are research questions your Inner Mad Scientist MUST have been experimenting for that brought about those blessings now in real time. From the nature of the blessings, you can creatively postulate the research questions your mad scientist wanted to have answered in the experiment. Always remember, you can't do this analysis wrong. Trust what comes up for you, and the process will become easier with time and practice as you harvest more and more power out of the supposed powerless events and influences in your life. Play with it and come up with several possible research questions. Your beakers are boiling! Now, turn up the heat!

Tip for Step 6: Findings

This may be a hot and active experiment still happening, full of dynamic, electrical-arcing energy or molding, test-plate cultures. Or, maybe, this wild experiment just concluded. Because of your proximity to the experiment, a tendency may arise to classify all of the findings (answers to your research questions) as "undetermined" just because of the freshness of the event or influence being analyzed. Nonetheless, go ahead and see what answers you can determine as conclusive even at this point. Self Expression Directives reveal themselves from the blessings and findings you identify, so at least proposing some answers is important.

Now that you've been "tipped," take your story through Steps 3 through 7 of the Discovery & Expression process.

Eyelids are beginning to flutter on this new life you have created!

MuuuuuuuAAAAAAAAAHaaaaHaaaaHaaaa!

A new life form is placing its feet on the ground!
Your creature now stands!
Revel in your life-generating magnificence!

MuuuuuuuAAAAAAAAAHaaaaHaaaaHaaaa!

Embrace 2—Homeplay 3
because to Be Cause: Your Present (Expanded)

As your next Embrace 2 Homeplay, apply the 7-Step Discovery & Expression Method you just completed to each of the remaining four Serious and Significant current time events/situations/influences you identified in Homeplay 1. Work on this gradually if you need to, but steadily, and come back to the book when you are finished.

Embrace 2—Homeplay 4
Insight & Awareness Questions

Let's pause a moment and look at what you found in and through the Self Expression Directives you have intuited from applying the 7-Step Discovery & Expression Method to your Present. Take some time to write out your answers to the following questions in your Back Forty Freedom Fliers Journal.

1. In what direction are your seemingly unwanted events, situations or influences pointing you in terms of living fuller, freer and happier from here on out?
2. What have you Discovered that will now Express from these events or influences, which you may now recognize are happening *by* you, not *to* you?

These questions in themselves reveal where we want to go by using the Discovery & Expression Method to address both our past and present previously unwanted situations or events in life: to a place of power in having created it all. Your answers reveal your specific flight plan.

Life is a rip-off when you expect to get what you want. Life works when you choose what you got. Actually, what you got is what you chose. To move on, choose it. —*Werner Erhard*

When, from an observer's point of view, you can own and be amazed by the mechanics and magnificence of your incredible, growth-directed antics of experimentation, you get more freed up and flexible around any urgency or tragedy of the moment, past or present.

You realize that there's a purpose to it all. Even if you haven't deciphered it yet, your entire life has been and continues to be a uniquely powerful laboratory for the discovery and expression of something. A directional pointer is encoded in every situation; that pointer, identified by you as your Self Expression Directives, enables your life to become more aligned with who you came here to be and what you came here to do. Your life ceases to happen to you and starts to occur as happening by you and always for you.

When we begin to switch our "to"s in life to "by"s, we start stepping into our already pre-existing, though perhaps mostly unconscious, power to create. Realizing that creative power makes for a radical second half of life.

You are never who you "are" or who you've been. You are who you're becoming. And who you're becoming depends upon the story you are telling yourself about your past and present. Change your story, change your life.

> *When we begin to switch our "to"s in life to "by"s, we start stepping into our already pre-existing, though perhaps mostly unconscious, power to create. Realizing that creative power makes for a radical second half of life.*

As we continue in our quest for a Back Forty of play, passion and purpose, we'll take this idea of where and how life occurs even further. What if, even beyond life happening *by* us, we might arrive at a point of understanding that life is happening *for us, through* us, or even *as* us?

Whoa!! Just let that idea shake up your whole Mad Scientist mood!

MuuuuuuuAAAAAAAAHaaaaHaaaaHaaaa!

SECOND SEPTENARY ACKNOWLEDGMENT

This is bold and brave Homeplay that you are conducting. It's not to be taken lightly. Congratulate yourself! If you've fully engaged in the ideas presented thus far, perhaps even begun to uncover for yourself your own perfectly designed life-and-times for the Discovery and Expression of who you came here to be and what you came here to do, you are likely in a uniquely small percentage of humanity. Breaking out of the seductive and hypnotic matrix of "this is how life is," as you are doing, is pioneering, courageous and inventive.

Just like the early global explorers, when pursuing a truth that the world is actually round and not flat, you put yourself in a vulnerable position of being laughed at, ridiculed and mocked. Yet, most innovative ideas are thought to be crazy at first. Then, as more and more brave souls begin to think outside of the "normal" box, many originally foolish ideas become "but of course!" aspects of everyday life.

> *You are never who you "are" or who you've been. You are who you're becoming.*

Granted, it may be a while before most folks choose to be responsible for the creation of their own lives and experiences, but that's not your concern or mine. It's what we can do for our Self in creating our own life in the here and now that matters. If we do that for our Self, ideally it has impact far beyond us as individuals.

I salute you. And me. Yay for us!

CELEBRATING RADICAL IDEAS

As I close Embrace 2, I'll share some quotes of inspiration to support your continued incorporation of this radical idea of ultimate responsibility and, therefore, power in and over your own life.

The difficulty lies not so much in developing new ideas
as in escaping from old ones.

JOHN MAYNARD KEYNES

Every really new idea looks crazy at first.

ALFRED NORTH WHITEHEAD

I can't understand why people are frightened of new ideas.
I'm frightened of the old ones.

JOHN CAGE

Be not astonished at new ideas; for it is well known
to you that a thing does not therefore cease to be true
because it is not accepted by many.

BARUCH SPINOZA

A mind, once stretched by a new idea,
never regains its original dimensions.

OLIVER WENDELL HOLMES

A person with a new idea is a crank until the idea succeeds.

MARK TWAIN

> **Don't be afraid of new ideas. Be afraid of old ideas. They keep you where you are and stop you from growing and moving forward. Concentrate on where you want to go, not on what you fear.**
>
>
>
> TONY ROBBINS

> **New ideas pass through three periods: 1) It can't be done. 2) It probably can be done, but it's not worth doing. 3) I knew it was a good idea all along!**
>
> ARTHUR C. CLARKE

> **The future is built on the flow of new ideas.**
>
>
>
> PAUL MEYER

Next, you'll take your newfound power, the Be Cause of your past and present into discovering the gifts and talents you'll be carrying with you into your Back Forty future. In Embrace 3, you will inventory and discover all the natural gifts, talents, skills, knowledge and knacks that you've amassed in a Front Forty full of experimentation and determine which of those will serve you best in your second half/best half. You may find that who you are now is a completely different human being than who you were ten, twenty, thirty years ago.

YOUR GIFTS

Our deepest fear is not that we are inadequate. Our deepest fear is that we are powerful beyond measure. It is our light, not our darkness that most frightens us. We ask ourselves, who am I to be brilliant, gorgeous, talented, fabulous? Actually, who are you not to be? You are a child of God. Your playing small does not serve the world. There is nothing enlightened about shrinking so that other people won't feel insecure around you. We are all meant to shine, as children do. We were born to make manifest the glory of God that is within us. It's not just in some of us; it's in everyone. And as we let our own light shine, we unconsciously give other people permission to do the same. As we are liberated from our own fear, our presence automatically liberates others.

MARIANNE WILLIAMSON, *A Return to Love*

FRONT FORTY SADDLEBAGS

Ideally, at this point in your getting The Back Forty lay of the land, a couple things are starting to happen. First, you're beginning to sense the possible perfection of everything that has come before this moment in your life's Front Forty/first half. Embraces 1 and 2 of the Back Forty journey have given you a method for discovering that perfection, which reveals previously unseen blessings. You might call it the "method to the madness" of your past—and of your present.

Second, this awareness of perfection has offered you an opportunity to requalify everything that you've previously held as limiting you and your future in any way. You are beginning to see that no limits exist when you discover and run with your Self Expression Directives, which Discovery & Expression analyses of life's laboratory experiments have made evident and will continue to reveal. The discovery process never stops.

Building on this start, we want to initiate an inventory of the skills and talents we have accrued thus far in life—the gifts we developed and utilized in that first half of ardent experimentation. Many of the blessings we've uncovered or will continue to uncover through ongoing "because to Be Cause" Discovery & Expression analyses will likely include great skills, talents and abilities emerging through the course of our life's lab experiments. For example, your sense of humor, your ability to persevere, your uncanny knack for organizing, your innovative mind, which can envision whole new approaches and solutions, all of these may actually be blessings that came from previously held "bad things that happened to me."

We want to recognize and magnify the value of those abilities because, after all, we put a lot of time into constructing events and circumstances so we could specifically gain those gifts, be who we came to be and do what we came to do! Plus, as we acknowledge the existence of the gifts and talents infused in us, we open the door to realizing that we have lots more gifts on the way. We're not limited to or by only those past experiments and their derived talents. Beyond magnifying those gifts through our newly attained awareness of them, the subsequent attention we give to them and beneficial use we make of them, we want to consider that it's even possible to multiply their number—to grow even more perfectly designed gifts and talents—through further consciously designed experimentation and Discovery & Expression analyses as we move forward.

In compiling an inventory of the gifts and talents that you'll carry with you through the gateway to your Back Forty, you'll include an entire spectrum of

- gifts developed in traditional ways (e.g., education, training);
- still more gifts and talents uncovered through excavational and reflective means (e.g., gifts you previously have not realized that you've gained); and
- even additional gifts pointed out by independent observers (e.g., what others see about you that you don't).

This "Embrace 3: Your Gifts" and the next chapter, "Embrace 4: Your Values," will uncover the personal anthropological finds that your Front Forty has set you up to reveal in your radical, playful, passionate and purposeful Back Forty.

Embrace 3 is particularly important because many of us have gotten used to ourselves at this point in life. Most of us are no longer a mystery to that person in the mirror. We think we know all too well and are absolutely convinced of that person's capacities, boundaries, limitations and what is and isn't possible for him or her.

Moreover, we think we really know the extent and capacity of our Self— the highest level of conscious being that we're equipped to become. So, we are the equivalent of a day-in, day-out roommate with ourselves, passing by without noticing our own immensity. As opposed to reveling in utter awe and wonder at the ineffable magnificence of that person in the mirror, as the Broadway song goes, we've grown accustomed to our face. Inasmuch as your unique gifts and talents go mostly unnoticed, lost in the wallpaper of your everyday life, you likely never celebrate them. Now, I encourage you, urge you, to begin to do so. By focusing on and celebrating your gifts, you'll empower those gifts with more vitality than they've ever had and set your Self up for a limitlessly talented Back Forty. Therefore, it's necessary to gain renewed awareness of your Self, that being in the mirror, likely still yet to do what it came here to do. Think about it: if your BEST Self Expression in life is still ahead, you ought to know what materials you're going to use to build it!

> *Most of us are no longer a mystery to that person in the mirror. We think we know all too well and are absolutely convinced of that person's capacities, boundaries, limitations and what is and isn't possible for him or her.*

We often focus on what we don't already know or have in terms of skills, talents, gifts, capacities and resources. We claim, "If only I had this or that [talent/ability/opportunity], then I'd be able to be and do what I want." Yet, if we would get deeply in touch with who we already are and what we're already truly capable of, we'd be moved to tears. That is exactly the kind of Self-awareness and Self-appreciation you want to bolster as you prepare for your biggest game ahead. And, that's the purpose of the upcoming Embrace 3 inventories.

> **There is a Fountain of Youth: it is your mind, your talents, the creativity you bring to your life and the lives of the people you love. When you learn to tap this source, you will truly have defeated age.** —*Sophia Loren*

THE LYNCH MOB

In Wild West movies, you'll often see a cowboy or two travelling across a wide expanse of territory, perhaps crossing barren plains for days or weeks. They carry in their saddlebags everything that will sustain them along the way, so they're smart to check their inventory before beginning their ride. Similarly, in crossing over into your second half/best half of life, you're wise to tally up the assets you've collected in your Front Forty saddlebags.

One pervasive and bothersome crowd we want to acknowledge and come to terms with as we set out to discover our Wild West wonder-full-ness is *the lynch mob*.

You know them well. They're depicted prominently in old western movies, and they've run you out of town many times before. The lynch mob always shows up just when you start to free your Self from whomever, whatever and however you've been in the past. They get especially riled up when you get uppity about your unique voice or Self being heard and acknowledged. Those are grounds for stringing you up for good.

> *If we would get deeply in touch with who we already are and what we're already truly capable of, we'd be moved to tears.*

Beginning to appreciate your unique and special gifts and starting to recognize that you are so loved by a beneficent, all-inclusive Universe that you've been endowed with certain talents and capacities that make you absolutely distinct from everyone else is getting a bit bold and downright lawless. The lynch mob doesn't take well to folks stepping out of their prescribed (often self-prescribed) place. So, learning to acknowledge and celebrate your own greatness may dredge up all sorts of programming from childhood. Stay-in-your-place, lynching voices from the past can arise. The mob may burst into shouting some version of these accusations:

"Well, just who do you think you are? God's gift to the world?"

"Look at you on your high horse. You really think you're something, don't you?"

"Oh, so you think you're better than everybody else?"

"Don't get so high and mighty. Your poop stinks just like everybody's."

"Be careful: remember, what goes up must come down."

Or, maybe they speak through you in seemingly more mature, refined and intelligent tones like:

"That's all fine and good, but I don't have time to take an ego trip around how great I am."

"No thanks. I don't want to become arrogant or pompous."

"I've already done that introspective work and already know my gifts. Thank you, but I'm good."

Whether in disguise or not, when you begin to explore or declare your wonder-full-ness, the internal lynch mob has their torches lit, their pitchforks in hand and are out on the road confronting you, convincing you to turn around and head the other way. They speak in various voices and reason in various ways, but the message is always the same: do not go there.

The lynch mob says that you're wrong to even get close to discovering your Self because, when you do, you'll start tooting your own horn and become an obnoxious ass. They've told individuals this for so long, in so many different words, in so many different customs and in so many different cultures on the face of the earth that it seems to be a universal dictum: do *not* know (much less celebrate) your own wonder-full-ness!

Fortunately, there's a new sheriff in town and things are going to be different around here. Let's get freed up! Why? Because. . .

The saddest thing in life is wasted talent, and the choices that you make will shape your life forever. —*Chazz Palminteri*

Let go of the fear of becoming an obnoxious ass! What if it's possible to simply get a good, sober and responsible inventory of the gifts and talents you've picked up along the path of life lived thus far without becoming egotistical? Possible? Yes! And, it's harmless. Plus, I propose that, if you give this Back Forty-gateway, gifts evaluation process its due, it will actually wake you up to storehouses of hidden aptitudes and capacities you have right now, right under your very feet! Best of all, it will enable you to better help others by using those gifts you didn't even know you had.

See how apparent self-centeredness becomes a blessing?

> *What if it's possible to simply get a good, sober and responsible inventory of the gifts and talents you've picked up along the path of life lived thus far without becoming egotistical? Possible? Yes! And, it's harmless.*

MuuuuuuuAAAAAAAAHaaaaHaaaaHaaaa!

Embrace 3—Homeplay 1

Affirmation

So, let's open up this inventory-explorational Embrace 3 with an initial exercise. Get out your Back Forty Freedom Fliers Journal and be ready to take some notes.

I want you to say the following bold sentence over and over to yourself out loud. Slowly. Deliberately. With your eyes closed. No rush. Repeat it to yourself ten times and only open a corner of an eye to make a mark on your journal page after each repetition, so you don't have to remember to count. Simply concentrate and be present to the feelings these words evoke within you.

"I am brilliant, gorgeous, talented and fabulous."

After repeating the above sentence 10 times, quickly write in your journal the thoughts that come up for you after doing so. What are the immediate and strong responses that you get from your inner voice? Jot down anything that you hear. Words, sentences, memories, body sensations, voices, anything at all that occurs in your experience. Be honest. Give yourself a moment to listen and record what you hear, see, think, and feel.

Now, take a few minutes to answer the following *Back Forty Insight & Awareness Questions* in your journal:

1. Does the internal lynch-mob immediately discount the validity of the statement you repeated?
2. Does the lynch-mob completely deny your right to even speak it, based on the circumstances, conditions or situations you're facing in life right now?
3. Does that inner voice go so far as to say, "What junk! This is all a retread of some self-help platitudes written long ago to make me feel good. This is stupid. I'm done with this book!"

If any of these lynch-mob responses describe your experience, just take notice and become aware of them. You don't need to do anything about it right now.

On the other hand, your inner voice may not be critical; it may even be openly receptive and accepting of the statement. It might agree, saying *"Yes, yes, yes! This is true. This affirmation resonates with me!"* This could mean you have somehow dodged the prevailing lynch-mob laws of keeping egos in check. If so, this saddlebags inventory of gifts and talents should be easy for you. Enjoy it with abandon.

For whatever reasons and to whatever degree the lynch-mob voice may be confronting you, don't be persuaded to pass over Embrace 3 and not complete the exercises. Just notice the voice. It has an opinion for you to be aware of. Simply recognize that *a voice,* posing as friend or foe, has some response to the statement you repeated. If you'll merely acknowledge the existence of that voice and its opinion, without either buying into it or resisting it, you have a good chance of keeping your Self independent, open and available for this Homeplay inventory process. The voice is not You, who you really are. It's just a voice. Practice thinking for your Self outside of the dictates of that voice.

> *The voice is not You, who you really are. It's just a voice. Practice thinking for your Self outside of the dictates of that voice.*

YOUR SHINE

Here's another "what if?" question:

Just what if each of us *is* actually "brilliant, gorgeous, talented and fabulous"? What if that *is* the case, regardless of your voice's supposed evidence or proof to the contrary? What if that *is* who you are at your very core, and what if any seemingly contradictory appearances, circumstances or conditions playing out in your current life don't mean squat?

I assert that, underneath all the conditions or challenges you may currently face, lies within you a true foundation of greatness and magnanimity that you may simply not be in touch with at the moment. Yet, as certain as the sun will rise tomorrow, there's a core awesomeness shining within you—your Self—that you don't know, the knowing of which will make a second-half lifetime of difference. And, if you can bring yourself to consider that to be true, for even a moment, it suggests that any appearance of disarray in your present-day life is simply an illusion. The disarray isn't real, it just *appears* to be real. What's really going on is experiments!

As you discovered with Embrace 2: Your Present, experiments always point you toward your greater Self-expression yet to be revealed. Do not let your ongoing and necessary experiments—which, as you may be noticing, are the nature of life itself—dim the light of your very real and substantial shine.

To reiterate a portion of the quote that began this chapter. . .

And as we let our own light shine, we unconsciously give other people permission to do the same. As we are liberated from our own fear, our presence automatically liberates others.

> *There's a core awesomeness shining within you—your Self—that you don't know, the knowing of which will make a second-half lifetime of difference.*

For you to let your own light shine, first and foremost you must know what that light is. You must prove to your conscious, often argumentative mind, which dismisses most of the claims of Self wonder-full-ness you ever attempt to make, that you, indeed, possess substantial, unique gifts and talents to be shared.

If you accept that this "light" is not just in some individuals, but in all, and that you too are here to "make manifest the Glory of God" within you, your most important question might become, *"Wow, I wonder what that unique light within me is!"*

While growing up, I was once given a "treasure-hunt" birthday party, where I was directed to notes with clues that led me to gifts hidden all over the house. Consider the exercises and surveys that follow to be notes and clues guiding you along the path of discovering your own gifts, your own light within.

And, as we embark on this treasure hunt, a last note regarding the lynch mob for the humble or unassuming: just drop the false humility right now, all right? If you don't take on a commitment to your own unique greatness, nobody else ever will. . .or can.

The process of being who you came to be must start from *within*. If you have assets that are not recognized and invested wisely, just like in business, you're being irresponsible and careless. The Parable of the Talents in biblical scripture tells of a master who puts his servants in charge of his business while away on a trip. Upon his return, he evaluates them on their steward-ship of his investments ("talents"), rewarding those who reaped value and reprimanding the one who squandered the assets. It's no accident that the word "talents," a measure of goods and value in biblical times, also relates to you and your own uniqueness. If you don't reap all the value from that uniqueness, it's tantamount to squandering all that's been given you by your Front Forty experiments.

If necessary, just for the sake of these Homeplay surveys and exercises, play a game and look at yourself from the perspec-tive of an overbearing, doting and gloat-ing grandmother. You know the type: prais-

> **The process of being who you came to be must start from within.**

ing her grandchild incessantly, finding every tiny reason to proclaim the child as God's gift to humanity, so much so that you, the grandchild, become incredibly embarrassed. Well, be like her. Go so overboard in self-acknowledgement with these inventories that you verge on embarrassment through such Self-awareness!

Whatever it takes, just let go of the old conditioning we all grew up with that says don't toot your own horn. If you don't begin realizing all there is to toot about your Self and start tooting right away, your uniquely enliv-ening and awakening Back Forty wake-up call may forever remain a tootless wonder.

"Hey there, Brilliant, Gorgeous, Talented and Fabulous. . .what's Your Shine?"

SURVEYS

On the farm, some of the greatest riches are not ones seen by the naked eye. For example, the oil reserves or other mineral rights underground are sources of wealth far beyond those seen above ground. Such riches require geological surveys to assess.

We're going to do our own versions of geological and even archeological surveys to account for the inherently valuable, though perhaps not immediately perceived, assets that you're bringing with you into your Back Forty life ahead.

We'll approach this insightful inventory process in two ways:

Internal Surveys

1. Things I do better than the average Joe/Jane.
2. Activities I most enjoy doing that give me "**JUICE**," (**J**oyful **U**nification—**I**ndividual **C**ommuning with **E**ternal).
3. The elements behind Surveys 1 and 2—my raw talents or building blocks.
4. Specialized skills, knowledge, experience, education, training or resources.
5. Lists of people I think have the best jobs in the world, and why.

External Survey

A survey to discover what others observe as my greatest gifts, talents and skills: a 360-degree assessment to identify what others see that I don't.

Through these surveys, we'll detect "Your Shine" and uncover the gifts, talents and capacities that make *you absolutely DISTINCT from everyone else!*

As demonstrated earlier in the book, I'll put myself on display. You'll watch me discover and find "My Shine" in inventories I conducted for my own awareness when first engaging in The Back Forty. Use my assessment as an example for conducting your own inventory. But do keep in mind that my Shine is not Your Shine; nor is yours mine. So, don't get stuck with any particularly personal elements I uncover. Just use my inventory as a model or template for yours and be just as authentic and acknowledging of what's true for you as I'll be for myself.

Please, heed the stop signs along the way. Breezing through such critical, Self-reflective material won't provide the awareness necessary to design your radical second half of play, passion and purpose. So, do yourself the favor of Homeplaying as you go, not later. Your Back Forty happens now, not later.

Lastly, I invite you to approach these surveys from the creative space of inquiry versus being intent on finding an immediate, goldmine answer. Just as the earlier "because to Be Cause" process required creative imagination, simply allow yourself to ponder and percolate on these surveys and what they evoke for you to consider. One insightful clue leads to another. Enjoy the treasure hunt.

To kick off the baring of my own gifted soul, here are the things I believe I do better than the average Joe or Jane:

1. Communicate and express ideas, both written and verbal.
2. Friendly comfort with all types of people until or unless I realize they are "important," upon which I can get intimidated.
3. Humor and quick wit.
4. Technically adept: can figure out new electronics or app.
5. Disciplined: have been able to work from home for the last thirty years because I don't focus on the fridge or friends.
6. Focused: can eliminate all cluttered surroundings from my vision as I zero in on a particular project.
7. Have some understanding of human nature.
8. Lover.
9. Affirmative prayer.
10. Conversationalist: good at talking with people.
11. Public speaking.

12. Counseling and coaching.
13. Discipline-oriented parenting, noting the word "discipline" actually means "teach."
14. Singing.
15. Daredevil/high adventure activities.
16. Drawing/artwork.
17. Physical fitness activities.
18. A reader and assimilator of ideas.
19. Inspiring leader.
20. Risk-taking.

Ready, set, get out your Back Forty Freedom Fliers Journal and prepare to write!

Embrace 3—Homeplay 2
Internal Survey 1: Things I Do Better Than the Average Joe/Jane

This first survey is fairly straightforward and can be assessed from an overall view of your life, daily activities, affinities, and talents you get complimented for. This can include professional or career talents as well as basic, personal life skills. At this point in your evolution, you do a lot of things better than the average Joe or Jane. Simply list out anything you do fairly well.

As mentioned before, forget my own particular "Shine" factors and focus on yours. Don't stop until you've come up with at least 20 Things You Do Better Than the Average Joe/Jane. Keep going beyond that if you like, but definitely DON'T stop until you have a minimum of 20. Disregard any lynch-mob, inner-voice that says you can't come up with at least 20. Also, don't discount something you used to do but don't now do consistently. Inconsistency isn't necessarily a deal breaker.

If you begin to think you can't write any more, know that it's the very NEXT ones you'll list that will be absolutely golden: talents so deep or invisible that you've never even considered them as gifts. When you have at least 20, then and only then, move on.

Now that you have your list, referring to it, answer in your journal these *Back Forty Insight & Awareness Questions:*

1. What did you notice from creating your list of 20?
2. Did you experience resistance to completing 20? If so, why do you believe you did?
3. What items showed up that you hadn't really considered before?
4. Which gifts do you most enjoy engaging in?
5. How might you share your gifts in better or bigger ways?
6. What gifts might you develop and express more?

Here are notes from my own Back Forty Insight & Awareness exercises:

- I reminded myself of my love for creatively expressing ideas, whether through writing, speaking, singing, performing, etc. These are the things I enjoy most.

- I hadn't really considered my ability to pray "affirmatively" as a unique talent but, when I stop to consider the gratitude and compliments I receive from individuals after praying with them, it's good to recognize it. (Affirmative prayer is a style of praying in which, rather than beseeching or pleading, one prays believing that they already possess whatever they are praying for, so as to mentally and spiritually open the door to receiving whatever it is. It aligns with the scriptural encouragement to "Pray believing that you already have, so that ye may receive." We'll talk more about affirmative prayer in "Embrace 7: A Presence.")

- I'd like to grow more in the avenues of writing and speaking. I've never truly given writing its due as a regular activity in my daily life. However, I've known for a long time that speaking is an area I want to expand into.

- I've always enjoyed performing karaoke when out of town, on vacation, etc., but I've never made a point of engaging in it regularly at home. I could put this playful, "vacation-mode" element of fun into my life on a more regular basis.

JUICE

Let's move on to another survey to explore for even deeper riches of insight and awareness about what makes you special. Let's talk about JUICE!

You know that feeling you get when time seems to stop? Like when you spend four hours doing something but think it's only been ten minutes? Some call it "being in the zone." That feeling is a good clue as to what gives you **JUICE** (**J**oyful **U**nification—**I**ndividual **C**ommuning with **E**ternal). I believe this zone feeling, when time stands still, puts us in touch with the Eternal Being (Oneness) that we were and all remain part of before it seemingly dispersed into separate bodies and identities with different names and stories: before it broke out into you and me. When an activity detaches us from time, it connects us with the timeless from where we touch the Infinite. Our JUICE *is us* tapped into the bigger Self.

You might ask what makes an activity I enjoy doing, that gives me JUICE, a gift? Here are a couple answers.

First, if you enjoy doing something and it gives you JUICE, then there's a built-in, developmental process causing you to become better at whatever that activity is, even if you may think you stink at it right now. You do it, you enjoy it, you get lost in it, it gives you JUICE. You do it more, you enjoy it more, you get lost in it more, it gives you more JUICE. All the while, you become more "gifted" in that particular activity because, as you continually engage in it, you learn and grow in your facility with it, regardless of how "good" you may be at it.

> **When an activity detaches us from time, it connects us with the timeless from where we touch the Infinite. Our JUICE is us tapped into the bigger Self.**

Second, even if you listed activities that you rarely practice, those are still gifts in that they serve as guides and treasure maps toward that which energizes you. Fact is, you'll always express your light brighter in the world when you're in the vibration of joy. Therefore, having roadmaps toward joy—knowing where you can find it and engaging in it as often as possible— will always serve to translate your many other activities (joyful or not) into a greater contribution on the planet. You might call these JUICE activities your "joy translators" in that they have you radiate more joyfully in everything else you do.

Knowing where to fill your joy tank and ideally doing it often is a gift and allows you to offer a greater vibrational benefit to the planet.

Here's my JUICE list:

1. Writing, wordsmithing, and finding creative ways to express ideas.
2. Expressing humor and wit.
3. Performing in front of people, speaking, singing, dancing.
4. Facilitating groups, moderating.
5. Interviewing notable people to reveal their unique experiences, ideas and wisdom.
6. Traveling to new places, being out-and-about.
7. Coaching people toward what's possible.
8. Getting outdoors, especially by the water.
9. Meeting new and different people, learning other cultures.

10. Engaging in existential and ontological philosophies.
11. Physical fitness, working out, running.
12. Learning golf.
13. Attending personal development seminars and workshops.
14. Long drives without rush, especially up the coast.
15. Flying.
16. Playing video games with my son.
17. Reading mind-expanding materials, great works, classics.
18. Meditating and visualizing.
19. Making a sale; producing income.
20. Watching educational and informative programming on PBS.

Embrace 3—Homeplay 3

Internal Survey 2: Activities I Most Enjoy Doing That Give Me JUICE (Joyful Unification—Individual Communing with Eternal)

Basically, the question to ask yourself is *"When do I become most lost in my activities and check out of the here and now?"* As you make your list, don't edit yourself. Just list all the activities you enjoy doing that give you JUICE. Again, don't let yourself stop until you have identified at least 20. List more if you like. Press beyond the moment when you think you can't come up with more. Remember, the next, perhaps slightly more hidden ones, can be absolute gold.

Next, answer in your journal these *Back Forty Insight & Awareness Questions* for JUICE producing activities:

1. What did you notice from creating your list of 20?
2. Did you experience resistance to completing 20? If so, why do you believe you did?

3. What items showed up that you hadn't really considered before?
4. Which gifts do you most enjoy engaging in?
5. How might you share your gifts in better or bigger ways?
6. What gifts might you develop and express more?

I share my own Back Forty Insight & Awareness so that you can observe me learning to think differently. A radical Back Forty of play, passion and purpose demands that we think in new ways.

• When first constructing my JUICE list, I noticed a tendency to put the serious, "more important" and work-related items first and the seemingly "luxury" and when-I-have-time-for-them items second.

At one point, I actually began to re-order the list, even while still writing it, based on some culturally accepted, work-before-play ethos. However, upon noticing that mindset, I decided to leave my list as it was, unedited, in the order the thoughts occurred. I encourage you to do the same. Allowing myself to operate in ways contrary to old models of thinking may hold further insights.

> *Knowing where to fill your joy tank and ideally doing it often is a gift and allows you to offer a greater vibrational benefit to the planet.*

This brings up a point to consider. Be aware of the pull to edit your thoughts when engaging in these processes. Don't edit! Trust what comes. A good motto to operate by is "First thought, best thought." In flowing with first thoughts through these inquires, more of your own personal wisdom will creep out. If you allow it, that deeper wisdom may surpass your current, surface understandings and standard, logical patterns of thinking. Truth is, your present way of thinking got you here. Whether "here" is a rough neighborhood or a comfortable home, to get where you want to be next, you'll need to think differently. So, regard first, unedited thoughts as sacred and see what insights you gain from looking back at them. Also, allow my own tendency to prioritize certain JUICE-producing activities over others (work before play) to raise your awareness of any similar segregation between activities that seem "important" and those that seem more like playful "luxuries" in your own list.

- What if my "luxury" and "when-I-have-time-for-them" activities are just as important and reap just as much overall benefit as my "serious/more important/work-related" ones? I might ask myself, how is the energy from seemingly frivolous, JUICE-producing gifts and talents being suppressed or untapped because I treat them as secondarily important and, therefore, engage in them less?

    Certain items on my list—writing, singing, dancing, golf, traveling to new places, physical fitness, flying, getting outdoors and watching PBS—are all examples of what I might consider "playful luxuries" that come after "work." Yet, some individuals make their entire living specifically in and around those areas! So, I might reconsider what's possible in my future beyond the hard and fast lines I've drawn for "work" and "play" based on the past.

    Plus, even if I never made a dime directly from any of those more playful activities, how might they rejuvenate, uplift, and energize me in ways that *can* impact the dimes I collect elsewhere? What if belting out a karaoke song a day has me attracting more paying clients? If I can begin to treat "luxury" gifts as justifiably equal in importance to those I associate with work and income, who knows what new paths I may forge in life? Who knows how my current career might be directly or indirectly enhanced by these sideline pursuits? The possibilities are exciting!

To explore this insight even further, I reviewed my list again and put an "I" next to the activities I consider important (more serious and work-related) and an "L" by those I tend to engage in when I have the time (what I might consider luxury or play). Here's that list again, now annotated:

1. Writing, wordsmithing, and finding creative ways to express ideas (L)
2. Expressing humor and wit (L)
3. Performing in front of people, speaking, singing, dancing (L)
4. Facilitating groups, moderating (I)
5. Interviewing notable people to reveal their ideas and wisdom (I)
6. Traveling to new places, being out-and-about (L)
7. Coaching people toward what's possible (I)
8. Getting outdoors, especially by the water (L)
9. Meeting new and different people, learning other cultures (L)
10. Engaging in existential and ontological philosophies (L)
11. Physical fitness, working out, running (L)
12. Learning golf (L)
13. Attending personal development seminars and workshops (I)
14. Long drives without rush, especially up the coast (L)
15. Flying (L)
16. Playing video games with my son (L)
17. Reading mind-expanding materials, great works, classics (L)
18. Meditating and visualizing (I)
19. Making a sale, producing income (I)
20. Watching educational and informative programming on PBS (L)

This list-segregation process created even more Back Forty Insight & Awareness for me:

• Actively carving out time each and every day to write and express ideas creatively can be a source of not only luxurious JUICE for me but could also very well be a path into The Back Forty I envision for myself. Actually taking the step to move forward with this book rather than waiting until some "better" or "more appropriate" time, which never comes, is a step in that direction.

- Also, rather than wait until the book has been completed, I see that I can engage in the "luxury" of speaking and conducting workshops by creating venues to share and explore these ideas even while still in the process of documenting them.

- This is completely out of left field ("first thought, best thought"); but, through engaging in these insights over the last couple of days, I woke up one morning with the idea that my "luxurious" joys of creative writing, wordsmithing and wit could be used to start a hobby I've only considered once before, just after college— writing country music lyrics! If there's a genre that most creatively uses words, wit and turn of phrase, it's country music, which I grew up with and have always loved.

As you can see, inside a process of identifying your JUICE-giving activities while also becoming aware of how you hold them in terms of practical versus playful, unexpected new possibilities and completely wild ideas can arise. You don't necessarily need to take immediate action on every insight. Yet, it's exciting to simply notice the potential for radical, second-half shifts!

Embrace 3—Homeplay 4
Ranking Internal JUICE Survey

Engage in this process yourself. Go through your own list of "Activities I Most Enjoy Doing That Give Me JUICE" and put an "I" (important) by those you tend to consider more serious and/or work-related and an "L" (luxury) by those you tend to include in your life "when you have the time."

Now, answer these *Back Forty Insight & Awareness Questions* in your Freedom Fliers Journal:

1. What do you see for yourself out of distinguishing your JUICE activities as important versus luxury?
2. Where might you re-orient your life to bring more time and energy into those luxurious activities that give you JUICE?

These questions and your answers to them can alter your second half of life, based on any insights you get. What new insight and awareness are you having about the way you've been thinking? How could you think differently moving forward?

MY RAW TALENTS OR BUILDING BLOCKS:
The Elements Behind My Better Than Average Joe/Jane and JUICE Lists

Let's continue with yet another survey, this one taking us even deeper into underground resources than the previous ones. Here, we want to list out our basic, raw or primary talents that enable us to do the things we do better than the average Joe/Jane and do those activities that give us JUICE. We want to get to the driving source(s) of those previous lists. We look behind or beneath those activities and compile a list of what makes it even possible for us to do them.

Reviewing my previous two lists, here are the elements I see at the source of them:

1. Fascination with language and its use
2. Quick wit
3. Quest for positive attention
4. Inquisitiveness into how things work and the unknown
5. Social butterfly
6. Fascination with human nature and potential
7. Discipline
8. Playfulness
9. Helpfulness
10. Drive
11. Logical thinking
12. Spiritual orientation
13. Boldness
14. Creativity

For this particular survey, I placed my "what-I-do-better" and "what-gives-me-JUICE" survey answers in front of me and simply scanned them, asking myself,

1. For someone to be good at that, or to have interest in that, what would their basic make-up have to be?"
2. What basic elements would be required for someone to have an interest or skill in that?

For example, at the top of my lists were "communicate and express ideas, both written and verbal," and "writing, wordsmithing, and finding creative ways to express ideas." So, it naturally follows, upon asking the above questions, that a basic *fascination with language and its use* (e.g., writing, speaking) must be present.

Sometimes it might not be so cut and dried, but clear nonetheless when we peek below the surface a bit. For instance, when I see that I have listed activities or skills such as humor and quick wit, public speaking, inspiring leadership, performing in front of people, singing, and dancing, then I must figure that I'm someone with a *quest for positive attention.*

I will not—and encourage you not to—get caught up in any self-judgments, like whether it's good or bad to have a quest for positive attention. Psychoanalysis is valuable, but that is not what we are doing here. This process is simply to get up underneath your gifts and talents to notice—with judgment-free awareness—what raw abilities and drives make up the unique You.

Many of these raw abilities and interests may have come in response to Front Forty laboratory experiments, your serious and significant events or influences. Even if they may have come about as a reaction to some "bad" thing that happened to you, it doesn't diminish their value. They are a legitimate part of who you are. If you consider that all of those laboratories were to help form you into, or, better yet, inform you of, who you're here to be and what you're here to do, then it's truly all good!

This particular list may seem pretty basic, but that's the point—you want to get in touch with the fundamental building blocks of your talents, gifts, and interests. Like a Periodic Table of Elements in chemistry reveals the atomic structures underlying the substances of this world, you want to uncover what's underneath and comprising your substantive expressions of gifts and talents.

> *Like a Periodic Table of Elements in chemistry reveals the atomic structures underlying the substances of this world, you want to uncover what's underneath and comprising your substantive expressions of gifts and talents.*

Why? Because developing a greater awareness for the "method behind the madness," the foundational aspects of your uniquely gifted make-up (your "Shine"), helps you find new and broader ways to express those same basic elements in everything you do.

Realize that there is no right way to do this analysis, and note that there's no magic number of elements that lie behind your skills, talents, and interests. *You can't do this process wrong!* The point is simply to dig deeper and deeper into You so that You can see what You see for whatever insights You get.

Embrace 3—Homeplay 5
Internal Survey 3: My Raw Talents or Building Blocks

Go ahead now and create your own list of "My Raw Talents or Building Blocks." Here again are questions that may facilitate your discovery. Ask them in relation to each item in your lists.

- For someone to be good at that, or to have interest in that, what would their basic make-up have to be?
- What basic elements would be required for someone to have an interest or skill in that?

As previously recommended, write your first thoughts into your journal without editing what comes up and without sitting in judgment of it.

Now, answer these *Back Forty Insight & Awareness Questions* in your Freedom Fliers Journal:

1. What did you notice from creating your list?
2. Did you experience resistance? If so, why do you believe you did?
3. What items showed up that you hadn't really considered before?
4. Which raw talents do you most enjoy using?
5. How might you expand these elements in better or bigger ways?
6. What raw talents might you develop and express more?

SPECIALIZED SKILLS, KNOWLEDGE, EXPERIENCE, EDUCATION, TRAINING, AND RESOURCES

This next internal inventory survey, which will amaze you when you fully begin taking stock, recognizes the gifts of specialized skills, knowledge, experience, education, training and resources that are already in your possession.

Undoubtedly, you've taken immense ground in these areas, ground which is undergirded with valuable minerals. Without inspecting or surveying that ground, those riches, often lying only inches beneath the surface, remain untapped. They bless nobody and definitely not you. Truly taking stock of these lesser-noticed treasures can create a gusher of awareness.

Here's my list, which includes overlapping items from earlier surveys:

1. Ability to convey ideas, written and verbal
2. Speaking and teaching
3. Developing, promoting and conducting workshops and trainings
4. Conducting teleseminars
5. Coaching for success
6. "Backdoor" or stealth job search/career transition knowledge and related training ability
7. Recruiting/headhunting skills, knowledge and ability
8. Spiritual counseling and prayer treatment
9. Network marketing skills, knowledge and ability
10. Internet marketing
11. Home business setup and success principles
12. Book writing, editing, publishing and promotion
13. Acting and performing
14. Enrollment and the ability to engage the participation of others
15. Dealing with custody and single parenting issues

16. A member of inspiring, transformational communities, in which I am a spiritual counselor

17. Connected one or two degrees apart from top individuals in the speaking, inspirational and career counseling arenas

This survey requires you to revisit it a few times, likely over a day or two, because you won't necessarily notice all those underground treasures in one sitting. Yet, as you focus on it while believing and knowing that there *absolutely is such a list inside you*, like a squirrel in winter, you'll remember where you've buried lots of nuts just in time to chew on them.

Realize that your "skills, knowledge, experience, education or training" doesn't need to come through organized channels of learning (classes, courses, educational institutions, etc.). Many people learn and utilize far more in the "school of life" than they ever learned, retained or used from formal education.

It's been said that a college education is more about learning *how to learn* than it is about any particular field of study pursued. Because every field on the face of the planet is ever-evolving, often what you learn in college becomes obsolete almost the moment you walk out the door. So, the time spent in formal education might be more a period of proving to oneself or to a future employer that you have the capacity to learn and develop skills and knowledge, the ability to be trained and developed, than it is about the subject area itself. Therefore, much of the treasure to be mined from your Front Forty in the way of skills, knowledge, education and training may be things you've simply learned along the way, planned or not.

For example, I possess an ability to coach and support individuals in the area of custody disputes over children *not* because I chose to study that area but because I went through a custody dispute myself. I may not have all the technical or legal answers, but I'm a good resource for experience, strength, hope and discoveries gained through my own challenges stemming from that life event.

Too often, life gives each of us incredibly powerful "educations" that get wasted because we fall victim to the situations or events surrounding those educations rather than owning them and growing from them. That's why we took time with Embrace 1: Your Past and Embrace 2: Your Present to expand your ability to render your serious and significant events or influences to be fruitful and abundant with blessings, findings and directives that better your life rather than being dark clouds constantly raining on your life's parade.

Considering not only what I learned about the family law system, but also the insights I gained about myself, my personality, parenting and areas in which I'd like to personally improve, I've often considered those three years and the half-million dollars invested in that custody battle to be my best "education" to date. I'm still reaping enormous rewards from the changed human being I became Be Cause of it.

> **Many people learn and utilize far more in the "school of life" than they ever learned, retained or used from formal education.**

When I was growing up, a famous slogan for the NAACP stated that "a mind is a terrible thing to waste." Similarly, any education brought on by a life event, situation or circumstance, whether pre-planned or not, is a terrible thing to waste. As you did in Embraces 1 and 2, owning that education and claiming to have put yourself into those particular schools for your own greater-yet-to-be Self allows you to appreciate (i.e., grow in value) the huge amount of hours, expense, trauma, blood, sweat and tears invested.

Doctors, Lawyers, and PhDs pay a price for success by persisting through incredibly challenging schools of study. They deserve to reap the rewards of their hard work. So do you! Therefore, don't discount your own particular "schools" as being any less fruit-bearing than formal ones. Just because you didn't officially enroll in an institution of learning doesn't mean you didn't *pay* for it. You most certainly did. Now, pick the fruit!

If you've attended the school of hard knocks, then let those hard knocks land upon a door of abundant blessings that now opens up for you.

As for the last element in this list, "resources," realize that we are all tapped into resources, some right under our noses, that can be activated or recharged to help us fulfill who we came here to be and what we came here to do. Having a clear direction helps you utilize resources most effectively; but often your resources alone can assist in creating clarity around your direction.

Relationships, who-knows-who connections, circles of influence, and awareness of the material and intellectual assets you possess (and those possessed by people you know) are incredibly valuable resources. They should be considered a gift. Realize that you know, or know of, certain individuals for a reason. If you haven't understood, acknowledged or activated those reasons yet, don't discount their value. They are simply assets that have been sitting around underutilized. Choosing to appreciate (grow in value) those gifts as you move forward can make a radical Back Forty difference.

> *If you've attended the school of hard knocks, then let those hard knocks land upon a door of abundant blessings that now opens up for you.*

Capitalizing on your contacts and connections is like discovering old interest-bearing certificates of deposit and cashing them in. Reconnecting to folks you know *in a contributory way* blesses everyone because we all like feeling connected and being helpful wherever we can. I cover how to best tap into relationships around career and business in my book *Never Apply for a Job Again: Break the Rules, Cut the Line, Beat the Rest*. Later, in a survey in *this* book, I'll show you how to tap into relationships to support the fullest expression of your Back Forty life in general. For now, though, take some time to begin your own list of Specialized Skills, Knowledge, Experience, Education, Training and Resources.

Embrace 3—Homeplay 6
Internal Survey 4: Specialized Skills, Knowledge, Experience, Education, Training and Resources.

Know that you are abundant in skills, knowledge, experience, education, training and resources. Pull out your Freedom Fliers Journal and, just like the other lists, don't stop writing until you've come up with at least 15 to 20 items. Then be sure to revisit your list later today or tomorrow, as more come to mind.

Now that you have your list, answer these *Back Forty Insight & Awareness Questions* in your Journal:

1. What did you notice from creating your list?
2. Did you experience resistance to completing 15 to 20 items? If so, why do you believe you did?
3. What items showed up that you hadn't really considered before?
4. Which of these do you most enjoy tapping into?
5. How might you share these specialized skills, knowledge, experience, education, training, or resources in better or bigger ways?
6. Which of them might you develop and utilize more?

DREAM JOB

Finally, as a fun and future-oriented way to conclude these internal surveys of your gifts and talents, here's one final survey that will open up even more awareness of the hidden treasures lying within you.

Who, in your opinion, have the best jobs in the world? Why?

You may be wondering what admiring the jobs of other people has to do with you. The answer is: a lot. When you appreciate the talents, gifts, and roles of others, it means you are acknowledging the presence or desire for the presence of those talents, gifts, and potential roles within and for you.

Other people are mirrors. What we appreciate, respect and admire in others, we value (or aspire to see) in ourselves. The mere fact that a person's particular work stands out for us among the infinite possibilities of folks on the planet whose work we could admire means something. It's a signal that whatever they possess in terms of character, ways of operating or other personal qualities, those same traits may lie within us, albeit, perhaps, only in acorn state.

Granted, any particular individual may command a physique, skills, talent or experience cultivated over years of dedication to a field you've never even considered tapping into. You may never be able to actually do what they do. Yet, treasures of insight can be obtained from noticing who fills the roles you admire and why you admire those roles and individuals.

> **What we appreciate, respect and admire in others, we value (or aspire to see) in ourselves.**

How can noticing someone else's great job be *your* gift? The great roles you perceive as being fulfilled by others give you a divining rod for discovering nascent, dormant or untapped talents or qualities within your Self or to at least demonstrate a similar element in your own life. Similar to our "luxury" activities gleaned from the prior "JUICE" survey, just noticing can point the way and everything we see can serve as a roadmap and JUICE translator.

For example, if that person whose job you admire is a sports hero or a Nobel Prize winning physicist, it's unlikely that you'll ever be able to do their job. However, an uncultivated ability within you, by noticing it in them, might come closer to being expressed in your own life. It won't be an exact match, but sometimes even something close or inspired in a similar direction can prove valuable.

As an illustration, here's my list compiled several years ago when first engaging in these surveys myself:

1. Charlie Rose.[6] Host of the twenty-seven-year Public Broadcasting System (PBS) talk show of the same name. Charlie interviewed the greatest and most talented individuals in virtually any field of endeavor on the face of the planet, from politicians to philanthropists, from Nobel Laureates to actors, singers, authors and spiritual and business leaders. You name them, he interviewed them. What a job! Of course, it looked all rosy on-screen, but he had to do tons of research to have it look that good. Again, what a job! For me, to imagine being *paid* to do research (e.g., read the guests' books and research the topics they present), to educate myself in all of these areas and then to sit down in a collegial way with influential and intelligent individuals, many recognized as the experts in their fields, to glean their wisdom in a major media format. . .that job seems like about the closest to heaven one can get with feet still on earth!

2. Oprah Winfrey. Included for many of the same reasons as Charlie Rose, yet with the avowed and accredited role of also being a *thought leader* herself. In addition to associating with people who are doing amazing things, she leads people into areas that she deems as forward-moving for the planet. She has been touted as the most influential person on earth today. She handles her role of influence boldly and courageously, yet in such a compassionate, authentic and available way as to include viewers and listeners who would never be exposed to certain ideas otherwise. What a job!

---

6 NOTE: *This is not an endorsement of the individual nor addressing any controversy but, rather, distinguishing one of his roles, which I admired.*

3. Tony Robbins, T. Harv Eker and other motivators and workshop leaders. Obviously, they developed their materials and built themselves from the ground up to where they are now. However, to now have teams scheduling their lives so that they can show up and motivate, that seems like heaven. Of course, they have to be the leader and incredible manager of their own organizations to elicit the support of their teams. I don't take lightly their continued driving force and the years of their building up to this state. Yet, what a job!

4. The late Dr. Wayne Dyer. Self-proclaimed as not simply a motivator but an "inspirer," Wayne Dyer didn't work the popular workshop/seminar circuit of many personal development gurus, but rather operated more like a traveling and lecturing mystic. Whether teaching to an auditorium of 500 people or taping a PBS show to be broadcast throughout the country, he was both a devout and almost monkish researcher and writer in his Maui retreat, as well as a spiritual statesman and professor conducting lectures and talks. He worked a seemingly annual pattern: hibernating in Maui to write his next book and then hitting the lecture and PBS circuit to share his newest ideas. What a job!

5. Esther and the late Jerry Hicks. Although Jerry has passed away, together this couple were messengers of the philosophy of Abraham including a body of work known as "The Law of Attraction." The teachings, which Esther continues, are mind expanding. It is their blessed-by-a-message role that has them on my list of people having the best jobs in the world. Like others throughout history who have fulfilled similar roles, they are open recipients of life-altering information, which they disseminate. They enjoy and benefit personally from the teachings received, and then perform service by getting that information out to interested and waiting ears. The opportunity of sinking

into beneficently offered wisdom and then being a messenger of it. . .what a job!

6. Hosts of Travel Channels or other "tour guides." I include "tour guides" in quotes because anyone hosting a show that takes the viewer somewhere else, to a physical place or even into a new body of knowledge, qualifies as having what I consider to be the best job in the world. While vagabonding through Europe after college, I remember using *Let's Go: Europe* published by Harvard Publications. Throughout my travels, I thought, "Wow! What a job! The students writing this book got to travel the world and then write about it! They got paid to explore!" This goes for creators of restaurant guides, travel or nature shows, documentaries or programs of any educational nature in which one is exploring and sharing information. To be able to explore and play in the areas of your interests and be paid for it, what a job!

This brings up a bit of Back Forty Insight and Awareness: I'll surely come up with further additions to this list, as I'm now more fully engaged in the inquiry and watching even more acutely the world of work being performed around me. However, at this moment I'm already observing a pattern in my list, an overall theme of "learn, then teach" or even "learn while teaching" through the various venues of disseminating information: television, seminars and workshops, lectures, books, audios, etc. Given this is a consistent pattern in the individuals I consider as having "the best jobs in the world," this is an area to which I am called for greater development and Self-expression.

Embrace 3—Homeplay 7
Internal Survey 5: People I Think Have the
Best Jobs in the World and Why

It's time now to get out your Back Forty Freedom Fliers Journal again and create your own list of people who you think have the best jobs in the world.

You'll obviously notice folks in distinctly different fields than I do. That's because you have a distinctly different inner makeup of gifts, talents, proclivities and interests, along with a sensitivity and radar for individuals who resonate with that makeup.

Come up with five or more people who you believe have the best jobs in the world, and then explain why. These people do not have to have a name; they might be "lab technician" or "rural route mail carrier." To get the most insight available, be sure to outline *specifically* what it is about their roles that intrigues or inspires you.

You might make the list as a stream of consciousness, writing one name or occupation after another, letting your mind flow. Then go back and describe the aspects of those "best jobs" you are drawn to.

Now that you have your list, complete this survey by answering in your Journal these *Back Forty Insight & Awareness Questions*:

1. What did you notice from creating your list?
2. Did you experience resistance to identifying five? If so, why do you believe you did?
3. What individuals showed up that you hadn't considered before?
4. Which of these types of roles or functions would you most enjoy tapping into or playing with?
5. How might you, right now, build the elements and flavor of the types of vocations you identified into your life or career in bigger ways?
6. Which of these individuals might you study and learn to model more?

As with all Back Forty methods and processes, these surveys are intended to be incorporated into your approach to life. Stay awake for the next several days, or better yet forever, to the myriad of ways and means through which people employ themselves in their areas of fascination.

Keep observing who, for *you*, has the best job in the world. Who is actually doing work that seems so playful that it's hard for you to conceive of them getting paid for it? Keep adding to your list. Write down in detail why each job is so attractive to you and why you feel they are so blessed to have it.

You get more of what you focus on. The more consciousness you put toward this survey on an ongoing basis, the more resonant elements that you admire will be attracted into your own life. Get ready to have your eyes opened to alternative paths for planning and living your own radical, playful, passionate and purposeful Back Forty.

MID-CHAPTER ACKNOWLEDGMENT

Hooray for you! You've already accomplished a huge amount of discovery through the Internal Surveys presented in this chapter. Hopefully, you've been able to assess and inventory not only your Shine factors that you already knew were in your Back-Forty-bound saddlebags but also some new treasures in You that you didn't even know existed.

> *Get ready to have your eyes opened to alternative paths for planning and living your own radical, playful, passionate and purposeful Back Forty.*

External Survey

The Back Forty Information Campaign

At this point we must realize that we have thus far been operating as scientists observing our own experiment. We're noticing patterns and arriving at valuable insights independently, but a scientist can never be removed enough from his or her own experiment to see it with complete objectivity. We are intertwined with our own observations, our awareness undoubtedly shaped at least to some extent by our opinions and biases about ourselves.

What if you could get a 360° assessment to identify what others see about you that you can't see yourself? What if your own observations could be confirmed or even expanded upon through the collective observations of others? Corporations and other organizations pay consulting firms big bucks to conduct 360° evaluations to assess how their leaders and managers show up for customers, vendors, employees, etc. Since companies, political parties and even notable individuals pay billions of dollars annually to conduct market research on how they are perceived by the outside world, wouldn't it be a gift to be able to get such input free of charge? You bet!

Ironically, at the same time as you can only see yourself through your own eyes right now, you've been broadcasting a clear and consistent message of who you are out into the world and may be completely blind to what that message is! Beyond simply confirming your own self-assessed inventory, what if you have gifts and talents that others see but you're completely blind to? Of course, there's also a chance that your own personal assessments could be refuted, but wouldn't that give this entire process more credibility and point you toward more reliable truth? The answer, of course, is yes.

So, let's now tap into other people's perspectives of you! The upcoming external survey can be incredibly illuminating. It also requires significant courage and openness. You'll need to be willing to get outside of your own reality and step into the reality of the world as it sees you. Sound scary? That's okay. I promise that in doing so you'll get some eyes-wide-open awakenings that can truly transform your experience of yourself and your life.

That phrase "the reality of the world as it sees you," can seem very dicey. You don't want your life to be dictated by the world's perceptions because if you live only by the "good opinion" of others, you lose your Self. That said, often much wisdom, insight and knowledge can be gained when we're willing to hear harmonic opinions of what could be our blind spots. As musical harmony occurs when there's agreement (accord and congruence in pitch), harmonic opinions carry the weight of aligned perceptions. Though our lives should never be *dictated* by the perceptions of the world, we can benefit from being *informed and educated* by those outside perceptions. Information never hurts. It's what you do with the information that matters.

It's interesting to note that rarely is our blindness to ourselves a case of *over*rating, that is, perceiving we are better than we truly are. More commonly it's a case of *under*rating. Because of the predominately self-critical nature of the human psyche, we're much more apt to discount our talents, gifts and abilities than to fly a false flag of confidence.

Some individuals, however, are an exception to the commonality of undervaluing oneself and may have experienced early-life laboratories that gave rise to grandiosity, which can be just as problematic as a lack of self-value. However, most self-inflation is rooted in a deep lack of self-esteem. The "ego-trip" is usually compensation for or resistance against the awareness of a complete void of self-appreciation.

Although this survey should not be taken lightly in terms of what it can offer, it is also not to be belabored or treated with apprehension. As a matter of fact, fully diving into and robustly completing this survey alone can be the single most fun, uplifting, enlightening and transformational takeaway of this chapter, if not the entire book! Plan right now to have fun with it!

> *Though our lives should never be dictated by the perceptions of the world, we can benefit from being informed and educated by those outside perceptions. Information never hurts. It's what you do with the information that matters.*

The Mindset

That said, as you engage in this survey, I'm going to challenge you to practice operating in two minds simultaneously. One survey, two minds.

In one mind, I want you to *play* with this survey. Make it fun! Implement it with the highest expectations that you will glean absolute gold from it. In terms of mineral rights, you can hit whole new veins with this survey.

It's important to regard every bit of input you get from this exploration as a sacred gift. Consider all participants as "messengers" from the Universe. I encourage you to bless each exchange of information beforehand as being *exactly* the right message for you to hear from *exactly* the right person.

Be enormously grateful upfront for all who choose to participate and acknowledge and appreciate their willingness to go outside of their comfort zone to assist you. Your participants are literally courageous angels. It's challenging to be open and honest with another person, especially if it includes sharing something delicate. Approaching this unique opportunity from a sacred, appreciative and grateful space will infuse it with the energy necessary to experience the extreme blessing that it is.

In the other mind, I want you to take from this survey only that which serves you—and leave the rest. Receive all the information that comes to you graciously and gracefully, yet treat it like a coat. Try it on and see if it fits. If it does, keep it, and be grateful. If it doesn't, let it go, and be grateful.

Throughout—*and this is the crucial point*—maintain extreme gratitude for the person who was willing to offer you the coat! Whether you like and choose to keep the coat or not, you were given a gift! The key to success with this entire survey is to come from a place of gratitude, openness, and willingness to receive and appreciate what you get from this sacred outreach.

The List

Your first action step in your Back Forty Information Campaign is to create a list of the people surrounding you in your life, people who know you best. Then you are going to reach out to them for input about your gifts and talents. Your list can include family members, friends, partners, co-workers, bosses, staff members, employees, clients, vendors, associates, classmates, group members, team members, church or activity members and so on. Basically, any individual with whom you interact in your life who has a personal sense of you will be a fit for this survey and is a viable target for approach.

You may be thinking, *I'm going to approach people?*

Of course, you're going to approach people! If you don't begin approaching people in a mutually beneficial way, you'll miss your opportunity to approach the world as a whole with your uniquely special purpose for being on the planet!

Let's just get over any sense of weirdness right now, okay? Be willing to give up the natural human tendency toward smallness, fear and isolation. That tendency would have us believe that self-analysis alone, locked up in our closets by ourselves, pondering our navels, will sufficiently enable us to give the fullest gifts we came here to give. No! Giving your fullest gifts will always involve others; so get used to it.

> *If you don't begin approaching people in a mutually beneficial way, you'll miss your opportunity to approach the world as a whole with your uniquely special purpose for being on the planet!*

By the way, if you feel a desire to just skip this survey with the rationalization that you'll come back and do it later, please just notice it's the lynch-mob inner voice that's talking. Right now, that voice sounds very logical, because the lynch mob doesn't want you to complete this survey! Want to know why? Because you think the feedback you'll get will be "negative" and will make you feel bad about yourself—and that's exactly where the lynch mob wants you to stay—unaware of *who you really are* and convinced that you are not enough. The truth is you'll be absolutely blown away by who you find out that you are for others!

The lynch-mob voice will give you lots of good reasons for why this survey isn't such a good idea, when, in fact, it is a SPECTACULAR idea!

Remember, the lynch-mob inner voice is cunning and deceptive and wants to keep you from knowing your wonder-full-ness. If you keep listening to it, you'll keep getting more of what you already have. If you want something different, you need to *do* something different.

So, don't die with your potential intact! Glean every bit of this Back Forty call-to-action to finally realize and become who you came here to be and do what you came here to do.

You bought this book. So, I encourage you to *do* this book. Be courageous by getting input from outside of the internal lynch mob!

The world listens and hears you a certain way. Learning how that particular listening is constructed can open up a whole new world for you. Living only in your own concept about yourself will never get you the input and feedback necessary for you to consider, understand and incorporate, much less begin to manage, the "listening" that the world has of you and what you're here to do.

You are about to write down in your Back Forty Freedom Fliers Journal *everyone* from your past or present in any arena of your life who you believe knows you well. You won't necessarily get input from all of them, so don't worry about that right now.

> **If you want something different, you need to do something different.**

In my list, it took substantial courage right off the bat, starting with my then-current girlfriend, most recent girlfriend prior to her, my ex-wife and my eleven-year-old son! NOTE: Significant names have been changed to protect the innocent.

Here's the list from when I first conducted this survey.

1. Lenka, girlfriend
2. Hunter, son
3. Adrianna, most recent prior girlfriend of two years
4. Claire, ex-wife
5. Anne-Marie, long-term friend and fellow single parent
6. Brian, Connie, Sue, Frank, Marleen, Bob, Wendy, Justin, Micah, Stephanie, Anai and other current and past associates in a network marketing organization
7. Savitha, Bill, Mike, Frank, Steve, Bethann, Peter, Joyce, Ram, Tushi and other former career-coaching clients
8. Ntino, Escott, Charlie, fellow scoutmasters in my son's scout troop
9. Jewel and Larry, parents
10. Jane and Jim, former in-laws
11. John, Morris, Paul, Daven, Ed and other men's club buddies
12. Pat, former coach and personal-development friend
13. Sarano, former coach and mentor
14. Otto, Mark, Jai, Sharon, Steve and other former "accountability buddies" in self-development programs
15. Gayle, web and computer assistant
16. Mark, fellow former recruiter and career coach
17. Vince, friend and fellow way traveler
18. Liz, friend and speaker buddy
19. Ward, friend and mentor
20. Jim, mentor
21. Coco, Kathleen, Stanley, David, Linda and other former spiritual counselors and fellow church community members
22. Lori, roommate from a few years ago
23. Michael, advisor in a network marketing organization
24. Brian and Doug, long-term friends and high school buddies

Embrace 3—Homeplay 8
External Survey: Information Campaign List

Here are a few tips and guidelines to help you get started on your own list:

- Don't edit yourself. Just make a list.

- Use free-flow writing to get the unedited list out of your head.

- The order of your list doesn't matter. Later you may notice that you've first listed people you interact with most on a daily basis or that you have begun with those in your inner circle, moving out from family to friends to coworkers to community, etc. Just list people however they come out, making no judgments and only asking yourself, *"Who do I interact with, or who have I interacted with in the past, in any capacity that they may have some sense of me?"*

- In compiling your list, notice which people come to mind whom you *simply don't plan* to approach, the ones you're certain would be of *absolutely no value whatsoever* for your purposes. Maybe you're thinking to exclude them because of it being a not-so-perfect relationship? Nobody's going to twist your arm. You're over there with a book in your hand and I'm over here pulling for your freedom. This is an honor system. You'll play this survey the way you play it. Yet, I offer you this bit of advice: since you may conduct this kind of survey only once in your life, you owe it to your Self to play it big just this one time. Include them too! There's good information out there! If you only stick your toe in the water for input from "safe" people—people whom you trust to tell you what you already perceive about yourself or, at best, will push your edge of awareness only slightly—you'll get some value, but you won't get all that's available.

- If you're willing to include even those "don't go there" individuals on your list, I guarantee you'll experience mind-blowing insight. If you deep-dive into this survey headfirst and bare-ass naked, I promise that you'll get so much supportive input—even from sources you would have never expected—that you may get hooked on this process for life!

- Be careful not to eliminate people because you think they won't understand what you are doing. Keep your judgment of them and their ability to comprehend out of the picture. You might just be surprised.

- Lastly, don't be concerned if people are on the border of familiarity, that is, whether they know you well enough to respond. You'd be amazed at what people are able to glean about you in only the most cursory or limited relationships. Who knows? It may be one of those more borderline relationships that gives you a nugget of insight that "incites" you in a way that wouldn't have happened otherwise. Again, choose for your Self how wide and deep you're willing to play, but I encourage you to play BIG and go for it!

Okay, here you go! Pull out your Back Forty Freedom Fliers Journal and start writing. To begin, list *at least* 20 people or groups of people and their relationship to you. If you really want to make this a blowout, insightful and illuminating process, go for more, as many as you can legitimately determine may have some sense of you. 40? 60? 100?

You may notice a tendency for your list to slow down considerably at some point. Realize that you're only halfway! A good doubling of what you've already listed remains still to go! Just press through that first stopping point, which may simply be resistance, to find the next half of your list. Realizing how many people are in your life who really know you well is a great wake-up call itself!

The Context

This external survey process will only be valuable to the extent that you make it *extremely safe* for participants to truly open up with you. Your ability to have others feel such safety will require a certain internal preparation on your part. The value of the *content* you receive will depend on the *context* you create around their offering it. So, before we discuss the how-tos of approaching these folks, what you'll *say* to obtain their input, you must be very clear about your intentions, that is, who you will *be* in requesting their input. You want to establish a context of energy, purpose and gratitude around this survey. This will uplift and inspire everyone to participate.

You also want your participants to get the feeling of being appreciated by you upfront, *even before they've given you any input* whatsoever. How do you achieve that? First, by letting them know how much you truly honor them and are grateful for the fact that they know you well enough for you to request this input from them.

Be prepared: they may initially think otherwise. They may believe that they don't know you well enough. But, that's usually just because of fear. People don't want to risk doing harm to others or themselves and will only stick their necks out when they are convinced that they can *only* do good, that there is literally *no way* they or you can lose, but only win. For you, it's the win of insight into your blind spots—what you can't see about yourself—that will incite you into new awareness, new actions and new paths. For them, it's the win of being able to contribute input that makes a difference in your life. Win-win.

"Oh," you might ask, "how do I guarantee that?" Here's how: You must decide for yourself, upfront, if there is *any way* someone can lose by giving you their honest input. If there is, you can't request input from them! (Hence the section earlier on mindset.) Plain and simple: you just can't set up someone to lose. If you can't wrap your mind around the sheer blessing that a particular person's input can be, regardless of the nature of the input, you'll have to *take them off the list* of potential participants.

Now, if that knocks almost everyone off your list, you're in trouble. . . at least as far as this powerful survey is concerned. It means that your fear of the opinions, assessments and feedback from others is greater than your desire to get some independent, amazing and life-changing awareness of your Self.

As mentioned before, the information you get will likely lean far more heavily toward how awesome you are in ways that you never knew and can't see. Yet, you must be willing to receive some constructive input as well. Even if some of that input has an edge or two, it's worth it to at least investigate. As I keep emphasizing, you'll generally gain much more awareness of the "goodies" about yourself that you don't see than the "baddies" that you see all the time.

And that leads to the biggest context-setting question of all: can you just eliminate "good" and "bad" from your vocabulary altogether, at least as far as this survey goes? That is one of the keys to making the Information Campaign safe. Unless you make it *really safe* for people to give you everything they've got by conveying the message that you're open for any and all input, you won't stand a chance of gleaning what you really want to hear: something completely unexpected that totally *rocks* your world, the knowing of which could make a huge difference in pursuing your purposeful Back Forty.

To reiterate: *the overall context you want to create is one in which everyone involved in this survey, you and your invited participants, can only win.*

If you are feeling this is too much to ask of the people in your life, consider this: it's been said that the greatest contribution you can make to someone else is letting them contribute to you. So, you're giving the people you ask a gift through this survey! If you truly believe that, then you'll approach people in such a way that they'll believe it too. *Only then* will they take the time and make the effort to participate and do so honestly.

One final note on context: Many times in life I've received external input that didn't serve me at the time but did later at some point down the road. Maybe you've experienced that, too? Having been put in your "doesn't serve me now" pile, the external input sat unused until one day it popped out of your memory as relevant.

So, adding them up, you'll get three valuable gifts through engaging in this survey:

1. The gift of information that's immediately uplifting, empowering and relevant, with insight that completely serves as a catalyst. This will likely be the majority of input.
2. The gift of information that doesn't serve you presently, which you'll gratefully set aside in a mental folder, perhaps to be perused later (a minority of input).
3. The gift of information that doesn't serve you at all, which you'll immediately delete from your mental hard drive altogether (again, a minority of input).

> **What you really want to hear: something completely unexpected that totally rocks your world, the knowing of which could make a huge difference in pursuing your purposeful Back Forty.**

A final, incredible goodie that will come from this survey is that you'll reconnect in a heart-centered and authentic way with lots of people you may have either lost touch with or to whom you've simply not shown this "real" side of yourself. The opportunities for greater depth in those relationships, the exchanges and updates of information that will take place and even the career- and business-related synchronicities that may occur, will deliver blessings you would have never expected from a chapter about embracing your gifts!

The Method

Enough context; let's get on with some content! Potentially you could use one of several avenues to obtain the input you want: ask personally face-to-face or over the phone or write via text, email or the postal service. For the purposes of getting the most input in the most efficient way while creating a greater likelihood that the people on your list will participate, I recommend a structured, *written* approach.

Human beings are built to keep their guards up and to avoid sticking their necks out. They don't want to run the risk of hurting anyone or of being hurt. So, they'll quickly look for a way out if they perceive any exposure on their part. With the dearth of information they'd have if a spontaneous conversation began, they'd quickly be on guard to find a way out, to protect themselves. In contrast, a written communication gives someone non-pressured time and space to consider your request before they respond. Plus, an email offers the added convenience of easy return reply.

Here's a good rule to play by: If right now you have the email address of someone on your list, then email them. If you don't, send them a handwritten note, text, or social media message to get their email address. Once you have an email address, you want to paint the full picture of the request upfront. Before you give them any chance to answer yes or no on whether they'll participate, you want them to not only understand *why* you are making this atypical request but also and more importantly *how there is no way they can lose* if they accept your request. If they truly understand that they can only bless you by participating, the majority of those you contact will participate. We all love safe opportunities to contribute and make a difference.

Incite Request E-mail

When conducting this survey myself, I sent the email below to each person on my list. I playfully *and privately* called it an "Incite Request" because 1) I hoped to receive valuable insight; and 2) I hoped to be incited to take the information I'd get and run with it into a radical Back Forty of new possibilities!

Watch closely at how I weave in the *context* of the request so that I will receive the most abundant, honest, and helpful *content* from each person.

Email Subject Line: Request

Dear [Person Who Knows Me Well],

I'm writing to you in what may seem a somewhat formal way only because I'm looking for a bit of unique support and feedback from you that requires some explanation. I'm currently engaged in a research project to gain a better understanding and assessment of my personal gifts, talents, and assets. This is part of an overall process of becoming better focused in both my career life and my life as a whole, so as to best discover and fulfill my purpose.

As someone who knows me in the way you do, I'd like to ask for your help in giving me some feedback on a few questions. This need not take more than 10 minutes of your time, because I am looking for your first thoughts. (More is wonderful, but just a few minutes of first thoughts would be greatly appreciated.) And, I want to emphasize that your honest and straightforward responses are specifically what I am looking for.

I understand that your time is valuable. I also understand that you, like many people, may be reticent to offer input on such a personal matter because you may feel you don't know me well enough or don't want to risk telling me something "challenging." Let me assure you that I do not approach this request of you lightly and that I've given great consideration to asking for your specific feedback. Through our unique history and interactions, I feel that you know me in a unique way and that your particular perspective in answering these questions will benefit me greatly.

[NOTE: This might be a good spot to personalize any e-mail with a bit about your years of knowing each other or the unique dynamics of the relationship if you haven't known this person for very long. However, I actually found that the text above, as written, was appropriate for just about everyone, so I rarely added more.]

Therefore, I assure you, on my honor, that you can only serve and support me by giving me your authentic answers to the questions that follow. Whatever you offer will be taken as a gift and a contribution, and I will be forever grateful. Hopefully, as I incorporate your gracious feedback into my discovery process, not only I, but the world, will benefit from my being more pointedly on purpose.

Please feel free to simply respond by email.

In all areas in which you know me or even areas in which you have just a sense of me:

1. What do you see as my strengths, my strong suits?
2. What do you perceive to be my greatest gifts, talents, assets, and abilities?
3. What areas of endeavor would you see me most excelling in? In what roles would you see me most happy and fulfilled?
4. What do you see as my areas for improvement, my weaker suits?
5. What do you perceive to be the areas of endeavor for me to avoid?
6. Anything else related to my becoming more on purpose that you'd like me to know?

Again, 10 minutes maximum is all I'm asking, and any more than that is up to you. Thank you for your valuable time and attention, and I promise to treat everything you have offered me as a blessing.

If, for any reason, I have a question in attempting to best understand a comment you've made, I hope you won't mind if I call or follow up. I wanted this first contact to be in writing, however, so that you could both understand my request as well as have the freedom to respond in your own thoughtful way.

Gratefully,

Darrell W. Gurney

There are several underlying reasons why the email above is worded the way it is. Let's break it down. First, notice in the first paragraph that I say "a research project to gain a better understanding and assessment" rather than "a process of self-discovery" because I don't want to have anyone thinking this is some airy-fairy thing.

Also, notice that I begin the second paragraph with "someone who knows me *in the way* you do" instead of "As someone who knows me *well*" or "As someone who knows me *as well as you do*," because, again, they may not feel that they know me well at all. This takes away their objection of not knowing you well enough to participate. This is driven home more in the next paragraph. However, in that paragraph, I removed the phrase "you may feel you don't know me well enough" when there was no question the person did.

I invite you to incorporate as much of my exact wording into your own emails as you wish. A lot of psychological consideration went into it. As the communication itself states, it's a bit formal, but you want something precisely worded so that you convey the *context* in such a way to get the most responses and the most accurate *content* from your respondents.

> *Since companies, political parties and even notable individuals pay billions of dollars annually to conduct market research on how they are perceived by the outside world, wouldn't it be a gift to be able to get such input free of charge? You bet!*

One caution, even if you use this exact basic form for each email: I recommend that you not simply cut and paste. The last thing you want in such a personal appeal is for people to feel that you are sending them a pre-fabricated e-blast. My advice is to actually read each and every outgoing communication from beginning to end before sending it to be sure that it makes sense as it pertains specifically to the intended recipient, and even personalize it if you can.

Also, if someone is an employee or relates to you as a superior in any way, you must make it truly safe for them to respond so that you get full and accurate information. People can feel uncomfortable enough by simply engaging in this process, but even more so if a professional relationship is involved. They surely won't give you unbiased information if they feel their standing with you could be adversely affected. *Make it safe* and *keep it safe.*

Lastly, one final bit of advice: As you review the list of people you'll be contacting, you *will feel* some resistance, especially if you've been bold enough to include some of the dicier relationships in your life. You'll notice a tendency to first send some easy ones and to hold off on the more challenging requests. That's understandable, but when you get to the difficult ones, adopt a tip from Nike, Just Do It!®

Embrace 3—Homeplay 9
External Survey: The Incite Information Request

Go! Jump in, have fun, and expect miracles!

Send them all out! My first request came back fully answered in only ten minutes with some interesting and affirmative feedback, so don't burden your mind with the weight of wondering, pondering or debating. Just send them out all at once and move on to the next chapter in the book as your responses trickle in.

Remember, you can't lose.

But, for your Back Forty future's sake, DO NOT move on until you've completed sending out your requests. It can truly alter who you know your Self to be. Yes, it may take you a few days to get the requests out. Yet, what good is rushing through the book without the benefit you came to get?

Send the rest, if you haven't finished.

Embrace 3—Homeplay 10
External Survey: Capturing Inciteful Responses

When you review your own Back Forty Information Campaign Incite Responses, have your Back Forty Freedom Fliers Journal out for taking notes. Otherwise, you may quickly get overwhelmed and forget particular insights as they begin to pile up. The Back Forty Insight & Awareness you will receive will begin to blow your mind. So, jot them down in your journal immediately, as soon as they come up.

Also keep all the email responses you receive. We will come back to those emails and to the reactions you record in response to them in Embrace 6, where you'll begin to put together all the puzzle pieces of You that you've been gathering.

Don't Stop.
Continue to record your insights and awareness
while you proceed through the rest of Embrace 3 and Embraces 4 and 5.

I sent out eighty-four Back Forty Information Campaign Incite requests, all by email because I knew these people strongly and generally communicated with them via email. I received twenty-four responses to my questions, including replies from both members of one married couple and many responses after sending a follow-up request a month later. Don't assume that people don't want to respond if you don't hear from them. They're just busy and need helpful reminders.

Here's an example of the way I handled the second request/reminder. I just forwarded the original "sent" email to the same person again with the following additional message in the forward. Perhaps you're not working on a book, so leave that part out.

Incite Request Reminder (1 Month)

From: Darrell W. Gurney
To: [Person Who Knows Me Well]
Subject: FW: Request

Hi [Person Who Knows Me Well],

Just wanted to remind you, if you can take 10 minutes, I'd really love your input on the following research I'm doing. Not only are these responses providing me valuable personal information that I am soaking in and taking to heart, but it is an exercise that I am recommending in a book I am currently working on.

Your input to me is completely confidential, and I sent this request to only certain individuals whose thoughts I particularly wanted. So, if you can review the request below and take a few minutes right now, I would truly appreciate it.

Cheers,

Darrell

-----Original Message-----

From: Darrell W. Gurney
To: [Person Who Knows Me Well]
Subject: Request

Hi [Person Who Knows Me Well],

I am writing to you in what may seem kind of a formal way only because I am looking for a bit of unique support and feedback from you that requires some explanation. . .[remainder of forwarded original message]

I will share with you my own "incite-ful" feedback from my Back Forty Information Campaign. You can view it online in a free downloadable document at https://thebackforty.com/book. I am sharing the replies I received not because of the particular details but to demonstrate for those of you who can't imagine opening yourself up for such input from others, the wondrous opportunity it affords.

Over time, The Back Forty Information Campaign offered huge insights to incite me into various forms of exploration and play. I've never had a more comprehensive and detailed list of what's great about me nor been blessed with such a thorough survey of my awesomeness (and my weaknesses) from those who know me best. It has been as much a mirror of reflection to look into as any above a bathroom sink, and I've been consistently amazed at the treasure trove of direction and opportunities for Self-expansion offered by onlookers that I never would have seen or realized on my own.

Embrace 3—Homeplay 11
External Survey: Capturing Insights and Awarenesses

I trust that you've gained a greater awareness of your uniquely gifted nature through your internal surveys and the Information Campaign responses you've received so far. If not, please consider engaging in this chapter a second time. It'll be worth it.

If you do revisit this Embrace, consider the first time through as simply a warm-up, to have you begin recognizing and appreciating your Self in new ways.

Your own fulfilled and purposeful Back Forty will depend on your awareness of the individual and unique being that you are and of what you bring with you into your second-half expression.

Assuming you've gained some insight, you can be excited that so much more insight is still to come as your Back Forty Incite Responses trickle in. While that's going on and before you move on, here are a few last questions to answer in your Back Forty Freedom Fliers Journal. Hopefully, you'll begin actively expressing your Shine factors now, not later, though you can revisit these questions when your forthcoming Incite arrives.

1. What are the greatest insights you've gained about your Self in this chapter?

2. What major components of your life and work would indicate that you're fully Shining?

3. In what ways can you take action on the insights you gained in this chapter? What specific actions can you take? By when will you take them? What results are you committed to producing out of those actions?

4. What would an ideal day look like when you're Shining as brightly as possible?

[AS A LAST REMINDER: Keep track of who has responded to your Incite Request; and, when a month has passed, send out one reminder email to those who haven't.]

THIRD SEPTENARY ACKNOWLEDGMENT

You are gifted. . .and Shining!

What you've accomplished in this chapter is amazing. Do you realize that most people *never* look into themselves to discover their talents, gifts and uniqueness, much less muster up the courage to go out and ask for feedback from others? You are a truly brave and determined individual, obviously committed to untethering your potential!

You are getting in touch with your unique gifts and talents, so that you will be well aware of what you carry with you as saddlebags provisions when you cross over into your purposeful Back Forty.

Congratulations! You are awesome!

> *Your own fulfilled and purposeful Back Forty will depend on your awareness of the individual and unique being that you are and of what you bring with you into your second-half expression.*

As you continue your Back Forty embraces, begin to appreciate and allow your special Shine to be expressed. It's time to start "Shining" now!

Shine on! As you bring your unique light into the next Embrace, we'll create a similar saddlebags inventory of the Values you're bringing into your playful, passionate and purposeful Back Forty.

YOUR VALUES

Your values become your destiny.

GANDHI

YOU AT YOUR CORE

In "Embrace 3: Your Gifts," we dug deep beneath the surface to appreciate your wonder-full-ness. The underlying gifts and talents you discovered are included in the "mineral-rights" wealth you'll bring into your personal Back Forty and are part of the foundation upon which you'll build your second half/best half of life. Another part of that foundation will be your values

Solid and consciously held values establish a centered place from which to weather turbulent storms while also serving as a divining rod pointing toward fulfillment. Revisiting your core values in times of great change or consciously establishing new ones can be stabilizing. Even in ordinary times, regularly assessing certain shifts in transitory values such as work/life balance can provide peace of mind through various seasons of your life.

Depending on the individual, early-in-life, more ego-centric career ambitions toward wealth or fame may rank high, while concerns for stability, world contribution or life balance may seem less important. This early, internal and often unconscious values-ranking system then shapes how we choose to express ourselves in our careers: the actual fields in which we work, the types of companies or entrepreneurial endeavors we pursue, the roles we fill within those organizations and the way in which our work melds with other areas of life.

But then we mature. We conduct laboratory experiments, in both career and life. Those experiments give us new information. That new information may then shift the underlying foundation of values we've built everything on top of. All of a sudden, things start to crumble, at which point a new, *consciously designed* foundation of values is needed to reach our life's *next* Self-expression.

Accordingly, knowing your *current* Life Expression Valuation, or Life E-Valuation for short, can reveal either the method to your madness or the overall sanity of your direction. It can allow you to release obsolete values and move on to the next, higher expression of your Self.

When was the last time you E-Valuated your life? You're not the same person you were twenty or thirty, or even ten, years ago. In sequential stages of life, our values reflect drastic differences in what's important to us. Is there a chance that some of your underlying, foundational values have shifted without you even noticing? Perhaps who you presently are *at your core* has yet to be uploaded into your conscious awareness because you've been too busy to realize that you've changed!

> **Without an awareness that a values upgrade has taken place, we keep trying to propel the hardware of our engagements and activities with old software.**

Without an awareness that a values upgrade has taken place, we keep trying to propel the hardware of our engagements and activities with old software. In doing so, we may notice a sense of disconnect. Our old operating system just doesn't cut it anymore.

One of the most centering saddlebag inventories you can bring into your playful, passionate and purposeful Back Forty is a clear sense of where your values are today. So, let's use this chapter to survey your value system—to see what it tells you about where you are now, how you want to grow, and who you are becoming.

E-VALUATION SURVEYS

Below, you'll find several values surveys, each constructed in a particular way yielding distinctly different Back Forty Insights & Awarenesses. Give yourself ample time to play your way through each survey to see what you glean.

Your E-Valuation surveys will be:

1. Feeling & Experiencing Values
2. Being & Interaction Values
3. Orientation & Focus Values
4. Work Element Values
5. Workplace Environment Values
6. Top 10 Regrets
7. Top 10 Rejoices/Pledges
8. Final Expression Valuation

Though these surveys provide tremendous clues into your Self at this point in your life, don't be overly analytical as you move through them. Just go with the same "first thought, best thought" gut instincts you utilized earlier. It's less about being exact and specific than simply getting an overall sense of your current values. Realize that every item on these lists can be considered valuable and important, and it may seem challenging to choose one item over another. Nevertheless, you'll have to make some decisions. Simply play with it and enjoy the process.

We're all wired by the particular shaping influences of our own Front Forties to place weight on certain elements of personal life and work over others. Having a clear and current understanding of your own weighted values is the result you're looking to achieve here, not a right answer or a better-than-someone-else's answer. There's no right way to be. And you can't do this process right, or wrong. It's simply about your individual Self-discovery.

Embrace 4—Homeplay 1
E-Valuation Survey 1: Feeling & Experiencing Values

Get out your Back Forty Freedom Fliers Journal to capture insights as you go along, and let's dive into the first survey: what you value most in terms of what you want to feel or experience in life. It will be enlightening to get a glimpse of how you hold each feeling and experience in relation to the others. Simple as that.

Rank the following set of 20 Feeling & Experiencing Values in order of importance to you. Number them 1 through 20 with 1 being what you hold as highest in value and 20 being the lowest priority. Here are some tips to get you started:

- Some explanations have been added to the 20 main values listed, but your understanding of these words may be different. Use whatever descriptive words or meanings you associate with these concepts. It may be helpful to cross out my explanations and write in your own even before ranking.
- One way to proceed, as you rank from your #1, highest value onward, is to ask yourself, *"Of all the remaining items on this list, if I could have only one more, what would it be?"*
- A similar, reverse method to check yourself after ranking them all is to start back with #1 and compare it to #2 with the questions, *"Would I choose to have #1 before #2? "Would I choose to have #2 before #3?"* working your way down again.

Those are just some ways to approach it, but don't be overly meticulous. Keep it fun and easy. Even if you have some tough choices to make, remember that it's not life or death. Just go with your gut and *without* self-judgment. You can't do this wrong, and you can't do it right. You do it the way you do it.

Feeling and Experiencing Values

1. _____ Achievement—success and contribution
2. _____ Worthiness—value and self-esteem
3. _____ Wisdom—deep knowledge and insight
4. _____ Spirituality—sensing a bigger plan or direction
5. _____ Serenity—inner calm and peacefulness
6. _____ Affluence—prosperity and material comforts
7. _____ Thrill—excitement and adventure
8. _____ Autonomy—independence
9. _____ Wellbeing—physical, mental and emotional health and vitality
10. _____ Approval—appreciation, acknowledgement and recognition
11. _____ Intimacy—primary relationship, romance and deep love
12. _____ Camaraderie—fellowship and friendship
13. _____ Fun—joy and playfulness
14. _____ Family—proximity and bonding of close relations
15. _____ Legacy—having an impact
16. _____ Fairness—equality for all
17. _____ Global welfare—world peace and brotherhood
18. _____ Beauty—aesthetics of nature and the arts
19. _____ Security—safety and certainty
20. _____ Style—flair and fashion

[REMINDER: I've placed these [STOP] signs after surveys and exercises to alert and encourage you to complete the task just given before proceeding further. The gold is in the Self exploration, and only you can do that in your own Homeplay.]

Now, answer these *Back Forty Insight & Awareness Questions* in your Freedom Fliers Journal:

1. What do you notice from ranking your list?
2. Did you experience resistance or confusion? If so, why do you believe you did?
3. What items ranked higher than you would have expected?
4. What items ranked lower than you would have expected?
5. Have these values changed over time? If so, why do you believe that is?
6. How might you express your highest current values in bigger and better ways?

Congratulations on playing. Now, we are going to look at what you value most in terms of how you want to "be" and how you want to interact with others in life.

Embrace 4—Homeplay 2
E-Valuation Survey 2: Being & Interaction Values

Rank the following set of 20 Being & Interaction Values in order of importance to you. Number them 1 through 20 with 1 being what you hold as highest in value and 20 being the lowest priority. Just go with your gut, without self-judgment.

Once again, I've added some explanations to the twenty main values listed but use whatever words or meanings you associate with these ideas. Cross out mine and put in yours, if necessary, before you start ranking.

Being & Interaction Values Survey

1. ____ Competent—skilled and capable
2. ____ Authentic—truthful and genuine
3. ____ Self-Sufficient—autonomous and free
4. ____ Self-Expressed—sharing gifts and ideas
5. ____ Creative—inspired and inventive
6. ____ Accountable—where the buck stops
7. ____ Determined—driven and ambitious
8. ____ Brave—daring and heroic
9. ____ Trustworthy—honest and steadfast
10. ____ Dependable—reliable and responsible
11. ____ Supportive—encouraging and compassionate
12. ____ Smart—intelligent and quick
13. ____ Friendly—gracious and affable
14. ____ Reasonable—sensible and practical
15. ____ Progressive—embracing change, progress and improvement
16. ____ Tolerant—open-minded and forgiving
17. ____ Reverent—respectful and honoring
18. ____ Graceful—refined and elegant
19. ____ Patient—enduring and accommodating
20. ____ Orderly—neat and tidy

Again, kudos to you for playing. Now, answer these *Back Forty Insight & Awareness Questions* in your Journal to gain some understanding even beyond the ranking process itself.

1. What do you notice from ranking your list?
2. Did you experience resistance or confusion? If so, why do you believe you did?
3. What items ranked higher than you would have expected?
4. What items ranked lower than you would have expected?
5. Have these values changed over time? If so, why do you believe that is?
6. How might you express your highest current values in bigger and better ways?

Now, let's survey what you consider to be the most important in your Orientation & Focus in life to gain another insightful glimpse at your values foundation.

Embrace 4—Homeplay 3
E-Valuation Survey 3: Orientation & Focus Values

Rank the following group, again in order of importance to you, numbering them 1 to 16 with 1 being what you hold as highest in value for the orientation and focus of your life and 16 being the lowest priority. Feel free to write in whatever words or meanings you associate with these ideas. It's your world that matters, not my own definitions.

Orientation & Focus Values Survey

1. _____ Freedom—operating independently without many constrictions

2. _____ Influence—impacting people, situations and organizations

3. _____ Stability—grounded, conventional and preferring what is foreseeable

4. _____ Spirituality—cultivating awareness of a greater power or presence

5. _____ People—interacting with others in community, friendships and close relationships

6. _____ Growth—pursuing ongoing education, training and personal development

7. _____ Winning—driven to overcome obstacles and come out ahead

8. _____ Service—selflessly helping others or contributing to a cause

9. _____ Adventure—seeking to explore, see and do new things

10. _____ Creativity—original and inventive from a unique vision

11. _____ Directing—calling the shots and responsible for results

12. _____ Balance—blending all aspects of life into a unified whole

13. _____ Riches—amassing large amounts of money, property or other assets

14. _____ Proficiency—being the best at what you do, the expert in an area

15. _____ Family—focused on the welfare and primary relationships of home

16. _____ Joy—doing what is joyful and fulfilling

Now, answer these *Back Forty Insight & Awareness Questions* in your Freedom Fliers Journal:

1. What do you notice from ranking your list?
2. Did you experience resistance or confusion? If so, why do you believe you did?
3. What items ranked higher than you would have expected?
4. What items ranked lower than you would have expected?
5. Have these values changed over time? If so, why do you believe that is?
6. How might you express your highest current values in bigger and better ways?

Next, we're going to look at what you value most in terms of work-related values and elements you would like to emphasize in your career.

Embrace 4—Homeplay 4
E-Valuation Survey 4: Work Element Values

You'll engage in this Work Values/Elements Survey a little differently. This time, score each value independently. Rate each on a scale of 1 to 3 in terms of its importance to you with 1 being a higher priority and 3 a lower priority. As always, change the explanations to fit your own understanding of these ideas.

Work Values/Elements Survey

1. _____ Teamwork—solving problems or addressing issues through group efforts
2. _____ Stability—permanence of a job and assurance of income

3. _____ Risk—going into unchartered waters of a situation,
   idea or industry

4. _____ Wealth—in a position to receive a great deal of money
   and amass assets

5. _____ Precision—dealing with meticulous and strict matters
   or materials

6. _____ Challenge—dealing regularly with tough issues and
   problems to be solved

7. _____ Learning—engrossed in topics involving higher
   knowledge or development

8. _____ Pressure—intense involvements where time and
   performance are critical

9. _____ Beauty—focus on areas involving aesthetics and
   the emotions

10. _____ Management—directing the efforts and results of others

11. _____ Solitude—working primarily alone with little
    interaction with others

12. _____ Flexibility—opportunity to manage work
    responsibilities around own schedule

13. _____ Stimulation—finding enthusiasm and joy in the work

14. _____ Exposure—on the front line and working with the
    outside world

15. _____ Competition—going head to head with others or
    outside entities to win

16. _____ Artistic—engaging with materials and projects of a
    creative nature

17. _____ Diversity—work that involves continually changing
    duties and roles

18. _____ Association—known as belonging to an organization
    or enterprise

19. _____ Authority—definitive decider of directions and actions
    to be taken by others

20. _____ Acknowledgement—noticed and appreciated for the work
21. _____ Wide Impact—affecting community or society as a whole
22. _____ Freedom—calling my own shots and determining my way
23. _____ Camaraderie—growing deeper connections with others and coworkers
24. _____ Ethical—abiding by a code of principles important to me
25. _____ Helping—being of direct assistance to individuals in need
26. _____ Smart—the most astute on a subject
27. _____ Originality—designing new ideas or approaches to old problems
28. _____ Constancy—a steady and predictable focus of attention and workflow
29. _____ Impact—able to affect overall courses of direction or groups of people
30. _____ Volume—a large amount of issues or items to be dealt with

Now, answer these *Back Forty Insight & Awareness Questions* in your Freedom Fliers Journal.

1. What do you notice from scoring each element?
2. Did you experience resistance or confusion? If so, why do you believe you did?
3. What items scored higher than you would have expected?
4. What items scored lower than you would have expected?
5. Have these values changed over time? If so, why do you believe that is?
6. How might you express your highest current values in bigger and better ways?

Before the next survey, let's take a moment to touch down again and reconfirm there are no right or wrong answers to these surveys. You are just gathering information for your Back Forty best half of life.

Embrace 4—Homeplay 5
E-Valuation Survey 5: Workplace Environment Values

Now, we're going to look at what you value most in terms of Workplace Environment Values. The environment in which you work shapes your overall career experience, and your work life will be happiest and most productive when it reflects or at least approximates your values.

In this survey, score items on a scale of 1 to 5 (1 = absolutely required; 2 = highly desired; 3 = desired; 4 = unimportant; 5 = avoid completely).

Workplace Environment Values Survey

1. _____ Balance—valuing the holistic individual, including family and personal life
2. _____ Independence—involving little interaction with or dependence upon others
3. _____ Communication—front-line contact with people in or outside my organization
4. _____ Management—presenting opportunities to direct and supervise the efforts of others
5. _____ Velocity—emphasis on a rapid pace and volume of activity
6. _____ Low Stress—offering consistent, reliable and frustration-free work
7. _____ Adventure—supporting bold actions or risky endeavors
8. _____ Affiliation—where development of close personal relationships can be expected

9. _____ Exacting—involving clear-cut, rigid or meticulous processes or standards

10. _____ Freedom—autonomy and control over schedule and direction of involvements

11. _____ High Pressure—involvements and settings of an intense and time-critical nature

12. _____ Artistic—emphasis on projects involving artistic media

13. _____ Significance—centering on matters of extreme import and magnitude

14. _____ Appreciation—where individual contributions are noticed and recognized

15. _____ Leadership—encouraging authentic influence rather than chain of command

16. _____ Teamwork—stressing group engagement and accomplishment

17. _____ Loyalty—mutual high regard between individuals, management, and organization

18. _____ Status—involved in high-profile work or with an organization of popular regard

19. _____ Equal Opportunity—valuing and rewarding all individual contributors

20. _____ Beneficence—generosity of the organization in terms of benefits and perks

21. _____ Portability—offering moves throughout the organization, country or globe

22. _____ Challenging—pushing the personal envelope in terms of overcoming and growth

23. _____ Physical—engaged in work of bodily skill or strength

24. _____ Hierarchy—structured around conservative lines of control and decision making

25. _____ Enthusiasm—work of an exciting nature or involving invigorating elements

26._____ Fulfillment—affording opportunity and structures to reach one's highest potential

27._____ Diversity—involving people and ideas from varied cultures and backgrounds

28._____ Like-mindedness—alignment with organizational values, ethics and goals

29._____ Expansion—where one can anticipate upward growth and development

30._____ Mobility—incorporating a high degree of travel

31._____ Contribution—priority on serving humanity and the world as a whole

32._____ Liberal—unstructured and flexible in terms of goals and direction

33._____ Variety—including diverse and constantly shifting areas of involvement

34._____ Intelligence—high regard for knowledge, expertise and professional development

35._____ Community—located within an area that fulfills personal and family needs

36._____ Stability—a structure that ensures continuity of work and reliability of income

37._____ Profits—enabling highest personal earnings and asset development

38._____ Creativity—involved in designing new ideas or approaches

39._____ Competitive—emphasizing challenge among co-workers and/or other organizations

40._____ Environment—workspaces which enhance social, creative, and ergonomic comfort

Now, answer these *Back Forty Insight & Awareness Questions* in your Freedom Fliers Journal.

1. What do you notice from scoring each element?
2. Did you experience resistance or confusion? If so, why do you believe you did?
3. What items scored higher than you would have expected?
4. What items scored lower than you would have expected?
5. Have these values changed over time? If so, why do you believe that is?
6. How might you express your highest current values in bigger and better ways?

And an additional summary question:

7. Drawing from the five values surveys taken thus far, what are your greatest insights about what's important for you to express now? E-Valuate yourself and journal on your three greatest insights about where you are now and the directions you see that you want to move in life, in work, in your overall Self-expression.

Way to play! Completing these surveys and answering the corresponding Insight & Awareness Questions may not have been easy. They're neither simple to run through nor quick to evaluate. They require time, thought and balanced consideration. Kudos for completing them. If you're like me, you'll find a wealth of Back Forty Insight & Awareness on this side of that hurdle.

If you would like to see my own Embrace 4 Values as expressed in my answers to the surveys and in the personal insights I gained from the surveys, please visit Appendix B at the end of the book.

OK, now for something completely different!

FROM HERE TO HEREAFTER:
Top 10 Regrets

Regret: a distress of the mind from sorrow for what has been done or has failed to be done[7] (e.g., issues without closure, things said or left unsaid, unfulfilled expectations, dashed intentions).

Beyond values related to career, relationships and overall life, it's important at this midlife waystation to gain clarity around what simply matters most to you *each and every day*. Fulfilling on your playful, passionate and purposeful second half will come about more powerfully when you're clear about your single-eyed track—and stay on it. With all the previous treasures (Self Expression Directives and Gifts) you've already mined from your years of R & D, as well as all the gold you'll discover moving forward, you'll want to make the most of every solitary minute in your Back Forty. To do this, you will have to be in touch with your deepest core values.

> **Fulfilling on your playful, passionate and purposeful second half will come about more powerfully when you're clear about your single-eyed track—and stay on it.**

One way to get to those deepest values, to assess your current life path and potentially design a new one is to engage in a little mind-game process. Ask yourself the question, *if life wasn't going to continue much longer for me, what values demonstrated by my life as lived thus far would I look back upon and shift if I had the chance?*

Though I wish you as many wonderful years of cultivating your playful, passionate and purposeful Back Forty as you'd like, there are no guarantees. None of us knows how long we have left on this earthly playground. With that in mind, let's take a safe, little field trip into Almost-Outta-Here and see what we observe.

---

7 Dictionary.com

Let's say you found out from some unquestionable source that, without any incapacitating illness or even the faintest preliminary sign of illness, you would definitely keel over three years from today. What then?

You might think, "I *do not* want to go there!" but *do* go there with me. *Do* complete these final values surveys because they will give you a powerful experience of the insights and perspectives you would have were you really almost outta here.

For starters, what would you think about the very next moment after being told unquestionably that you would die in exactly three years? Perhaps you'd first go through what has been proposed as the natural stages of grief identified by Elizabeth Kubler-Ross: denial, anger, bargaining, depression, and acceptance.[8] Years of scholarly debate have taken place as to the veracity of these stages but, debate aside, here's the point: once you've gotten past the shock of your imminent demise and reached acceptance, what would you do moving forward into the days, weeks, and months ahead? Where would you now put your time, attention, and energy? I'd say that you might want to recalibrate, reorganize and revitalize your life in various ways. And, driving any such forward-focused makeover would be your deepest core values. Those most fundamentally important values are what we're looking for in this survey.

Embrace 4—Homeplay 6
E-Valuation Survey 6: Top 10 Regrets

First, set aside at least a couple hours or even half a day to move through this Homeplay. Don't rush it. You'll probably need ample time at the beginning to even convince yourself of the premise of your certain death in three years in a sufficiently real way to have it rattle everything you need it to. Getting into that mental space first is necessary.

Take some quiet time to truly create this scenario in your mind. To get yourself in touch with the feeling of the shocking news, you might try to close your eyes and imagine yourself in a medical office or a hospital and, after

---

8 Kübler-Ross, E., On Death and Dying *(Routledge, New York, 1969).*

waiting for a prognosis, your doctor comes in with a dour look and informs you that you've contracted a recently discovered, rare, progressive, incurable *and yet not incapacitating* disease that will take your life within the next three years. You will feel fine throughout that time.

If this exercise seems frightening to you, you might call up a friend or loved one and simply tell them that you're going to do a deep-dive process in a book. Don't go into detail because the likely ensuing conversation could derail you or cause them concern. Just say you want to have someone aware that you're doing a personal, introspective process and that if you don't follow through with calling them in a few hours, to please call you. Say you'll be happy to share the details of the process with

> *You might want to recalibrate, reorganize and revitalize your life in various ways. And, driving any such forward-focused makeover would be your deepest core values.*

them afterwards and, perhaps, what you gleaned from it. It may sound silly to make that call, yet having a "safe person" on alert allows you to really let go and go deep into the emotional space of your impending death.

Now, get out your Back Forty Freedom Fliers Journal and write your answers to these *Back Forty Insight & Awareness Questions*:

1. Assuming you've accepted it, how do you feel about the fact that you will die three years from today? What emotions come up? Anger? Sadness? Disappointment? Remorse? Defiance?

2. Now look underneath the emotions you have identified and get in touch with the source of those emotions—*your regrets*. Use free-flow writing to explore your regrets. If one regret after another comes spilling out, try just listing the regrets first. Then

go back and delve into them in detail. Uncover and elaborate on as many as possible and *no fewer than your top 10*. Make note of all the reflections that these regrets give rise to. If you feel upended, distraught, anxious, frenetic, and/or remorseful during this exercise, you're probably engaging in it really well.

Be sure that, if you do this exercise over a period of days, each time you begin and end you come back to the awareness that this is simply a mind game. And be sure to make your beginning and ending notification calls to your "safe person," if that supports you.

Darrell's Regrets

I took this deep dive myself when first engaging in the 7 Embraces; my answers reflect my feelings at the time. Though all these Freedom Flier surveys can yield different results when taken at different points in our lives, I believe this exercise in particular could be done more than once. It enables us to get present to the importance of this moment, now, at various points along our path of staging (versus aging). Until we train ourselves to wake up time and time again to the preciousness of every single sliver of life, it's all too common to fall asleep yet again.

My own answers below reveal the insights I gained from the surveys. I share them to demonstrate the process. Don't limit the length of your writing to mine. I wrote volumes beyond what you see here and condensed my sharing to the most poignant insights, simply to assist you in priming your own pump to let it flow.

You'll see me sharing nakedly from my depths to support you in taking an authentically deep dive yourself. The process isn't necessarily pretty, nor are the thoughts and reflections that arise organized or rational in any way, but who looks pretty or thinks clearly when they're about to transition to the hereafter? Let your mind go where it goes. Simply track and document it.

Question 1: My Feelings about My Impending Death

To get the most out of this, let go of any idea that this is a cute, interesting, innovative or even distantly fascinating conceptual survey, and just dive in all the way: blood, guts and all. Let the tears flow, the snot run, and fully feel any pangs of hopelessness and/or profound sorrow. This experience could be the best gift you ever give your Self.

> *The process isn't necessarily pretty, nor are the thoughts and reflections that arise organized or rational in any way, but who looks pretty or thinks clearly when they're about to transition to the hereafter?*

Darrell's Feeling About His Death

First, in contemplating my death, I'm overcome with sadness. When I put myself in this situation and believe it, as if it were truly so, I begin sobbing. I feel an overwhelming sense of unfinished business, along with the heartache of not being able to look forward into an undefined, indeterminate, long life ahead.

Underneath the emotions, what has me feel so much regret at the derailing of this train I've been riding called "my life" is a sense that I just didn't "get there." I never seemed to get situated, stable or on track with the bigger picture or impactful difference I wanted to make on the planet. This quote comes to mind and expresses my regret best:

> **This is the true joy in life, the being used for a purpose recognized by yourself as a mighty one; the being thoroughly worn out before you are thrown on the scrap heap; the being a force of Nature instead of a feverish, selfish little clod of**

**ailments and grievances complaining that the world will not
devote itself to making you happy. —*George Bernard Shaw***

I definitely don't feel I ever reached the "true joy in life."

Question 2: My Top 10 Regrets

Remember, my sharing here is authentic and raw and any thoughts upon hearing the news of imminent death are not organized, rational or pretty. I have no intention to be maudlin, but getting real for the sake of the exercise is what I'm going for. My feverish and selfish regrets begin to pour forth.

Darrell's Regret #1: I deeply regret that my relationship with my son has never been experienced or expressed to the deepest degree of love I've always felt.

I worked hard to maintain my relationship with my one and only son and, yet, never experienced a bonded-love or heart-felt relationship with him. Since he was born, I could cry at the drop of a hat when tapping into the wellspring of emotion surrounding him. I even used this propensity as a "substitute" when conjuring up necessary tearful emotions onstage in my acting days, given they were so easily accessible.

Yet, I feel that I had to be my son's disciplinarian and teacher of life skills for most of his adolescence, given a unique co-parenting relationship. When necessary, I always opted to ensure that he grew up to be a responsible adult rather than to simply be his buddy. Therefore, teaching life lessons, responsibility, pursuit of excellence, the value of a dollar and hard work, etc., always took precedence over just hanging out with him as a pal or being "liked." Yet, now I feel that he'll always remember me as tough and strict and not appreciate that I was simply doing my job to raise him to be a responsible and capable adult.

At the moment, he's still a teenager and a typically challenging teenager to teach. But, given that I'm leaving the planet in only three years, when he'll be eighteen, I'll have no opportunity to experience the adult-son fruits of my labor. I fought to stay present in his life, worked hard to give him the influences I thought he needed; and yet I'll be gone before any of it is appreciated or fulfilled. I deeply regret that my relationship with my son was never experienced or expressed to the deepest degree of love I've always felt.

Darrell's Regret #2: I never really experienced my concept of a great life of difference-making that, as a kid, I wanted to fulfill.

I never really experienced my early concepts of "success." I dabbled in different things, made a few bucks here and there, but never experienced what I'd call wealth—something I dreamed of as a teenager. I also never wielded any substantial influence to change people's lives. It seems I never found a way to put my ego in service to something bigger than myself.

I always admired powerful and influential leaders, be they politicians, speakers, spiritual leaders, business barons or inspiring authors and deeply wanted to play at that level. What began in my teens as a bold desire to have a big impact in the world—reflecting on George Bailey's famous line from *It's a Wonderful Life*, "I'm shakin' the dust of this crummy little town off my feet and I'm gonna see the world!"—turned into basic survival attempts to recover from midlife's one-two punch. I never reclaimed my ignorance-is-bliss, perhaps ego-laden, mojo of confidence after the devastating custody suit and humbling bankruptcy. I never realized the great life of difference-making that I was so sure I would fulfill.

Darrell's Regret #3: I regret that I had so many grand ideas of books to write and businesses to build but didn't get them done.

Something was always more pressing to be dealt with than the seeming luxury of time spent pursuing dreams. I also had internal resistance to accomplishing those goals. I said I wanted those dreams, but subconscious fears of both failure and success gave me plenty of circumstances and good reasons for not achieving them. I'm left now with the feeling that I was nothing more than a dreamer. [I reflect on a line from Macbeth's soliloquy, which seems to summarize my life, *"A poor player that struts and frets his hour upon the stage and is heard no more. It is a tale told by an idiot, full of sound and fury, signifying nothing."*]

Darrell's Regret #4: I regret having worked so hard without having more fun.

Especially because I didn't reach the success I'd always envisioned; but probably even if I had, I regret having worked so hard and not focused more on fun. As an adult, I dropped the playful activities that I used to get lost in when younger, my creative expressions that provided laughter and joy. I let them go in an adult quest to "make it" or "be somebody." [I reflect on the movie "Citizen Kane" where the multi-millionaire, power-wielding main character, on his deathbed, uttered "Rosebud." The last thought on his living mind was his favorite sled, named Rosebud, and those simpler times as a child.] Similarly, I dropped playing my trumpet right after high school. Also, after an early stint of training and performing in Los Angeles, I dropped acting to focus on being a single dad. I rationalized that there were only so many hours in the day and that I didn't have the space for continued auditions or play-acting. I needed to get "serious."

Darrell's Regret #5: I never seemed to establish and maintain a solid, through-thick-and-thin, deep, enduring relationship with a woman.

I never experienced the deep, enduring love between a man and a woman that I thought life afforded. As I came of age in the context of adult relationships shaped by the '80s, '90s and new millennium, rightly or wrongly, I began to discount the possibility of true, enduring love. I participated in every relationship workshop I could find; became an atypical, communication-savvy male; and grew to be psychologically and ontologically aware. But, apparently, none of that made a damn bit of difference. I could never seem to establish and maintain a solid, through-thick-and-thin relationship with a woman. [I reflect on how Carl Jung so deeply mourned the loss of his wife, his soulmate, in his later years. I always wanted to experience that depth of love with someone.]

Some of my relationships "education" even had me realize that I might be too relationships-wise for a guy, that I should be more of a typical, simple, uncommunicative, no-clue-about-relationships male. But, even trying to dumb myself down didn't work; it felt inauthentic.

I told myself it was difficult as a single father, especially of an older boy, to find a woman willing to jump into that situation. Most single women I dated wanted to be #1 and couldn't accept that their role as #1 would have to be shared with my son.

Even though I was a single dad requiring lots of accommodation for someone to even choose to be with me, I still wanted a woman who fit my desires on every level. I refused to budge from wanting them to be sexy, hot, attuned to personal development, spiritually aware, highly self-expressed (both in life and sexually), adventurous and willing to play big in life. Perhaps I should have lowered my expectations or standards.

Now, in my mid-forties, with all the baggage that both another person and I would bring into a potential relationship, it seems impossible that youthfully nostalgic, deep, abiding, and through-thick-and-thin love could ever happen. It appears that untainted younger folks, who have built that ideal together over time, still have a chance. But, us scarred and "wiser" folks, who've been around the block a few times, must let go of the fantasy that unconditional love could now ever override the strong probability of no-fault divorce.

Darrell's Regret #6: I regret that I didn't get around to seeing the world as much as my early wanderlust would have dictated.

Coming from my roots, it was a big deal to travel and live in Europe right after college. (As a matter of fact, just going away to college was atypical.)

It opened me up beyond the standard American, ethnocentric and myopic understanding of the world. It answered my yearning for a wider view of life on the planet while stimulating a thirst to discover that people are basically the same everywhere. I subconsciously wanted to prove to myself that, no matter what cultures, colors or religions were out there, it's the man-made lines of demarcation on a map that give us the illusion of separation.

Yet, within five years of coming back to the U.S., I owned a home in Los Angeles and had a wife wanting a child right away. I got tied down. Not that I would have chosen anything other than my son, but I wish I had found a way to get around the world more, either before or after him.

Darrell's Regret #7: I regret that I didn't read everything I wanted to.

I wasn't raised in a heavily reading family, but my mother tried hard to segment me out when I was young. She seemed to want to influence me to both read and use vocabulary beyond the levels of my immediate environment. Therefore, I always had a romantic fantasy of being well-read and deeply knowledgeable. I often regretted that without college entrance guidance I opted for being a business major because it was practical. [I reflect on my mid-20s, after college, when I purchased an old set of The Harvard Classics, thinking I would grow in wisdom through reading them from front to back. Their creator designed the set for exactly that reason: to give someone a solid, liberal arts education even outside of institutional higher learning. From an estate sale, I also picked up an old set of The Great Books series and similarly thought I'd while away pipe smoke-filled hours reading them in my "study."]

I actually did put together a study in my first house, a truly Harvard-esque smoking room with burgundy walls, globe wallpaper trim, dark wood furniture, a roll-top desk and lawyer bookcases. The scene I created was akin to a stage set from some play involving old-world wisdom. Problem was, I was a guy with a first-time mortgage, newly married to a woman wanting a child quickly. I rarely engaged in the "great thoughts" for which I designed the room, only once carving out enough consistent time to read Dostoevsky's *The Brothers Karamazov* (Volume 52 of The Great Books series). It was one of the thinnest volumes, so it seemed like a manageable place to start. It was also an unmanageable place to end.

Darrell's Regret #8: I regret the other things I didn't do from my "101 Things to Do Before I Die" list.

I never took flying lessons. I never went up in a hot-air balloon. I never sang before audiences. I never hosted a TV show. I never wrote a best-selling book. I never conducted life-changing seminars and workshops. I never took my parents on a European vacation. I never gave as generously and anonymously as Elvis. Hell, I'm so out of touch with my "101 Things to Do Before I Die" list that I don't even know what I regret not doing!

Darrell's Regret #9: The paths I chose in life left me questioning whether I succeeded in my parents' eyes.

As silly as it may seem for an adult man to regret that he never "made it" with his parents, I feel I didn't fulfill on my potential in a way that had me seem successful in their eyes. Their idea of success was far different from mine, and it's not that I regret having taken my own path instead of the one they would have envisioned. I simply regret that the path I chose did not leave me feeling that they saw me as successful.

Darrell's Regret #10: I regret all the times I didn't treat people with kindness, respect, and love.

In a quest to get things done efficiently and effectively, I didn't always take time to consider my effect or impact on people. I had a particular issue around "customer service" for most of my life, mostly holding that phrase as an oxymoron. I also had my share of ego issues that inevitably shaped my interactions with family, friends and the world at large. [I reflect on the life of gentle, loving, soft-spoken Gandhi. How much I wanted to be like him, but never achieved such extreme self-transformation. I also remember hearing direct experiences from people who'd brushed closely with death, and how they now hugged their loved ones more, took more time to care, listen and understand. A quote comes to mind that I read somewhere but failed to implement: *"Be kinder than necessary. Everyone is facing some kind of battle."*]

There you have it: my Top 10 Regrets from the time I initially took these surveys and completed the exercises offered in this book. You should know that the entire fabric of my life has dramatically shifted since originally outlining these regrets years ago. So, believe me, the effort is worth it. But, rather than share about all my personal transformations since then, let's just stick with the Embrace 4 process for now, because it's what you do with this survey that matters most.

Embrace 4—Homeplay 7
E-Valuation Survey 6: Top 10 Regrets (Revisited)

Have you dug into your own Top 10 Regrets and associated reflections to the same authentic, ugly and maybe even depressive level as I did? If not, go back to your writing and deeply throw down what's true for you when you're about to be history. Spend time delving deeper. I've been called, by those who know me, one of the most positive-minded people around. Yet, I can't encourage you enough to get down and dirty, even sad and remorseful with this. In the same way that my life is now completely transformed from what it was several years ago when engaging in this exercise, I assure you that, if you get real now about your deepest regrets, major shifts can happen for you too.

> *In the same way that my life is now completely transformed from what it was several years ago when engaging in this exercise, I assure you that, if you get real now about your deepest regrets, major shifts can happen for you too.*

FROM HERE TO HEREAFTER:
Top Ten Rejoices/1,095-Day Pledges

After getting present to my Top 10 Regrets and then pulling myself out of despondency, I could begin to envision a pathway to "the true joy in life," as George Bernard Shaw puts it. Yet, I was faced with a pointedly sincere question: was I *really* willing to live from this moment forward as if I truly had only three years to live?

A famous Jewish proverb says, *"If not me, who? If not now, when?"* My question for both of us, you and me, is, from all the Back Forty Insight & Awareness that's flowed from these values and regrets inventories, what will we actually *commit to implement* and *be held accountable for* as we live the next 1,095 days of our lives? *That* is a Back Forty life-altering question.

This would be an easy question to skirt past with a quick "yes," and then just finish the survey with lots of good, worthwhile intentions. However, intentions alone have no value and do little good. What counts is intention followed by action. So, are *you* really willing to live from this moment forward as if you truly had only three years to live? I hope you join me in saying a genuine yes.

Embrace 4—Homeplay 8
E-Valuation Survey 7: Top Ten Rejoices/1,095-Day Pledges

While remaining in the mind-game of knowing that you're almost outta here, write out your "pledges" in a list and number them Rejoice #1, Rejoice #2 and so on. Don't try to prioritize them, just list them as they come up. To help you formulate your pledges (commitments), try asking your Self the following questions, writing out your answers in your Back Forty Freedom Fliers Journal:

1. Since I won't be incapacitated in any way, on what will I now spend my time and energy in my next remaining 1,095 days?

2. What are the most important things to get done in the time I have left? Starting with my regrets, how can I transform each one into something worthy of rejoicing?

3. What commitments (1,095-Day Pledges) would I like to make, given what I've now seen from my regrets matters most to me?

It may be helpful to approach your list by writing at least one Rejoice/Pledge to correspond to each of your top ten regrets.

Darrell's Top 10 Rejoices/1,095-Day Pledges

Again, baring my soul—so you will feel safer baring yours—I share my original, amalgamated and condensed answers to the above questions. To a great degree, my pledges correspond directly to the regrets. Given the list of regrets showed me what I don't want, the related pledges confirm what I do want. . .and how I'll respond. (Note: you may have written more than my condensed sharing here but, if my answers stimulate you to write more on the questions above, for sure take the time to do so.)

Darrell's Rejoice #1: Transform and develop my relationship with my son.

I was never a deadbeat or uninvolved father. I've worked really hard to keep my son engaged in programs, activities and church so he would, as he has, develop character, responsibility and integrity. Yet now, with 1,095 days left to spend with him during some big years in his life (finishing high school and moving away from home), I want to experience a deeper connection as well as playfulness with him, things I put on the back burner while getting my "job" done as his single father.

Though his growth in responsibility and character are still always my primary concern, I want to have more fun with him before I'm gone.

[Two reflections come to mind around this. First is the 1993 movie *My Life*, wherein Michael Keaton, learning that he's going to die, leaves a video-log for his soon-to-be-born son so that his son will, one day, know exactly *who* his father was. Second is an image burned into my memory from college when I saw my 6'6" friend, on the front porch of his parents' home, kiss his 6'6" dad *on the lips!* I remember thinking how different this was from my own upbringing, yet it symbolized the kind of deep, father-son relationship I would love to model one day.]

Given my son is now a teenager in high school, this may be a challenge. Soon, I'll have even less personal time with him, as he gets more into friends and girls. Yet, I can't write off the prospect of closeness with him as "too late" because I have at least the next three years to shape this relationship. I'll need help, and mentoring.

Darrell's Rejoice #2: Transform my relationship with success.

I want my life to end with a feeling of having been successful. I don't want some gnawing feeling of disappointment for a life only partially-lived, only partially-fulfilled and only partially having made a difference. What counts is the score at the *end of the game*, not after the first half or third quarter. I want to feel that I scored a win before the final whistle blows.

With only three years left, I obviously won't accomplish my past pictures of success. However, perhaps that's perfect. Had those pictures been true to form or real for me, I probably would have achieved them. Therefore, I'll transform my relationship with "success" and redefine it such that it's not some ending place with a certain amount of money, notoriety and security, but rather, a way of living and being. Redefinition is a good thing, given that my earlier concepts of success may have been immature. [I reflect on what some great thinkers have said about success:

To laugh often and much;

To win the respect of intelligent people and the affection
of children;

To earn the appreciation of honest critics and endure the betrayal of
false friends;

To appreciate beauty, to find the best in others;

To leave the world a bit better, whether by a healthy child, a garden
patch or a redeemed social condition;

To know even one life has breathed easier because you have lived.
This is to have succeeded.

—Bessie Stanley or Ralph Waldo Emerson

Success consists of going from failure to failure without loss
of enthusiasm. —Winston Churchill

Try not to become a man of success, but rather try to become a
man of value. —Albert Einstein

Life is a succession of moments. To live each one is to succeed.

—Corita Kent

It is on our failures that we base a new and different and
better success. —Havelock Ellis

It's interesting that none of these great-thinker quotes on success
mentions any amount of money, notoriety or security, the attributes very
often held as signs of success.]

Darrell's Rejoice #3: Damn it! I'll finish this book, The Back Forty, *an idea
I've nursed for over ten years.*

I've nursed this book concept for over ten years and, for fear of failure
and/or success, I've subconsciously thrown every possible reason,
condition and circumstance in the way of fulfilling on it.

Everyone who's been introduced to the idea—the basic premise that the first forty or so years of life are simply R & D, research and development, with what follows (The Back Forty) being an opportunity for purposeful fulfillment—has been uplifted and inspired. Yet, I've effectively sabotaged myself into a paralysis of analysis in sharing the idea more.

I've become mired in questions like *who am I to write a book on this subject?* I've also had some intellectual critics, those whose opinion "should" matter, review parts of the rough initial manuscript, and I have found myself immobilized by their critique. But, at this point, I only have 1,095 days left! Who the hell cares what they think? I've heard we must be sure not to die with our music still in us—and this is my song! Damn it, I'll sing it—even if it's the worst Karaoke on the planet! [I reflect on a quote by Stuart Wilde: *"I understand that how others judge me is about them. I look 'em in the eye, I tell 'em who I am, and if they don't like it, fuck 'em!"*]

Darrell's Rejoice #4: I'll put performance back into my life.

Karaoke has lived in my psyche, like many creative pursuits, as a luxury, something I associate with joyous, free times rather than a regular, self-care activity like going to the gym or getting a haircut. Just what if the urge to create and perform warrants as much of my attention as a regular haircut? I obviously haven't operated as if that were the case, but I intend to now.

Given I'll still need to pay the bills to provide for myself and my son, I can't just go join the circus to fulfill this rejoice. I need to get this book written and out of my hands a hell of a lot faster, given I only have 1,095 days; but I don't want all that time spent behind this laptop (!), so I'll put a karaoke night into my schedule once every week, at a minimum.

I'll also find a play to perform in, perhaps, a small community theatre production. It will be interesting to experience performing for the sake of performing as opposed to the underlying reasons behind my pursuit of acting before: to get somewhere, to be somebody, to be noticed and "discovered." I'll observe my internal reaction to joy for joy's sake and perhaps discern a different JUICE it provides.

And, as ludicrous it may be to attempt to develop my embouchure again after 30 years away from my instrument, I'll pick up my trumpet and begin to toot my own horn.

Darrell's Rejoice #5: I'll find my soulmate before heading back to soul.

I've questioned the idea of a one-and-only soulmate because I believe many individuals we might connect with could create a bond at that level. But I do believe in finding those who are seemingly a "perfect fit" because I've seen it happen with others. I've just never made it a priority to find her myself and have used being a single dad as an excuse.

I've met romantic partners in many places, yet I've never launched a pointed campaign to find "the one." I've stayed away from the various dating websites, always leaving it to the Universe to bring someone to me, wherever I might meet them.

Yet, "wherever" has no definition to it. I wouldn't buy a wherever house. I wouldn't take a wherever job. I wouldn't go on a wherever vacation. Certain necessary criteria are called for in the bigger aspects of life. Though I've compiled my "perfect partner" attributes list, I've never engaged in a systematic campaign to find the proverbial foot onto which the slipper fits.

No, I've simply met who I've met and mentally checked off (or left unchecked) the appropriate qualities and qualifications on the list. Many times, even with lots of items still unchecked, I've tried to make a relationship work anyway. Of course, none of us are list-perfect, and I've always thought I should be more sensible and live in the "real world" of relationships, which I've defined as make-do, "satisfice" (a combination of being satisfied and making a sacrifice) and work, work, work to make the relationship work.

Obviously, that approach *hasn't* worked.

So, I'll give the dating sites a try. I'll focus on the ones that whittle down to "who you are" through questions. That seems to be the smartest way to initiate exploration between people before the pressure (and hormones) of meeting in person come into play.

I'll actually write out my ideal list, segmented into musts, high desires, and negotiable elements, and I'll stick to it. I'll make a conscious, campaign-like effort to find/attract her and then see what the Universe has in store for me.

Perhaps she won't even show up through my campaign or dating-site efforts. Maybe the simple act of consciously choosing that it *is* possible for me to attract "the one" could shift my entire energy and have me manifest a deep and eternal love before I leave for the Eternal.

Darrell's Rejoice #6: I'll take on that a life of travel is still possible for me.

I've always dreamed of taking my parents on an extended European vacation. Right now, I'll begin a savings fund for that. I'll set aside all of my reasons about not having the flexibility, funds or freedom to accomplish such a trip and create a new reality around it. I'll put the intention into a time structure, scheduling it into the calendar, to consciously begin to draw it toward me, along with all the necessary circumstances, conditions and wherewithal to make it happen.

Darrell's Rejoice #7: I'll begin reading the great and classic books that I've amassed and fantasized over.

It's critical that I break the back of the beliefs and logic that has had me not do the reading I've always wanted to do. For too long, I've entertained thoughts of not enough time in the throes of my daily life or that such unrelated-to-business or not-fixing-me reading is a luxury I can't afford. I will now *make the time*—carve it out—so as to satisfy my literary hunger.

Given my 1,095-day predicament, in just a few short years I'll be in the place of All-Knowing anyway. Nonetheless, I deserve the experience of discovering and enjoying great wisdom while still in human form. Granted, this pledge will require sacrifice and redirection of my time and efforts, as will all my pledges. Yet, chasing only the carrots of life without the experience of living fully *in this very moment* must end. For my remaining 1,095 days, I will focus on the enjoyment of the journey rather than some illusory destination.

Darrell's Rejoice #8: I'll dust off, revamp and fulfill on my "101 Things to Do Before I Die" list.

Given the drastic lifestyle shifts required by only the first seven recalibrations above, it would be easy to simply write off any possibility of fulfilling on my "101 Things to Do Before I Die" list. But, that fatalistic thinking (pun intended) doesn't allow for the possibility of unexpected openings or miracles coming from out of the blue.

So, though I haven't reviewed or revised my 101 list in several years, I'll dust it off and revamp it. I'll hold these Top 10 Rejoices/1,095-Day Pledges as "musts," yet I'll refresh my awareness of the 101 List if only to appropriately engage my reticular activating system (RAS).

The RAS is the bundle of nerves at the stem of the brain that filters out unnecessary information. It acts as the gatekeeper of information, so the important stuff gets through including opportunities we'd not normally see. For example, if we decide we want to buy a Tesla, what do we see on the road everywhere? Teslas. Basically, when we want something, we just might see new ways to get it with the help of the RAS. So, even if I expend only a minimal amount of effort in revamping my 101 List, the mere fact that I'm newly aware of these desires will undoubtedly draw forth from the Universe unique occasions for their fulfillment.

Darrell's Rejoice #9: Achieve "success" in my own eyes.

Perhaps the best thing I can do to achieve "success" in the eyes of my parents is to achieve success in my own eyes. For all I know, I may have already succeeded in their eyes. However, even if that's the case, it can never fill the hole of success-awareness within me. So, through effectively recalibrating my remaining-life efforts in the ways outlined in my Rejoices and, in particular, Rejoice #2, I'll render myself successfully regretless and successful regardless.

Darrell's Rejoice #10: Create and adopt a 1,095-Day game around the motto "Be kinder than necessary. Everyone is facing some kind of battle."

I'll need structures for reminding myself to bring this intention into conscious awareness. Perhaps incorporating it into a daily prayer? After a lifetime of, perhaps, falling short of this mark, it would be an accomplishment of huge proportions to live my remaining days in such a way that this statement becomes the epitaph on my gravestone. That's a final game worth playing.

There you have it: from several years ago, an amalgamated and highly condensed version of my own Top 10 Rejoices/1,095-Day Pledges from which I began to live out my next three years and still endorse today, as if I still have only 1,095 days left.

Embrace 4—Homeplay 9
E-Valuation Survey 7: Top Ten Rejoices/
1,095-Day Pledges (Revisited)

As always, what's most important is you and your process here. Did you fully allow yourself to go deep in your own survey? Have you truly explored how you'd alter your ways if you knew these next few years were your last? You might say, "This just sounds like a bunch of New Year's Resolutions, most of which are never kept." To some degree, that may be true. People often get rah-rah riled up and then do nothing about it. But it is also possible to treat this like an opportunity to gain heart-attack wisdom without the heart attack. If you do, your own Back Forty of play, passion and purpose will be a much more wonderful, second-half experience.

So, review what you've written to make sure you've taken the opportunity to accomplish this transformational deep dive. If you find you haven't, spend more time with your Back Forty Freedom Fliers Journal until you feel you have exhausted the personal changes you'd like to make at least for now and the next 1,095 days.

Finished? If so and if you haven't already, organize your answers into a list of your Top 10 Rejoices/1,095-Day Pledges, placing them in order of importance to you.

Embrace 4—Homeplay 10
E-Valuation Survey 8: Final Expression Valuation

To fully complete Embrace 4: Your Values and bring it all together, answer these questions in your Back Forty Freedom Fliers Journal. The questions will help you extract your core values as they have revealed themselves in your responses to your values surveys.

1. What are my biggest realizations from the values list-ranking surveys earlier in the chapter? What do these surveys show me in terms of what's most important as I move into my Back Forty?

2. What are my biggest realizations from my Top 10 Regrets and Top 10 Rejoices/1,095-Day Pledges? What do these surveys show me in terms of my deepest, core values as I move into my Back Forty?

Here are my responses extracted from my own survey answers.

My main Back Forty core values seem to center around:

- loving and empowering relationships
- authentic and unabashed Self-expression
- contribution and consciousness as the measure of success
- continuous education, growth and development

These are very different from my more youthful, egotistical, and, perhaps, immature values of wealth, fame, and fortune. Building my 1,095 remaining days (and many more, if I'm lucky) around these newly E-Valuated pillars will be worth living for.

A final insight of mine is that I absolutely need to be surrounded by a community of individuals similarly intent on fulfilling on such a life-shifting re-E-Valuation of their own. Fulfilling on such a deep dive and such powerful pledges for living life on a new path can only be realized with the support of and accountability to others. It will take discipline. Once the tears have dried and the snot has been wiped away, the pull to return to my Front Forty ways of being is simply too strongly ingrained to be faced alone. Accordingly, another huge element for me is creating and remaining in an aligned, possibility-driven, Back Forty community.[9] This ranks at the top of my second-half/best-half values system. If you

---

see such a need of this for your Self as well, perhaps we'll be able to help one another.

We must all suffer from one of two pains: the pain of discipline or the pain of regret. The difference is discipline weighs ounces while regret weighs tons. —Jim Rohn

FOURTH SEPTENARY ACKNOWLEDGMENT

Well done! It's truly wondrous to participate in discovery with individuals willing to ask the tough questions and who are eager to do the dirty-handed digging required to consciously design their "wasn't just going to happen anyway" Back Forty life. For the most part, human cultural tendency is to simply fall prey to the beliefs that we are *a certain way* and that life is already set and on track, going a particular direction with no real possibility of change.

You are defying that. You are now literally breathing life into your second-half/best-half Self. To *inspire* means to breathe into. Thank you for that inspiration and resuscitation. It helps us all. But my words of acknowledgment for you, at this point, will hopefully pale in comparison to your own words of appreciation for and acknowledgement of your Self.

You are now approaching the gate dividing your research-and-development focused, because-based Front Forty years of life from your consciously designed, Be Cause-based, Self Expression-directed, gifts-aware and values-awakened second half—your radical Back Forty of play, passion and purpose. I'm grateful that you're on this path with me and all the other Freedom Fliers. Together, by supporting one another in our new contrarian ways of thinking, we stand a chance of turning around the societal mindset from the Down-and-Out Model of aging to an Up-and-Out Model of staging—for the sake of our biggest games yet to come.

Thank you for your willingness to become a Freedom Flier. See you in the Back Forty!

PART III

EMBRACING
YOUR
BACK
FORTY

YOUR INITIATION

Everything that is today could not be if it were not for that which was before.

ABRAHAM

FLEXING INTO THE FUTURE

Life may become really interesting and exciting now, if it hasn't already.

You've now been exposed to an alternative view of your life as lived thus far. It suggests that everything that's ever happened to you has been absolutely perfect, necessary and required for you to pursue your unique direction and purpose. This view sees you as a victim of nothing or nobody from your past or present. Rather, it asserts that you have caused and continue to cause all of life for your own Self-fulfillment.

You've also been introduced to the notion that your entire first half of life has simply been R & D, research and development, to support who you came here to be and what you came here to do. It's even been proposed that your biggest game is still ahead of you in a playful, passionate and purposeful second half.

Lastly, it's been demonstrated that, along your path of Front Forty R & D, you've acquired unique gifts and talents and have aligned yourself with certain values to sustain and propel the new You through the gate into your own Back Forty.

Wow. . .and whew! All of this is pretty radical thinking! It may take some time to adapt to, much less fully incorporate, this new mindset. Luckily, the awareness process you've begun is a no-turning-back proposition. You can't "unthink" these concepts. Not like you'd even want to forget all this, yet a stretching of the mind has definitely taken place that you simply can't reverse.

The mind, once stretched by a new idea, never returns to its original dimensions. —*Ralph Waldo Emerson*

In yoga or any other regular routine of stretching you can't expect to perfectly bend any particular way on the very first try. It takes time, repetition and consistent practice before you reach certain levels of flexibility. We first notice the limits of our present capabilities through pain. Yet, when we back off just a bit, breathe into the pose and hold it easily and gently, the pain slowly surrenders. Eventually, we discover that we can stretch much farther when we've given ourselves the necessary time, patience and practice.

Similarly, some pain may occur associated with the stretching of the mind you've been practicing in this Back Forty philosophy. For instance, it may be logically clear that life becomes much more powerful when you own your past and present, including all the events, circumstances, situations and influences that have impacted your life. Yet, you may have some pain or even a strange sense of loss associated with giving up victimhood.

Victimhood, your old story and "good reasons" (forces outside of yourself) for why life looks the way it does and having something or someone to blame (even yourself) may be so ingrained that your mental, emotional and spiritual bodies have stiffened, if not atrophied. Learning to stretch your mind and beliefs to consider new ideas like these pushes you outside of your comfort zone and may even have psychosomatic physical benefits.

Past tendencies to discount yourself and your awesomeness by mini-mizing your unique gifts or the rigidness of an old values system may have decreased your youthful and hopeful spirit of flexibility. Maybe it's been a long time since you've flexed the muscle of Self-appreciation? When did you last view your Self with wonder and amazement or get tickled and even blown away by your own capabilities? Have you become fixed inside a narrow range of unquestioned or obsolete (for you) values?

> *As you gradually relax and breathe into a Be Cause stance, you'll notice that your comfort zone, power and ideology begin to stretch and expand progressively over time.*

As you gradually relax and breathe into a Be Cause stance, you'll notice that your comfort zone, power and ideology begin to stretch and expand progressively over time. Simply relax into it. Easy does it. One day at a time. Move forward with patience. Just keep practicing and exercising with these ideas and, most of all, keep breathing.

NOW the stretch is on!

WAKE UP CALL FROM MIDLIFE HAZE

Coming to terms with midlife is a hugely critical embrace in and of itself. We can be blindsided by it before we even know what hit us. The sooner you recognize that an actual Back Forty "Initiation" is going to take place or has taken place and call it for what it is, the sooner you'll be empowered by what's about to or has already begun to happen for you. The key word is *for* you, not *to* you.

Shift happens. You can't stop that fact of life. But recognizing what's hap-pening as an initiation instead of "my life is going to hell in a handbasket!"

allows you to be powerful in the face of shift rather than downtrodden and walking around with shift all over your face.

Your midlife initiation may have you observing habits, patterns, beliefs or idiosyncrasies you've never noticed before. If you don't like what you see, you can get caught up in disempowering self-analysis, self-doubt or self-beratement. When you wake up and see what has heretofore been hidden in the blind spots of your life, you might feel foolish, judgmental or even angry with yourself. *"How could I have done that?"* or *"I should have known better!"* are just a couple of the sharp self-punches we take to the gut.

> **Shift happens.**
> **You can't stop that**
> **fact of life.**

Yet, through your Front Forty Discovery & Expression analyses and your gifts and values surveys, in a Back Forty frame of mind, you begin to appreciate the complete and total order of your perfectly timed wake-up call; and it becomes possible to embrace the absolutely perfect past and present that got you here as well as look forward excitedly to your new Self Expression-directed future. This new mindset gives you a powerful grip on the reins of the unique passage called Midlife.

The danger lies in not recognizing that an actual initiation is happening for you and that what may now seem like chaos has another side to it. Instead of making the changes you have the new awareness to make, you can get stuck in the conduit of change itself. An initiation is meant to be a passageway, not a forever state.

Some have called this initiation "midlife crisis," and many have become stuck in the bowels of it. This is not how it should be. To be duly initiated into The Back Forty means to be embraced by a profound and joyous "Welcome!" as you pass through the gateway into your life's second half.

What lies ahead will unfold to be the fullest and most satisfying part of your life! However, your attention will be deflected from this golden opportunity if you remain fixated on the vehicles that drove you to the initiation ceremony, that is, the life situations, events, conditions and circumstances that probably prompted you to pick up this book.

Unlike other life passages ritualized by celebrations (e.g., birthdays, bar/bat mitzvahs, retirement), initiation into midlife often occurs unnoticed or acknowledged only with distaste. Often what happens on the road to midlife isn't pretty, so we're not excitedly jumping up and down about it. So, let's change that. We do so by changing the midlife context.

Remember from Embrace 1: Your Past that context shapes the way we perceive any particular content? Then, let's shift the context of "midlife crisis" to "midlife opportunity" by focusing on the golden opportunity ahead versus the ugly

> *This new mindset gives you a powerful grip on the reins of the unique passage called Midlife.*

vehicles that drove us to the party, and by seeing everything as perfect and exactly what needed to happen to get us where we are.

Many of us have experienced or seen hazing take place, whether in school or social circles. It's sometimes used to ritualize the initiation of someone into a new group or community. It can involve subjecting the inductee to embarrassing acts, physical challenges, roadblocks or gauntlets to be passed through. Generally, hazing is characterized by mental, emotional and sometimes physical strain. It's designed to break the individual down so as to surrender to the larger group and gain "acceptance."

Playing off of that metaphor, though hazing is illegal and detestable in mainstream society, it is easy for us to think that the Universe seems to reserve Its right to initiate us into midlife however it so chooses. We can each list the seemingly offensive licks to the backside we've received from the midlife paddle as we approached the gate to our second half—that humbling or even humiliating stuff of "midlife crisis."

Complaining to the Universe about the hazing has gotten us nowhere. (We are, after all, complaining to our inner Mad Scientists when we do so.) Resisting and griping about our own unique past and even present hazing process only slows down what could be a quick trip through the gauntlet of initiation where we come out into a full Back Forty welcome and membership. Hating the hazing process of initiation only puts us more into a victim role. On the other hand, seeing the apparent hazing as a gateway into our own radical Back Forty can actually give us a reason to get excited!

Inside the context that says your first half of life was simply research and development for your own radical, playful, passionate and purposeful second half, you might choose to respond to the apparent midlife blows of initiation with, *"Oh goodie! I'm obviously being inducted into the Back Forty Club!" "Thank you, may I have another?"* may become your mantra because you know that what follows the blows to your backside is a *backside of life* that's off the charts. Contextualizing the hazing makes all the difference, so being context armed and ready definitely helps.

In college, I was invited into a men's organization called The Tejas Club. The members arrived at my dorm room one night around midnight, woke me up, took me outside and engaged in a friendly, spoken ritual on the back steps of my dormitory, followed by an early morning road trip for cinnamon rolls to a local, all-night bakery. For several months afterwards, I experienced a formal, respectful and honorable initiation process into the club. The point is: I didn't know they were coming that particular night. They simply showed up at midnight. In the same way, you'll rarely know when your initiation into The Back Forty is coming; but you can be alert, ready, willing and accepting of your midnight call when it does. Setting the context as a "midlife opportunity" ahead of time allows you to fully embrace the initiation process. When you do, what you may have initially interpreted as the pain of change transforms into a mysterious, healing adventure.

It's likely that your own midlife initiation has already begun, though perhaps unnoticed and definitely not celebrated. I say "likely" because something drew you to this book and has inspired you to endure the mental stretches required to get to this Embrace 5.

Your mission, therefore, if you choose to accept it, is to transform your own probably negatively held wake-up call into a welcomed, if not sought after, opportunity for a new life. The first step in that transformation is to understand and recognize the tell-tale signs that you are entering, or perhaps have already entered, the gateway to this fraternal/sororal order of midlife opportunity.

YOUR BACK FORTY INITIATION

Knowing when you get to/got to the Back Forty gate will allow you to best contextualize and incorporate the midlife opportunity you now have rather than remain overwhelmed by the gauntlet itself. Like when you are standing at a directory map in a shopping mall that declares, "You Are Here," you'll be able to recognize and appreciate where you are now and envision where you want to go.

As described, the exciting initiation into our Back Forty often goes unnoticed because we don't recognize that our "midnight call" has occurred. It may just appear that life somehow became a blurry series of rapid-fire, unfortunate events. I call it the "Morassive Thrust of Midlife," combining the words "massive" and "morass." That "Big Swamp" can well describe the confusing and muddled situations and circumstances that tend to characterize what's called midlife crisis.

But wait! That sure sounds like a victim story, doesn't it? Being overtaken and befuddled by circumstances is just another form of "because," isn't it?

Yes, however, you now have the ability to take any seeming untoward situation, event, circumstance or influence from your past or present and Be Cause it! Anything and everything mucky that has either brought you to or is occurring within the process of your initiation can be Be Caused into your designer goodies, your Self Expression Directives, just like you did in Embraces 1 and 2. You have that power. Plus, the Cause Scene Investigator (CSI) process will give you a good estimate of your actual Back Forty Initiation Date. And, that awareness gives even more power.

> *You now have the ability to take any seeming untoward situation, event, circumstance or influence from your past or present and Be Cause it!*

So, let's, for a bit, step back into your CSI role to take stock of and locate when your own particular initiation occurred.

Embrace 5—Homeplay 1
Initiation Identification

To begin, pull out your Back Forty Freedom Fliers Journal and give your Self ample time to write on these *Back Forty Insight & Awareness Questions*. Your answers will get you started on identifying when your initiation into the Back Forty may have occurred or begun to occur.

1. When was the last time you remember things clicking along rather smoothly? Life always has problems to solve and inevitable ups and downs, but when was the last time you remember a preponderance of ups over downs?
2. When were things progressing along at a steady, upward pace?
3. When did you last feel relatively happy and secure?
4. At what most recent point were you moving toward your goals and dreams with a general sense of peace and high expectancy? Where were you? What were you doing?
5. What were the major activities going on in your life in that generally "up" time you've identified?
6. Why were you involved in those activities/areas?
7. Who were the players around you, the significant relationships?
8. What were your prevailing attitudes about life?
9. At that generally "up" time you just located, before any prolonged poop hit the fan, what happened *first* to change that sense of life moving ahead smoothly, happily, and/or securely? What event or series of events began to take place? List them out.

Here's an amalgam of condensed, authentic and unretouched answers to the questions above from my own inquiry several years back.

The last time I recall things moving along at a smoothly flowing and forwardly progressive pace was in the late 90s. I was getting used to single dad life and my business was strong. In 1998, two years after my divorce, I had my best earning year ever in the recruiting business and began to ponder writing a book.

The book was about the recruiting business, but it wasn't necessarily because I loved recruiting. I thought I should write my first book around something that I knew and use that experience to move out of the office and ideally onto a speaking and workshop-leading platform. (I've subsequently learned that it's best to write on something you want to delve into, not something you want to leave!)

Overall, it was a good book and it won some awards. Little did I know that this book about using "headhunters" would hit the market at the worst possible time: the outset of the 2001 recession.

In the late 90s, however, life was good. I was bringing in money and naively envisioning best-selling authorship. I began building an office support staff, enjoying my best earning year ever and eliminating debt from the lower earning year before (the year of the divorce). I felt excited about life and the possibility of becoming an author. I was enjoying my five-year old son's activities.

I moved easily in and out of a few dating situations, more to simply avoid being alone than to find a relationship. I then participated in a men's personal development weekend, where I learned that I really needed time alone to get to know myself better after my divorce. So, I began surrounding myself with a team of men and stayed away from more relationship-based female interactions. I remained on a men's team or various forms of it for a couple years. Eventually, I dropped the structured men's groups to pursue spiritual counselor training with my church and to sing in the choir. I'm sure I had many concerns but, in retrospect, it seemed like an overall heavenly time of positive and forward movement.

Rightly or wrongly, after my biggest earning year ever in 1998, I tried to put my business on autopilot so that I could focus on the book project. I was so tired of recruiting, even in the face of my windfall year, that I decided I'd take a big risk and go for writing the book. Basically, I tried to set up my staff to handle the recruiting business on their own. Bad move.

Though I showed up in the office quite a bit, my efforts were focused on publishing and promoting the book. I trusted that my administrative staff, some of whom were complete newbies in the field, could make enough placements to keep the business going. They made a few, but they were too few and far between to keep the business afloat.

At that point, I began making some bad financial decisions, drawing on a home equity line to press forward, hoping to sustain the business until more placements occurred and my "best seller" book was published. Bad business planning, naiveté and magical thinking were the order of the day.

In retrospect, now understanding that I am the Be Cause of my life, I can see this decision in one of two ways: either it was a function of unworthiness, a self-sabotaging backlash at having earned more than I ever had the year before, *or* it was a desperate drive to get out of the recruiting industry before the good money enticed me to stay.

Having just dug myself out of divorce-related debt a couple years earlier, I was again using credit, attending book conventions and spending loads on the production of my self-published book. I'd like to say that I went way over budget in my book publishing efforts, but that would be a lie. I didn't go over budget at all because I never *had* a budget! I simply sought the best deals I could on everything—editing, design, printing, etc.—and operated on a pay-as-you-go basis. With no plan whatsoever, I forged ahead into a huge publishing debt.

Unfortunately, the pay-as-you-go, book-publishing non-plan, along with the new-millennium slow-down in the recruiting business, put me $100K in debt—right before the September 11 attacks of 2001 and oncoming recession.

To deal with the debt, I decided to sell my house, where I'd lived for five years as a married man and another five as a single dad. I rationalized that it was a good change because I needed to move past the reminders of my former marriage that still surrounded me: same furniture, same paint on the walls, same junk we had moved in with still in the closets.

My ex-wife had made a clean break by getting a new place when we split up, starting over completely with her buyout funds. During the breakup, I naively thought that the stability of staying in the same place would be good for me because I inherently abhor change. In the end, however, by moving out years earlier, I believe she got an emotional head start on releasing our marriage.

It took nine months to sell the house, all at a time when my business had whittled down to only three of us: me, myself, and I. I had let go of my staff due to the tough employment market, which is deadly for headhunters. I was completely beaten by the stale economy. Plus, while attempting to take back the reins of placement activity to survive that tough market, I felt like a foreigner to the job, having stepped away for so many months.

Based on my book, I started receiving calls to speak at a few career conferences. At one of these conferences I became reacquainted with career coaching, which I had experienced myself at age twenty-four, when new to LA; and I decided to shift my career in that direction. Selling the house, I moved into an apartment and was just getting my motivation (and rationalizations) together to "start over" when a two-year custody suit hit me like a bag of bricks.

From that wallop forward, it was a long, hard road of emotional and financial recovery. My midlife "ship" had come in, but it didn't carry a treasure trove. And two-year-long, half-million-dollar custody suits create much more than a wake behind them. Think tsunami.

The fact is that all of us can only do the best we can with what we know at any moment in time. And, what we "know" at any particular point in time includes not only our skills and knowledge of the world, relationships, business, life, etc. but also only our then-current level of Self-development. All of us, in wiser, more mature, less desperate and more experienced times will always make different choices. Yet, at any point in time, we can only live life forward, drawing from our then-current resources, not from those we may gain later. That's the whole point of the Back Forty mindset: to be able to move forward more freely when we discover what we've learned about our Self, life and our direction in it by engaging in the first four Embraces.

This Cause Scene Investigation (CSI) Homeplay is not meant to rub your "mistakes" in your face. On the contrary, you conduct these analyses to eventually come to peace of mind and a sense of freedom from realizing that you have never made any mistakes. Rather, you've given yourself the environments and laboratories to refine your Self into who you came here to be in order to do what you came here to do. Remember the maxim for this entire Back Forty philosophy:

> *You conduct these analyses to eventually come to peace of mind and a sense of freedom from realizing that you have never made any mistakes.*

Your entire life has been (even in the worst of times) and continues to be a uniquely powerful laboratory for the discovery and expression of something.

It also helps to keep at the forefront of your mind and the tip of your tongue the anchoring affirmation of your incredible Mad Scientist prowess:

MuuuuuuuuAAAAAAAAAHaaaaHaaaaHaaaa!

YOUR INITIATION TIMELINE
AND BACK FORTY BIRTH DATE
Embrace 5—Homeplay 2
Initiation Timeline

After you have thoroughly completed your work on the *Insight & Awareness Questions* in Homeplay 1 above, turn your Back Forty Freedom Fliers Journal sideways and onto a fresh page, and get ready to plot out your **Back Forty Initiation Timeline**, a diagram of the major life occurrences you have written about above. The graph will track the points in your life when they occurred and will plot their relative impact on you as you experienced them.

- An illustration of the Initiation Timeline graph can be found on the next page. Draw a similar graph in your Journal.

The following is an overview of the steps to fill in the graph.

- Decide the age (your age) at which you will start the time period to be examined. Make it *well before* the "up" period you described in your answers to questions 1 through 8 above. This exploration can go back many years, all the way back to school or childhood or birth if you like. However, I recommend that you start with a smaller, more manageable time period and then expand later if you wish.

- Along the left axis (vertical line), create a scale moving up in value from −10 to 0 to +10. The 0, as you see, is in the middle of the left, vertical axis.

- Along the horizontal axis, chart out your years starting on the left with the first year in your chosen time period when things were generally "up" and long before the point you isolated in question 9 above. If you begin at age 30, for example, then evenly space the years between age 30 up to present.

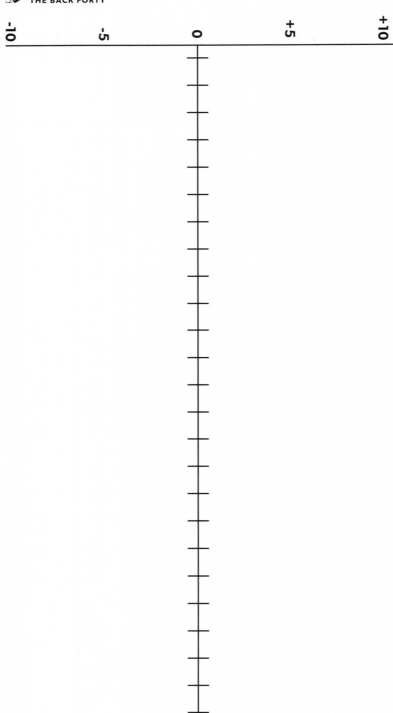

Back Forty Initiation Timeline Graph

- Next you will plot out your highs and lows along the chart with single dots, writing in the greatest things that happened to you as a +10 and the worst things that happened as a −10 and neutral impacts as 0. You will place a dot for each at the spot where the age at which the event occurred converges with the high/low level (10 to -10) of the event.

For demonstration purposes, before you start filling in the graph, I'll share my own abbreviated sequence of life events compiled from my exploration several years ago and then show you how I plotted those onto my own Back Forty Initiation Timeline.

Be well aware, I journaled heavily on the period covered in my timeline, mentally proceeding through each year and recalling the significant events and their respective rankings (-10 to +10). What you see here is merely a short list of events I pulled out of that journaling. I've outlined these with just a few words for the sake of brevity. Yet, I fully encourage you to journal as much as you can on the period you have chosen so as to accomplish a comprehensive walkthrough and resulting list of your own events. (Sometimes slowing down and really thinking back over time brings up events and situations we've conveniently forgotten.) Remember, however, that you're simply passing through the past. Don't hang out or get stuck there. Only revisit long enough to document the events and assess their relative perceived highs and lows on your own unique path of initiation into The Back Forty.

Lastly, don't get distracted by my events. Simply skim through them. They only demonstrate another individualized version of moving into midlife chock-full of enormous R & D, change, challenge and ultimately growth, probably a lot like yours. Pay only passing interest to my unique details. It's the process itself that I want you to focus on so you can duplicate the process and gain clarity around your own Back Forty Initiation Timeline.

Here's the events I recorded. The numbers represent my age.

27—Met Claire, LA Marathon, became office sales manager

28—NY Marathon, started business

29—Got married, became seminar director, bought house

30—Began acting

31—Studied with Sandy Meisner, son born, bought Mercedes

32—Founding member Sanford Meisner Center for the Arts,
    2 plays, commercials

33—Joined West Coast Ensemble, plays, commercials

34—Separation/began divorce, post-divorce fling

35—Men's team, began Agape classes (4 years to practitioner), best
    earning year ever

36—Continued best earning year, wrote first draft of
    recruiting book

37—Began publishing/debt mounting, focused on book

38—Business slowdown/dot-com burst, put house on market

39—Stock market crash, recession, sold house and paid off
    publishing debt ($100K), apartment living,
    began coaching, custody arbitration cum lawsuit

40—Custody suit (ten days in court over six months),
    big custody debt mounting, Maui Writers Conference,
    agent/publisher *Back Forty* interest

41—Custody suit ends, $125K debt, focus on individual/group
    coaching, biggest months income-wise through coaching
    (Jan and Feb 2004, $20K), Quantum, began
    network marketing

42—Met Adrianna and moved in together, challenging
    two-year relationship

43—Moved to Glendale, network marketing

44—Breakup/move; renewed coaching/teleseminar focus,
    met Lenka and resumed network marketing

45—Working network marketing hard, moved on after Rome,
    refocus on coaching

46—Financial markets collapse, breakup, put together first
   resume in 20 years, began outplacement consulting,
   moved again

After completing the list, I then assigned plus or minus values to the
events and charted them on the Initiation Timeline graph.

- An illustration of the Initiation Timeline graph can be found on
  the next page.

Now that you have an illustration of how this works, take some time,
perhaps even a couple days to complete *your* Initiation Timeline Graph.

- Review the events you have written about. If you have a lot,
  pick the most significant of them to chart.
- Match the events to your age, assign them a value (-10 to +10)
  and then place a corresponding dot for each event on your scatter
  plot graph. Here again are the detailed instructions for plotting
  the graph:

  ○ Plot out your highs and lows along the chart with single
    dots, writing in the greatest things that happened to you
    as a +10 and the worst things that happened to you as a
    −10 and neutral impacts as 0.

  ○ Place a dot at the spot on the graph where the age at
    which the event occurred converges with the value of
    the event.

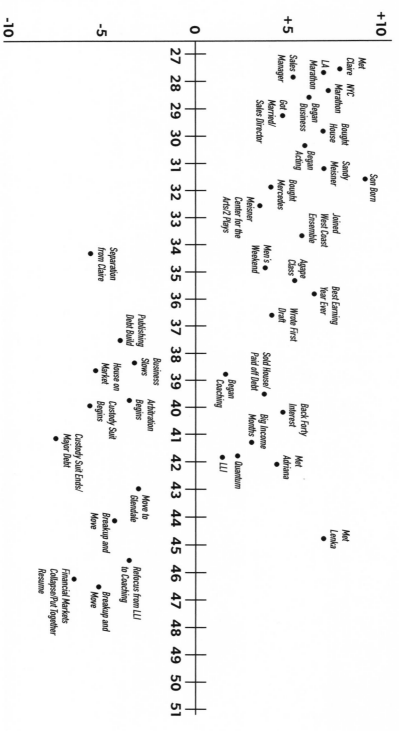

Darrell's Initiation Timeline

YOUR BACK FORTY TREND LINE
AND INITIATION DATE

Your final objective in this Initiation discovery is to determine a trend line, which in turn will reveal the approximate point in time of your Back Forty Initiation.

- On the next page, you'll find a graph showing how mine turned out. Use it as an illustration for constructing your own Trend Line.

As can be seen from my timeline and approximated trend line, my Back Forty Initiation occurred around age forty-one. Of course, depending on the specificity of my trend line, it actually could have been anywhere between ages forty and forty-two.

Remember, this is a rough approximation of my initiation. It was built subjectively, based on my recollection of the most significant events during the range of years I chose and the subjective relative value I gave to each event. I could, of course, have selective memory and be performing an irrational retrospective downgrading or upgrading of particular experiences. In the end, this is a very gut-feeling type of process, so we have to trust our gut. This exploration is completely organic and rational only to each individual engaging with it. But, even though subjectively created, mine gives me something to work with—a point in time to build context around and gain a new footing upon.

Embrace 5—Homeplay 3
Back Forty Trend Line

Look at your Initiation Timeline chart and apply your best guesstimate to sketch the average trend line from your earliest age on the graph to present. For example, if the first and second events occurred at nearly the same time and are +8 and -4 respectively, your trend line would start at +2 (about halfway between the two). Repeat this process from left to right,

Darrell's Back Forty Initiation Trendline

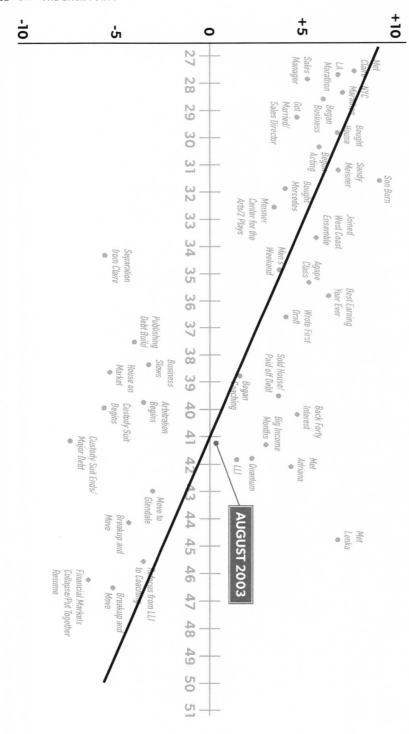

- Met Claire
- NYC
- Bought House
- Marathon
- LA
- Sales Manager
- Began Business
- Got Married; Sales Director
- Began Acting
- Sandy Meisner
- Bought Mercedes
- Meisner Center for the Arts/2 Plays
- Son Born
- Joined West Coast Ensemble
- Men's Weekend
- Agape Class
- Best Earning Year Ever
- Wrote First Draft
- Sold House/ Paid off Debt
- Began Coaching
- Big Income Months
- Back Forty Interest
- Met Adriana
- Quantum
- LLI
- Separation from Claire
- Publishing Debt Build
- House on Market
- Business Slows
- Custody Suit Begins
- Arbitration Begins
- Move to Glendale
- Focus from LLI to Coaching
- Custody Suit Ends/ Major Debt
- Breakup and Move
- Financial Markets Collapse/Put Together Resume
- Breakup and Move
- Met Lenka

AUGUST 2003

+10 · +5 · 0 · -5 · -10

27 28 29 30 31 32 33 34 35 36 37 38 39 40 41 42 43 44 45 46 47 48 49 50 51

continuing to draw the line through the average value of events in close proximity. Then take a look at where the line crosses 0 (neutral). That is the approximate point your initiation began. Don't worry about being precise. An approximation is sufficient to empower you in determining Your Initiation entry date into The Back Forty and your approximate age at that time.

For myself, I'll claim my Back Forty Birthday as August 5, 2003 when a particularly poignant situation ended: my two-year-plus custody suit!

Identification of your Back Forty Initiation Date is a symbolic anchor around which to build context and upon which to gain your new footing. If left unidentified and unexamined, vagueness around the Morassive (morass + massive) Thrust of Midlife (i.e., the big swamp) will be like a fog overcoming you. It will refuse to dissipate.

Embrace 5—Homeplay 4
Back Forty Initiation Date/Back Forty Birthday

To disperse the fog and gain crystal clear clarity, in your Back Forty Freedom Fliers Journal, take time to journal, outline, explore and examine the approximate date that your Back Forty Initiation Trend Line is pointing to as Your Back Forty Initiation. A particular year is sufficient. However, if you want to be playful and choose a specific point within that year, based on a unique event (or your incredibly specific calculations), you'll now have a designated date to forever celebrate as your "Back Forty Birthday." Your Initiation Date, your Back Forty Birthday, is an anchor point of celebration and inspiration for you to think and do things differently in your future.

> **Your Initiation Date, your Back Forty Birthday, is an anchor point of celebration and inspiration for you to think and do things differently in your future.**

If you think this process is meant to playfully minimize the significance of your particular version of midlife hell, you're right, it is. If you think I'm making light of your own slippery slope into the swamp, you're correct. Light is good. Light is the only way out of darkness. And, remember, yet again: your entire life has been—even in the worst of times—and continues to be a uniquely powerful laboratory for the Discovery and Expression of something.

GATE-OPENING SERIOUS AND SIGNIFICANT EVENTS

From the beginning of our Back Forty exploration together, you've discovered that out of your past and present experiences it's possible to discern certain essences and qualities. You now have the opportunity to carry them—Your Self Expression Directives—with you through the gateway of your midlife initiation and forward into your Back Forty life.

So, let's put your understanding of that same Discovery & Expression Method to good use and apply it to any new Serious and Significant Events that have shown up in your Initiation Timeline, that is, events or influences that you did not analyze in Embraces 1 and 2.

Truly, if you haven't already taken each and every one of these newly surfaced or resurfaced morassive, *below-the-neutral-line* midlife events you just listed in the timeline process all the way through a CSI because to Be Cause transformation using the Discovery & Expression Method we used in Embraces 1 and 2, now is the time.

Now? you might say. Yes, now. Which other *now* would be the best time to use this flight plan to completely free your Self and begin anew!

To help you be brave, I'll share an analysis of one of my Midlife-Opportunity Significant and Serious Events that began right before my Back Forty birthdate.

Discovery & Expression Analysis: Midlife Opportunity
Darrell's Experiment: Custody Suit

Step 1: Serious and Significant Event or Influence
Choose and name a serious and significant event or influence.

"Custody Suit"

Step 2: Victim Story
Tell the story in full (as it occurred then) victim form.

My first marriage of five years ended in divorce. We went through the legal process rather easily, hiring a do-it-yourself divorce service to handle the paperwork for our own, self-styled settlement agreement. It was five years after the divorce when the real trouble started.

My former wife prospered in her Hollywood studio development career for the next five years while I did well in my recruiting business. I even wrote my first book toward the end of the '90s to teach folks how to best use executive recruiters. Our son was two and a half years old when we split. We divided our time with him equally on a half-week schedule.

As noted, unfortunately, the economy fell out dramatically in 2001, right after that book hit the shelves. Recruiters were leaving the profession in droves due to a lack of positions to fill. Even I moved out of recruiting into career coaching. A book on how to best use recruiters, therefore, became useless and a hard sell; and a huge chunk of change had gone into publishing it. My plan to sell my home and use the equity to pay off my significant book publishing debt created an environment of opportunity for my ex, who continued to thrive on her increasing, studio-executive salary. For years, she had wanted to move closer to her work in the Valley. Though we both still lived on LA's Westside and shared custody of our son, in her financially superior position the time was ripe to handle sour grapes. Though the purely procedural process of divorce had been smooth years before, plenty of scars and unhealthy dynamics continued in our relationship. This was payback time.

I was just starting over, now in the career coaching world, when I received legal documents from her. The documents proposed that she move to the Valley and have our son full-time, with me only seeing him every other weekend. (The Valley is only twenty-five miles from the Westside but a mini-lifetime away in LA traffic.)

That wasn't the biggest rub though. Switching from five years of 50/50 joint custody to every other weekend—that was the kicker. Our son was seven at the time. He and I had participated in the local YMCA Indian Guides and Cub Scouts for over three years, YMCA swimming and basketball, AYSO soccer, church on Sundays, and many neighborhood activities. I was very involved in his life, but my ex's proposal didn't mention that. And so began a legal battle that would span two years and a half-million dollars in legal fees.

After an initial failed arbitration, a year passed with paperwork shuffling back and forth between attorneys. This was followed, as required by the court, by us both undergoing extensive psychological evaluations lasting a few months and, finally, ten full days in court spread over six months.

Thanks to an insightful, female judge, the suit ended with relatively similar custodial arrangements as existed before. However, now the attorneys had Harvard University fund coffers ready for their kids. Not so for our son.

It was not only the untruths and enormous debt that had me feel victimized, but the slings and arrows of a negative psych evaluation that struck my core. Fortunately, the judge didn't buy the evaluator's opinion because my "father fitness" had been proven in spades during the case. I didn't buy it either, but the psych evaluation did point out some traits that gave me pause and subsequently served to get me down on myself.

The inner-voice inherited from an overly critical father expressed itself, yet again, in full force. So, in the end, I "successfully" defended in the hard-fought custody battle but lost the self-esteem war. I found myself at age forty, a single father, back in an apartment, career-less and with a ton of debt and a cowering self-concept.

Step 3: Blessings
Identify the phenomena (blessings) coming from the event or influence.

- The storm created a subsequent peaceful co-parenting world because in the process we both learned enormously about ourselves and our respective contributions to our son.
- The suit tested my tenacity and persistence, tempering those qualities within me just as quality steel is forged.
- The process awakened an awareness of the reckonings from the trails I've left behind: the impact on others I've had in relationships (e.g., my former wife). It magnified the critical importance of keeping those trails as clean as consciously possible when moving forward in life.
- The psych evaluation had me look deeper into the thinly veiled dearth of self-esteem from which I operated in life.
- The debt I incurred opened up completely new worlds for me in multiple ways, outlined in the remaining blessings.
- This particular debt caused me to become aware of a pattern of other debt situations following my divorce years earlier. Interestingly, I had never once had any debt issues prior to my divorce.
- The debt forced me to seek support outside of my Lone-Ranger-ness so as to be inspired by the experience, strength, and hope of others with similar debting issues.
- The debt had me examine underlying spiritual issues surrounding debt, money and abundance: forgiveness, integrity, regrets, worthiness, deserve-ability, surrender, service, appreciation, and more.

- The debt had me face some tough choices, which everyone must make at some point in life: to forge forward or fold; to get bigger or succumb; to persist with faith or to shrink into isolation and stagnation.

Step 4: Hypothetical Research Questions
Determine the hypothetical research questions I may have been experimenting for in the laboratory.

1. Can a guy already known for his blind tenaciousness expand that ability even more in a seemingly no-win situation?
2. Can a strong-willed guy who has developed his way of dealing with people and life catch a message from the Universe to change?
3. Can fake self-esteem be replaced by true Self-esteem?
4. When pressed to the edge of a financial cliff, will the Lone Ranger remove his mask?
5. Can the spiritual and social dynamics of debt serve to advance life? Can debt be a teacher?

Step 5: Owning the Lab Design
Declare my ownership of the laboratory and its design—how I picked the perfect lab assistants and ideal lab environments.

LAB ASSISTANTS
My greatest lab assistant in this experiment was my son's mother, my ex-wife. I hired her well. Extremely well! Plus, given the obvious blessings of this serious and significant "because," I'm eternally grateful for having invited and created her participation.

It's critically important that I truly take responsibility for hiring her and for delegating her tasks because, for so long, I blamed her, her particular past and her particular upbringing for "doing what she did to me." Boy, is that last bit a serious and significant "because" statement, or what?

Yes, to absolutely OWN the whole thing is where the rubber meets the road in the Discovery & Expression analytical process. To realize that I hired someone to be my wife, and then ex-wife, who had experienced a childhood involving a similar custody case with a mother who, some present at the time say, had similarly besmirched the father. Now, if this sounds like I'm still blaming my ex or her mother, realize that I'm not. REALLY, REALLY, REALLY!

What I'm saying is that I hired as laboratory assistants an ex-wife and a mother-in-law with background stories that would allow me to justify myself as a victim! If their "resumes" for the job hadn't been so compelling or convincing, then the experiment could never have taken place!

Realize that it's possible that someone else could have been in relationship with my ex and with her mother without needing the elements of their history to justify victimhood. For instance, my ex's current husband of many years is doing very well in relationship with my ex and her mother. It's just that I obviously *needed* that unique experiential history in the qualifications of my own laboratory assistants to be able to run the experiments I needed to in order to access the blessings, findings and directives that flowed from them.

The point is this: everyone is running their own laboratory experiments. . .all the time. . .simultaneously. . .with some shared lead and supporting lab assistants. . .but to different ends.

Every experiment is different. Every individual's needs and therefore subconscious research questions are unique. Every soul came here to experiment, test and even retest certain questions to arrive at their own Discovery & Expression conclusions. What appears to be a must-have quality or element in the staffing of one person's laboratory experiment is not even listed in the job description of another person's experiment.

Yet, we're all inter-connectedly conducting these experiments all the time: causing, causing, causing, simultaneously, while in one another's constant employ as reciprocal lead and supporting lab assistants. Amazing isn't it?

LAB ENVIRONMENT

Two main environmental "climates" were needed for this experiment. First was the tense, power-struggle relationship that remained between my ex and me, even five years after our divorce. As outlined in the blessings, I see now how patterns of my own arrogance, inflexibility and anger had sown seeds of rebellion on her part, just as societies ruled by imperial, out-side forces also rebel. This long-incubated desire to strike back was simply waiting for the right time, the perfect opportunity.

Second and providing that perfect opportunity were the respective financial situations that existed in our divorced relationship. At the onset of the custody suit, I was in the middle of a career change, renting an apart-ment and pulling together income in whatever ways I could. On the other hand, my ex, in a Hollywood heyday of increasing salaries and bonuses, felt quite strong, as was her deserved right. So, opportunity knocked. The disparity in our financial and employment situations made the timing right.

You may only hear the above as me again blaming her if you don't understand that *I am taking complete responsibility* for setting up the envi-ronment and situation. I personally and solely designed the *perfect* labo-ratory environment required for my experiment.

Step 6: Findings from Research Questions
Determine the possible findings from my experimentation.

A. *Question:* Can a guy already known for his blind tenaciousness expand that ability even more in a seemingly no-win situation?

    Findings: Yes. At times I just couldn't imagine being able to go for-ward, yet I did. I remember one particular day, the day the psych evaluation came out recommending that my ex have custody, when I faced the biggest question: after nine months of legal expenses and putting all of life on hold, do I still move forward or do I fold?

    My experience was that in the family law system, even with all the advances in the rights of and stronger attitudes toward fathers in the last few decades, the dad is still pretty much behind the eight ball in an already precarious standing in a supposedly fair and equal forum. But, to then have a non-supportive evaluation, even my attorneys sensed a kiss of death for my case.

Yet, as I sat watching my son from my meditation chair while he slept in my bed that night when my parents were sleeping in his bed, their being in town to lend me money, I remembered my son's Cub Scout Motto: Do Your Best.

Had I done my best? Had I given it everything I had? Was I done doing my best or was I willing to simply put it all on the line, go all in for what I believed to be true—that my son needed my presence in his life as much as his mom's? It was at that moment that I decided, Whatever It Takes.

Of course, practical and rational minds (many of them surrounding me) might have said, "Cut your losses" or "It just ain't worth it." But I was obviously experimenting with stretching an outer limit that practicality and rationality couldn't reach. Whether smart or not, it was my experiment, and I was obviously committed to the lab test.

B. *Question:* Can a strong-willed guy who has developed his way of dealing with people and life catch a message from the Universe to change?

Findings: Yes, and obviously with a will that strong, it took a huge bag of bricks to catch my attention. Two and a half years and a half million-dollar legal production is a noticeable wake-up call to change!

C. *Question:* Can fake self-esteem be replaced by true Self-esteem?

Findings: I guess this is, in the end, what I actually paid for. Had I not organized this experiment I might still be operating over the top of the self-esteem chasm that existed before. At least now I've begun to plumb the depths of it, to shine light into its cracks, crevices and sinkholes, which have for so long created instability in anything I built. Better yet, I've begun a conscious and sustainable land-fill process.

D. *Question:* When pressed to the edge of a financial cliff, will the Lone Ranger remove his mask?

Findings: Maybe not the original Lone Ranger because Hollywood would never let a hero appear to "give in." Yet, as a metaphorical Lone Ranger, the whole financial test and debt experience have served me well. I've explored and learned about the spiritual dynamics of money and debt. Removing my mask has come in the form of letting go of resentments, replacing fear with faith and isolation with fellowship. I've gained a wisdom that all debt is a function of unforgiveness, and I've grown more peaceful and serene by realizing that I'm only as sick as my secrets. So, this particular Lone Ranger has learned to drop the mask more and more.

E. *Question*: Can the spiritual and social dynamics of debt serve to advance life? Can debt be a teacher?

Findings: As described in the Findings from Question D above, the answer for me has been completely and undeniably yes. If everything in life has a reason, if we've Caused everything as part of our individual experiments, then debt, too, can serve as an amazing gift and life-altering teacher, if we take complete responsibility for it.

Step 7: Self Expression Directives
Identify or simply postulate Self Expression Directives arising from the event or influence.

- **"Never Give Up! Never Give Up! Never Give Up!" (purported to be the shortest speech ever, given by Winston Churchill)**
- **Do Your Best**
- **Wake Up and Listen to the Universe**
- **Get Real**
- **Humility**
- **Authenticity**

Embrace 5—Homeplay 5
Discovery & Expression Analysis: Below the Line

Now it's your turn to take your Midlife-Opportunity events through the 7-Step Discovery & Expression Method to bring all of these below-the-line, swampy events and influences from because to Be Cause. This extra unloading of baggage from your Front Forty life will bring into your Back Forty a lightness that will allow you to fly further faster. Take a few days to complete this if necessary.

INITIATION INSPIRATION

In the morassive thrust of midlife, our flight pattern seems to move further and further askew from what we want. We may mourn the innocence and excitement of youth, especially in the areas of relationships, career, earning potential, and growth opportunities. Our youthful, ignorance-is-bliss confidence is gone, and perhaps vibrant health and vitality are now but vague memories of the past. Back when life seemed simpler, we had fewer all-encompassing concerns; we hadn't yet accumulated so much baggage and ballast bags.

Well, guess what? This is not the end. Far from it. This is an opportunity for the beginning.

After having outlined and plotted your trend line in the way described above and having analyzed your below-the-line events to extract their Self Expression Directives, some questions may arise for you.

From viewing my own trend line, an obvious question comes to mind:

"Does this mean that being initiated and living in The Back Forty is about having a life below the line?"

The answer is, of course not! There would be no JUICE in that! The idea is to move back above the line and, ideally, to trend upwards from here on out. This can happen through the work you've been doing. It happens when we truly let go of all the weight that brought us below the line in the first place: the weight of not only the many Serious and Significant Events or Influences addressed in Embraces 1 and 2 and just now in Embrace 5 but also the weight of the mistaken significance we ascribed to them.

Other questions that may come to mind are:

"So, when do things change?"
"When does my trend line turn upward?"
"When do I get to BE those Self Expression-directed essences and qualities?"
"When do I get to fulfill on my saddle-bag inventory of gifts and values?"

Here's an easy answer to all of those questions:

Today is the day! You and I get to BE all of that right now!

Your Back Forty Birthday, which you have just identified, denotes waking up into a new world of purposeful direction for your remaining time on the planet. Consider it the halftime buzzer in this game called life. You huddle, review, evaluate, inspire, ignite and then get out there and win your second half of life, regardless of whether you feel you won the first half or not.

And you do it now, because there's no sense waiting any longer! You get to fulfill on all of your laboratory experiments immediately—and from this point forward! Your Initiation Date/Back Forty Birthday is your day of celebration because you now realize that living in the old ways of "because," minimizing your inherent gifts and lacking current and distinct values just doesn't set any kind of upward trend toward a radical Back Forty! Once again, that dog don't hunt!

What happens next depends on the choice you make at this midlife juncture. To get stuck in your Initiation without recognizing it as the passageway and midlife opportunity that it affords is to risk becoming self-absorbed and stagnant rather than building some much-needed self-esteem and autonomy.

Years ago, at the beginning my own Back Forty adventure, I identified and Be Caused my Top 5 Serious and Significant Events or Influences. You may remember from Appendix A the event involving my luggage being stolen at Newark International Airport. At age twenty-two, I lost everything that reminded me of who I was. This seemingly tragic event, however, had me expand into a bigger world of elevated experience beyond the small-town life I'd been living.

Metaphorically, losing your "bags," having them stolen, throwing them over the side or just setting them down and walking off is the BEST thing that can happen to you as you move into your Back Forty. *And*, if you want to harvest the goodies of your second-half/best-half life, letting them go is essential.

Similarly, all the accoutrements and personal security blankets you've acquired on the road of life thus far, be they self-limiting beliefs, galvanized judgments about the way things are or the way life is or die-hard opinions of yourself and others can and will only hold you back from the new experiences that The Back Forty has to offer.

Distinguishing and gaining clarity on the way life was trending *before* your Back Forty Birthday, followed by the actual Midlife Initiation itself, creates an opening for a playful, passionate and purposeful future. In the same way I lost my "bagged" identity at age twenty-two, you now have the opportunity to release your own Front Forty identity and any significance behind it. As you pass from your Front Forty to your Back Forty, consider putting on a name tag that reads "Who am I NOW?" to represent the engaging inquiry of those joining the Royal Order of The Back Forty Freedom Fliers.

Your Back Forty can fly as high as you're willing to let go of the ballast that's been holding you down: living with "becauses" and being unaware of your Self Expression Directives to deliver, blind to your Gifts to express, and oblivious of your current Values to embody. All of that held you below or barely above the ground of midlife. In contrast, as a newly inducted Back Forty Freedom Flier, you'll experience new heights and enjoy broader views as you drop your ballast bags.

If and when we are each able to take full responsibility for our lives as lived thus far—like WE created it ALL for our own GOOD—then we're headed to a place of Oneness, where we will find no bad guys and no good guys. We may become beacons of a novel idea that there's never anybody or anything to blame—not even ourselves. More importantly, we may begin to experience and express deep gratitude and appreciation for everything having occurred exactly as it did, simply for the Be Cause of it.

> *Your Back Forty can fly as high as you're willing to let go of the ballast that's been holding you down.*

Granted, walking through the Royal Order of the Back Forty Freedom Fliers gate requires plenty of creative Cause Scene Investigation Homeplay, like you've done here, to assess and compile all the many and varied Self Expression Directives your laboratories have afforded you. But, if you're willing to re-engineer all those serious and significant events or influences through the mindset of your Mad Scientist, who has resided within you from birth, you'll take ownership—the keys to a huge laboratory for your own continued design of a radical, playful, passionate and purposeful second half of life.

FORGIVENESS IS OPTIONAL

At this point, I'd like to make a shout-out for forgiveness. I know, I know: I've spoken at length throughout the book that what has happened in your life is not the fault of others or of yourself. Accordingly, forgiveness of others or even of yourself would be unnecessary when you've taken full responsibility for your life having occurred exactly as it has.

I stand by that idea. However, sometimes our old patterns, belief systems and internal wiring have remnants that can be addressed quickly and easily by just taking actions that filled the bill in our earlier, less conscious days—in this case, forgiveness.

If the idea of forgiving all of those individuals and all of the serious and significant events or influences in which those individuals were involved appeals to your senses, I encourage you to practice it *radically*! Sure, on the conscious, causal side of this Back Forty philosophy, you now know it's not required. However, if the unconscious side of your Self can feel more freed up and become enlivened even more quickly through forgiveness, what have you got to lose?

When contemplating activating the power of forgiveness in your life, it's important to remember that forgiveness at a spiritual level is not so much for another person as it is for yourself. Just like judgment and criticism of others are akin to poison we ingest while expecting others to be harmed, forgiveness is, in an opposite way, a blessing we give to our Selves imagining that it is meant for others.

Forgiveness can be given in more than one way. If you don't want to necessarily do it verbally with the person or organization involved, which may have them feel criticized or judged if they are operating in the world of "because" (as if they could have actually done something to you that you didn't hire them for) then just do it within your own heart and mind. One way to do it is to create a forgiveness ritual around ALL of your laboratory assistants and laboratory environments and then just release any holds on those old employees and settings in one fell swoop.

If you want to play life at an elite level, you can go so far as to actually acknowledge and thank them for the difference they've made in your life, for having done well the job for which you hired them! Again, this can be done verbally, engaging with those you are thanking, or within your own soul. If verbally, just be prepared to share in a total-owning and non-critical way how you came to this gratitude and acknowledgement. Sure, this may be a bit hard to explain; but, hey, if you got freed up to see your life's design in this new way, why wouldn't you want others to get a glimpse of it, too? However you approach forgiveness, if you are called to it, the result is that more weight, more baggage will drop away, making you lighter and more agile as you pass into your Back Forty best second half.

Rites of Passage

To fully honor and appreciate the significance of our Back Forty Initiation, let's take a moment to explore the concept of rites of passage. We see these rites take place throughout the world, where various cultures acknowledge transitions from one era to another in a person's life. Some common ones such as baptisms, confirmations, bar or bat Mitzvahs, school graduations, weddings, retirements and funerals are all marked with ceremony.

Much has been written about rites of passage in particular and their significance in general. I encourage as much in-depth exploration of that topic as you'd find helpful to understand the rite of passage that we are celebrating here: your passing through the gateway into your Back Forty life. At whatever age it occurs, you now come into a stage of life you have experimented to create that will be playful, passionate, and purposeful because of the work you have done and the baggage you have dropped.

You might be getting a sense that this transition into your purposeful and fulfilling second half of life can be one of the most important rites of passage you'll ever experience. Yet, because it hasn't been celebrated, nor perhaps even recognized, your passage may have occurred as simply an embarrassing and isolated slippery slope into swampy conditions evoking self-criticism, cynicism and resignation.

Well, we are changing that now! Get out the fireworks and strike up the band! Celebrating Your Initiation gets you past the tendency to hold this transition period in contempt and to, instead, shower it with appreciation.

Through recognizing, distinguishing and appreciating midlife as a doorway between worlds, you can detach from the heaviness of the unique gauntlet through which you may have passed and simply get on with the task at hand: fulfilling on your reason for BEing on the planet! What was heretofore midlife crisis has become your midlife opportunity!

> *Through recognizing, distinguishing and appreciating midlife as a doorway between worlds, you can detach from the heaviness of the unique gauntlet through which you may have passed and simply get on with the task at hand: fulfilling on your reason for BEing on the planet!*

Embrace 5—Homeplay 6
Initiation Rite

Pull out your Back Forty Freedom Fliers Journal and take some time to write your thoughts on the following *Back Forty Insight & Awareness Questions*:

1. How do you relate the concept of Rites of Passage to your own midlife opportunity? Write out any and all insights.
2. How has your initiation served you? Why would you (your Mad Scientist) have chosen it to be exactly as it is and was?
3. What is the weighty ballast—the "old self"-perpetuating baggage—that you've now been given the opportunity (or have been forced to) let go of in order to move through your initiation into your second half?
4. How might you support, in a celebratory way, your own Back Forty Initiation—your separation from your Front Forty and entrance into your second half? When will you do so? Who will you invite? How will you make it joyous?
5. From this point of Your Initiation, what does Back Forty Freedom look like for you? Describe it.

6. What initial Back Forty Insights & Awareness are you having related to the **F**ormula of **U**nique **S**elf Expression (**FUSE**) that you came to light? Who did you come here to BE? What did you come here to DO? (We'll be looking at this again in "Embrace 6: Your Purpose," so don't worry if right now you have only bits and pieces of an answer. Just begin to inquire.)

Duly initiated, you are now invited into a spirit of fellowship with other Freedom Fliers who are questing for a meaningful future. Join with others who've also come to the edge of their Front Forty, ready to cultivate and harvest from their Back Forty. None of us can advance through what's ahead with the same old plan we've been using. No, playing forward requires a new vision and new tools—all of which we're now building together.

Like joining clubs and organizations in your younger days when you were discovering and forming your initial concepts of Self, you are now being inducted into a new era and fellowship in which your sole intent is to express your **F**ormula of **U**nique **S**elf Expression, to light your **FUSE** of who you originally came here to BE and what you originally came here to DO.

> **Are you ready to light your FUSE?**

Are you ready to light your FUSE?

FIFTH SEPTENARY ACKNOWLEDGEMENT

As you embrace, rather than resist or bemoan, your particular trajectory into The Back Forty, you can choose to feel a certain honor and level of accomplishment that you made it to the checkpoint of Your Initiation. Like the racing video games I used to play with my son, you only get to continue driving if you make it to the next checkpoint in the time allotted. And, you made it! Now, this is when you move on to the remainder of the game called your best half/second half of life with you consciously aware of your Self's role in it. . .and making the most of that awareness!

As you conclude this chapter, not only in the book and Front Forty of your life but also in your heart, mind and spirit, rejoice in what lies ahead. You're now a member of an admirable order, duly initiated into the conscious evolvement of your greatest-yet-to-be. The hazing is over and your Royal Order of The Back Forty Freedom Fliers badge has been well earned.

I salute you!

YOUR PURPOSE

"I was bewildered and worried that my entire scale of values was untrustworthy. . .I confessed that I had a burning desire to be excellent, but no faith that I could be," Martha said to me, very quietly. "There is a vitality, a life force, an energy, a quickening that is translated through you into action, and because there is only one of you in all of time, this expression is unique. And if you block it, it will never exist through any other medium and it will be lost. The world will not have it. It is not your business to determine how good it is nor how valuable nor how it compares with other expressions. It is your business to keep it yours clearly and directly, to keep the channel open. You do not even have to believe in yourself or your work. You have to keep yourself open and aware to the urges that motivate you. Keep the channel open."

AGNES DE MILLE, *Martha: The Life and Work of Martha Graham*

LIVING IN THE QUESTION

"**W**hat is my purpose?"

"What's it all for/about?"

"Why am I here?"

"What am I here to do?"

. . .and a myriad of similar existential inquiries have resided in more minds, kept more people awake at night (and daydreaming during the day), been at the heart of more addiction, have preceded more shifts in direction and sold more books than perhaps any other questions known to man.

So, will this chapter be the end-all, be-all answer to these questions for you? Of course it will not. This Holy Grail is one that humanity has pursued throughout history and no silver-bullet, ultimate "answer" has ever been found.

I don't personally plan to ever stop asking the questions and I encourage you to keep asking, too. We will always arrive at a next level and those next-level answers, which can't be heard from the level we're at, won't come if we quit asking. Early on in my quest, I came across a bit of wisdom which, still in the midst of my very human drive to get "the answer," I could never seem to shake off—"perhaps getting the answer is the booby prize."

So, here's the biggest question you *will* need to answer for your Self, one that will shape any real meaning or results you'll derive from The Back Forty:

What if this way of experiencing life doesn't promise you an an-swer to your purpose, per se, but infuses within you the ability to live powerfully inside of a purpose-directed question itself? Can that be enough?

Standing in that frame of mind, I've allowed myself to enjoy books, courses, programs and inner work of a personal development nature with-out a nagging pressure or necessity to get the ultimate answer. "Inquiry" has been mentioned several times as you've moved through the Embraces. Now, for the remain-der of this book and for your entire Back Forty ahead, I want to introduce you to inquiry as a *practice,* a practice that may calm what is

> **"Perhaps getting the answer is the booby prize."**

perhaps your own insatiable desire to get *the* answer. Living in inquiry is a lot more fun and a lot less frustrating.

INQUIRY VS. ANSWER

What is inquiry? Dictionary.com defines inquiry as "a seeking or request for truth, information or knowledge" as well as "the act of inquiring or of seeking information by questioning; interrogation."

Nowhere in those definitions, nor anywhere else, will you find that the word inquiry involves *getting* an answer. You'll only see references to the act of seeking and questioning. Therefore, to establish appropriate expectations for The Back Forty ahead of you, I invite you into the power of inquiry.

Inquiry is engaging in a question that explores ALL possible answers; it is knowing that far more than any one, single, solitary or finite "answer" exists. Just because something is "true for you" or somebody else doesn't mean it's actually "true." Inquiry involves examining every inch of possible ground that a question unearths without any urgency to arrive at a one-and-only answer lickety-split.

> *Just because something is "true for you" or somebody else doesn't mean it's actually "true."*

You may eventually choose to adopt the particular and personal answers to life's most perplexing questions that most empower you. Doing so too quickly, however, can have you making uninformed choices. Also, think about it: when you've arrived at any "answer" for yourself in the past, you've actually stopped the questioning process, which may have left you closed off, fixed and in danger of obsolescence.

Your answer in the past may have taken the form of the ultimate romantic relationship or life partner. It may have been the job, career or business that was, at the time, the perfect fit. It may have been some religious or other group with certain beliefs or views on life and the world.

It may have been the attainment of money, position or prestige that you thought would provide your answer to life. In other words, your past answers may have shown up in a myriad of forms. Yet, as life progressed, those answers may have fallen short of being the be-all and end-all to your highest Self-expression. They were simply your best "answers" available at the time and may have since become obsolete.

In your second half of play, passion and purpose—your Back Forty of infinite possibilities—there's no room for obsolescence. When it comes to **Embrace 6: Your Purpose** being realized, the power and practice of continual inquiry is essential.

Why? Often, we quickly latch onto "answers," thus limiting ourselves, simply to resist being in the void of an inquiry. Have you ever noticed, when you give yourself the opportunity to truly contemplate an idea, even richer and more profound *possible* answers arise beyond the first-blush conclusions you initially come to, answers that carry you to yet another level of inquiry?

Don't avoid the void. —*Michael Beckwith*

Consider this: what if the magnitude of the questions you seek to answer in life were so BIG that they could never have any final answers. What if a finite "answer" didn't even exist? What if the act of engaging in the questions themselves carried a life-altering power all its own?

> *When it comes to Embrace 6: Your Purpose being realized, the power and practice of continual inquiry is essential.*

Perhaps that's the secret behind the powerful and purposeful lives of some of the greatest individuals to ever walk the planet. Martin Luther King, for example, lived inside a question akin to "how do we live as equals?" Gandhi lived inside a question like "how do we live in peace with independence and freedom for all?" Mother Theresa lived inside a question on the order of "how do we serve as our brother's keeper, supporting the unwanted, the unloved, and the uncared for?"

Those are enormous questions (one could even say, problems) inside of which these individuals lived day in and day out. They didn't exhaust or frustrate themselves inside a futile, short-term mindset of thinking they would one day get a final answer. Rather, they functioned within and contributed to the world from the enormous power given to them by being courageous enough, bold enough and tenacious enough to live *inside of*, to live *surrounded by*, and to *make their very bed on top of* the questions themselves.

Whether or not these celebrated luminaries ever approached or achieved any actual answers to their questions, the very act of *living inside the questions* gave them supernatural powers. They experienced insights, established movements, authored situations and created history-making impact—results—that never would have occurred had they not engaged in the *big* questions. Perhaps that's exactly why they became luminaries.

Can we do that? Can we adopt our own versions of some BIG questions and reap enormous empowerment from inquiring into them? The answer is *yes*! We don't necessarily need to change the world, but we can inquire, and by doing so, possibly change ourselves and the course of our own lives.

It seems counter-intuitive to *choose* to take on a big problem if you know upfront that you'll never find "the answer." For example, how does an individual, much less humanity as a whole, ensure themselves a second half of play, passion and purpose such that they leave the planet fully Self-expressed and completely used up? That is a BIG question alluding to a big problem. It can seem overwhelming. Yet, it can open up endless possible avenues of inquiry.

Perhaps that's where your true power and purpose live: forever engaging in that BIG question itself. Personalizing it. Dialoging on it. Experimenting with it. Venturing into new territories individually and with others because of it.

> *How does an individual, much less humanity as a whole, ensure themselves a second half of play, passion and purpose such that they leave the planet fully Self-expressed and completely used up? That is a BIG question.*

If you stick to only easy, manageable questions in your second half, you'll just be playing it safe. You'll end up focusing with a tiny gaze on just the little problems you believe you can handle, the ones you think you can answer, like how to pay the light bill. Survival, though necessary, is a weak foundation upon which to build a radical Back Forty.

The funny thing about playing it safe and small is that you actually never get any final answers to those little, piddling questions either. Even if you only deal with the tiniest questions, you never really *handle*, once-and-for-all, their nagging, persistent and constant demand for answers. Over and over again you may ask, "How do I pay the light bill?" "Okay, now, how do I pay the light bill?" "Okay, NOW, how do I pay the light bill?" You'll think that you got it handled, but it comes up again and again!

So, the ultimate question boils down to this: if you'll never get final and absolute answers to either the trivial questions or the BIG questions, do you become stronger living inside of BIG questions or small questions? What size of question empowers you the most?

One line of thinking says that the size of the worldly problems you're willing to engage in determines the quality of your life. Want to lead a big life? Then take on some big, worldly questions. Want to experience a small life? Worry primarily about paying your bills and surviving.

The only thing worse than being blind is having sight but no vision.
—Helen Keller

Interestingly, when we take on very BIG problems in life, those that reach beyond the small self and directly impact the Higher or overall ONE Self—that bigger body of humanity we're all a part of—often the smaller, survival-oriented problems just tend to get handled. The light bill just happens to get paid while you're shining your greater light in the world, all the while in service of kicking some major, BIG-problem butt.

The game you'll play in life is up to you: luminary or light bill? Both involve light, but one carries a lot more kilowatts. One involves radiance and Presence. The other represents only subsistence and, perhaps, even decadence.

I propose that your future radiance as a Back Forty luminary lies inside of your capacity to take on BIG questions and inquire into them without letting them deceive you into thinking that you've lost any power from your inability to find a definitive answer. Your midlife opportunity is to gain absolute *em-power-ment* (power put *in*) from simply exploring the possibilities that arise from the inquiries themselves.

> *The game you'll play in life is up to you: luminary or light bill? Both involve light, but one carries a lot more kilowatts.*

One last point about The Back Forty practice of inquiry: for it to be worthwhile, rather than simply a luxurious head trip, you must still have a driving determination to truly find the "answer"!

"Whaaaaat???? He just told me to give up any need for the answer. Now he's telling me to be hell-bent on finding it????"

These dual intentions, letting go of the need for the answer while retaining the drive for discovering the answer, may seem contradictory; but stick with me here. This duality is a paradox, for sure—but a paradox with power.

Just think about how luminaries operate in life. They live inside of BIG, virtually unanswerable questions and, as we've discussed, gain power from that alone. At the same time, they take deliberate and concerted action *on a daily basis* toward finding solutions as if they still might arrive at their ultimate answer. They are empowered by the inquiry itself and take actions every day, where the rubber meets the road, as if their lives depended upon the actual answering of their questions.

Think of it like this: luminaries model an attitude of being absolutely and unquestionably *committed*. However, at the same time, they are *not attached*. That's the catch! Commitment to finding an answer is great fuel for action. Attachment to getting an answer is a deadly killer of valuable and worthwhile inquiry.

Embrace 6—Homeplay 1
Living in the Question

Considering all this, ask your Self a couple of defining questions, record-ing the questions and your answers in your Freedom Fliers Journal. Your answers to these questions will determine the ultimate value you'll get from this book and The Back Forty message and practice as a whole.

1. If I don't expect a final answer for the big questions I'm asking, but rather engage in the questions themselves (inquire) such that I'm empowered to alter the course of my life, can I be satisfied with that?
2. If the process alone of inquiring into The Back Forty's 7 Embraces allows me to create a radically more playful, passionate and purposeful second half, will that be worth it?

For me, obviously, the answers are unequivocally yes.
How about you?

Commitment to finding an answer is great fuel for action. Attachment to getting an answer is a deadly killer of valuable and worthwhile inquiry.

This book was originally written for *me*. It was written through me to me and for me. It was some-thing I personally needed to read. It has provided a whole new future for my life that wasn't going to "just happen anyway." I can only hope and pray that it provides actionable inspiration for you as well.

In my own personal relationship with the Back Forty message, I've chosen to give up the need for ultimate answers. Yet, I'm also willing to operate as if my life depends on getting the answers to move both myself and others forward.

I venture into the laboratory of this Back Forty experiment—the book, the movement, and my own next forty to fifty years—with a commitment to engage, inquire and try on some new thoughts, all with an attitude of non-attachment. How about you? When it comes to Your Purpose, can you be committed and, yet, not attached? If so, we can really play in the realm of extraordinary possibilities! If you're not sure, I encourage you to simply keep exploring while staying open to the possibility of non-attachment.

For the power that comes from inquiry alone, I invite you to dive into the inquiry of Embrace 6: Your Purpose. Let's use all the Self-awareness you've gained thus far in your Back Forty journey to explore the many possibilities. Such an inquiry versus attachment to finding the "answer" can and will yield valuable fuel to the fire of your soul.

A little story sums up the point. When first testing the waters of these Back Forty concepts, my wife and I designed our first Back Forty **INFUSE** (**I**gniting a **N**ew **F**ormula of **U**nique **S**elf **E**xpression) Live 3-Day Event. The Back Forty philosophy had already supported huge transformations in our own lives, and we wanted to see how these ideas would land with others. The event allowed us to experiment inside a contained "Laboratory Environment" of discovery in the midst of our own "Laboratory Assistant" participants.

One particular participant came into the course under a lot of pressure to get the monumental question we've been discussing handled, once and for all: "What is my purpose?" She was, and is, a very accomplished, connected and spiritually aware individual and is personally and professionally associated with many outstanding world luminaries. It was an honor to have her in the course, as it is with anyone who chooses to engage with us in this new, co-created conversation for a radical, second half of life.

Upon arriving at the Embrace 6: Your Purpose segment of the program, the pressure was on—on her, by her. She now had to deliver to herself the "answer" to this nagging question because through all of her other evolved and empowered efforts in life, she had not found a resolution. Needless to say, she was a too tense to get it because, as mentioned above, no easy answer exists. Plus, pressure never helped anyone resolve anything creatively and lovingly.

Her need to deliver it *to herself* became her perceived need *for us* to deliver it to her. It seemed that she unconsciously placed the weight of realizing her "answer" on our shoulders. I believe she felt some initial disappointment at not having had that answer simply and easily given to her on a silver platter. She did, however, leave the course empowered and became a great supporter of our work.

Considering her experience, here is a great riddle you can use to boost your popularity at any party: "what is the most important part of a jigsaw puzzle?"

Take a moment to consider the question before reading on. The punchline lands better when you've truly pondered the conundrum.

Ready?

The picture on the box! Until you know what the puzzle looks like when it's put together, you're pretty much connecting pieces in the dark. Many want to be handed a full picture of their purpose and provided a box lid-of-life answer to measure their progress against while pulling together the pieces of their own, puzzling life. On the other hand, many others have, for their entire lives, pursued becoming free of exactly that.

Back Forty Freedom Fliers fall in the second camp. A radical, playful, passionate and purposeful life doesn't work the way a store-bought puzzle does. As a Back Forty Flier, the last thing you want is to have your life fit any picture on a box that someone else designed. There's only one unique YOU in this lifetime. Only you have your one-of-a-kind combination of experiences, influences, lab experiments, Self Expression Directives, Gifts, Values and Back Forty Birthday. If YOU don't discover and express your unique YOU, igniting your own **F**ormula of **U**nique **S**elf **E**xpression (**FUSE**), it will be forever unexpressed.

The picture that comes together from your own, personalized, puzzle pieces of life could never be designed by anyone who's come before you nor by anyone who'll come after you. Plus, nobody would ever design it in exactly the way you will, *even if* a one-in-a-trillionth chance occurred where they possessed the very same pieces! What you construct from the pieces of your own Front Forty puzzle will—and can only be—unique to who YOU came to be and what YOU came to do. And, as the Jewish proverb instructs, if not YOU, who? If not now, when?

> **Modern man lives under the illusion that he knows "what he wants," while he actually wants what he is supposed to want. In order to accept this it is necessary to realize that to know what one really wants is not comparatively easy, as most people think, but one of the most difficult problems any human being has to solve. It is a task we frantically try to avoid by accepting ready-made goals as though they were our own. —Erich Fromm**

> *If YOU don't discover and express your unique YOU, igniting your own Formula of Unique Self Expression (FUSE), it will be forever unexpressed.*

So, learn from the story of the INFUSE course participant's experience and know that you'll need three elements for a truly *embracing* inquiry into Your Purpose: *patience, creativity and a loving spirit.* Let go of the idea of a single, final and perfect answer. Let go of any pressure to figure out Your Purpose, and just stay in the inquiry. Simply and patiently love yourself into a creative space where the dots can somehow get connected.

If you do so, you'll have a very good chance that an overall inspiring second-half picture of your life will begin to emerge. Be open for that bigger picture to take form. It did for me and for many others who've taken this Back Forty ride of Discovery and Expression.

> *Know that you'll need three elements for a truly* **embracing** *inquiry into Your Purpose:* **patience, creativity and a loving spirit.**

> **Be yourself; everyone else is already taken.**
> **—*Oscar Wilde***

A READY-FOR-PRIME-TIME PURPOSE REVIEW

Let's lay out on the table all the pieces of the YOU puzzle you've already discovered thus far as you've travelled across your Front Forty acreage toward your playful, passionate and purposeful Back Forty. Then, we'll explore some further mindsets from which a low pressure, easy and graceful sense of purpose can emerge.

Embrace 1 and 2: Your Past and Your Present

You've embraced this moment, and everything that has come before it.

As you own Your Past and Your Present, transforming your becauses into Be Causes, realizing that it's an ongoing process to do so unceasingly, you free up your future.

You can now feel empowered by every single thing that has ever happened to you because you see the perfect design behind it all. You can appreciate the laboratory experiments that your Inner Mad Scientist set up for the development of your greater Self-expression.

Realizing that you've never been a victim of anyone or anything, you can Be Cause and fully OWN every aspect of Your Past and Your Present. In so doing, you'll Be Cause your future as well. Your Self Expression Directives, deduced from earlier experiments, point toward that Self-designed future.

We say that The Back Forty is about experiencing a "radical" second half of life and that the freedom that arises from embracing your past and present is the very foundation of that possibility. You may consider "radical" a bit of an overstatement. But think about it: isn't it radical to think that you can live the rest of your life with no limitations, only empowerment, from Your Past and Your Present?

Embrace 3: Your Gifts

You have inventoried and embraced your unique gifts, talents and capabilities. Your original "plan," so to speak, of what you thought your life would be about (e.g., what you studied in school, your initial career, that particular person you married, etc.) might not have supplied all of the skills, talents, and circumstances required by your ultimate plan, called Your Back Forty.

Therefore, your first half of life has been chock-full of unplanned and unexpected learning opportunities (laboratory experiments), which have enabled you to acquire the requisite gifts and talents to become who you came here to be and to do what you came here to do, shining all the way. This cache of gifts and talents developed in the throes of your Front Forty is immense. You can now appreciate the multiple capabilities you've been equipped with for the Big Game that you came for, but may have yet to play.

Embrace 4: Your Values

You've embraced what matters most. In the same way that your gifts and talents expanded in unforeseen and unexpected ways through the lab experiments called your life, your values took on new hues and priorities as the experimentation of your first half prepared you for the second. What really matters now and what you're willing to do for it has changed.

In having taken time to inventory and get crystal-clear about Your Values, you're able to focus your time and talents on what matters most NOW —including your 1,095 Day Pledges— distinct from what mattered most in your unthinking, catapulted-into-life first half.

Embrace 5: Your Initiation

You've embraced Your Initiation into Your Back Forty. You've stopped to celebrate the Rite of Passage that such initiation offers.

Declaring a Back Forty Birthday and drawing a line of demarcation between your Front Forty of unconscious research and development and your radical second half of purposeful fulfillment is an essential and defining ritual. It allows you to not simply "begin again" but to actually *begin*. Who you came here to be and what you came here to do STARTS NOW. The first half, your Front Forty, simply got you here.

I was conscious of a profound sense of relief. I felt as if I was walking with destiny and that all my past life had been but a preparation for this hour and this trial.
—Winston Churchill, on his 1940 election to Prime Minister of England

A metaphor I use to distinguish The Front Forty from The Back Forty is a chocolate chip cookie. When it comes to the cookie, what it's all about for me is the chips. I'm in it for the chips. The cookie is simply a vehicle to bring on the chips. Similarly, your Front Forty cookie is simply a carrier, an enabling mechanism, to bring forth your sweet Back Forty chips.

At this point then, your first-half Front Forty has gotten its job done! And *you* got *your* job done! You did everything exactly the way you were supposed to, according to your own grand design, and you've now passed through the gate into your radical Back Forty. Woohoo!

You're ready to move forward to embrace two more elements that contribute to the vastness of your Back Forty ahead. Interestingly, the final two Back Forty Embraces arise to be embraced simultaneously: Your Purpose and A Presence. As you progress through this and the next Embrace, it will become increasingly apparent that you can't fully embrace one without the other.

UNPATTERNING AGING

No doubt, you're beginning to experience a significant number of insights, revelations, "aha's," inklings of direction and even burgeoning freedom from your analysis of the Research & Development experiments that you've conducted thus far in life.

Does the R & D stop now that you've passed your initiation and are headed into your second half of play, passion and purpose? Heck no! Are you kidding? It's not like you'll now stop setting up laboratory opportunities to grow even more in all the ways necessary to be who you came here to be and do what you came here to do. And, it's not like you'd want to! Your Big Game is yet to come! Your ultimate card has yet to be played! Your best crop is yet to be harvested—or maybe even planted!

Think about it: approaching your next half/best half of life from a context of conscious and proactive Research & Development is absolutely the most empowering and future-building way to go. It flies in the face of the generally accepted direction that society says we're to follow when getting older.

> *Your Big Game is yet to come! Your ultimate card has yet to be played! Your best crop is yet to be harvested— or maybe even planted!*

Many of us grew up programmed to believe that getting older involves three patterns. First, we're supposed to gain a certain amount of "wisdom" from our experiences, wisdom which is to then serve as a guidepost or divining rod in determining our way forward. Second, we're told to work hard early in "the earning years" in order to reach a time when we deserve and want to sit back, take it easy and "do what we really want to do and not what we have to do." Third, as we grow older, it's understood that we'll naturally shrink our circles of friends and influences to those who fit our then perceived "truths" about the world and how to live in it.

What if those three patterns, supposedly characteristic of our later years, aren't accurate or even desirable? Starting with that as a

> *Think about it: approaching your next half/ best half of life from a context of conscious and proactive Research & Development is absolutely the most empowering and future-building way to go.*

research question, let's inquire into those generally accepted patterns. You may notice definite downfalls in subscribing to them as you move forward. Remember, in an inquiry nothing is either all right or all wrong. That's why it's called an inquiry: no easy answer, or even any answer at all.

Pattern 1:

The Value of "Wisdom" Gained

First, let's consider this concept of progressively gaining "wisdom." Perhaps it has an Achilles heel to be exposed.

Consider this: if you gain "wisdom" from your experiences in the old-fashioned "because" way of living (i.e., victim, at effect), then that wisdom can become your prison cell. For example, from a limited number of serious and significant events or influences that occur in your life, you might decide *for the rest of your life. . .*

> . . .the way you're supposed to be
> . . .the way men are
> . . .the way women are
> . . .the way work and career are
> . . .the forms and avenues in which your self-expression
>   is allowed
> . . .who you are
> . . .what's possible or not for you
> . . .and many other fixed views
> *yes, for the rest of your life*

Many of your most shaping, serious and significant events or influences took place in younger days before you had the capacity to see that whatever happened wasn't about you. These events or influences were simply the three acts of someone else's opera that you showed up in the middle of. However, you learned to survive in those situations and in life by making certain decisions about yourself and the world: how to behave, who to be, what to watch out for.

Be the good boy/girl. Just be quiet and it will all be over. Those who are too close are not safe. Something is wrong with me. I'd better watch out or I will be taken advantage of. I am not enough. If I love them, they will leave. Marriage screws things up. These are just a few of the myriad directional life decisions that can come from Front Forty serious and significant events or influences when we respond to them as "becauses."

Based on those decisions, all of life going forward gets shaped by a lens or filter through which you see every remotely similar situation as a potential repeat of that first one. The father who left you shapes the way men are perceived. The mother who dominated you shapes the way women are perceived. The religion or belief system you were indoctrinated into shapes the way all things of a spiritual nature are perceived. The wife or husband who cheated on you shapes the way relationships, trust and intimacy are perceived from that event forward. On and on, your life becomes limited through so many shaping incidences and by what you surmise from them. This is your "wisdom."

You then proceed to react to life in the present through the decisions made and survival mechanisms developed in those first, formative incidents from the past. For example, having survived your father leaving as a child, when difficulties or issues start to occur in a relationship, you toughen up and erect a wall of impenetrability. "I won't be hurt by this. I'll make it on my own. I don't need anyone." These or similar mindsets might be the early, survival-based program you pull out to run again. It worked then. This looks like then. It'll work now (or so you proceed to think and react). You don't necessarily think it through consciously, but the program runs in the background, nonetheless.

As another example, if you were somehow mentally or emotionally damaged by an early religious experience or in some way sold a belief system bill of goods, you may operate from an unconscious but ongoing survival mechanism that says people and events exhibiting too much zeal are unsafe, so you keep yourself at a distance.

Living by such unquestioned, because-based "wisdom" nets you a view of life that is self-perpetuating. There's no end to the evidence you can rack up when perceiving life through a filter. Every slightly similar event becomes further proof of the overall world view that you've established for yourself. Your world, thus, becomes smaller. You take fewer risks. You move life into a box. Your future becomes set.

In contrast, living life from the Be Cause-based context of R & D, which you've already accomplished in your embrace of your Front Forty and which you're conducting right now and will continue to engage in ad infinitum as you move forward in your Back Forty, creates more and more openness to life while providing access to becoming the fullest YOU.

Review, if necessary, to call them to mind the slew of Self Expression Directives you have collected so far and recorded in your Freedom Fliers Journal. Think about it: have any of those Self Expression Directives you've discovered through the "because to Be Cause" exercises you've completed thus far pointed to anything other than your fullest Self? No! Have any determined who and what you should avoid? No! Have any segmented out only certain instances when and where you're able to be your true Self? No! Have they in any other way focused on limitation of any kind? No! (If they have, you'll want to reread the first two chapters and refine your process.)

Inside of R & D living, no one or anything is wrong and nothing out there needs to be avoided! There's only living forward, using certain pointers, which we call Self Expression Directives, to move toward becoming your fullest Self. These directives are *always* toward the positive: more freedom, more joy, more love, more Self.

Inside of R & D living, "bad stuff" does not and cannot happen to you. Life is your friend, and it can only give you laboratory-based opportunities to grow, events and influences to pull out your greater yet to be. Any old-fashioned "wisdom" of who you are, what you're to avoid and your supposed "proven" limitations only gets in the way and shrinks any big games of Self you may now want to play.

I want to be clear: I'm not saying you haven't gained information in your Front Forty R & D that has some value, such as information that has led you to refrain from participating in certain activities, utilizing certain substances or engaging with certain types of people.

However, if you've truly analyzed the serious and significant events or influences that originally spawned ideas of avoidance, you'll see that the Self

Expression Directives coming from those analyses point in a positive direction such as "love myself," "find happiness within," "attract and engage with loving spirits." Such directives broaden life, not shrink it. Movement toward positive, growing-of-Self directions that come from R & D living can only make life better and your enjoyment of it richer. You continually move forward through a context of highest expression of your Self and the expansion of that Self in the world.

> *Inside of R & D living, "bad stuff" does not and cannot happen to you. Life is your friend, and it can only give you laboratory-based opportunities to grow, events and influences to pull out your greater yet to be.*

As such, your world becomes more open and safe. You become more directed toward inner qualities, resources, capabilities and capacities that have you feel more one with life. This beats the old, crotchety, cynical, secluded and righteous ways of being that the engrained, former concept of "wisdom with age" offers you.

Pattern 2:
The Drive to Retirement

The second pattern, which says we work hard in our first half to allow ourselves to kick back in the second half (i.e., retire) is similarly limiting—though very much a sacred cow. The proposition is based on the idea that you have only a certain amount of time to "make it" before you get to be "free." It promotes the real joy of life as eventually being found in *not* engaging and *not* being involved in the activities, endeavors and building of things with others. It persuades you that a life free from the time-focused productivity of "work" is better. It seduces you into believing that an unstructured, carefree life beats a more structured one of intentional, directional and purposeful creation.

Yet, through my experience in supporting people around their careers, I've found that for many of those who've worked hard, engaged earnestly and played well with all the cards they've been dealt, when they remove themselves from the card table, a certain life blood drains out. A "good retirement" is supposed to be the ultimate goal, but Mai Tais on the beach and golf only go so far. With too much time on their hands, many retirees begin to notice that body parts and mental capacities start to diminish in stamina and dynamism. Underutilized, the infrastructural machinery (a.k.a. the body) necessary for Spirit to fulfill on a purpose begins to fall apart without such directedness toward purpose.

> **The tragedy of life is what dies inside a man while he lives.**
> **—Albert Schweitzer**

On the other hand, if your work life has been unceasing hell and you've never found any avenues in which to fully express your Self and your unique gifts and talents, then perhaps this idea of retirement with a bunch of nothing in the future, with no direction and no purpose, surely beats the misery you've experienced in the past. If that's you, consider that withdrawal is not your only option after an exhausting, unsatisfying first half. You can still discover something rewarding and be energized by it. Similarly, if you are in a position of absolutely needing to continue working and earning and feel cheated by that fact, you can, at any age, experience a Back Forty Initiation and Be Cause the rest of your career as an inspired engagement that you wouldn't have wanted to miss.

> A "good retirement" is supposed to be the ultimate goal, but Mai Tais on the beach and golf only go so far.

So, is the "make it now so I can kick back later" cultural message of retirement an empowering one? Choose for yourself. Whether you are where you want to be in your life or not, whether in your mind you've "made it" or not, when choosing keep in mind that you can *always* design a more fulfilling Back Forty, an expanded life with even bigger contributions and greater freedom from the stress and struggles of your past.

Impossible?

No. When you emerge as the greater Self designed by a past of R & D, it's absolutely possible. The Self Expression Directives derived from all those initial lab experiments can give you access to advanced abilities to create greater results with more ease and grace.

Nonetheless, often those who feel they've "made it" say, "But I don't *need* to do anything now. I'm set. I'm enjoying my life. I did my hard work. I'll simply be a consumer now. Thanks, and you go for it. I'm good."

We each make our own choices. But, can you imagine what it would be like if each of those who've already "made it" pointed their new, R & D-enhanced, more evolved Self toward a greater purpose than retirement? What impact could that have on worthwhile initiatives in the world? What difference might that make in their own longevity and experience of a life well lived? What if we were all like Jimmy Carter, who keeps going and going and going?

Though partially quoted earlier, this full George Bernard Shaw quote is even more poignant now:

> *Underutilized, the infrastructural machinery (a.k.a. the body) necessary for Spirit to fulfill on a purpose begins to fall apart without such directedness toward purpose.*

This is the true joy in life, the being used for a purpose recognized by yourself as a mighty one; the being a force of nature instead of a feverish, selfish little clod of ailments and grievances complaining that the world will not devote itself to making you happy.

I am of the opinion that my life belongs to the whole community, and as long as I live it is my privilege to do for it whatever I can.

I want to be thoroughly used up when I die, for the harder I work the more I live. I rejoice in life for its own sake. Life is no "brief candle" for me. It is a sort of splendid torch, which I have got hold of for the moment, and I want to make it burn as brightly as possible before handing it on to future generations.

Personally, the handed-off torch of vitality beats the handed-down drive to retirement any day. That pattern is not for me.

From a mile-high view, we can see that the concept of retirement is based on a "Down and Out" model, which society says is the direction aging inevitably takes us. We're supposed to rise, grow and expand in the front end of the bell curve, moving up towards our forties and fifties: get an education; earn a living; create and invent; establish relationships; build a family; amass a bunch of stuff; save for the future; etc.

Can you imagine what it would be like if each of those who've already "made it" pointed their new, R & D-enhanced, more evolved Self toward a greater purpose than retirement??

Then, when we get "over the hill," it's understood that we'll begin a slow descent: become locked into an industry or career that's no longer fulfilling; endure breakups and restructurings in love and relationships; face the loss of loved ones; exhibit diminished interest in risk-taking, new ideas and new things and thus experience reduced creativity; encounter decreased earning potential and live on stored nuts (savings) like a squirrel; possess less bodily agility; and experience diminished sex drive, energy, stamina and so on. Down and Out.

The "Down and Out" Model

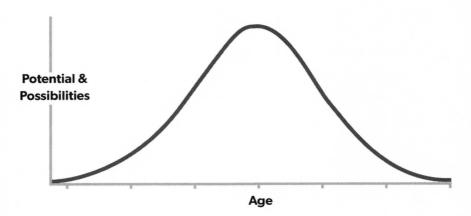

Potential & Possibilities

Age

Of course, everyone doesn't live by this pattern, thank God! But a majority does. Perhaps the above degradation list doesn't apply to you and you see this as a gross generalization. I hear you. Many discussions around the trajectory of life and retirement are sensitive. Yet, I encourage you to truly look to see if this isn't the generally accepted message and direction that Western society promotes: Down and Out.

What if it didn't have to be that way? What if it actually isn't that way? What if the only reason the concept of Down and Out is still in place is because we haven't thought bigger, better and beyond those societally sanctioned, handed-down-to-us belief systems? What if that's all it really is, a load of BS, belief systems, not reality?

A final promising and intriguing question is this: what if our concepts and thoughts of what life is about, and for, can be transformed into a more promising graph and fulfilling game in the form of an "Up and Out" model?

That is what The Back Forty is all about.

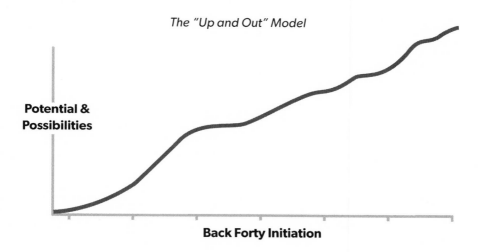

The "Up and Out" Model

Potential & Possibilities

Back Forty Initiation

In The Back Forty, we're empowered by the premise that we have yet to be *who* we came here to be and have yet to *do* what we came here to do: no matter what our age, no matter what we've already done or haven't done and no matter what we've been through.

The Back Forty embraces a new game to build our mindset around—the Up and Out model—in which we start exploring from a place of inquiry what it takes to actually play bigger as we mature.

A contrarian approach to aging is the idea of *staging*. As discussed briefly in this book's opening, "The Lay of the Land," in the Up and Out model, like a series of sequential rocket boosters required to thrust a rocket into space, each stage of life lifts us higher and increases our momentum, then drops away just as the next level kicks in to take us even higher. The graphic above captures the idea of a new burst of Self-expression igniting just where the last stage of growth leaves off, beginning with our Back Forty Initiation.

> *The Back Forty embraces a new game to build our mindset around—the Up and Out model—in which we start exploring from a place of inquiry what it takes to actually play bigger as we mature.*

However, fair warning: if you truly begin to operate from this new, contrarian belief that you can and will express even greater creativity, experience even more play, engage in even more fulfilling relationships, enjoy even more health and vitality and engender even greater personal contributions as you mature, then anything in the way of that new belief system will need to come up and out to be dealt with, starting with your *personal* BS.

You'll need a brainwashing! Washing out your old belief structures will take many forms. Mentally, you'll begin to notice that limited, closed-minded, "wisdom"-based thinking doesn't serve you anymore. You'll become aware of your risk aversion and start to stick your neck out again in new fields of interest, romantic relationships with new or existing partners and new forms of Self-expression in activities, careers, business, etc.

You'll adopt a "play first" attitude, whereby you'll start taking action on initiatives and splendid ideas *even before* you have them all worked out. All of that usual preliminary planning so you "won't look foolish," which is simply a delay tactic, a way to play safe, will take a back seat to your simply getting on the court of new games and going for it! Planning to get started is *not* getting started. You'll detach from the score in those new games and will allow yourself to merely become curious again, playfully acting on your curiosities rather than talking yourself out of them. You'll start living in the inquiry of possibilities and feel engaged and empowered by them.

Physically, you'll begin to find ways to better maintain and sculpt your instrument for living, your body, so it will serve you for the longest possible second half, even if you didn't treat it so great in the first half. You'll begin to experiment with the idea that the body is an outward expression of the thinking taking place in the mind. In so doing, you'll shape your bodily experience with the vigor and vitality of a new, open and empowered belief system.

Emotionally, you'll free your Self from limited-thought baggage of the past, allowing your fullest, natural faculties of trust, love, excitement, joy and happiness to come out and play.

Long before the serious and significant events or influences that you examined in your Discovery & Expression analyses happened to you, you possessed an openness, an innocence, a vulnerability and a willing receptivity. Certain events then occurred that led to your bracing yourself with fortifications so you'd never be hurt like that again. Now seeing everything that occurred as perfect and designed by you to get you to be who you came to be and do what you came to do, you can fly without having to check any emotional baggage. You will have lost that victim baggage altogether! You'll start to entertain the joy of innocence again and become available to real miracles taking place in your life.

Spiritually, you'll open up to thoughts beyond what you've thunk before. Realizing that you simply can't have already gotten the whole truth about the secrets of life and the Universe from whatever earlier influences you had and perhaps clung to from a need to feel safe and in control, you'll begin to consider other ideas and concepts about life, love and humanity. You may even become a modern-day mystic, expanding your field of awareness into the all-things-possible, all-inclusive Universe.

> *In a nutshell, the Up and Out model has you ever spiraling upwards and outwards in possibility, consciousness and contribution until you make your final exit from the earthly stage, handing your brightly burning torch to future generations.*

In a nutshell, the Up and Out model has you ever spiraling upwards and outwards in possibility, consciousness and contribution until you make your final exit from the earthly stage, handing your brightly burning torch to future generations.

Live as if you were to die tomorrow. Learn as if you were to live forever. —Mahatma Gandhi

Pattern 3:
Shrinking Circles

A third societally sanctioned pattern of aging to be debunked in creating a playful, passionate and purposeful Back Forty is the one of shrinking circles.

Many have observed and come to expect that as we age we'll naturally shrink our circle of friends and influences into ones that fit our then perceived "truths" about the world and life. In the context of the Down and Out-patterned drives for "wisdom" and retirement outlined above, it simply makes sense to cut out people, ideas and experiences that seem like outliers to our sensibilities. When living from the because-based, unquestioned cultural conversation around aging, certainly you would rush to eliminate those damn radicals from your mind and sphere of interactions!

According to this generally accepted pattern, which I call The Incredible Shrinking World, your original, at birth, untainted, wide and expansive view of life and all that's possible in it shrinks as you age. As described earlier, you have experiences in life and from them you gain "wisdom," basing decisions on what happened *to* you in the past. You then see everything that happens from that point forward through that lens. Those perceptions then confirm your wisdom (beliefs/BS) providing "evidence" and "proof;" and you become even more certain of your "truths" regarding the way you are, the way they are, and the way life is. Ultimately, you become convinced you are "right" and choose to associate yourself only with those who subscribe to, or at least appease, your righteousness.

The Incredible Shrinking World

Believing is seeing. . .which confirms belief

RIGHT!

Seeing is believing. . . which validates perception

Think about it. Many of us have been guilty of statements like "the kids these days. . ." or "that music people listen to is just too. . ." or "back when I was a kid/teenager/starting out, the way it worked was. . . ." These aphorisms, lobbed upon us years ago by our parents and elders, start to come out of our own mouths! Righteousness reigns supreme! We know better than anyone else how *life is* and *should be lived*; and we become the image of the crotchety old man or lady, "a feverish, selfish little clod of ailments and grievances complaining that the world will not devote itself to making [us] happy."

Of course, that isn't to say that you need to associate with *all* types of people and circles of thought as you mature. You may have rightly learned in your first half of R & D that participating in certain activities or engaging with certain folks just doesn't serve you. However, as described earlier, any selective discernment of your future activities and associations filtered through a properly analyzed first half replete with Self Expression Directives will likely point you toward playing fuller, broader and more inclusively with others rather than retreating into self-justified isolation.

Life naturally desires expansion toward possibility and the miraculous. Holing up by yourself in your little, controlled, "I'm good. I know what I'm doing" world doesn't make for a fully Self-expressed Back Forty.

> **Life naturally desires expansion toward possibility and the miraculous.**

So, how about we shift the paradigm? If you're empowered by this new conversation we're inventing together, which says that you have yet to be who you came here to be and have yet to do what you came here to do, can you afford to shrink your mind and world into an ever-smaller circle of possibilities? Heck no! In your best half Back Forty, you want to be thinking thoughts you've never thought before! You want to be doing things you've never done before! You want to be engaging with folks outside of your current reality of self, others, and life!

> **Alice laughed. "There's no use trying," she said. "One can't believe impossible things."**
>
> **"I daresay you haven't had much practice," said the Queen. "When I was your age, I always did it for half-an-hour a day. Why, sometimes I've believed as many as six impossible things before breakfast" —Lewis Carroll, Through the Looking Glass**

When you consider that many of the newest advances in technology and business are birthed by individuals in their twenties, we have to seriously entertain that at least one reason is that they haven't yet been conditioned to limit their thinking. Thank God for untainted innovators! They quickly step beyond "the way things are" because they haven't been around long enough to be indoctrinated into "the way things are."

In your midlife opportunity, therefore, you have a dual charge. . .if you choose to accept it. First, you'll want to best utilize some of the valid and worthwhile knowledge and awareness you've gained in your circles around the sun thus far. Perhaps we'll call it a *refined* wisdom. Then, to benefit both your Self and mankind most powerfully, you'll want to relearn limitless thinking.

To do that, you'll need to participate in circles of thought and personal interactions that stretch your current sensibilities and that support such limitless thinking. You'll want to nurture for your Self an ever-widening and expansive world.

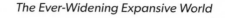

The Ever-Widening Expansive World

POSSIBILITY!

Playing First and Curiosity elicit more awareness and discovery

New awareness and discoveries elicit more Playing First and Curiosity

Welcome to The Back Forty! Instead of being stuck with the old "wisdom" lens and pattern of using every experience to prove yourself right about your existing views on life, love and humanity, which is simply a stay-safe control mechanism, become curious again and start operating from what Zen Buddhists call "beginner's mind." Open yourself up to new opportunities for awareness and discovery that in turn will elicit new possibilities. Begin to take baby steps forward into areas of interest, passion and purposeful direction, many of which have already been laid out for you in your recently mined Self Expression Directives, Gifts and Values inventories.

Let go of the die-hard need to have your explorations already worked out and ensured of "success." Begin to Play First before every "i" is dotted and "t" is crossed, and then both revel in and review your *experience of having played while you also gained more knowledge.* Don't wait for some elusive point at which you feel you have enough knowledge or skill to get started. That day never comes. Get started anyway.

> **Freedom is not worth having if it does not connote freedom to err.**
> **—*Mahatma Gandhi***

Establish a pattern of honoring your Self for the courage it takes to play, and then get out on the field and play again, over and over. After each game, come back into the locker room of your Back Forty community[10] for a pep talk and opportunity to evaluate what you've learned and how you've grown.

> **Establish a pattern of honoring your Self for the courage it takes to play, and then get out on the field and play again, over and over.**

An invented and *caused*-by-you Back Forty creates an ever widening and expansive view of life and all that's possible in it. More awareness and discovery of who you are and what you're truly capable of by Playing First brings about even more Curiosity as to how and in what ways you want to play bigger, which then repeats itself by generating more Play First. Like Pavlov's dog, your Self begins to salivate at opportunities to risk and try new things. You become bold, *causing* and conducting *consciously* designed R & D experiments with abandon. Your circles of life, experiences and relationships grow wider, richer and more fulfilling.

So, the choice is yours: Implode or explode? Experience a shrinking circle or an expanding world? Choose! And realize that with any resistance or hesitation to choose you're thereby making the default, societally-sanctioned, ingrained-pattern choice to shrink.

> **Implode or explode? Experience a shrinking circle or an expanding world? Choose!**

> **If I have the belief that I can do it, I shall surely acquire the capacity to do it even if I may not have it at the beginning. —Mahatma Gandhi**

---

10 See TheBackForty.com/book for sprouting groups of The Back Forty Accountability Alliance offering supportive environments to encourage Big Back Forty Games.

In a nutshell, you'll see your life through some lens as you add numbers to your earthly age counter. It will either be an unchallenged lens of unquestioned "wisdom" characterized by finding opportunities to be right, or it will be a generated lens of possibility focused on finding opportunities to learn and grow. "Generated" means it isn't going to happen without you creating it for your Self.

PURPOSEFUL R & D
Assessing the Risk

The good news to underscore and revel in is that R & D (research and development) becomes from this point forward a *conscious,* distinguished and empowering way of life. With this focus, so different from the undistinguished morassive thrust of midlife which mired you before, you become powerful. A conscious and proactive laboratory always beats the "big swamp."

R & D now becomes intently purposeful. Experiencing your second half as your best half requires that you step fully into the openings that this awareness creates. You'll want to stretch outside of any limiting comfort zones you adopted from a perceived-as-victim Front Forty and begin to rise up, step out and take risks!

However, before you now get scared and squirmy about the risks that lie ahead,

> *The good news to underscore and revel in is that R & D (research and development) becomes from this point forward a **conscious**, distinguished and empowering way of life.*

realize that taking risks is nothing new to you. The truth is, you've always taken risks. It's completely evidenced by your past. You just didn't know they were risks then, but it seems that you're pretty used to taking, enduring and surviving risks!

To you, at the time, in the unthought and catapulted-into-life experience of your Front Forty, it simply seemed that. . .

. . .this was the ideal person to marry

. . .this was the ideal single life

. . .this was the ideal trade or line of work to pursue

. . .this was the ideal major to study in school

. . .this was the ideal company to work for

. . .this was the ideal type of business to build

. . .this was the ideal religious faith to live by

. . .this was the ideal culture to be born into

. . .this was the ideal family to be a part of

Only after the fact, only after some serious and significant events or influences occurred inside of these by-design laboratory experiments, might you now acknowledge just how risky these ventures actually were! Ignorance was truly blissful!

The concept of risk is fallacious, anyway, when it's looked at through the Back Forty lens. Given your newfound awareness that every serious and significant event or influence is designed (by you) to point you toward your more fully Self-expressed future, you can now see that you can never actually *lose* from any actions you take moving forward.

You are now equipped to be a Conscious Collaborative Creator in the design of laboratory experiments moving forward. Just as you participated at a "soulular," unconscious, and development-of-Self level in the design and running of the laboratories of your past—playfully referred to as the Mad Scientist at work—you can now consciously and proactively set up those laboratories to secure more and more helpful findings and Self Expression Directives to further widen your world and your participation in it.

Your Formula of Unique Self Expression (FUSE) never burns out because you keep gaining Directives through not only the past and present events you've chosen to analyze, but from the proactive, consciously created experiments you design going forward, And, even though the gifts and values surveys were taken once, upon your initial encounter with this Back Forty exploration, your answers could be different in only a few years, after many more consciously designed laboratories. Your FUSE is ever-evolving and ever-expanding, which makes for next and next and next levels of greater Self-expression.

Of course, there will always be some laboratories put together by the Mad Scientist still playing a stealth role on the behind-the-scenes, skunkworks level, putting you into research experiments and laboratories for your highest and greatest growth. But now you can declare the formation of and integrate yourself into laboratory experiments of your own choosing, such as some of mine:

> Experiment: Radical Givingness
> Experiment: Creative Artist Meets Texas Cattleman Results
> Experiment: Understated and Overdelivered

Those are just a few of the consciously created laboratories I've personally designed and am beginning to experiment with. They all point to areas of my own consciously chosen growth and development. More labs, more Self.

You and I can construct and analyze our own labs in exactly the same way the Mad Scientist's labs were constructed, except for the different perspective of looking *forward* instead of back and in being Cause Scene *Instigators* versus Cause Scene Investigators.

Be Cause the Future

So, become an Instigator! Run your Mad Scientist experiments to purposefully design what is yet to come by using the 7-Step Discovery & Expression Method, which has been tweaked here for a forward focus on the future.

1. Choose and name a playful, passionate, purposeful or radical event or influence I'd like to create.

2. In full Conscious Collaborative Creator form, tell my story of what I am creating (the experiment I will set up).

3. Identify the phenomena (blessings) I intend to reap from the event or influence.

4. Determine the hypothetical research questions I'll be experimenting for in the laboratory.

5. Determine my ownership of the laboratory and its design, describing the perfect lab assistants and ideal lab environment and how I'll pick them.

6. Observe and document the possible findings from my experimentation, as I playfully engage in it.

7. Observe and document my Self Expression Directives from the event or influence, as I playfully engage in it.

Now, it's important to acknowledge that this proactive approach to Collaborative Creatorship of consciously designed laboratories still relies on our own "best thinking." For example, Step 5 above has us picking our lab assistants and lab environments, which we can only do based on our own cognizance. No doubt, these picks will be impacted by ego, comfort zones, beliefs and perceptions from an Incredible Shrinking World.

We might all agree that such proactively designed laboratories may not provide the same potential for growth as comes out of the Mad Scientist's skunkworks labs, where our current comfort zones or belief systems are not factored into the experiment. However, it's nonetheless a playful way to add a helping hand to the lifting up and expressing of our highest Self. Plus, it beats just sitting around waiting for our Back Forty field to plow itself.

Darrell's Forward-focused R & D

Here's an example of how I designed an experiment for my own Purposeful R & D. Similar to my note back in Embrace 1, I realize that the particular experiment I'm designing may not be something of importance to you or may even seem rudimentary compared to your own development. Just like picking your own Serious and Significant Events and Influences to analyze were your choice and independent from anyone else's experience of life, we also don't judge or compare the validity of our respective growth paths forward. We all have different trajectories in the Back Forty life we're creating, to be and do what we came here for. So, we play with what comes up for us, and appreciate what's there for another to play with along their unique path of growth.

Darrell's Experiment: Radical Givingness
Discovery & Expression Step 1: A Playful, Passionate, Purposeful or Radical Event or Influence I'd Like to Create

"Radical Givingness"

Darrell's Experiment: Radical Givingness
Discovery & Expression Step 2: Tell the Story of My Planned Experiment

I will grow confident within myself as being a "giver."

For years, and actually most of my life, I've had an internal vision and image of being in a position to give as a generous, benevolent and even philanthropic difference-maker on the planet. I've often succumbed to the idea of being limited in my ability to give based on income, resources, time, influence, availability, etc. Yet, I also know that, beyond perceived physical limitations, the spiritual truth of Abundance is that it is unlimited.

As stated in the Upanishads, "From abundance he took abundance and still abundance remained." With all of the spiritual studies I've engaged in, I've gained enough anecdotal and outside experts' evidence to be aware of that Truth. Yet, I've not personally taken on and created what I feel is demonstrative evidence in my own life that these principles are true. Being caught up in the "I'm busy" story, I've seen such benevolence as something for others who have, do or are "more" than I am. So, that is an experiment I'm excited to design a laboratory around.

I heard a minister once describe a bit of wisdom he received from his grandfather, who told him that there are two types of people in the world, the givers and the takers. He advised his grandson to always rush to get in line with the givers.

As an adolescent, I remember being impressed when hearing a story of how Elvis Presley would give anonymously in the most amazing ways. In one instance, he supposedly saw a newly married young couple goggling over a car far outside of their price range at a car dealership. The story goes that Elvis bought the car for them and had the owner of the dealership simply walk over and give them the keys, saying only that it was a gift from a friend.

I similarly remember seeing walls of $1,000 cancelled checks at Graceland when I visited his former home, checks which he seemingly sent to every organization or cause that reached out to him. $1,000 was a lot of money in the '60s and '70s. . .and still is!

As a young adult, the image of the man I'd like to be was my grandfather. He was critiqued by some as being someone who would "give you the shirt off his back;" and, admittedly, he didn't die with a lot of wealth left behind. And yet, he was one of the most loved, big-hearted, community-involved, contributing and jovial men I ever knew. He demonstrated life and giving in a way I always wanted to emulate.

Lastly, when getting some spiritual advice many years ago, I was advised that in any ways I can pursue selfless service, I will expand to allow more good into my own life. Makes sense and, yet, implementation is another thing. I always seem so busy.

These are just some of the influences that have caught my psyche over time around the energy of giving, beneficence and generosity. I'm interested in exploration and new discovery in this area. Though I have heard that "You can't outgive God," I like the idea of playing for it anyway and then being able to speak from experience.

Darrell's Experiment: Radical Givingness
Discovery & Expression Step 3: Identify the desired phenomena (blessings)

1. I'll experience new vitality, aliveness and joy around giving and serving.
2. I will have proven to myself certain spiritual laws of abundance and prosperity that I've only heard or read about.
3. I'll develop a new concept of myself as a giver, free from the past of seeming limitations.
4. My ego will be diminished as I practice selflessness.
5. I'll end up losing in my attempt to outgive God.

Darrell's Experiment: Radical Givingness
Discovery & Expression Step 4: Research questions

- Can a guy who has spent his life leaning toward the accounting side of relationships (watching, monitoring and seeking balance in the swinging give/receive door) move over in both mind and spirit to the give, give and give more side?
- Is it possible for an individual to shift fundamental internal wirings, orientations and sensibilities around abundance through a consciously designed and executed experiment versus the Front Forty unconscious initiators of major change (i.e., serious and significant events)?
- Can someone train themselves to act and be different than they have in the past and in so doing experience a radically different reality?
- Is Abundance truly unlimited?

Darrell's Experiment: Radical Givingness
Discovery & Expression Step 5: Designing the Laboratory

My Lab Assistants

The Lab Assistants I'll proactively choose for this experiment, while trusting that my inner Mad Scientist, the Universe, my Higher Self will guide me to others, will be individuals and organizations who play in the arena of giving.

I'll explore and find both individuals who simply provide for me an opportunity for random acts of givingness as well as business and philanthropic organizations that operate from givingness principles.

In the area of business, a wonderful training I experienced many years ago was to approach folks first from a "what can I do for you?" mode. The relationship starts from giving. Obviously, if everyone operated that way, instead of a me-first approach, everyone would be more taken care of.

I've always been called to connecting with the elderly, so I'll explore ways in which to interact and selflessly give time to those who may feel forgotten. I may even pursue hospice volunteering to serve as a final comfort while exploring what those final days or weeks in this physical realm are like for people.

I'll also seek out and associate myself with mentors around philanthropy, to watch and learn how they think and operate. I may even ask for personal interviews, to explore the personal insights and awareness that brought these individuals to such involvements.

My Lab Environment

My tendency to want to go big on things would have me focus on bright, shiny, big name causes and organizations. But that's just more ego. Simply waking up to the many small causes and initiatives to make a better world is where I'll focus. I'll watch for people who come into my life, where givingness in time, attention, support and service can make a big difference for them even though on a smaller scale. As the story goes, when a boy throwing beached starfish back into the ocean is told by a passerby that his effort was fruitless and that he couldn't possibly make a difference given all the starfish on the beach, he threw one more into the surf and said, "It made a difference for that one."

Darrell's Experiment: Radical Givingness

Discovery & Expression Step 6: Observe and document the findings from my experimentation, as I playfully engage in it.

To Be Determined!

Darrell's Experiment: Radical Givingness

Discovery & Expression Step 7: Observe and document my Self Expression Directives from my experimentation, as I playfully engage in it.

To Be Determined!

This proactive, consciously designed experiment gives me an exciting new arena of Back Forty life in which to play for more and more Self Expression Directives. Once this design is drafted, I'm able to utilize methods of Back Forty Big Game play[11] to actively dive into and conduct the experiment. I'll do my conscious design part, and A Presence will do Its.

As with all other exercises, inquiries and insights shared throughout this book, the real value comes for you in practicing them yourself, so let's playfully and proactively begin some experiments you would be interested in designing for the sake of your own Purposeful R & D of the future.

Embrace 6—Homeplay 2
Forward-focused R & D

First, do whatever it takes to become centered and relaxed in your mind. Close your eyes and relax. As always, let go of the idea that you have to do this "right." There is no "right" in play; there is only play. Trust whatever comes up for you as perfect.

Now open your Freedom Fliers Journal. This is where you get to be a kid in a candy store, with no limiting ideas of yourself from the past but rather operating as a free and innocent agent, capable of engaging in subjects, areas, projects, initiatives, dreams and desires of your own choosing. From all of your puzzle pieces pulled together during the course of these embraces—your awareness of Self Expression Directives from lab experiments conducted and your insightful surveys of Gifts and Values amassed

---

11 *See more about Back Forty Big Game Play at TheBackForty.com/book.*

as well as the general trajectory of your life thus far, look to see in what ways you'd like to grow. Come up with at least three possible experiments you might proactively design in pursuing Purposeful R & D for your second half/best half. They may come to you logically or intuitively.

Embrace 6—Homeplay 3
Forward-focused Discovery & Expression Design

Pick one of the above possible experiments and begin your design project. You haven't committed to actually doing it yet, so feel free to just play with it. Don't feel pressure to have it all figured or worked out. Any experiment is all made up from the get go. Just be inquisitive, interested and creative about it.

Take your chosen experiment through the 7-Step Back Forty Discovery & Expression Method for purposeful, future-focused research and development. As needed, refer back to the list that appears above in my Experiment: Radical Givingness for a brief description of each step; and here's an additional orientation to this future-oriented version of each step as well.

1. (The Experiment) In your Back Forty Freedom Fliers Journal, write "Experiment 1" at the top of a new page. Then, write a name for your first chosen Proactive, Purposeful R & D Experiment. Just make up a short title for it.

2. (The Story) Then as Step 2, tell the story in Conscious Collaborative Creator form of what you are creating and why. Let yourself go in justifying for yourself why this is a big game you'd like to play. Include all of the history you've had around this area: why it's important to you and the feelings, hope and possibility you'd like to create for yourself.

3. (The Blessings) In Step 3, set yourself up proactively to win by getting clear about the blessings that you anticipate or imagine will come out of your active engagement in opening up this new territory for yourself and your life.

4. (Questions) Next in Step 4, lay out what you're looking to prove with this experiment. Your research questions will give you a platform to postulate from an all-things-are-possible perspective, setting you up as a researcher with access to the levers and dials of life.

5. (Lab Design) As mentioned in my own proactive experiment design above, you can only call on lab assistants and create lab environments from what you already know, and yet that's something! Go ahead and let yourself think as far outside the box as you're capable of to include all the people, parts and ingredients of an ideal laboratory and lab staff. Know that A Presence within will bring forth all the other out-of-the-box elements you'll need. You're setting a stage here for discovery, which is Collaborative Creatorship at its best. Your hands are literally on the levers, dials, switches and circuits of creating life.

6. (Findings) Once you've designed these first five steps, now in Step 6 simply play, watch and document. You've set an intention; you've causally and actively put yourself on the playing field and now you can trust that the Universe will bring you the answers to the questions you posed and more.

7. (Self Expression Directives) You already know the power of Self Expression Directives coming retrospectively from your past and present. Now you get to play in the world of Self Expression Directives arising proactively from the future you're creating. Nothing's like having the keys to the vault of all the Self Expression Directives you could ever want. Those keys are

in your hands when you proactively design the Back Forty Self you want to grow. As you play, watch for and document the Directives you see cascading from your experiment, the directional pointers for your greater Self to be expressed.

If you're called to, you can right now lay out another proactive experiment, bringing it into possibility with the same purposeful Discovery & Expression Method. However, it's also okay to enter into passionate, purposeful play with one experiment for a while before adding another.

PURPOSE IMPOSTERS

With the three Down-and-Out life patterns out of the way and your now-familiar Discovery & Expression tool sharpened and in the ground again, ready for cultivating additional consciously designed, forward-focused R & D for your Back Forty Self, I invite you to now utilize your newly forming, un-patterned, willingness-to-risk and R & D-focused freedom to design a radical second half. An element of that radical second half is your sense of purpose.

As human beings, we so often seek to discover who we are, what we're here to do, and with whom we belong. Yet, when delving into the workings of the mind, we must recognize that all of these fundamental questions evoke answers born of the ego. In many ways, we need the ego; yet, from a Back Forty perspective, each of these areas of sought-after "knowledge":

- our sense of identity;
- our activities (i.e., what we ended up doing, career, business, involvements, etc.); and

- our concept of belonging based on already-established
  relationships

. . .have all arisen from a Front Forty, past-based ego, which doesn't necessarily set us up for an unrecognizable, unprecedented, or unpredictably
purposeful (radical) second half. A purpose based on programming from
the past will not provide for an authentically powerful Back Forty. Only a
purpose based on the future can do that. Therefore, we'll begin the exploration of that often elusive and enigmatic holy grail—**Your Purpose**—first by
distinguishing what your purpose is *not*.

For instance, as I began an inquiry into Purpose/Presence, when writing
the initial draft of this book, I awoke one morning fearful, feeling the complete bankruptcy of everything I was about to do that day. All the activity
I could see for the day ahead was based on what seemed to be a habit of
overcoming struggle. Through inquiring into a personal pattern of general
freneticism, I observed that the previous decade had been mainly survival-based living with a focus on overcoming familial and financial challenges.
I saw that an overarching theme of my life had been to "overcome struggles"
and that the struggles *themselves* had provided whatever sense of "purpose"
I had entertained up to that point. A constant, necessity-of-the-moment way
of living had my concept of purpose be nothing more than getting through
the next hour, day, week, month, or year.

That's generally how rock bottom feels. Only the next moment is in
sight, and anything offering some brief semblance of relief is sought after.
Perspectives and timelines become condensed to the immediate. Strangely
enough, a singular sense of peace and even seeming "purposefulness" can
reside in such a place.

The very act of getting down to basics creates, in a weird way, a much
simpler life. It's very alluring for sure. Forget about being responsible for
dreams, visions, personal or professional growth. The only question for the
moment becomes "how do I make the car payment?" Life is lived myopically.
Bigger inquiries don't happen because you can only focus on the urgency of

the now. Yet, survival is a weak substitute for purpose; the grandest design of purpose goes beyond mere daily survival.

So, that was what my "purpose" based on reactionary living from the past (what I call my Purpose Imposter) looked like for me. Yet, I'm no different from many. I see it everywhere in many people because I've lived it. However, when we recontextualize our history from the perspective of it all being R & D to point us toward who we came to be and what we came to do, an entirely different and empowering picture begins to emerge.

As you'll see when I lay out my own Puzzle Pieces of Purpose later in this chapter, this "Back Forty of Play, Passion and Purpose" perspective can offer a divining rod pointing toward a deep well of one's greatest Self-expression—the expression of Purpose.

> **Survival is a weak substitute for purpose.**

MORE PURPOSE IMPOSTORS

When we begin to truly inquire into purposeful living, a huge awareness of its opposite, *purposeless* living, comes into view and is easily found in ourselves and in others.

Busyness is one leading purpose imposter. Even the act of slowing down enough to ponder and perceive what gives you a sense of purpose is in itself difficult because of the illusion that busyness equals purpose. So, you stay busy, too busy to even consider purpose. You keep a thousand plates spinning in the air, rushing from one to thing to another on your massive and ever-growing "to do" list.

From my own experience, I found a morbid sense of safety and security in knowing that the next problem to be solved, the next task to get handled, was ready and waiting.

So, when can activity—maybe even a lot of it—be an expression of purpose? Perhaps it depends on the source of the tremendous activity: inspiration, or addiction. How can you know which it is?

Here are some questions to ask your Self:

- Does the activity in which I'm engaged arise from the infinite wellspring of a Higher Will? Or, is it simply my ego's way of avoiding the awareness of a *complete absence* of true purpose?
- Right now, am I engaging in this activity joyfully (from inspiration) or do I feel driven (by addiction)?
- Does this activity avail me unlimited energy and creativity or leave me frayed and worn out?

An interesting practice is to watch closely as your days, weeks, and months pass by. Observe the flows of excitement and activity and you may notice that the highs and lows of energy, inspiration, and joy often coincide with particular circumstances or events taking place.

Let's say you're single and you meet someone new. Now, a kaleidoscoping and cascading waterfall of thoughts as to what this could be or where this could go begins to thrill you. Or, maybe you receive a promotion at work. The prospect of continued progression up the corporate ladder makes you eager and enlivens your sense of long-term direction and security. Or, perhaps you own a business and just landed a new account or you recently received some great publicity. You're excited about how this might enhance your growth and operations.

These are all gleeful events, to be appreciated and not to be minimized. Yet, do they imply or give purpose? Is purpose simply derived from the winds of daily happenings or is it something beyond, beneath or above all that? Is "glee-mania" the best offering we can place on the altar of purpose?

It's important to realize that with the "ups" come the "downs." What happens when any of the above happy events change in character: the relationship or job or business opportunity doesn't pan out or runs its course? Again, the point is not to diminish the pleasure or even titillating rush that occurs when apparently good

> *Is purpose simply derived from the winds of daily happenings or is it something beyond, beneath or above all that?*

things come to us. The point is that it's important to recognize the shifting sand nature of building our sense of purpose upon them. Many people only wake up to the false sense-of-purpose "security" they've placed in relationships, jobs or finances when the divorce, layoffs or economic downturns inevitably occur.

However, flipping it around the other way, another false sense of purpose can be derived from playing the absolute reverse of such glee-mania— what one might call "the downside game." Having some form of crisis serve as the only consistent element in one's day-to-day experience is another way of substituting events and circumstances for purpose. Moving from one emergency to another as a way of life definitely precludes any higher mindedness. Dealing with and perhaps even subconsciously creating one form of chaos after another just to have something to solve, a next level of "peace" to get to, a weird but viable "reason to live" can be an addictive drug and an immediacy-of-the-moment impostor for true purpose.

Now let's take a look at some more sacred cows. As with all processes of inquiry, if the shoe fits, wear it. If it doesn't, simply move on with compassion for those for whom these shoes fit perfectly.

Having kids can be a substitute for purpose. This includes raising them with a focus completely on them (i.e., "sacrificing" for the sake of the kids). I'm not diminishing parenthood or the honorable intent to always put family first. Parenthood can actually be a portal through which one can experience being of purposeful service through other-orientation: focusing one's mind, attention and efforts on others. However, as a crutch or excuse for not living one's fullest Self-expression, the institutions of marriage and parenthood can be a sellout. What happens when the kids leave or, God forbid, you lose a child to some tragedy or illness? The "empty nest" syndrome arises when one's reliable sense of a "reason to live" has had the rug pulled out from under it. Also, marriages that have devolved into solely being about the kids tend to dismantle. Unchecked and without conscious context, such other-focused orientations around marriage can become an escape from or avoidance of a sense of true purpose.

Considering all of this, your own honest assessment and personal clarification of what purpose *is not* is necessary. Until you distinguish the false, you can't see clearly or be available for the real. Letting go of your own sacred cows of purpose impostors initially creates a void. . . and we hate voids! But as already quoted, "Don't avoid the void!" Until you can strip away that which keeps you running like a rat on a wheel, until you have the courage to sit in the "nothingness" that remains after the compulsive, thrill buttons have all been pushed, you can't and won't consider true purpose.

> *Until you can strip away that which keeps you running like a rat on a wheel, until you have the courage to sit in the "nothingness" that remains after the compulsive, thrill buttons have all been pushed, you can't and won't consider true purpose.*

PURPOSEFUL PROBES

In moving forward then, let's establish a basis for personal inquiry into what Purpose is for you. You'll start by engaging in some questions around purposeful living. Be clear, there are no "right" answers or any implications as to where your true purpose is or isn't. I firmly believe that the greatest answers to your purposeful Back Forty direction are inside of you. This is simply an inquiry to have you look below the surface of life to open yourself up for insights.

Embrace 6—Homeplay 4
Purpose Probe 1

To begin, pull out your Back Forty Freedom Fliers Journal and take some time to write on the questions that follow. Look and feel for yourself to discover which shoes truly fit while gaining clarity, understanding and compassion for those that don't.

Tip: When I repeat the same questions below or ask you to look again, I mean for you to put aside your earlier answer and come up with another. To truly inquire into something often means get-ting past some of our first-blush, surface answers in order to get to deeper truths underneath.

Purposeful Probes: Round 1

1. How busy are you in life?
2. What's behind your busyness? Meaning, what's driving it?
3. Look again: what's behind your busyness? What's driving it?
4. Look again: what's behind your busyness? What's driving it? Really, keep looking.
5. What does the word "purpose" mean to you?
6. Look again: what does the word "purpose" mean to you?
7. How much of your day are you present to purpose?
8. What are your purpose-imposter substitutes for purpose? Truly look and be honest with yourself.
9. How much, if any, have you substituted thrills for purpose?
10. How much, if any, have you substituted survival for purpose?
11. How much, if any, have you substituted a focus on others for purpose?
12. How much, if any, of your day do you experience being busy?
13. How much and in what ways, if any, do you substitute being busy for purpose?
14. Look again: How much and in what ways, if any, do you substitute being busy for purpose?

After you answer the questions above as fully and authentically as possible, answer these additional *Back Forty Insight & Awareness Questions.*

1. Which of these questions most intrigued you? Why do you think that is so?
2. Which of these questions most irritated you? Why do you think that is so?
3. What is your greatest insight, if any, from Purposeful Probes: Round 1?

Good probing. Congratulations. Hopefully, you're starting to get real with yourself. If any potential shoes fit, begin to distinguish the grip of those shoes and how they may be tripping you up from your true purpose being revealed to you.

If these questions intrigued or irritated you, that's good news: there's gold in them thar hills! Take some more time to journal on what fascinations occurred or which sacred cows got tipped, especially on the irritation front. Like a great coach once told me, look to see what gives you a charge (i.e., ticks you off) and investigate further into that. You'll find value to be mined and profound insights to be gained underneath the irritation.

In this Embrace 6: Your Purpose inquiry, as always, what matters most is your personal discoveries. Yet, for demonstration purposes, I'll offer my own authentic, condensed and amalgamated answers to these questions from several years ago. (I wrote much more and only offer the highlights of my own initial and hugely personal inquiry.)

Darrell's Purpose Probe 1

The idea of "poor substitutes for purpose:" I can relate to all of those listed and have practiced each.

As a busy-manic, I've positioned my purpose in my work and in feeding the voracious appetite of the "Make Money and Succeed!" monster. As an other-manic, I've placed my sense of purpose "over there" when in a relationship, substituting that other person's good opinion of me for my own. Additionally, I've allowed being a single dad, wearing the badge of courage from overcoming adversity and "doing his best" to substitute for a truly fulfilling purpose. My empty nest is coming soon, however, and that impostor will soon be out of a job.

But, mostly, I've engaged in playing the downside game as a survival-manic: living on emergencies and chaos, particularly around money. My already mentioned last financial whammy of a custody suit on the heels of a couple other periods of high debt advanced a now twelve-year cycle of one money concern after another. And, the problem with having money concerns is that it affects every other area: living arrangements, relationships, pursuing dreams, etc. Where I live, who I live with, whether I can even "afford" a relationship or the time-off to pursue my dreams, these are all impacted by money. In our world, money is a biggest, first domino that can take down the whole line.

With money being an issue for the last twelve years, I've substituted immediacy-of-the-moment little victories and a mission of "overcoming" for purpose. I've now played that game specifically for the last eight years instead of getting this book out. I first proposed it to agents and publishers in 2002. But at the time, I had more of my own R & D to accomplish first.

The above is just a small bit of what I saw for myself years ago when beginning my own Back Forty transformation. Yet, as stated, it's your story and it's how you're now going to tell it that matters most here. Change your story, change your life.

Embrace 6—Homeplay 5
Purpose Probe 2—Part 1

Let's take this inquiry to another level and get a sense of exactly what purpose looks and feels like for you. It's different for all of us. What one person might take for feeling purposeful another might consider indigestion.

Pull out your Back Forty Freedom Fliers Journal and write on this next set of *Insight & Awareness Questions*. Take time to really examine for your Self. Every shovel full of soil that you turn over from your Front Forty has the potential for gold in it.

Purposeful Probes: Round 2

1. Exactly when have you felt purposeful in life? Have you ever felt it? Get as specific as possible. Write about all the instances that come to mind.
   a. At what ages have you felt purposeful? Doing what?
   b. At what events, situations, and/or activities have you felt purposeful?
   c. Involvement with which people has felt purposeful?

2. Get in touch with the feelings you've had of being purposeful or "on purpose." Describe those feelings or the sensation of purpose itself, how it shows up for you.
   a. How does it feel in your body?
   b. How does it feel in your mind, your mental state?
   c. How does it feel emotionally, your general disposition and attitude?
   d. How does it feel spiritually, your sense of connection with something greater than you?

3. What themes or patterns do you see around the times in which you've felt purposeful?
   a. Are there patterns involving other individuals that relate to a feeling of being on purpose?
   b. See if you can list out three or more commonalities wherein purpose has been present in connection with others.
   c. Are any of these patterns related to what was discussed earlier as poor substitutes for purpose? Be honest with yourself, and look to see how much, if any, of an

underlying absence of purpose has had you base your identity on relationships, work, special events, or even survival and chaos.

4. Underneath the purpose impostors, if any exist, what can you honestly see and say have been the main ingredients of feeling purposeful in your life thus far? Make a searching inventory and list them out.

5. Why are you or why are you not worthy of having a true purpose for the rest of your life?

Okay, after you've completed answering the questions above as fully and authentically as possible, answer a few more:

1. Which of these questions most intrigued you? Why do you think that is so?
2. Which of these questions most irritated you? Why do you think that is so?
3. What is your greatest insight, if any, from Purposeful Probes: Round 2?

Once again, sharing highlights from my own very personal inquiry years ago, here are my authentic, condensed and amalgamated answers. Perhaps a bit long-winded, yet I want you to get a sense of the many avenues and byways this particular inquiry can take. Again, don't define your writing based on the length of mine.

Darrell's Purpose Probe 2

When I feel purposeful, I'm excited and feel that everything is clicking. I feel like the stars are aligned and everything is going according to some perfect plan. People around me are charmed and charming, encouraged and encouraging, receptive and giving. "Magic" seems to be in the air. Who knows if this is just describing flights of fantasy or grandiosity-thinking on parade, but it's a feeling I enjoy.

One instance which comes to mind first is when, at thirty-seven, looking for a distributor, I attended my first national book conference with my first book. I had such a sense of accomplishment that, seemingly, a wellspring of charisma was pulsing through my veins as I met people from far and wide throughout a huge conference hall with thousands of booths. Though the convention was in Chicago, a friend from my church in LA happened to be there promoting something of her own. She spent several hours walking around with me to various booths. At one point, she stated that I was "on fire" and exhibiting the same power, charisma, and magnetism of our famous minister back in LA. I felt that way: like I was on a mission.

In thinking about the feeling in my body, a seemingly infinite source of energy and vitality was present. I didn't need to sleep and only needed to eat to keep from passing out. The maintenance of the body was purely functional, as I felt my spirit was being set free.

I recall another time when I felt this way. At age twenty-seven, I was assisting as a volunteer at a two-weekend, personal development course led by a widely known transformational teacher. I remember needing so little sleep, maybe four to five hours per night, even though I was putting in sixteen or so hours of volunteering each day on those sequential weekends.

What was giving me this seemingly endless stream of energy? Possibility. The possibility that was present for not only me but the whole body of attendees. It was the conversation taking place—an inquiry into freedom from the past—and the inspiration that this freedom was mine to be experienced. It also didn't hurt that I was volunteering alongside my lover du jour, bringing the passionate conversation home each night into the bedroom.

That's what being "on purpose" looks like for me: a passionate energy that shows up in every area of life.

Another instance of feeling on purpose was when, just turning eighteen, I left my small hometown and moved to "the big city" to attend college. I had so longed to get away from what I felt was a limited purview of life that going back to that small hometown after college was not an option.

So, I immediately sought to become a "big man on campus" in my freshman dorm, ran for the student council of my school and got to know everybody everywhere. I have to ask myself in that instance was I "on purpose" or just driven? Was this an over-the-top compensation for feeling insecure and inadequate, a small fish in a big pond? Yes. Without a doubt. Yet, it's the feelings I associate (rightly or wrongly) with being "on purpose" that I'm looking to uncover here.

I'm noticing a bit of a theme of being out in the world, talking to many, serving and supporting many, being a hub of connections and relationships, being out on display while carrying a message. It's almost evangelical and bears a strong similarity to being a politician, but with more of a statesman feel and laudable intentions. Noticeably in this and the other purposeful situations I'm describing, my gifts and my values converge.

I remember feeling on purpose when, at age thirty-one, a flurry of new energy and possibilities occurred simultaneously with my son being born. First, I was a new dad, experiencing heightened responsibilities and a lot less sleep. Also, I was just finishing an eighteen-month acting program with one of the last original master teachers, Sanford Meisner. I had aspirations of big roles, exposure and "fame." I was making more money in my recruiting business, which proved some advice I was given by a friend who said, "Despite never feeling you have enough money to have a kid, the Universe just tends to provide when you do." Exciting new possibilities were afoot in many areas, and I felt like I was moving throughout each day from one life role to the other (husband, new dad, actor, businessman) without even taking time to "freshen my makeup."

On the flipside of my son being born, I also recall feeling very "on purpose" at age thirty-nine, when engaged in a two-year lawsuit to retain joint custody of him. For sure, a great deal of ego was involved; so, perhaps I have here an instance in which Imposter Purpose and real Purpose exist one superimposed over the other. I was incensed at the claims being made about me, and I wanted to prove myself "right" and "worthy" in continuing to jointly raise our son as well as also being motivated by a basic sense of justice. Therefore, I fought unceasingly and unwaveringly, putting every last and future dime on the line for what I felt to be a moral imperative.

At times, to my own detriment, I can fail to weigh the extreme costs involved in proving myself "right." This may have been one of them, and I became willing to sacrifice everything for the sake of it. Needless to say, a commitment to the fulfillment of justice (at least the way I perceive justice) can for me involve a sense of being on purpose.

I'm noticing yet another theme of single-minded focus. Each situation also offered an uncluttered sense of inspiration which allowed me to simply focus on the perspiration—the work to be done. There was an absence of doubt or self-condemnation and a feeling that the objects of my single-eyed attention, literally, meant the world to me.

I just recalled another couple of times of feeling on purpose. At age twenty-one, I spent two weeks one summer taking care of my grandmother as she recovered from a hospital stay, driving her around and being a supportive aid. Several years earlier, I had also spent time with my grandfather in the hospital before he passed, and even wiped his butt from the bedpan because he felt better having family do it than some nurse he didn't know. At fifteen years old, it created a humbling awareness of the circle of life.

So, the themes I'm seeing of being on purpose involve a sense of mission, overcoming, grandness, service, the bringing of a message and possibility, big love and single-minded focus—all reflective of my values and all allowing my gifts to come into play. I experience the state of my body as one of seemingly endless energy and enthusiasm and the state of my mind as one of directedness, focus, confidence and self-assurance; the state of my spirit, one of inspiration and bigness, feeling an equal and worthy part of the world as a whole.

A pattern emerges of being involved with some bigger picture or purview with ideas or concepts that rise above the mundane and have a sense of common humanity and universality to them. The only pattern I notice around the other individuals is that I'm giving or providing some-thing to them: a message, a service, a cause, a possibility. So, overall, I see common themes of being a messenger, a soldier for right, a purveyor of possibility.

Self-expression and shooting higher, while preaching "the good news" (possibility) and taking others with me seems to be the main motif of my feeling on purpose in life. An apparent dedication to justice for all and ensuring that everyone is privy to the same possibilities and poten-tial is central. For me, being purposeful occurs as a wholesome desire to reach out and give others a hand up, and to bring about a worldview of equality, authenticity, and Oneness.

As noted, some of these particular instances of feeling on purpose have also included elements of purpose impostors. When feeling I was going to "make it" with my first book and embark on a new career as an author and speaker, it was all about getting somewhere and "being some-body" with my creative work. This was also the case both when I grad-uated from an eighteen-month acting course with visions of grandeur about being "discovered" and, when coming from a small hometown, taking a huge university by storm. "Make it." "Be somebody." So, many of these were clearly about getting noticed and approved of, a massaging of the ego, rather than a nourishing of the soul.

This isn't to say that any of these endeavors were unworthy in any way or that I was not also on purpose with them (in a running-of-experiments way). It's just that a purposeful life in The Back Forty is not focused on feeding the ego. But, beyond that, the flavor of the rest of my above-noted instances of feeling purposeful actually seem honorable and worthy—not poor substitutes for purpose.

Embrace 6—Homeplay 6
Purpose Probe 2—Part 2

Now take a look at what you wrote. Did you allow your Self the right to be as verbose as necessary and pursue as many tangents in your own journaling? Feel free to review and sit with the questions above for a day or so, returning to write more if needed. The opportunity to uncover your patterns around purpose may never be better. Take whatever time needed for a thorough purpose probe.

ELEVATING WHILE RELAXING YOUR SENSE OF PURPOSE

Now, with this depth of probing insight underway, let's dig deeper in The Back Forty field to uncover how true Purpose occurs in your second half/best half of life. Let's start by looking more closely at the last question in Purposeful Probes Round 2, which deals with worthiness as related to purpose.

Growing up in a small town and then getting out into the bigger world, I assumed that one had to be a truly special person to have a purpose. I had heard of, and to a small extent observed, the likes of Martin Luther King, Mahatma Gandhi, Albert Schweitzer, Mother Theresa and other highly evolved individuals; and I developed a big, other-worldly concept about the unique kind of person who could validly claim to have a purpose. Contradicting my concept is the fact that, for the most part, the luminaries of purposeful living throughout history did not begin with a silver-spooned purpose already in their mouths. What if having a purpose is a both a right as well as an unavoidable obligation that we *all* have and are worthy enough to express, regardless of our particular stories, upbringings, conditions or levels of development/society/income/education?

If not you, who? If not now, when?

> *For the most part, the luminaries of purposeful living throughout history did not begin with a silver-spooned purpose already in their mouths.*

Especially for those over age forty, it's important to realize that true purpose is a real possibility for each of us—yes, even for little old you and me—even though many of us weren't necessarily raised to believe so. Given the discoveries we've now made in our Back Forty explorations and excavations, we've been able to drop a lot of weighty ballast in the form of critical judgment and assessment of ourselves, freeing up our energy for purpose-focused activity, perfectly designed by us, *right now*, *right on cue*.

So, you and I haven't missed the harvest. The heretofore uncultivated fertile soil of our Back Forty is just waiting for us to break ground. Who knows what we can plant or the kind, size or value of the purposeful harvest we can reap!

As we embrace true purpose, I perceive three areas of thought to consider, as expressed in the words of some of the luminaries mentioned above:

- A more daily routine purpose
- A seemingly privileged purpose
- An incremental and evolving personalized purpose

First, there are ideas which we can all relate to, and feel worthy to be in league with:

Whatever your life's work is, do it well. A man should
do his job so well that the living, the dead, and the
unborn could do it no better.

MARTIN LUTHER KING

We ourselves feel that what we are doing is just a
drop in the ocean. But the ocean would be less
because of that missing drop.

MOTHER TERESA

Nearly everything you do is of no importance,
but it is important that you do it.

MAHATMA GANDHI

The purpose of human life is to serve and to show
compassion and the will to help others.

ALBERT SCHWEITZER

Most of us can easily subscribe to the sentiments of those basic, purpose-leaning principles, yes? Do your job well. Follow your heart. Do what you do like it matters. Help others.

But, then what about ideas that begin to stretch our perceived limits of Self, sending us off into thinking that purpose is for those otherworldly beings with more time, drive, commitment, space and spirituality than we have to play big.

> **If a man has not discovered something that he will die for, he isn't fit to live.**
>
> MARTIN LUTHER KING

> **Spread love everywhere you go. Let no one ever come to you without leaving happier.**
>
> MOTHER TERESA

> **Man becomes great exactly in the degree in which he works for the welfare of his fellow men.**
>
> MAHATMA GANDHI

> **Do something for somebody every day for which you do not get paid.**
>
> ALBERT SCHWEITZER

Those quotes point to an ideal that may be a higher hurdle to clear, especially if we're just starting out on the true-purpose track. They all sound like good, glorious and even evangelical ways of living for the lucky ones who seemingly don't have to work and can devote all their moments to the welfare of their fellow humans. However, I dare say that many of us have not reached such spiritual/financial/worldly/time independence! We still have rent and mortgages to pay, families to support and accounts to fund for college as well as the future and our legacy to build.

Nonetheless, every human being has the right—and I would assert, the ability—to live a life of purpose. Here are a few final quotes upon which I want to base the rest of this Embrace 6: Your Purpose inquiry into your second half/best half of life. I encourage you to continue the inquiry long beyond this chapter. And to support that end, these quotes will give you what I find to be a far more forgiving and accessible path for embracing your purpose.

> **Take the first step in faith. You don't have to see the whole staircase; just take the first step.**
>
> MARTIN LUTHER KING

> **We must know that we have been created for greater things, not just to be a number in the world, not just to go for diplomas and degrees, this work and that work. We have been created in order to love and to be loved.**
>
> MOTHER TERESA

> **As human beings, our greatness lies not so much in being able to remake the world—that is the myth of the atomic age—as in being able to remake ourselves.**
>
> MAHATMA GANDHI

> **Humanitarianism consists in never sacrificing a human being to a purpose.**
>
> ALBERT SCHWEITZER

So, purpose comes down to just getting started, having it be about love, understanding that it's an inside job, and knowing that there's not a soul without the ability or right to embody a purpose.

That sets the foundation for an incremental and evolving personalized purpose, of which you are completely capable.

INQUIRING INTO PURPOSEFUL PRACTICE

With what you uncovered in answering Purposeful Probes Rounds 1 and 2 above, have you gotten a sense of what it feels like to be purposeful and/or on purpose in life? Hopefully you've begun to catch a glimmer of the feeling tone: the physical, mental, emotional and spiritual states you've associated with purpose throughout your life. Not that you're limited to or by your past experiences; they just serve as an initial marker and baseline for the Back Forty sense of purpose you want to invent.

If you didn't catch that glimpse and you made it through all of those questions without a single instance or memory of ever feeling authentically on purpose, all is not lost. You're just in a fresh and unique position of realization. You can begin to grow in awareness of your everyday life and activities while gauging them against a Geiger counter of purpose. When you feel on purpose, a shaking up of the status quo will become noticeable.

Whether or not you've identified some past or present activities that feel to you like being "on purpose," you might start by asking your Self, after each activity or engagement of the day, "Did I feel 'on purpose' then?" Carry around a small notebook or jot notes in your phone. Begin to put together a database of situations and instances from which to assess your personal experience of feeling purposeful. Rate each day or each significant engagement or experience on a scale of 1 to 10 in terms of feeling purposeful. Keep notes, revisit them, and look for patterns.

One critical caveat for those who didn't identify any past on-purpose moments: you must *be willing* to experience feeling purposeful! It's likely that, if you answered all of the questions above with absolutely no recollection of ever feeling genuinely on purpose, you may simply be unwilling to consider *any* of your experience purposeful or yourself *worthy* of experiencing purpose in life. On the other hand, even if you do recall feeling purposeful in the past, it may be such an atrophied or paralyzed muscle that your nerve endings are now dead.

How in the world can a person who isn't willing to feel purposeful become purposeful? Impossible! You must be willing to feel purposeful, and you start by being *willing* to be *willing*. Go out today and simply be willing to be willing that something you do, say, hear, observe or otherwise experience can light up a sense of purpose within you. When you keep doing that and take notes to reflect upon, you'll build a huge database of awareness from which to connect the pieces in your own puzzle of purpose.

I encourage you to engage in such a Purposeful Practice on a daily basis.

The future depends on what you do today. —*Mahatma Gandhi*

None of this is intended to put any pressure on you. Often much pressure is felt by those who really care about living their lives in a meaningful way, those who truly want to make a difference, to get that purpose thing *nailed down*. However, being intensely attached to figuring out Your Purpose can actually prevent it from revealing itself to you. Your Purpose can be frozen with stage fright, just behind the curtain, because it's somehow expected to leap out onto the stage like a premier danseur/prima ballerina with all the perfected and elegant moves already in place—when it's only right now just begun learning to dance!

Let's relax the pressure on purpose! What if, like anything else, purpose only requires practice? As with learning golf or even a new language, your purpose becomes easier to understand and engage in the more you simply keep your mind on it, take swings at it, begin to distinguish it and practice having close-calls with it.

What if, rather than "nailing" your purpose (like a coffin, a.k.a. getting an "answer"), you simply court it and create space for it to show up in your life?

Years ago, when in dating mode, I was encouraged to set an extra place at the dinner table and to kiss the pillow beside me each night, creating an energy of invitation for my lover to show up. What if you can court your purpose in a similar way? It may be the best dating you've ever done! More importantly, it puts Your Purpose in a state of ongoing inquiry versus pressure to get an "answer." If true purpose is king, then just like in the Broadway play *The King and I*, it's a process of "getting to know you, getting to know all about you."

Now, back to your purpose probe inquiry. This idea of **Purposeful Practice** has two dimensions: First, "practice" means learning to open up to it, develop a relationship with it, discover it and become better at it. Second, when you begin to sense what purpose truly *feels like* for you, then you want to become a Practitioner of Purpose. Whether you did, in fact, gain a sense of the feeling tones and themes of being purposeful in the course of completing the purpose probes or you're only now beginning to distinguish them through inquiring into purposeful practice, I have a very easy question for you: what if being "on purpose" is simply about doing more of what most of the time makes you feel on purpose? If this or that has you feeling purposeful, then do more of it! If feeling on purpose impacts you spiritually, then your general daily spiritual practice will include practicing purpose.

> *If feeling on purpose impacts you spiritually, then your general daily spiritual practice will include practicing purpose.*

Personalized Purpose

Who's to judge whether one person's activities and involvements in pursuing purpose are more worthy, valid, or laudable than another's? It's the individual experience that matters, and that's why you're reading this book: for *your* experience of a purposeful Back Forty. Absent the purpose impostors, each of us has a unique set of physical, mental, emotional, and spiritual triggers to inform us of what feels on track and purposeful. What causes you to feel purposeful is completely independent from what causes others to feel that way. You have a one-of-a-kind makeup, based on the Discovery & Expression experiments you've conducted in your one-of-a-kind Front Forty. Regardless of how divergent your and my feelings of being on purpose may be, if you and I feel on purpose more minutes every day than we don't, we're both doing ourselves and the world a big favor and an act of service. We'll always serve humanity better when we're playing on purpose.

Can purpose shift over time? Of course. The Back Forty is not static or confined. Your Purpose is fluid, and you'll want to continually experiment with what provides an experience of your greatest Self-expression. When the time comes for an even greater-yet-to-be vision for your Self, it will be revealed. As is often recited, "when the student is ready, the teacher appears." Until then, go forward confidently with what you've discerned and discovered thus far about who you're here to be and what you're here to do. Refer frequently to your Self Expression Directives and your identified second-half gifts, talents and values to see whether you're living from them. If you are, you may well be On Purpose.

Pursue what feels purposeful to you.

> *Refer frequently to your Self Expression Directives and your identified second-half gifts, talents and values to see whether you're living from them. If you are, you may well be On Purpose.*

I learned this, at least, by my experiment: that if one advances confidently in the direction of his dreams and endeavors to live the life which he has imagined, he will meet with a success unexpected in common hours. He will put some things behind, will pass an invisible boundary; new, universal, and more liberal laws will begin to establish themselves around and within him; or the old laws be expanded and interpreted in his favor in a more liberal sense, and he will live with the license of a higher order of beings. In proportion as he simplifies his life, the laws of the universe will appear less complex, and solitude will not be solitude, nor poverty, poverty nor weakness, weakness. If you have built castles in the air, your work need not be lost; that is where they should be. Now put the foundations under them. —*Henry David Thoreau*

Granted, you must maintain the body while, nonetheless, seeking to fulfill the unbounded Spirit within it. Otherwise, the Spirit will have no functioning vessel within which to delve into the depths of Back Forty possibility. So, pay the light bill while you nurture the light in your soul. Maintain the material world while focusing on the ethereal one.

But be alert. If you limit your Self to only the maintenance of the vessel, then you're in the "Body Shop" and your Spirit will be confined to the flesh. However, if you build purposeful "castles in the air," as Thoreau states, and build support structures underneath those castles to ensure sustainability, you will have achieved balance. Balance is the key.

> **If you limit your Self to only the maintenance of the vessel, then you're in the "Body Shop" and your spirit will be confined to the flesh.**

You can even play The Abundance Game at the same time as you engage in your Purposeful Practice! As a matter of fact, your playful, passionate, and purposeful Back Forty may include lots of external financial expansion, and even toy upgrades (i.e., "stuff"). Yet, all of these will carry a fulfillment of purpose when they arise from and are in service to A Presence, which we'll explore in the next chapter. As mentioned earlier, Purpose and Presence are intertwined.

Purposeful Lightness of Being: Stuff or Ballast?

Let's consider, for a moment, just how much stuff[12] you do, in fact, need or want in your Back Forty. Just how much stuff does it truly take to maintain the vessel, and do you really want more than that? Is purchasing that impressive new home, driving that shiny, cool car or dating that hotter-than-hot hunk or hunkette really required for vessel maintenance? We're programmed in our Front Forty to want over-the-top luxuries, but are they really needed? Sometimes, acquisitions such as those are only to show off

---

12 For a quick and lighthearted inquiry into the importance of your "stuff," search online for "stuff" + "George Carlin."

so that we can look special while still being confined to the Body Shop. They can feed the appetite of the ego while starving the soul.

I noticed my own desire over recent decades to minimalize my surroundings. When selling a house of ten years, I faced the accumulated stuff that a marriage, child, backyard and inexhaustibly devouring black-hole garage produced. In reaction and as a precursor to my own oncoming Back Forty initiation, I wanted to ditch it all and go live on a boat! I dreamt of having literally zero stuff! I thought there could be no life simpler and more freeing than one with only the things absolutely needed: a computer, a phone, food, a few shirts and pants, lots of books, and the internet! I even began talking to one particular yacht owner who was selling his long-time, 65-foot, live-aboard vessel in Marina del Rey, California.

From my then situation in life, it seemed like heaven. However, as the father of an eight-year-old, I knew it wouldn't serve my son to have such limited space, so I rented an apartment instead. Yet, when he neared the end of high school, my mind began docking again on that simple and footloose idea of a boat. I envisioned a live-aboard as a home base with a motorhome as a second residence. The idea was to travel the country, speaking, coaching, and conducting workshops with everything I needed right there with me. I could literally taste the feeling of freedom in that! So, following my own Back Forty path, I manifested part of that vision, buying and living for over four years aboard a sailboat docked in Marina del Rey.

I share that story because, if you believe your Front Forty didn't give you the stuff you wanted so that you could feel like you finally made it and you think your Back Forty should be focused on amassing all of that long-awaited stuff, you might want to think again about what would really make you happy and support your spiritual Self. Be clear, we make no judgment on the inclination to amass stuff. And, yes, you may pick up a new bauble or bead in your Back Forty, but The Back Forty isn't about the stuff—it's about the feeling, the experience, the vitality and the endless inspiration of being on purpose. That's what designing a playful, passionate and purposeful Back Forty is all about.

To that end, I propose that we now turn our attention toward *acceptance*. The funny thing about acceptance—finding peace with having just what you have and just what you don't have—is that you become freed up to be inspired and motivated by something other than showing the world that you "made it."

When you feel happiness, contentment, gratitude and appreciation for what you *do have* and then focus your days on engaging in the *feeling tone* and *activities* of being on purpose, you win in three ways: First the quality of your internal life improves. Second, by focusing on what's truly important for the fulfillment of your own unique Back Forty, becoming a practitioner of purpose, you may tap into something that actually brings more stuff! Again, nothing's wrong with stuff as an *effect* of being on purpose. It's just not ultimately powerful as the prime motivation for existence. What's interesting, however, is that, when the stuff comes because of being on purpose, it won't be about the stuff! It may come and may come with greater ease, but it comes as the gravy on top, not the meat itself. Third, when you truly practice acceptance and gratitude and simply focus on your *feelings* of being on purpose, if no more stuff comes, it won't matter. You're still happy and content!

So, just as in Embrace 5: Your Initiation, when you saw the opportunity to let go of the "becauses" that have weighed you down, you can similarly begin to let go of the ballast bags of "stuff" that may limit you from purposefully flying higher.

That's it! Toss some more stuff overboard.

Overall, you just can't lose by cultivating the acceptance, happiness, sense of contentment and inner peace that comes from focusing on what makes you *feel* on purpose, independent and unattached to stuff.

Embrace 6—Homeplay 7
Your Purpose and Your Stuff

First, pull out your Back Forty Freedom Fliers Journal and write a bit on the thoughts about purpose presented above. How and in what ways are these ideas relevant to you?

Then answer these *Back Forty Insight & Awareness Questions*.

1. Are you willing to take stock, on a daily basis, of what does or doesn't have you feel purposeful? Why or why not?
2. What role does "stuff" have in your practice of purpose? Explain.
3. Can you bring more acceptance and gratitude into your practice of purpose? Why or why not? If so, in what ways might you do that?

Finally, consider that your unique and individual purpose does *not* reside in one wooden chest (of all the wooden chests in the world), located on one solitary, sandy beach (of all the sandy beaches in the world), under one particular palm tree (of all the palm trees in the world), under seven feet of sun-drenched sand (of all the grains of sun-drenched sand in the world), only to be found by meticulous and strenuous charting and mapping of the globe.

That's not to say that your purpose isn't "special." It is and will always be for you, but that kind of perfectionistic, idealistic and narrow thinking keeps you off the playing field of continued R & D and away from fulfilling the Self Expression Directives you've already identified, which act as a divining rod to your purpose. Too much focus on finding the "answer" can result in its evading you. In contrast, Purposeful Practice—trying things out that appeal to you, that stretch you, that give you playgrounds in which to "play first" outside of previous self-concepts, in a word, designing and engaging in conscious experiments—allows for and promotes evolving your purpose and up-and-out living.

Rather than ponder your navel incessantly as to where your *ultimate* true north is or will be—a process that can dramatically slow down your gaining of experiences, conducting experiments and growing in awareness of expanded possibilities—I propose that you simply gauge your sense of purposefulness *in the moment* by how you *feel*. Simply move forward with the intention to engage in whatever most *feels* on purpose to you *right now*. Doing so will always take you to your next higher and greater realization of an *ultimate* true purpose, if there is one.

> *Simply move forward with the intention to engage in whatever most feels on purpose to you right now. Doing so will always take you to your next higher and greater realization of an ultimate true purpose, if there is one.*

PUZZLE PIECES OF PURPOSE

To gain some additional direction in pointing you to that "on purpose" feeling, let's take a general look at your **Puzzle Pieces of Purpose** to see what may be staring you in the face. You have an abundance of data at your disposal. You have

- your **Self Expression Directives** and other insights gained from your Discovery & Expression analyses of the multiple experiments you've conducted in Embraces 1, 2, and 5 and are still conducting in the present;

- a list of your unique **gifts** as you identified them in your surveys and as they were shared with you by others through your Insight/Incite email inquiries; and
- a list of your current **core values** assembled through extensive inventories.

These all add up to your Puzzle Pieces of Purpose at this moment. Combining these with all the additional data you'll gain when engaging in Purposeful Practice will allow you to begin forming a picture of who you came here to be and what you came here to do—**your purpose.**

Organizing Your Puzzle Pieces on the Table

This is a *lot* of data to get a handle on, so to illustrate what such a compilation of puzzle pieces can look like, I've laid out in Appendix C my own ever-evolving Puzzle Pieces of Purpose, some of which you saw earlier in real time as I embraced these integral elements of my own Front Forty. The organization of my puzzle represents just one way to bring the pieces into a document that you can return to time and time again. Of course, you'll organize your puzzle pieces in the way that works best for you, but Appendix C will give you an overview of the general content you're shooting for.

Embrace 6—Homeplay 8
Puzzle Pieces of Purpose—Part 1

Read through Appendix C to see how I have gathered all my directives, gifts, and primary values in one place.

Embrace 6—Homeplay 9
Puzzle Pieces of Purpose—Part 2

Now pull out your Back Forty Freedom Fliers Journal and begin to organize all your Puzzle Pieces of Purpose for *your* Self. This project may take a while to complete.

Here's a reminder checklist of items to include:

❏ A single list of all your Self Expression Directives, findings, and other insights from all your Embrace 1 Discovery & Expression analyses of past serious and significant laboratory experiments.

If you would like to first analyze another four or five Past Serious and Significant Events or Influences, go right ahead. There's no end to the number of these events and influences that you can analyze to extract more and more Self Expression Directives. These analyses rightly deserve to become a regular practice that you turn to every time you think of yourself as being a victim to anything from your past. You can always incorporate any new Directives into your ever-expanding, never-ending puzzle.

❏ A single list of all your Self Expression Directives from each of your Embrace 2 Discovery & Expression analyses of your present laboratory experiments.

Similarly, if you'd like to first analyze additional Present Serious and Significant Events or Influences, do so. These analyses can become your regular practice every time something happens in your present that has you feeling "at effect" and a victim. Such a practice, engaged in as a way of daily life, can quickly put you on top of any event, influence, condition, circumstance or situation that's taking place in present time, rather than being dominated by its weight or severity.

❑ A single list of all your Self Expression Directives derived from the serious and significant events or influences that you analyzed in Embrace 5: Your Initiation. You might combine this with your Directives from Embrace 1 because both sets are likely to derive from your past.

❑ A list or table of Your Gifts as you identified them in your self-surveys.

❑ A table or chart of your gifts, strengths and weaknesses as perceived from your Insight/Incite surveys of people who know you well. You might record how many times the same gifts or weaknesses are mentioned as I did.

❑ A list of the best jobs that you identified, who holds them, and a brief summary of why they are the best.

❑ A list of the top 5 values you identified in each of the values surveys that asked you to rank the relative importance of each value and a list of all the values you considered to be of #1 importance in the score-based surveys.

❑ A list of your Top 10 Rejoices/1,095-day Pledges.

Now that you've compiled your Puzzle Pieces of Purpose, vigorously shake them all together, throw them out into your life and see what forms! Easy as that!

Of course, that's a playful joke. There's nothing easy at all about incorporating that much data into one, simple, ticker tape, out-of-a-machine direction of purpose. Were it so easy, someone would have already invented an instant, just-add-water recipe for Purpose.

However, you do have tons of information, insight and ongoing tools now at your disposal to help you reflect on your purpose, on who you are specifically here to be and what you are specifically here to do. Maybe it's even compiled in a much more empowered and definitive way than you've ever had before. In the world of inquiry (versus getting the "answer"), you're in goldmine territory.

Embrace 6—Homeplay 10
Puzzle Piece of Purpose—Part 3

So, take a good, overall look at your pieces. Spend time reviewing them like an investigator or detective reviews all the facts of a case many times over to assess clues before making a determination that points to a path forward. By revisiting the details repeatedly, over and over again and over time, you set your Self up for an "aha!" moment of insight. And, if you're doing this exploration in alliance with other Back Forty Fliers, you have some wonderful material to share in gaining the perspective of others.

Darrell's Puzzle Pieces of Purpose Insights

From reviewing my own Puzzle Pieces of Purpose, as laid out in Appendix C, here are some insights I gleaned that I'll share with you to give you an idea of how to use your own compilation. These are just a few actions I can now take and games I can start playing with what I see.

1. I surely want to create a graphic display of all the Self Expression Directives into which I've invested so much time, effort, blood, sweat, tears and LIFE—first to honor my amazing Mad Scientist brilliance; second to remind myself, quickly and easily on a moment's notice and a daily basis of the directions I want to take in every interaction, every activity, every thought, every deed and every word I utter in my Back Forty. With the price-less investment I've made into these pearls of lab-tested wisdom, I surely don't want to just sit on them. I want to be consciously

aware at all times by having them graphically represented in my environment.

2. I can even design a weekly or monthly check-in system to regularly rate myself on a scale of 1-10 on how well I'm expressing the Self Expression Directives in my life. Without setting up such a playful "existence system," that is, a structure or plan to specifically keep these ideas in existence in my consciousness, there's always the chance I'll forget to be who I came to be as revealed by my Self Expression Directives. By putting these ideas into displays, calendars and fun Self-monitoring practices, I'll support my Self to engage more and more in these qualities. What I focus on expands, so building awareness and existence systems guarantees greater expansion of the me I came to be.

3. I can apply my responses to the question of how I might build the elements and flavor of the vocations I consider to be the best jobs in the world into my life right now. These insights are golden playgrounds of unlimited experimentation.

4. I might also create another graphic display of all my gifts and talents—my Shine—as well as the Back Forty Information Campaign Incite Matrix (shown in Appendix C) for moral support in times of self-doubt and to serve as another existence system. I've never had a more comprehensive and detailed list of what's great about me, nor been blessed with such a thorough survey of my awesomeness (and areas for development) from those who know me best. This is as much a mirror to look into each morning as any above a bathroom sink.

5. The Back Forty Information Campaign[13] from Embrace 3: Your Gifts offered huge insights to incite me into various forms of

---

13 *Access the extensive, insightful and inciting responses to Darrell's own Back Forty Information Campaign with a free download from TheBackForty.com/book*

exploration and play. I was amazed at how much the feedback from others aligned with many of my own concepts of Self as well as how it offered current and potential directions of purposeful pursuit. Besides the validation aspect, which was hugely Self-affirming, it's been a treasure trove of direction and opportunities for Self-expansion that I would have never been able to see or realize on my own.

6. E-Valuation surveys from Embrace 4: Your Values could not be more timely. It's one thing to know, in general, that I think and weigh things differently than I did X number of years ago. It's another thing to have it validated right in front of me. As I get into the relationships, projects, environments and consciously-designed laboratories of my playful, passionate and purposeful Back Forty, using a values Geiger counter of sorts will empower me. Rating each life element on a values scale of one to ten will enable me to make swift and deliberate movements, not wasting a moment when my energy and vibes don't jibe and not missing a moment of appreciation for a directed and values-based life when they do.

7. The power of my Top 10 Rejoices and 1,095-Day Pledges is simply priceless. I can use this initial survey as a reminder to not allow regrets to accumulate as I pursue my next half/best half. This is, obviously, not an exercise I want to engage in only once.

8. Though not specifically listed in my Puzzle Pieces of Purpose, in "Embrace 3: Your Gifts," there was a question following every survey on how I might express my gifts in better or bigger ways. I can institute ALL of those insights into pro-active, consciously designed research projects and laboratory experiments to develop further findings and further Self Expression Directives. In other words, I can use my gifts to organize my life's future activities.

9. Left to my own devices, these insights and powerful actions will likely remain simply good intentions. Alone, I can't be who I came here to be or do what I came here to do. I need support, as does everyone, so I put together an accountability group[14] and encourage you to do the same. Be supportive and supportable.

Those are just a few initial ways in which I see my own Puzzle Pieces of Purpose coming together. I can obviously create a multitude of pictures and experiments out of these pieces as I engage in Purposeful Practice.

Embrace 6—Homeplay 11
Puzzle Pieces of Purpose—Part 4

Now, going back to your own newly amassed and amalgamated information, insights and tools: what similar actions and games can you come up with for your own Puzzle Pieces of Purpose? Begin to postulate what it all points to. Start to marvel at all the puzzle pieces you can move around to fit various scenarios for your radical, playful, passionate and purposeful Back Forty. The picture is yours to design.

Once we believe in ourselves, we can risk curiosity, wonder, spontaneous delight, or any experience that reveals the human spirit. —*e e cummings*

Start to marvel at all the puzzle pieces you can move around to fit various scenarios for your radical, playful, passionate and purposeful Back Forty. The picture is yours to design.

Take some time to again review your compilations of directives, gifts, values, and other findings to get a broad perspective of all that you've uncovered and discovered. Play with it. Perhaps organize it

---

14 See TheBackForty.com/book for sprouting groups of *The Back Forty Accountability Alliance* offering supportive environments to encourage *Big Back Forty Games.*

in a manner similar to how I have (Appendix C). Let the pieces sink into your consciousness. Meditate on them. Then, pull out your Back Forty Freedom Fliers Journal and answer these simple questions newly *every day* for the next two weeks. Yes, the same questions, every day, for two weeks.

1. What do your pieces tell you?
2. Where and how are you inspired to move forward?
3. If the question of who you came here to be and what you came here to do were never to have a definitive answer and it was simply up to you to Be Cause, that is, to design laboratories, to realize and implement Self Expression Directives, to experiment and play, what would be your best educated guess on the directions for you to take right now? And, your next-best guess?
4. Who can you share this playful inquiry with to make it more real for you and even to hold you accountable?

PURSUING PRECESSIONAL PURPOSE

Were your purposeful second half of life to be simply formulaic in design, dictated by a picture on a box as you put the puzzle together, you'd have no opportunity to consciously create your life. It would be yet another "should" in life. If Your Purpose were that predetermined and easy to decipher, you could clearly tell whether you were on or off the path that you "should" be on.

Thank God that we are gracefully provided free will by the Universe! By the courageous stands we take, the bold choices we make, the wild possibilities we bake, and the "play first" forays we fake, it's absolutely possible to become mid-life "Purpose-sized" for a Big Game Back Forty Future.

"Purpose-sized" is when you accept that little old you are big enough, worthy enough and designed perfectly by life as lived enough to both have and fulfill on a purpose, while playing a big game.

Now that you are saddlebag-supplied with the awareness, insights and tools that you brought with you when you crossed over into your second half/best half, what's required is faith that the direction of your purposeful Back Forty will continue to unfold while you live in conscious inquiry.

> *"Purpose-sized" is when you accept that little old you are big enough, worthy enough, and designed perfectly by life as lived enough to both have and fulfill on a purpose, while playing a big game.*

Faith comes into full play in Embrace 7: A Presence. And, play it does! Plan, organize and decipher your life's design to prepare yourself; but, at some point, you must leave room for the Divine to take you from here to where you are to go.

And so it is that these two embraces, Purpose and Presence, evolve concurrently:

> Your Purpose: Allowing A Presence to Shine
>
> A Presence: Allowing Your Purpose to Align

Letting go of any pressure to zero in on some immediately defined purpose, you have the opportunity to adopt a playful, purpose-feeling attitude as you move forward. Building Purposeful Practice (integrating Directives, Gifts, and Values) into all that you do, growing in awareness of the feelings of purpose being experienced (or not) through your activities and interactions, taking to heart your Puzzle Pieces of Purpose while playfully and proactively creating laboratory experiments in the directions the pieces lead— all of these, taken together, will provide ample opportunities to calibrate your compass toward your own, ultimate true north.

I have nothing new to teach the world. Truth and Non-violence are as old as the hills. All I have done is to try experiments in both on as vast a scale as I could. —*Mahatma Gandhi*

Simply keep moving forward. Proceed with your Purpose-Feeling Compass in front of you, as your everyday companion leading the way. This very act of **precession** is where you place your faith.

The Law of Precession is a concept created by Buckminster Fuller, a mathematician, engineer, architect, inventor, philosopher, humanitarian, author and visionary; and it has a lot to offer us in causing and fulfilling on a purposeful Back Forty.

Plan, organize and decipher your life's design to prepare yourself; but, at some point, you must leave room for the Divine to take you from here to where you are to go.

By watching nature and how the grander scheme of life seemed to unfold, Bucky, as he was known, devised certain theories, one of which was The Law of Precession. He saw that what human beings consider *side effects* of events are actually nature's intended *main effects*.

You might immediately relate to the truth of this idea in your own life when you consider the "side effects" occurring from your Serious and Significant Events or Influences. Had your serious and significant events or influences never happened, you wouldn't be right here, right now gaining clarity on the perfection of their design inside of your unique life path. The side effects of someone else's three-ring circus, which you showed up in the middle of, became the main effects of your experience contributing to your becoming who you came here to be and doing what you came here to do.

In the process of uncovering the multitude of laboratory experiments you engaged in related to those events and influences, you may have had the thought, "Wow, I sure want to watch myself so that I don't cause those kinds of impacts on others!" Yet, as much as we'd like to have only the best effects and influences on our kids, loved ones, coworkers, partners, communities and society as a whole, to some extent we have to surrender to being spear carriers in other peoples' operas. That's not to say we don't strive to operate as responsibly as we can; but we can never know what another soul is, underneath their outer appearance/identity, experimenting for. We want to be consciously aware, sure; but we also can't get in the way of another individual's need for Self- Expression Directives from situations or circumstances in which we carry a spear. We're being a blessing for them, just as others are a blessing for us.

So, our mantra might become: Do My Best, Let A Presence Do the Rest.

Returning to Bucky's basic concept of side effects versus main effects, let's consider the honeybee.

Mr. Honeybee: He's Got the Whole World in His Feet

Mr. Honeybee flies around all day long, visiting one flower after the next.

What is he thinking, if anything? The best thought we might imagine him having is "Nectar! Nectar! Nectar!" What does he think his purpose is? "Get to the next flower and get more nectar!" That's as far as he's able to postulate (if honeybees could actually postulate) when it comes to his purpose. However, we, as smart and sophisticated onlookers, know that his real purpose is cross-pollination.

Without Mr. Honeybee "accidentally" carrying all that pollen from one floral wonder to another, we wouldn't have so many widely varied and beautiful flowers all around us let alone the vast majority of foods bees pollinate. Of the 100 crop species which provide 90 percent of the world's food, over 70 are pollinated by bees, so Mr. Honeybee is actually making life on planet earth possible!

Whoa! That's a big, heavy-duty purpose for Mr. Honeybee! Were he to carry

around such a heavy thought—that he is responsible for human kind's survival—it might weigh down his little body to the point he could not fly and
gather nectar. Yet, how many of us carry our change-the-world purpose
around as a great burden, or else burden ourselves just as heavily with a
dire need to find that purpose?

Bucky's Law of Precession is all about "the effect of bodies in motion on
other bodies in motion." His law states that any action causes a 90° effect to
happen elsewhere. In the case of the honeybee, even though we say that pol-
lination is the main effect of the bee's activity, we
have to admit that it is likely not the honeybee's
conscious purpose.

There are plenty of physics-related
aspects to this law, but let's focus more on
this "side effect" notion.

TRUE PURPOSE

In moving forward, while allowing
your Purpose-Feeling Compass to precede
you, you'll begin to move outside of your comfort
zones to express more of who you came here to be and what you came here
to do (by your best approximation at this point). As you consciously design
laboratories of experimentation (make life choices) following the pointers
you've received in the form of both internal and external wisdom gained in
the course of embracing your past, your present, your gifts, your values, and
your mid-life opportunity and as you adopt a "play first" attitude to simply
get moving before you have it all worked out, you'll be a body in motion having effects on other bodies in motion.

*If the intention in your forward movement is simply to add value, even with so
many ultimate questions of your true purpose still unanswered, neither you nor the
planet can lose.* You have no idea whatsoever of the 90° effects you'll have on
other bodies in motion, be they individuals, groups, organizations or communities. The idea is simply to keep moving and keep adding value to the
best of your ability.

Nothing happens until something moves. —*Albert Einstein*

People often consider their worthiness or capacity insufficient to live a life based on a purpose. They put such "idealism" on the back burner because, "Hey, I have to make a living!" Bucky believed that our job as human beings wasn't to make money but rather to add value to others. He even went so far as to estimate that 70% of the jobs on earth were not contributing to the actual life-support of people but were making money from money, moving papers around to desk after desk.

> *If the intention in your forward movement is simply to add value, even with so many ultimate questions of your true purpose still unanswered, neither you nor the planet can lose.*

Bucky personally had a spiritual experience[15] that caused him to commit to a precessional way of living, making nature's big-picture "side effects" his main objective. He resolved to only ever do the greatest good for the greatest number of people. With such self-discipline as his primary goal, he reasoned through this precessional 90° logic that he would always have enough money and other resources to support his life's journey.

His stand was that, just as the honeybee did not need to *earn* a living, were he, as a human being, to simply keep adding value to the survival of humanity, doing whatever he was uniquely designed to do, he would not need to *earn* a living either. He would be precessionally provided for.

[I] paid no attention to "earning a living" and found my family's and my own life's needs being unsolicitedly provided for by seemingly pure happenstance and always only in the nick of time and only coincidentally. —*Buckminster Fuller,* Critical Path

---

15 Fuller, R. Buckminister, *Critical Path,* (*St. Martin's Griffin, New York, 1982*).

This may be a big Back Forty idea to swallow all in one gulp. We often learn only gradually from such high-minded luminaries. Yet, here's a synopsis to put in your saddlebag: if you just keep moving forward with the intention of adding value, doing what your unique path and your Puzzle Pieces of Purpose have designed you to do, you can't help but move whatever true purpose you have more into realization, more into form.

Just like Mr. Honeybee, you may never actually know what the real, 90° side effects of your Purposeful Practice will be. You may never truly comprehend how your uniquely designed second-half will impact life both now and/or far down the road for others on the planet. Your job is to simply keep moving—and to keep adding value.

You may never know what results come of your actions, but if you do nothing, there will be no results. —*Mahatma Gandhi*

We can do all this while paying the light bill. Bucky called human beings "money bees" because, though our straight-line objective may be "Money! Money! Money!" the 90° effects of such single-focused efforts end up creating products, services, programs, technologies, art, structures, philosophies and all manner of other "byproducts" that enhance the lives of humans on the planet. So, don't worry that in focusing on making money you're negating your pursuit of a purposeful Back Forty

While you playfully engage with and inquire into Embrace 6: Your Purpose with all the tools now at your disposal, know that you are not going wrong when you're also thinking about making money. It's all about balance. Alongside all the high-minded consciousness, we require financial resources to support our next half/best half as we design and play a Big Back Forty Future Game. All focus on money for you and your family with no bigger intention of adding value has no balance. All lofty intention with no money for you and your family equals no balance. Just keep moving forward adding value while balancing your earthly needs and your higher calling, and Your Purpose *will* be fulfilled.

A final word about your Puzzle Pieces of Purpose. Just in case at the end of this chapter, you still wish you had a perfect, tied-up-in-a-bow, silver-bullet answer to what your particular Back Forty playful and passionate purpose is. . .think about this:

Have you ever been putting together a massive jigsaw puzzle? You know, the ones with hundreds or even thousands of pieces, and you become single-mindedly focused on finding one particular piece? You look all around. You spend tons of time and effort trying to find that uniquely shaped piece. You're distracted and almost paralyzed, completely attached to finding that one piece that will fit in the exact spot you're now trying to fill.

Ever been there?

What if, for the moment, you detached from the need for that particular piece and simply kept working with the all the other pieces easily available and accessible to you, the ones right in front of you? When you start filling in other spaces, moving towards completion of the emerging picture while looking at it from other angles, the overall image will start coming together even if you haven't found that specific piece yet.

> *If you just keep moving forward with the intention of adding value, doing what your unique path and your Puzzle Pieces of Purpose have designed you to do, you can't help but move whatever true purpose you have more into realization, more into form.*

When will you find that exact piece? WHO CARES? You simply *add value now* by filling in what you can with what you have in front of you *now*. The point is that progress is happening and you're moving forward and adding value while completing the puzzle. The picture is being formed and, as a precessional effect of following your inner impulses and creativity, gifts, values, and Self-expression Directives, just like Mr. Honeybee, you unknowingly will fulfill your true purpose. You'll eventually pull the entire puzzle together.

When you are born, your work is placed in your heart. —*Khalil Gibran*

If you choose to subscribe to the Back Forty's radical idea that you planned this whole trip. . .as you. . .to planet earth. . .in this lifetime. . .and that you knew who you came to be and what you came to do, then you are simply in the process of taking signals from what you've created thus far to point you in that Self-appointed direction. You, in effect, set up a treasure hunt through Front Forty life so as to finally arrive at these keys to unlocking the purposeful work originally placed in your heart.

> *As you playfully and passionately allow your purposeful work to unfold, A Presence begins to reveal "ItSelf". . . through you.*

As you playfully and passionately allow your purposeful work to unfold, A Presence begins to reveal "ItSelf"—that which cannot be named—through you, expressing both the presence you carry in how you show up in the world as well as A Presence that carries you in how you show up in the world.

SIXTH SEPTENARY ACKNOWLEDGEMENT

My end-of-chapter acknowledgements are becoming ineffable. This isn't for any lack of awareness of who you are and what it takes for you to accompany me in this Back Forty adventure but for the simple lack of words to express the honor and depth of courage from which you are operating.

> *Just keep moving forward adding value while balancing your earthly needs and your higher calling, and Your Purpose will be fulfilled.*

This is not easy stuff in which to inquire, but rarely did easy create anything extraordinary. I honor you now and in our remaining explorations together, in the unsaid of knowing who you are and what you're up to Causing for your Self and the planet.

A PRESENCE

As soon as man does not take his existence for granted, but holds it as something unfathomably mysterious, thought begins.

ALBERT SCHWEITZER

PURPOSE WITH A PRESENCE

Embrace 7 invites us to embrace **A Presence**.

Okaaaaay. But. . .

What is a Presence?

What is it to "embrace" A Presence?

How does that work?

And what does it have to do with Back Forty flying?

This final Embrace in launching your radical second half of play, passion and purpose offers possible answers to these questions, with an emphasis on *possible* because remember that a purposeful life is actually lived inside of inquiry, not in the finding of some "true" answer.

Not unlike our age-old pursuit of Purpose, most of us, whether we can articulate it or not, seek to know something greater than ourselves and to feel connected to it. That It, I would call "A Presence." As sharp as they may become, the Back Forty tools in our toolshed—our newly acquired R & D analyses, surveys and Puzzle Pieces of Purpose—are somewhat limited in how far they can plow our way forward. And, although we've engaged these tools more and more consciously and effectively as we've embraced our past, present and even "morrasive" midlife opportunity, for our second half to embody a *radical best* half in which to playfully fulfill our Purpose, it will require something boundless.

The Updraft for Flying Higher

What is that something boundless? It occurs in relationship with A Presence. When we are in alignment with A Presence, the Highest aspects of ourselves are attuned to and able to catch the warm wind of Spirit beneath our wings, or rather, our ascending Back Forty airship. We're able to avail ourselves of an uplifting energy flow in a collaborative way to more readily rise into our uniquely individual purposeful practice.

For your playful, passionate and purposeful Back Forty to begin with a stark demarcation, a gateway through which you cannot (and wouldn't want to) return, you must be willing to *think* differently and *do* things differently from here on out. The entire concept of personal development, regardless of the particular philosophy driving it, is based on exactly this premise: until you operate in new ways, you can't experience or know anything other than what you've experienced and known in the past. Considering different thoughts and beliefs and generating actions from them is a practice that requires cultivation. Such cultivation results in an outwardly-spiraling, ever-widening expansive world, as described in the previous Embrace.

Critical to changed thoughts and actions is recalibrating *where* we take our direction from and *whom* or *what* we listen to for guidance. For example, years ago, when writing the initial draft of *The Back Forty*, I experienced an extreme foundational shift: a need to let go of the ego's direction. As I confronted each Embrace, I began with only that Embrace's title. I wondered where the actual content would come from. Interestingly, I found that in letting go of my need to know where the words would come from, the book largely wrote itself—and did so specifically as a healing process for me.

Ego, that "identity" part of us that thinks we can handle everything on our own, can't bring about an entire paradigm shift in our thinking and life experience, let alone manifest it, because the ego is not interested in anything outside of its safe and well-worn paths, be they busy-manic, glee-manic, survival-manic or other-manic. Therefore, your and my radical Back Forties of life must draw upon something beyond our ego's cheap attempts to figure out our path and purpose. It is what's beyond the ego that we want to access.

For your playful, passionate and purposeful Back Forty to begin with a stark demarcation, a gateway through which you cannot (and wouldn't want to) return, you must be willing to think differently and do things differently from here on out.

Midlife is the time to let go of an over-dominant ego and contemplate the deeper significance of human existence. —*Carl Jung*

As wonderful as the blessings and directives from my experiments have been and as precious as my inventoried gifts and awareness of my current values are, I have discovered that all of it by itself is insufficient to have me fully be who I came to be and do what I came to do. Yes, I'm a good student and I'll squeeze out every bit of awareness that's possible from my Front Forty R & D

Critical to changed thoughts and actions is recalibrating where we take our direction from and whom or what we listen to for guidance.

and ongoing Back Forty experiments; but, for me, literally a death of the old self needs to take place so a new Self can take the lead. Egoic "bankruptcy" is a term that comes to mind. Not financial, but with the same sense of surrender and new beginnings. Not a bad thing, but a necessary evolution, which has led me to recognize that you and I have been Divinely and collaboratively shaped, carved, and sculpted for a reason. Our entire lives have been a uniquely powerful laboratory for the discovery and expression of *something*. Now, we have an opportunity to consciously serve that *something* as, with and alongside Its co-sculpting Presence.

> *Ego, that "identity" part of us that thinks we can handle everything on our own, can't bring about an entire paradigm shift in our thinking and life experience, let alone manifest it, because the ego is not interested in anything outside of its safe and well-worn paths.*

Very likely, if you've diligently mined Your Past and Your Present Serious and Significant Events or Influences, you've noticed that your Self Expression Directives not only point you toward the emergence of your greater Self but may also imply ways in which your Shine may be of service to others based on your unique journey.

For example, if you look at the Self Expression Directives from some of my past and present serious and significant events or influences as well as my comprehensive Puzzle Pieces of Purpose (compiled in Appendix C), is it any wonder that I'm writing this book or building a community to serve folks in transforming their Morassive Thrust of Midlife? Clearly, helping others clean out the big, midlife swamp is something I was designed to do!

Life is an exciting business, and most exciting when it is lived for others.
—Helen Keller

I assert that I co-created and co-sculpted my whole Front Forty, like Winston Churchill, as "preparation for this hour and this trial." And, guess what? I assert that you co-created and co-sculpted your whole Front Forty for *something,* too.

A Presence and You

The sculpting Presence with whom we have the opportunity to consciously co-serve and co-create is anything you want to call it.

Your Higher Self	Bhagwan
Divine Intelligence	Elohim
Nature	Jesus
God	Allah
Higher Power	Almighty
Universal Intelligence	All-Powerful
Yahweh	Great Spirit
Krishna	You Name It

Pick your own term of higher-intelligence endearment. In the words of Marianne Williamson, "It doesn't matter what you call it. It just matters that you call." Given that A Presence, which we seek to embrace, is beyond the natural, physical world, we can even call it the Supernatural, which simply means inexplicable by natural law. You don't even have to call "It" anything because what we call "It" doesn't necessarily reveal what A Presence is. So, for the moment, let's simply consider that one way to conceive of A Presence might be "all that is unseen and unknown," including all that lies in the sub-conscious, which is also beyond our handy, physical-senses access.

That what we now see did not come from anything that can be seen.
—St. Paul

Your fullest possibility for reaping a rich harvest and flying high in the Back Forty will be elevated if you can find a way to acknowledge that *something greater* is at work here than merely ego—beyond you, beneath you, behind you and/or within you. If you're feeling some resistance and it helps, just entertain "A Presence" as a hypothetical research question and approach the remainder of this Embrace as a consciously designed R & D experiment.

To address any concern upfront, know that I am not attempting to religiously convert you. This isn't about religion. You don't have to believe in anything. I just ask that you be *open to the possibility* that a higher aspect of your Self or of existence in general is available for you to tap into in a greater way.

I fully realize that many people have experienced some of their most impactful Serious and Significant Events or Influences specifically around religious or dogmatic belief systems, organizations or individuals. Left un-Be Caused, those incidents may continue to color and limit your access to "It," an internal source of wisdom, guidance and power to which this Embrace will point and invite you to open up to. So, for sure, you don't want to leave those serious and significant events or influences unanalyzed. They, too, are ripe to be transformed to enable an unprecedented Back Forty.

The wound is the place where the Light enters you. —*Rumi*

As I've said, each of us defines our own truth, but I personally stand for the *spiritual* basis of what you and I are here to do and achieve in this particular lifetime. Spirit is within us in whatever way we understand or conceive it to be. I'm simply restating a basic tenet that many live by: something bigger than me, my small s self, and I is contributing to the running of this show. Call It whatever you want, but there's *Something* beyond your Puzzle Pieces of Purpose at work here, and it is with that *Something* that you want to consciously align and co-create. An untapped storehouse—a Source— of infinite, co-creative power is waiting for you. Think about it: proactively designing laboratory experiments, consciously cultivating Self Expression Directives, all with the awareness of a powerful, co-creative Presence in cahoots! The possibilities are endless.

If you are empowered by The Back Forty philosophy, then why not dive into the unseen from which you co-created it all?

Embrace A Presence.

In doing so, you'll discover the equally co-creative power you possess for similarly designing your life moving forward—albeit consciously this time.

If you got to this point in the Back Forty Embraces without your own personal faith system being encroached upon, I've accomplished my intention, which is to offer this

> *Call It whatever you want, but there's* **Something** *beyond your* **Puzzle Pieces of Purpose** *at work here, and it is with that* **Something** *that you want to consciously align and co-create.*

material in a way that reaches the widest audience. Yet, at this point, for my Self to move forward and a Back Forty of purposeful direction to ensue, I must declare that I cannot personally fulfill on the grandest idea of my life being realized by relying solely on my own will, abilities, resources, and best-thinking, nor even by shifting around my Puzzle Pieces of Purpose while engaging in Purposeful Practice.

I believe that my and your greater-yet-to-be must come from *Something* working *with* and *through us*.

Our goal, then becomes to find the best ongoing ways in which to have It take all that we've discerned logically in this wonderful Back Forty exploration and help us sort those pieces into meaningful purpose.

> *I believe that my and your greater-yet-to-be must come from* **Something** *working* **with** *and* **through us.**

That may sound oh-so-easy; yet, surrender is usually the toughest game in town. So, for the balance of this chapter and for the remainder of this book, I will focus on ways to enter into a surrendered Embrace of A Presence.

A Presence in Precession

First, let's explore two definitions of the word "Presence":

1. "Something (as a spirit) felt or believed to be present."
2. "The fact or condition of being present."[16]

Regarding the first definition, when you live from "because," you're simply buffeted about by the winds of woe, living reactively to your experiences. However, when you place your Self as "Be Cause" in the matter of your life situations and life path, you gain a different perspective. You revel in what life has provided you—laboratories, Self Expression Directives and other R & D findings—and begin to feel your Self in alignment with the It—"something (as a spirit) felt or believed to be present"—working behind the scenes *with* and *through* you. We might even say that this newly forming perception is a 90° or precessional outcome because things you originally perceived as for your harm were actually meant for your greater, Self-evolving good.

In this philosophy, while holding ourselves as "Be Cause," we subscribe to the idea that we had a laboratory-design hand in everything that has occurred; but that doesn't mean that we are *the* cause. We begin to sense that our Be Causes are a co-creative process with A Presence. Playfully, we might consider "It" to be the Lab Boss, or Growth Opportunity Director.

You've conducted experiments, co-designed with It. Though you didn't realize or embrace the perfection of those experiments as they were taking place, you can now see that everything happened for a reason: for the Discovery & Expression of who you came to be and what you came to do. So, A Presence can be held as your collaborative, intelligent partner in Back Forty design.

Regarding the second definition, "the fact or condition of being present," when you live an empowered and supported life, not only in your

---

16 *MerriamWebster.com.*

highly discerned Purposeful Practice but through the unseen world of guidance and direction from It (A Presence), the very way in which you show up in the world alters. Your physicality and countenance offer a uniquely inspiring and attractive energy with "attractive" meaning magnetic, not good looks (though you likely become better looking too).

> **As we let our own light shine, we unconsciously give other people permission to do the same. As we are liberated from our own fear, our presence automatically liberates others. —*Marianne Williamson***

Your "presence" makes a statement and a marked difference in the world, in and of It Self. Have you ever noticed certain folks walking into a room and everyone literally *feels* their uplifting presence? Sure, you have. Of course, there's also the opposite of that—when someone enters a room and the energy drops. Fortunately, a unifying, positive energy flow is available for all of us to channel, to be room uplifters versus drop-downers.

> *Your "presence" makes a statement and a marked difference in the world, in and of It Self.*

A great example of where both definitions of presence shaped a life is that of Buckminster Fuller. Bucky demonstrated that fulfillment, prosperity and legacy can be traced to doing work aligned with your own truths (which you've now discerned from your Front Forty of R & D) and for the highest and greatest good of all. In his own life, he modeled a willingness to "let go," so to speak, and allow something beyond himself to co-direct the show.

In Bucky's book *Critical Path* (1982), he described coming to terms with his own guiding "It," which he called "nature." As an architect (among many other professions), his gifts, talents and values involved raising people's consciousness by improving their experience in the environments in which they moved and lived.

He wrote:

It seemed clear that if I undertook ever more humanly favorable physical-environment-producing artifact developments that in fact did improve the chances of all humanity's successful development, it was quite possible that nature would support my efforts. . .

. . .I must so commit myself and must depend upon nature providing the physical means of realization of my invented environment-advantaging artifacts.

Basically, he sought to forward the greater good of mankind through environmental design efforts and made an assumption that, in doing so, his efforts and needs would be supported by the Universe. Of course, that was a big assumption. Yet, a life of service and difference-making usually calls for some big assumptions or at least big attunement with *something* beyond oneself.

Bucky noted that no other human could validate his choices. Only "nature" could prove his assumptions valid. But he also recognized that he would need to pay close attention to the feedback from nature: to watch and see which of his efforts were supported and which weren't.

He continued:

I assumed that nature would "evaluate" my work as I went along. If I was doing what nature wanted done, and if I was doing it in promising ways, permitted by nature's principles, I would find my work being economically sustained—and vice versa, in which latter negative case I must quickly cease doing what I had been doing and seek logically alternative courses until I found the new course that nature signified her approval of by providing for its physical support.

I suggest you research Buckminster Fuller to see how his plan of a co-created, purposeful life played out. Interestingly, his particular choice in how to live came only after a particular "suicide" experience he underwent at age thirty-two. Experiencing his own version of "midlife opportunity" after his young daughter had died and he lost his job, he contemplated suicide so that his family could benefit from a life insurance payment.

Wikipedia says of him:

Fuller said that he had experienced a profound incident which would provide direction and purpose for his life. He felt as though he was suspended several feet above the ground enclosed in a white sphere of light. A voice spoke directly to Fuller, and declared: "From now on you need never await temporal attestation to your thought. You think the truth. You do not have the right to eliminate yourself. You do not belong to you. You belong to the Universe. Your significance will remain forever obscure to you, but you may assume that you are fulfilling your role if you apply yourself to converting your experiences to the highest advantage of others."

Fuller stated that this experience led to a profound re-examination of his life. He ultimately chose to embark on "an experiment, to find what a single individual [could] contribute to changing the world and benefiting all humanity."

This may sound familiar: apparently victimy events delivering one to a midlife opportunity, followed by a lifetime re-examination and then consciously designed experiments. Heard that story before?

Bucky then went on to experiment with thinking and acting differently.

I then realized that I could commit an exclusively "ego" suicide —a personal ego "throwaway"—if I swore, to the best of my ability, never again to recognize and yield to the voice of wants only of "me". . .[17]

---

17 *Buckminster Fuller,* Anthology for the New Millennium

Does this sound like any idea of "death of the old self [that] needs to take place so a new Self can take the lead" that you've ever heard of?

Here's why I use Bucky's life experience as an example. He modeled an effective "after-life"—after the death of the ego—and demonstrated what's possible for all of us through "egocide." Think about it. Suicide takes you off the playing field. However, egocide not only leaves you playing, it allows a greater YOU to play, and serve, in even bigger ways.

The ego is sacred territory to most people. Talk about someone's ego, and it's as if you're talking about their mother. Funny enough, in many ways, you are.

> *Think about it. Suicide takes you off the playing field. However, egocide not only leaves you playing, it allows a greater YOU to play, and serve, in even bigger ways.*

Your ego is deeply attached to and replete with your personality and identity, most of which was birthed from your Front Forty laboratory experiments. If you're now choosing to truly take on a new Back Forty skin, then what's inside of that skin must reflect that newness. The old, small self must make way for the expanded, perhaps-yet-unknown, yet-to-be-expressed-through-you, larger Self.

Bucky demonstrated that allowing the ego to die is a sacrifice we can all choose to make so that a higher Self can intensify within us. It can then use us for Its own purposes, which It can and will validate, and even fund. And, remember what Bucky was told: that his particular purpose and significance would be forever obscure to him, but he would be doing his job in merely converting his experiences to the wellbeing of others (i.e., moving forward and adding value).

Of course, Bucky is not the only example of this collaborative relationship with the Universe. The lives of many known and unknown difference-makers reflect this principle. Yet, Bucky's concept of Precession (discussed in "Embrace 6: Your Purpose") with all of its ramifications for purposeful, second-half living makes him a ripe and relevant testament to what's possible from just such a reconstitution of one's Self.

The main implications of Bucky's example for your own Purpose-Feeling Precession, when you begin to embrace and align with A Presence operating with and through you, are:

1. It's important to develop your attunement (getting "in tune") in discerning how and in what ways your path is being supported (or not) by A Presence. Your work and activities become not so much about you or your personal desires and goals as much as about what "It" also endorses. This may require breaking up your old self-concept in terms of the roles, habits or ways of being and doing in which you've perceived yourself as either capable or not in the past so that your collaboratively designed and directed Self can rise and shine.

2. As a factor of attunement, it's critical that you develop your internal and external listening and observation skills. Hearing guidance from within—from the unseen—is the only validation you require to make your own bold assumptions and step forward in new directions. At the same time, observing guidance from without (the course-correcting playground of the Universe) gives you a truing mechanism for continual adjustment. Thus, you must grow in your ability to perceive and follow or act upon the right signals both from within and from without.

3. As a requirement of internal listening, you'll want to grow more in touch with your feelings and develop the ability to discern feelings of fear based on unthought reactionary "wisdom" of the past from feelings of guidance and intuition based on openness and receptivity to life being your friend. Guidance and intuition increasingly become your Back Forty tools of direction, replacing all the head-logic you've depended on for a lifetime.

4. Focusing on guidance and intuition moves you more toward the heart and away from fear. As mentioned in Embrace 6, Bucky transformed his relationship to earning a living and found his needs being "unsolicitedly" provided for. You too may begin to let go of your clinging, fear-based attachment to material needs and "stuff" through knowing that what you need can and will be placed before you at the moment you truly need it, even if at "the absolutely last second."

5. As a result of all the above, you can and will develop the courage to take actions consciously and deliberately, proactively establishing laboratories of Discovery and Expression, boldly declaring your Self as a "play first" student, and letting It become an increasingly present, collaborative sidekick— *A Presence* in your everyday experience.

> *Guidance and intuition increasingly become your Back Forty tools of direction, replacing all the head-logic you've depended on for a lifetime.*

A practice of Purpose-Feeling Precession supported by A Presence goes even further in taking away the pressure to find some specific "true" purpose. Precession gives you the liberty to co-create your purpose and allow for its continual formulation simply by moving towards what your Self is called to do, while adjusting and course-correcting as you go about your Purposeful Practice. You'll soon realize that your purpose and your path to it are unique, making it less likely that you will get stuck following someone else's picture or path. That's not to say that you won't engage in joint laboratory experiments with others and enjoy the laboratory assistance of groups and teachers along the way, but it will always be for the greater awareness of who *you* came here to be and what *you* came here to do.

Even if, and when, you join a cause or organization to contribute and make a difference, you'll be doing so inside of your own unique and individualized Purpose-Feeling Precession. That alone makes the cause or organization all yours to co-creatively dance alongside A Presence within, playfully, passionately and purposefully.

> *Precession gives you the liberty to co-create your purpose and allow its continual formation simply by moving towards what your Self is called to do, while adjusting and course-correcting as you go about your Purposeful Practice.*

**When I don't know who I am, I serve you.
When I know who I am, you and I are one.
—*Ramayana*, Hanuman to Rama**

Most important, you'll learn to let go of the need for control and just start moving forward with massive action. As long as your action adds value, your precessional impact (90° side effects) will come about to bless the world simply from your forward movement. Purpose-Feeling Precession infused and partnered with A Presence is, therefore, your main objective.

When you are inspired by some great purpose, some extraordinary project, all your thoughts break their bonds: Your mind transcends limitations, your consciousness expands in every direction, and you find yourself in a new, great and wonderful world. Dormant forces, faculties and talents become alive, and you discover yourself to be a greater person by far than you ever dreamed yourself to be. —*Patañjali*

TOOLS FOR TAPPING INTO IT

By way of your heart, mind and soul, let's explore and develop ways and means for plugging into your own, all-providing, infinitely intelligent, directionally focused, Back Forty-fostering "It." The more you are in tune with It, the more It can do with and through you. So, for the balance of this chapter and the book, we will explore some ways in which you may increase your ability to embrace A Presence and, thereby,

Allow

Your Purpose to Align

and

A Presence to Shine.

Full disclosure: I'm no guru with some ultimate answer for best aligning with A Presence and tapping into It. I'm just a guy on the bus of life like you and can't know your particularly best access points. Yet, through a lifetime of experience as a spiritual and personal development junkie, I've encountered, experimented with, engaged in, practiced and utilized a decent array of methods to expand my awareness beyond the self and into the Self. I haven't done everything, but I've been exposed to my fair share and continue to be an avid student of new modes of connection.

So, I'll share several tools that have supported me—some foundational ones in heavy detail and others with lighter descriptions. Ultimately, use what works for you and leave the rest. However, I encourage you to be open to experimentation, to "play first," giving all the methods that call to you a decent road test before possibly scrapping them. You may find that one or more of them will become lifelong companions. Others that you only test and toy with could very well put you on a playing field that opens you up to other information or methods that It directs you to, because what we need to know or hear often comes in circuitous ways. It's simply about trusting your Self to explore *new* ways to partake of *new* directions by utilizing these several accesses to Source—A Presence beyond you in scope but accessible to you through the core of your being.

I encourage you to reach out to share with me some of the new discoveries you find on your unique path, so I can be blessed by our joint and reciprocal efforts toward Allowing A Presence to Shine and Our Purpose to Align.

Meditation

Regardless of any religious and/or spiritual influences you may have from your first half of life and no matter what directions you'll pursue in your Back Forty, learning to turn your focus within through various forms of meditation can only serve to form a stronger relationship between you and It, giving you access to an enormous field of potentiality.

In my coaching practice, I've been called into corporate organizations to help "problem children" fit better within a company's culture, as a last-ditch effort before they're fired. Though highly regarded in terms of the professional value they may bring to the table, these individuals often stretch what management can bear in terms of behavior, negative effects on staff, and the general downer mood they foster.

My initial work with these "bad boys/girls" always involves a variety of introspective processes, such as 360° evaluations and other assessments. However, I often giggle inside when I discover that the most effective tool in facilitating these massive personality turn-arounds is simply teaching these hellraisers how to meditate!

The ego is birthed early in life from the limitless variety of serious and significant events or influences we've each experienced, which, when held in the because/victim fashion, help establish personality and our presentation in the world. Without growing a certain self-awareness to hold us in check, we simply operate from subconscious instincts, fears, drives and compensatory mechanisms born from those early experiences.

> *Learning to turn your focus within through various forms of meditation can only serve to form a stronger relationship between you and It.*

One of the main reasons the ego runs amok creating the strife and negativity we see in the lives of others (and ourselves) is that, without an internal checks-and-balances system with It at its center, ego is the only one running the show. Like a popular movie from years ago, it's a child "home alone" without any responsible adults present.

Conscious thought doesn't happen without effort. Without an intention toward greater awareness, the ego generally operates on autopilot. A good metaphor for relating to such an unconscious existence is the story of deaf, dumb and blind Helen Keller. At the age of seven, she was given the gift of language through the persistent efforts of Anne Mansfield Sullivan. Learning sign language and realizing that everything had a name gave Helen a whole new world that literally didn't exist before. She described her life prior to language as "only darkness and stillness. . .without past or future." Without language, she operated by instinct, like an animal. With language, she became a unique, sentient being.

In the same way, meditation and the other alignment tools presented here provide an intentional avenue to enable an awareness of Self and to break out of unconscious, rote and instinctual ways of being and living. It is a language of the soul.

Meditation provides access to ways of thinking and being outside of the default. The following is an example of one upgrade in consciousness you might gain from meditation. Someone cuts you off in traffic and your immediate reaction is to flick a finger at them; but instead you are able to ask yourself, "Hmm, what's really going on here? Why am I so on edge that I can be so easily swayed away from my peace?"

Of course, none of us is perfect—as I'm always apt to demonstrate beyond a shadow of a doubt—and we can all be particularly raw and reactive at certain times. Yet, if you learn to spend more time seeking peace within your Self, the chances increase of your both reacting more peacefully to the outside world and proactively bringing more peace to that outside world.

Your life becomes a masterpiece when you learn to master peace.
—Unknown

How does experiencing and bringing more peace with you everywhere you go relate to Your Purpose? Simple: more peace, more flow; more peace, more joy; more peace, more availability and receptivity to direction; more peace, more right action; more peace, more accessibility for something greater than you to work with and through you.

　　Basically, Your Purpose faces a steeper, uphill battle of being realized when there's tension in and around you, your relationships and your surroundings; when your life is all drama. You want to subdue the drama and foster an environment that invites peace. The more you take responsibility for your own life drama, actively seeking to decrease tension and Be Cause your own situations and circumstances instead of hiding in the default of becauses, the more you create a space in which It can collaborate and help redirect the show.

> *If you learn to spend more time seeking peace within your Self, the chances increase of your both reacting more peacefully to the outside world and proactively bringing more peace to that outside world.*

You do not need to leave your room.
Remain sitting at your table and listen.
Do not even listen, simply wait.
Do not even wait, be still and solitary.
The world will freely offer itself to you
to be unmasked, it has no choice.
It will roll in ecstasy at your feet.
　　　　　　　　　　—Franz Kafka

> *The more you take responsibility for your own life drama, actively seeking to decrease tension and Be Cause your own situations and circumstances instead of hiding in the default of becauses, the more you create a space in which It can collaborate and help redirect the show.*

　　Rather than have your daily direction dictated by the busy-manic, glee-manic, survival-manic, or other-manic purpose impostors, give A Presence the time and attention necessary to speak to you, to guide you. This, however, (and here's the rub) requires a huge shift in thinking. Rather than regard all of your *doing*—the endless tasks, reminders and to-do lists

Give A Presence the time and attention necessary to speak to you, to guide you.

of incessant activity—as the most important aspect of your day and plunging headfirst into *doing-ness*, set aside and invest time in your Collaborative Creatorship with A Presence. That time to *be is* just as, if not more important, than anything you'll do. *Being* enhances, if not trumps, *doing* every time.

So, what can we do to foster being? Try

- regularly scheduling time to sit in silence so that you can actually hear;
- repeating or contemplating an empowering affirmation, scripture or quote of some kind to plant new seeds of thought in your mind;
- stepping outside of your fixed, square surroundings and taking a walk in nature; and/or
- engaging in an activity that you find consistently relaxing, that eases your mind of concerns so that new, stress-free thoughts can enter.

Prayer, which I'll address later, is also a wonderful tool for tapping into It; but, even foundationally and beyond prayer, which is still an active *doing*, it is vital to *still the mind* and listen.

In addition to thinking that our perpetual activity is the answer, we often think that the answers we seek exist outside of us and we have to go get them from others. However, when we make a daily practice of listening beneath the monkey mind that has been running the show with all of its "best thinking" firing on all cylinders, we begin to hear an inner wisdom full of insight, pointing us in our most appropriate directions.

Slowing the mind doesn't come easily. Because of associative thinking (randomly linking one thought to another and another), our unchecked mind can run amuck and travel great distances of time and location within micro-seconds of a brain synapse. For example, in sitting to meditate some years ago, I closed my eyes, focused on my breath and then had a thought. . .

> **When we make a daily practice of listening beneath the monkey mind that has been running the show with all of its "best thinking" firing on all cylinders, we begin to hear an inner wisdom full of insight, pointing us in our most appropriate directions.**

. . .of that email I didn't respond to yesterday, the one where they are waiting for my proposal to speak, which then sparked a memory of the guy I didn't call back late last night, the one who will help me on my show ideas, and he's in Orange County and I want to meet him, and "Oh Yes!" isn't there a meeting of the professional association I want to look into down there tomorrow? Maybe I can schedule to meet with him then, but I haven't heard back from the association president, so I wonder if that deal is going to come through. Boy, I really hope so! I could use more exposure because things have been slow lately as I've focused on developing my speaking business. This darn economy has so many good people scared that they are holding back on getting the help they need, which is making me scared because I need to help people to make a living. I want to get more savings in the bank for my son's college, as well as pay back my folks for the custody-suit loan and, man, this financial challenge has been hanging on a long time. . .

On and on it goes, all in the course of milliseconds!

Though sometimes consciously and productively used in inventive, creative endeavors such as when brainstorming a new brand or product solution, unchecked, daily-life associative thinking is a fierce and wild animal. We are subjected to it ongoingly, which causes a great deal of distraction and ineffectiveness. This is especially true in the Digital Age, when we're barraged by triggers from every direction.

Don't take my word for it; give it a try right now! Close your eyes, sit in a relaxed posture and try to focus only on the breath coming in and out of your nose. Think of nothing else, not even of this book or the fact that you're doing an exercise in the book, and see how long you can focus *only* on the feel of the breath coming in and out of your nose, cool on the inhale and warm on the exhale.

How long did you last? Did you start by focusing solely on your breath? Did you even notice when the first thought came up to distract you from the breath? If so, how did you deal with it? Did you let it go as soon as it came along, or did you engage with the thought? Did you allow it to take you to other related thoughts? Did you simply fall asleep?

I've practiced daily meditation with only a few periods of hiatus for nearly thirty years, and I still get swept away by flurries of associative thinking. Of course, I try to be diligent. But taming the wild beast of the mind is no simple task and generally requires years of practice.

Perhaps you'll never achieve some elusive state of bliss or nirvana during meditation. That's like hoping to one day find a unicorn. But you'll still gain tremendously by simply noticing, while learning to detach from, the constant chatter of the associative-thinking, ego-directed mind. The relentless chatterbox and its incessant clogging of your mind's eyes and ears can block you from seeing and hearing newly. It can prevent you from obtaining guidance in your role as Collaborative Creator. Meditation can counterbalance or even neutralize the noise, helping you to gently build a muscle for managing your mind without succumbing to monkey chatter.

Though blissful, nirvana-inducing meditation sounds like an attractive goal, your access to all that The Back Forty has in store for you can be gained simply by cultivating the ability to be still. From that stillness, you open your Self up for greater direction.

Enlightenment is being immersed in and surrounded by peace at all moments in our lives. —*Nisargadatta*

With consistent and diligent practice of quieting your busy mind for five, ten, fifteen, twenty or thirty minutes of meditation once or twice a day, you'll open your Self up to a greater Mind of peace from which to gain centeredness and direction.

There's yourself, and then there's your Self. There's your mind, and then there's Mind. Your playful, passionate and purposeful Back Forty is best managed and directed by the dynamic duo of Mind/Self versus mind/self.

> *Meditation can counterbalance or even neutralize the noise, helping you to gently build a muscle for managing your mind without succumbing to monkey chatter.*

As mentioned earlier, there are many forms of mediation. They range from focusing on the complete quieting of the mind to the practice of reciting mantras or scriptures and from sitting in initially uncomfortable floor positions to active movement through nature. People ascribe the term "meditation" to a whole host of mental and physical expressions.

Winston Churchill wrote on the therapeutic benefits of painting, which took his mind away from the more serious concerns of wartime leadership. Thomas Edison used to fish alone for an hour a day, without bait so the fish would leave him alone too. Then, he could think. Albert Einstein used a form of "analytical meditation" to sort through great insights into physics and the workings of the Universe.

Those are more active types of meditation, which we might each find our own versions of. However, the practice of doing nothing—no thoughts, no distractions, no activities, no to-dos, *nothing*—is a path to awareness that we can all benefit from. It requires that we consider "quiet time" to be an investment rather than a luxury you only get to enjoy once all the to-dos are handled. If you wait until you have enough time to meditate, that time will never come.

What a thing it is to sit absolutely alone, in the forest, at night, cherished by this wonderful, unintelligible perfectly innocent speech, the most comforting speech in the world, the talk that rain makes by itself all over the ridges, and the talk of the watercourses everywhere in the hollows! Nobody started it, nobody is going to stop it. It will talk as long as it wants, this rain. As long as it talks, I am going to listen. —Thomas Merton

Embrace 7—Homeplay Alignment Practice 1
Meditation Trial Run (Posing for Still Life)

Whether you're currently engaged in a regular practice of meditation now, have known about it for years but never gotten around to it or are just becoming acquainted with the idea, I recommend devoting at least some period of each day to quieting the mind in these ways.

A Place

Set up your environment to support the mediation time you've allotted to be safe from distraction. Arrange your space and schedule your time to be free of anything that could disrupt a complete span of focused "nothing." Find a quiet location and, if necessary, use earplugs to drown out any nearby noise. Tell your family, roommates or friends that you're not to be interrupted and, if you feel uncomfortable doing so, just find some place outside of the house, such as in a park or on a balcony. Turn off all cell phones, instant messages, social media and computers, anything that could pull your consciousness back towards busyness and all those things *to do*.

Down the road, when you've gained some mastery, you may not require totally quiet spaces or earplugs and may even find yourself meditating in the middle of rowdy chaos! However, give yourself the healthy benefit of a low-distraction start. You likely already have so much noise going on in your head that you won't want any added, external challenge.

Meditation is not contemplation either, because it is not thinking at all—consistent, inconsistent, crazy, sane. It is not thinking at all; it is witnessing. It is just sitting silently deep within yourself, looking at whatsoever is happening inside and outside both. Outside there is traffic noise, inside there is also traffic noise—the traffic in the head. So many thoughts, trucks and buses of thoughts and trains and airplanes of thoughts, rushing in every direction. But you are simply sitting aloof, unconcerned, watching everything with no evaluation. —*Osho*

A Time

If at all possible, set up a time structure. You'll trust the process and your practice more long-term when it's regularly scheduled and reliable versus a willy-nilly, catch-as-catch-can effort. Get ready for your meditation by setting a gentle alarm reminder to go off at the end of your time so that you're not distracted by checking how long you've been meditating. Make sure it's not a harsh or disturbing alarm.

Focus

Once your space and time has been arranged, settle yourself into a simple, comfortable position, sitting erect on a couch or chair with your hands in your lap. You do not need to sit in some uncomfortable Eastern, mystical, or contortionistic position on the floor because it may distract from your intention, which is to have no distractions. Avoid lying down, however, as this can bring about sleep, which, though relaxing, is not the primary goal.

Begin with five minutes at the beginning and end of your day. In the default and rote busyness of life, it's an honorable commitment to invest even five minutes, so don't go too fast or expect too much of yourself too quickly. That would just be more of your ego trying to "win" or conquer something. You could quickly burn yourself out with frustration. Over time, as you become more accustomed to the practice of stilling the mind, you can gradually increase the amount of time you set aside.

Don't, however, make yourself wrong if you do, in fact, fall asleep when first beginning to meditate. The process is new to the body and the mind, so the first reaction to such non-active, non-thought may be for you to check out completely. Gradually, over time, you'll be able to maintain an easy, awake and relaxed awareness, supported by focusing on the breath.

The goal is to be awake, aware and simply still, so that the mind can slow down. You'll not only get used to but look forward to the experience of pursuing an awake and aware mind without chatter. When the default, never-ending chatter is experienced as passively as a soft breeze or light and airy clouds moving overhead, you'll have the opportunity to experience BEing beyond the usual attachment to your smaller self. The small self wants you to notice and run with the chatterbox thoughts, but the larger Self begins to exert mastery over those thoughts, being centered and unmoved.

The psyche is transformed or developed by the relationship of the ego to the unconscious. —Carl Jung

It will help to always remember that there's nowhere to *get to*. Nowhere is not a destination our driven-for-something-to-show-for-ourselves mind is geared towards. Slowly, you'll experience an internal reorientation, allowing yourself to be non-goal oriented and non-objective focused while still conscious.

Your practice is to be "Now Here."

Intention

Just before starting, declare for your Self your intention for the next five or more minutes. Use your own words, perhaps something like

It's my intention to spend the next [x] minutes allowing myself to practice stillness. I'll allow myself to *practice* with no attachment to a result of any kind. I'll take it easy and simply focus on the breath coming in and out of my nose, watching only it, feeling only it.

When thoughts of any kind arise to take my focus away from the breath, I'll simply notice the distracting thought as quickly as possible and then refocus on my breath. I won't judge myself if and when my mind strays. I'll simply devote this time to judgment-free awareness and a still mind. I give myself the right to merely practice.

Then, do that. Simply *practice*. You might even call this your daily period of "practicing A Presence."

As I said, start small and build up over time. Benefits will start to accrue from devoting time each day. They'll range from simply feeling more peaceful or centered throughout your day to more effective and focused in your activities to calmer and more relaxed in your interactions with others. One bonus effect may even include the faint hearing of an internal voice of greater Self-compassion and direction than you've ever heard before.

Beware: the ego will try to jump in and have you judge yourself and your meditation practice! That's because the ego knows its days of absolute control over you are numbered if you catch on to this powerful tool. Persevere, be gentle with your Self and keep investing time into developing your sense of Self beyond the ego.

> *Slowly, you'll experience an internal reorientation, allowing yourself to be non-goal oriented and non-objective focused while still conscious. Your practice is to be "Now Here."*

Meditation becomes one of an increasing number of areas in Back Forty life in which you grow in mastery but do not master and one of many Back Forty mountains you begin to scale but can never summit. You can never "win" at meditation or graduate from it, but its development as a tool in your Back Forty awakening to A Presence is significant.

Over time, while developing increased compassion for yourself and your associative mind, you'll begin to notice some random, quiet moments in which you are free from the chatterbox. With luck, your human *doing* results

> *Meditation becomes one of an increasing number of areas in Back Forty life in which you grow in mastery but do not master and one of many Back Forty mountains you begin to scale but can never summit.*

orientation will give way to your human *being* as you start to hear something calling to you above and beyond the frantic activity.

Now you must learn that only infinite patience produces immediate effects. This is the way in which time is exchanged for eternity. Infinite patience calls upon infinite love.
—A Course in Miracles

Practice

Initially, give yourself a specific number of days in which to practice meditation, to fully explore it so that you don't cut yourself off just when you might be on the verge of a worthwhile experience or insight. I suggest thirty days to begin with. Don't feel the need to ramp up your time so that you'll "accomplish" twice as much each day. This is specifically *not* about accomplishing; and if you bite off too much too soon, you may simply stop altogether.

Metaphorically, consider this practice to be like discovering and exploring a local park in a brand-new town to which you've just moved. Give yourself five or ten minutes daily and don't try to see the whole park all at once. Just make your daily visit to the "park" a routine.

Later, consider the underlying principle (not the specific durations) described in an interview with Mahatma Gandhi. When he mentioned that he meditated two hours each day, the interviewer asked, "What do you do when you are too busy to meditate?" Gandhi replied, "I meditate four hours a day."

Meditation is a good, consistent Back Forty tool. *Just be willing* for this practice to enhance your life in unknown ways. If you've known of meditation for years, have practiced in the past or are a current practitioner, be willing to have a new experience. If you've lapsed, forgive yourself and recommit. Stepping away from practices that have supported your well-being in the past can actually be a blessing because upon returning you get to appreciate, all over again, the benefits of having good, consistent tools in your life.

So, now, find a quiet spot to be alone and sit quietly for five minutes. If you have a watch or phone alarm, set it. Then close your eyes and pay attention to your breath as it enters and leaves your nose. When thoughts come, turn your attention back to your breath and nose.

Now write about your experience in your Back Forty Freedom Fliers Journal and schedule your regular meditation times for the next thirty days.

> **I have discovered that all human evil comes from this, man's being unable to sit still in a room.**
>
> BLAISE PASCAL

> **Sitting is the gateway of truth to total liberation.**
>
>
>
> DOGEN

> **Be a spot on the ground where nothing is growing, where something might be planted, a seed, from the Absolute.**
>
> RUMI

No thought, no action, no movement, total stillness:
only thus can one manifest the true nature and law of things
from within and unconsciously, and at last
become one with heaven and earth.

LAO TZU

I exist as I am, that is enough,
If no other in the world be aware I sit content,
And if each and all be aware I sit content.
One world is aware, and by the far the largest to me,
and that is myself,
And whether I come to my own today or in
ten thousand or ten million years,
I can cheerfully take it now, or with equal cheerfulness,
I can wait.

WALT WHITMAN

Don't go outside your house to see flowers.
My friend, don't bother with that excursion.
Inside your body there are flowers.
One flower has a thousand petals.
That will do for a place to sit.
Sitting there you will have a glimpse of beauty
inside the body and out of it,
before gardens and after gardens.

KABIR

> ## To the mind that is still, the whole universe surrenders.
> LAO TZU

> ## "Rocks pray too," said Grandad. "Pebbles and boulders and old weathered hills. They are still and silent, and those are two important ways to pray."
>
> ❧
>
> DOUGLAS WOOD

> ## Watermelons and Zen students grow pretty much the same way. Long periods of sitting till they ripen and grow all juicy inside, but when you knock them on the head to see if they're ready, sounds like nothing's going on.
> PETER LEVITT

Weeding the Core Beliefs Garden

Having your second half/best half colored and enhanced by those things you've always really wanted—loving relationship/partnership, fulfilling career, abundance, optimum health and fitness, harmonious family ties, adventure and more—is, indeed, possible. It simply requires taking responsibility for your first half of research and development and paying attention to the Core Beliefs Garden that grew inside of your Front Forty *being-ness*.

Most of the time, we engage and interact with life on a surface level with our egoic drives, fears, judgments, automatic reactions and emotional triggers calling the shots. We rarely investigate to uncover the belief systems, and resulting ways of being, operating behind and underneath.

Greater Self-awareness, perception of the You beyond the automatic, chatterbox activity, will likely be one result of your continued practice of meditation. That Self-awareness will have you notice with greater discernment your thoughts and patterns of thinking.

If you want to go deeper, outside of your meditation practice itself, you can do so by beginning to uproot the very belief systems behind the monkey-mind thoughts and patterns of thinking.

To be playfully accurate, we might say that we "thought" more than we think. Having a thought doesn't mean you're actually engaged in thinking. Thoughts simply come and go, incessantly, all day long. You have no control over that, but you can begin to discern and even dismantle the old, antiquated belief systems behind your "thoughting," which in turn can have you more available *in the now, to the now*. And, being more present, you're free to actually think.

Playing off the metaphor of The Back Forty, that big, uncultivated, fertile patch of land behind the farm and the next half/best half of our lives

> *You can begin to discern and even dismantle the old, antiquated belief systems behind your "thoughting," which in turn can have you more available in the now, to the now. And, being more present, you're free to actually think.*

ahead, it's important to consider what you intend to cultivate and grow in your future. You can newly plant anything you want in this radical second half of play, passion and purpose. However, it pays to be mindful of *what* you tracked in with you from your Front Forty terrain, especially the existing belief systems (BS) stuck to the bottom of your boots.

You've already planted and cultivated a Core Beliefs Garden in your first half of life based on all that happened to you: your Serious and Significant Events or Influences and the familial and cultural environments in which you grew up and lived. Most of your Core Beliefs Garden grew out of "because" given that the seeds of those beliefs were planted without conscious consideration. For example, a deep subconscious conviction that "you can't trust men" or "you can't trust women" or "you can't trust x" wasn't consciously planted when a particular event happened to you, but it was planted nonetheless. Additionally, the Shrinking World dynamic explored in Embrace 6 provided more and more evidence for you to be "right" about the decisions you made about the way you are, the way others are, the way life is and the way you had better *be* to get along (e.g., funny, cautious, quiet, perfect).

Now, however, you're being given the opportunity to plant new seeds and *consciously* grow your Back Forty Beliefs Garden. Proactively designing your Core Beliefs Garden is foundational to what Back Forty crop you'll bring to fruition. As you contemplate what you'll nurture in your Back Forty, you want to be consciously aware of the substratum on which everything depends. So, don't track in what you don't want growing!

One way to assess what's stuck to the bottom of your boots is to take a Core Beliefs Inventory. To become an observer of one's Self requires a high level of consciousness; nonetheless, a Core Beliefs Inventory is a bit like covert, counteragent espionage because attempting to see how the mind operates while still operating in that mind is tricky business. However, some simple practices can help you accomplish it.

Have you ever walked down the street or been at an event where you think you recognize someone and do a double take: a quick, surprised second glance back to catch another look? That's similar to what you're attempting in meditation and through a Core Beliefs Inventory—a double take on the mind itself, sneakily catching the mind being the mind so as to observe how it operates. Sometimes what you see isn't so pretty, so it can be helpful to have some understanding and compassion for where you've been and how your experiences have shaped you. Although there is no definitive "truth" about the way anything in life *is*, the illusion of "truth" unconsciously runs things from a fixed position until the illusion is unmasked. Accordingly, it's refreshing and hopeful to know that your Front Forty Core Beliefs only run your life until you become aware that they're simply beliefs and not "the truth." Beliefs may be "true for you" in the moment, but beliefs can change and can be changed.

I liken how Core Beliefs operate to the dynamics of superstition. Something is only recognized as a superstition once it's revealed to be a made-up belief. Before it's recognized as a superstition, it's basically running the subconscious as "the truth." It's just "the way it is." For example, if I unconsciously believe a black cat crossing the sidewalk in front of me bodes for a bad day, I will unthinkingly have a bad day because of it. However, if I realize that the supposed bad luck arising from a black cat or from stepping on a crack or spilling salt or walking under a ladder are only superstitions, then they have no effect on me. A superstition unmasked has no power.

From the Back Forty discovery process you've engaged in thus far, it's hopefully becoming clear that before you were given the opportunity to Be Cause them, many shaping and defining incidents from your past formed your psyche and ways of being in the world. What situations and people to avoid; how to behave; what you're capable of; and what you should or shouldn't expect from yourself, from others, from life—all of these decisions and more—were made early on from the belief in your being a victim to people and events.

> *It's refreshing and hopeful to know that your Front Forty Core Beliefs only run your life until you become aware that they're simply beliefs and not "the truth."*

Just because you've hopefully begun to gain power over those serious and significant events or influences on a conscious, Be Cause level doesn't mean the seeds they planted so many years ago won't continue to germinate and grow more weeds if given the soil to do so. Although you may now consciously declare your independence from the formative "stuff" that happened to you, left unchecked, the Core Beliefs Garden—what forms and grows in the subconscious—may still overrun what you are intending to grow in your Back Forty.

So, in preparing your Back Forty patch of life for a completely new crop, you cannot stop at the conscious level. That would be like mowing down the surface remains of previous growth without fully plowing up the old roots and bringing air and light to the soil underneath. Only when you get to the roots of your unconscious beliefs do you have a chance of eradicating those that do not serve your Back Forty purposes.

The first step in getting to the root causes is to begin to question why you believe the things you do. The next step is to start playfully challenging those beliefs (superstitions). A conscious, Back Forty-style Beliefs Garden inventory and replanting practice prepares the ground for second half/best half experiences, distinct and radically transformed from your Front Forty life and times.

In the realm of psychology, the term "post-traumatic growth" is associated with some core belief inventory models. The theory suggests that supposedly "bad stuff" happens to us. Then, we grow to become stronger and better human beings through the resilience and fortitude developed as a result of such trauma. In the process of that growth, we often shed old beliefs that once kept us trapped.

If you research stories of individuals who experienced something traumatic or life-altering and then went on to live lives of new awareness, you'll see this pattern. Examples include former gang and cult members, etc. After a defining incident of some type, they suddenly had the ability to distinguish their old belief systems as no longer true for them.

We in The Back Forty would name this phenomenon differently. Instead of giving it a because-based name that places emphasis on what happened *to* us, we would more likely call it "co-created Self-expression expansion." Clearly, the Back Forty interpretation offers a more proactive stance. The psychological explanation is that you were, indeed, a victim but grew stronger in your reaction to it. The Back Forty philosophy claims that you designed firsthand what took place to "Be Cause" your growth.

Regardless of which perspective chosen to describe it, the phenomenon results in more freedom. If you make a practice of unearthing and dismantling your beliefs behind or originating from the "bad stuff" that happened to you, you'll become more present and available to life as it *can* be. You'll experience fewer limiting and constricting beliefs and more of A Presence can seep through.

Various core beliefs inventory assessments constructed by PhDs and psychiatrists are available online; I won't attempt to duplicate those assessments

> *If you make a practice of unearthing and dismantling your beliefs behind or originating from the "bad stuff" that happened to you, you'll become more present and available to life as it can be. You'll experience fewer limiting and constricting beliefs and more of A Presence can seep through.*

here. However, I fully encourage your researching some of these core beliefs inventory protocols and engaging in them.

Here, I'll only offer one simple tool, which comes from a more ontological approach than a psychological one. Ontology, the study of *being,* is a body of inquiry that has engaged analytical minds since the days of Plato. The basic principle of ontology is that most of our core beliefs project themselves through how we *be* in life, not just what we say or even what we do.

Who you are speaks so loudly I can't hear what you're saying.
—*Ralph Waldo Emerson*

Darrell's Core Beliefs Garden Inventory

By way of example, here's an ontologically-based Core Beliefs Inventory I conducted for myself some years ago in and around the area of romantic relationship. Even with all of the Front Forty personal development studies and programs I'd experienced, I hadn't produced the breakthrough I wanted in the area of finding my, what I'll call, Divine Right Partner. One evening, spurred on by an ontologically oriented seminar I was attending, I grabbed a spiral notebook and began, through free association, to write down as many answers as I could to the following question: who or how do I *be* about dating?

Nope. No typos in that question. It's just wording that doesn't sound like a typical question. Don't get caught up in the semantics. What I was basically asking myself was, "How is it that I hold dating in my heart of hearts or psyche of psyches? What are my deepest ideas, concepts, beliefs, fears, questions, concerns, doubts, interpretations, etc. about dating? And, therefore, who or how do I show up *being* around dating?" My ideas around each of those internal elements defines who *I am* at my core about dating, and that definition sources who I'm *being*.

Here's what I discovered when I allowed myself ample time (and many pages) to free-associate many answers to the posed question: who or how do I *be* about dating?

But first, I'll ask you to forgive how my inventory was written; it has been extracted directly from the quickly recorded, chicken-scratch spiral I wrote it in. I didn't want to make it look "pretty" because self-digging isn't always pretty, and I want you to also feel free to be messy and unedited. *This is raw, vulnerable, judgmental and maybe even stupid stuff.* It came right out of my small, inner, protective-of-self world at the time: good, bad and ugly. Actually, mostly bad and ugly.

- Dating is hard. There are feelings of rejection and not-good-enough to be avoided and protected from, and then there are feelings of judgment of others and avoiding hurting others' feelings.
- Dating is not fun but a necessary task in order to find someone to be in a relationship with.
- It's hard to find someone to be in a relationship with.
- Everybody—them *and* me—have so many issues and scars and deep psychological and ontological and subconscious triggers and traps that finding someone I can fit with long term is impossible.
- Relationships are and require hard work involving intense and vigilant communication, clearing and completion, and real fun and joy can only take place when those elements are religiously honored.
- The gorgeous girls will be shallow.
- The really smart and/or funny girls will be plain and won't turn me on.
- Women older than me are to be avoided because their looks are on the downhill slide.

- Girls half my age wouldn't be interested in me and definitely wouldn't have depth, intelligence or maturity about life to be able to form a long-term and real relationship.
- Girls don't want sex as much as I do.
- Girls aren't as interested in adventurous and non-traditional sex and lifestyles.
- Women are unreliable and can't be trusted.
- Women don't want or wouldn't admit to wanting no-strings-attached sex.
- A woman can't really care about me if she's intimate with other men at the same time.
- I am not worthy of the best gal and I must learn to accept and make do with less than the best.
- I can't have a relationship work.
- I don't pick well.
- Love is dangerous, enemy territory.
- I have to be super confident to attract and keep a woman.

If anything I wrote from the depths of my fearful, small "s" self triggers you, you can choose to make room for my humanity or not. I dare say each of us has our own inner, protective and world-dissecting small s self, and engaging in any of these self-exploration processes is useless unless we're honest. Being honest doesn't make it right. It just makes it honest. And you can't clean house until you honestly acknowledge the dirt.

If you're a woman reading my dating beliefs inventory, you may laugh or be offended at my ignorance. If you're a man reading it, you may also laugh or even subscribe. But what you see in my inventory is a lot of unearthed core beliefs. Obviously, each of these raw statements represents an idea or decision that got planted into my Core Beliefs Garden at some point. For sure, I didn't come into this lifetime with these rigid views already in place. Stuff happened to plant them. Now, this type of Belief Inventory process doesn't always provide an immediate "Eureka!" insight, but it does stir the pot a bit, allowing the conscious mind to begin to slowly investigate and explore the workings of the often-irrational subconscious. That's what happened to me.

Clearly, each of the deeply-rooted statements of "truth" I uncovered put its own death knell on my prospects for a wonderful relationship. Yet, only a few days after the inventory, I began to zero in on this one particular idea: women are unreliable and can't be trusted. Upon greater reflection, this singular revelation stopped me cold in my tracks because I saw below it the belief that "I can't trust a woman with my heart."

I literally sat in amazement. For the first time, I realized that, despite all of my diligent and earnest efforts to meet "someone special," I had a Core Belief that from the outset rendered any possible romantic match dead in the water!

I can't trust a woman with my heart.

I didn't actively *think* that. I never even found myself *thoughting* that. Yet, I was absolutely *being* that.

Since my divorce, I experienced a string of relationships lasting six to twenty months each, totaling eight romantic relationships over the course of eighteen years. I became active on multiple dating sites and took every opportunity to meet a new person through the various venues in my life: church, personal development programs, conferences, coffee shops, etc. I was charming and affable and got into relationships with absolutely great women! Yet, nothing ever stuck. Go figure.

Granted, I thought I was *really* committed and believed I was earnestly doing everything in my power to find my princess. Yet, my dating activity itself was built upon sinking sand—a substratum of "I can't trust a woman with my heart." So, no house of relationship could ever stand the test of time. It would only last so long before a sinkhole would form and this or that partner would help my protection-focused egoic subconscious prove, once again, my unthought but as-lived Core Belief: I can't trust a woman with my heart.

What was really running the show wasn't my stated and heartfelt commitment to partnering in a long-term, committed relationship. No. What was really running the show was a deeper commitment to keeping myself "safe."

If you want to know what you're committed to, look at what you've got.

If this sounds psychological in nature, it's really not. It wasn't that I developed a neurosis from a traumatic experience but rather that I had made unconscious judgments and decisions from early Serious and Significant Events or Influences and those previously-authored decisions were running my life. I never actually *thought* the decision "I can't trust a woman with my heart." I *became* the decision. It's who I was *being*, and it shaped all of my relationships with women.

The bonus from such a self-revelation was that I could begin to walk back through my romantic relationships, uncovering all the "evidence" from earlier serious and significant events or influences that had served to form that core belief. I identified events from long before the custody suit, even before my divorce, going back to my teenage years or earlier. It was like following breadcrumbs through a forest of belief, reaching back to some formative decisions I subconsciously made even around my mother! An added

> *If you want to know what you're committed to, look at what you've got.*

benefit to the outcome of this beliefs excavation process was that, having brought these old events to light by the sorting and inventorying of core beliefs, I now had the opportunity to Be Cause all of those earlier formative events.

Most assuredly, you too possess substratum Core Beliefs undermining the surface-level, consciously claimed commitments you are declaring in the design of your own radical, playful, passionate and purposeful Back Forty. When moving toward what you most desire now, or toward whatever elements of a fulfilling Back Forty life (including your Rejoices/Pledges) that you find missing despite your earnest desires and efforts, Core Beliefs inventories such as the one I shared can serve to uncover limiting "truths" from your past and expose them as superstitions.

All that we are is the result of what we have thought. The mind is everything. What we think, we become. —*Buddha*

Choosing to Be Cause your past cuts down the weeds of old beliefs and supports the planting of new beliefs, reducing overgrown areas of Front Forty frustration. Your Back Forty is, thus, consciously planted and maintained. And, you'll experience more of A Presence when you proactively and consciously co-create in certain foundational areas of your life the elements and conditions you really want.

As an inspiring side note to my own detailed Core Beliefs Inventory process around dating, within several months of conducting that inventory, I was in a relationship with my loving partner and now wife, Alexandra, with whom I've been designing this whole Back Forty world of possibility ever since.

> *Choosing to Be Cause your past cuts down the weeds of old beliefs and supports the planting of new beliefs.*

Embrace 7—Homeplay Alignment Practice 2
Weeding Your Core Beliefs Garden

As mentioned, these types of deep dives into our Core Beliefs Garden are supported by an ongoing practice of meditation which relaxes the mind for unexpected insight to be revealed. Yet, feel free even now to begin to think on a particular area that just doesn't seem to work in your life, no matter how much time, attention, thinking, analyzing, effort and exhaustion you may have invested or endured. Isolate a particular area, as I did, and then practice a self-inquiring, stream of consciousness list similar to mine. Answer the question "Who or how do I *be* about [your challenge]?" Don't think, just write. Don't judge yourself or your thoughts, just put them down. Give it a round or two and combine that inventory of beliefs with some silent meditation over the course of a couple days and see what pops out for you. With a bit of relaxed, open and aware practice, you'll be surprised at the subconscious, substratum belief systems that will begin to reveal themselves to the light of day.

Not Wanted/Wanted Posters

A bonus that comes with your introspective Back Forty growth is not only more conscious awareness of what you now really want as part of your second half/best half of life but also conscious awareness of what you now *really don't want* as well.

A common method of crime-fighting communication in the Wild West of the United States was "Wanted" posters bearing the name and often the image of a sought-after bad guy. They were posted on the front of sheriffs' offices and inside courthouses. In my own childhood, they still hung from the walls of post offices.

Those Wanted posters displayed the bad guy as the object of desire. In our Back Forty use of Wanted posters, we're going to flip around that Wild West tool and make our *Wanted* poster announce in bold terms *the desired* or *heroic elements* we want to be expressed in our lives and our "bad guys" will be pasted on our Not Wanted posters.

> **The soul attracts that which it secretly harbors, that which it loves, and also that which it fears. It reaches the height of its cherished aspirations. It falls to the level of its unchastened desires—and circumstances are the means by which the soul receives its own. —*James Allen***

I've spoken at length of your Back Forty opportunity to now be who you came here to be and do what you came here to do. Another way to clarify that for yourself is to get crystal clear on who you *didn't* come here to be (anymore) and what you *didn't* come here to do (anymore). Discerning the contrast of what you, now, *don't* want is a critical first step toward gaining clarity around what you, now, *do* want. So, in addition to Wanted posters, we're going to print up some *Not Wanted* posters as well.

Often, when people really want to change something about themselves or their lives, they handicap themselves by making wrong who or what they're changing away from: who they've been, the choices they've made, the people they've associated with—the Not Wanted elements in their lives. However, when you move *away* from something or some old way of being out of fear, force or judgment, and especially when you do it with a lot of energy (as is a common practice), you're actually less powerful than if you move *toward* something based on vision, passion, and joy.

> *Get crystal clear on who you didn't come here to be (anymore) and what you didn't come here to do (anymore). Discerning the contrast of what you, now, don't want is a critical first step toward gaining clarity around what you, now, do want.*

Pain pushes until vision pulls. —*Michael Bernard Beckwith*

Sure, it's easy to look down in contempt upon the sad criminal on the Not Wanted side of the poster and clearly see his/her/its despicable characteristics, but are you as clear about the attractive looks and countenance of the hero you want to see on the other *Wanted* side?

Most if not all of us have entertained a first half of life that once generated a fair share of complaints about the way things were, the cards we were dealt or the fact that we don't have much to show for it all. But, that's just the old, Front Forty victim campfire song. By de-victimizing ourselves as we've now learned to do, we've ideally rendered ourselves more complaint free about the way the Front Forty turned out. We co-created it the way we did to become who we're becoming and we gained, from all of it, the blessings of Self Expression Directives pointing us toward our greater yet to be.

Even with the Embraces and playful transformation we've engaged in thus far, we've not bypassed being human. You and I may have some very

382 THE BACK FORTY

> *When you move away from something or some old way of being out of fear, force or judgment, and especially when you do it with a lot of energy (as is a common practice), you're actually less powerful than if you move toward something based on vision, passion, and joy.*

tangible complaints right now, and we'll definitely have some in the future. We're not going to instantaneously "because to Be Cause" every moment in our lives going forward. We save that process for the big, serious and significant events or influences.

But it's what we do with those seemingly inconsequential, petty complaints and sprouting victim situations that will either keep our Back Forty field spirited and brightly lit or belabored and dim. This is where the Not Wanted/Wanted Posters come in. Through the use of Not Wanted posters, any lingering first half-of-life complaints or current, fresh, ripe, real-time complaints can be transformed into productive, forward movement.

Not Wanted Posters serve as clarity magnifiers revealing our little, random bitches about life that build up like dust under a rug. Even though these piddling complaints aren't noticeable to the naked eye, they're still there diminishing the integrity of our space and keeping everything messy. Often, we're not even clear about what we don't want. We only sense some nagging anxiety or antsy-ness lying just under the rug of our conscious awareness.

So, getting clear about what's behind or beneath that resident anxiety (Not Wanted) can be very helpful. Learning to locate and put words to what is Not Wanted helps us no longer wallow in negativity and instead use each and every Not Wanted criminal as a pointer to a hero, to what's Wanted.

We want to magnify and enhance our moments of the Wanted and weaken and lessen our focus on the Not Wanted because when we become clear about what we want and focus on it, we enter into a space of gratitude, appreciation and joyful anticipation, where we're always more available to A Presence moving through us than when we're in a negative, judgmental, complaint mode.

Not Wanted/Wanted Posters get it all up close and personal, so we become clear about the choices we're making on where to put our energy of attention. That choice of focus will determine your resident being-ness in life as either grateful or gripe-ful. In so determining, you'll either invite A Presence to collaborate more in your daily life, or you'll wave It on to pass you by.

> *We enter into a space of gratitude, appreciation and joyful anticipation, where we're always more available to A Presence moving through us than when we're in a negative, judgmental, complaint mode.*

Embrace 7—Homeplay Alignment Practice 3
Not Wanted—Wanted

It goes like this: pull out your Back Forty Freedom Fliers Journal and turn to a clean page. Draw a line down the middle. On the left side, write "Not Wanted" at the top and on the right side, "Wanted." Down the left side, write out some short, simple sentences describing the things you're currently experiencing that you don't like and don't want.

To keep it simple to begin with, just look at *today*, nothing more. Write out five things that you do not want to experience or have as a result of your day. Consider your general mood and any underlying concerns, anxiety or antsy-ness you may be feeling. Flesh them out and put words to them.

For example, in conducting this exercise[18] several years ago, I looked at my day ahead and wrote:

---

18 *Inspired by the works of Abraham-Hicks.*

NOT WANTED

i don't want today to be unproductive.

I don't want to be concerned about income.

I don't want to get out of control with unexpected distractions or technical issues.

I don't want my computer to overheat and shutdown.

I don't want to become groggy and less effective because of this cold.

WANTED

Now do it yourself. Find five things that you don't want as part of your experience of *today* and write them out. Even if you've practiced this tool before, come from beginner's mind and be willing to engage with this simple exercise now, just for the day ahead of you.

Now that you have five things you're clear you don't want as part of your day, use that crystal-clear clarity as a launch pad for declaring what it is that you *do* want instead. In my example below, you will see that what I wanted was the direct opposite of what I didn't want.

NOT WANTED

I don't want today to be
unproductive.

I don't want to be concerned
about income.

I don't want to get out of control
with unexpected distractions
or technical issues.

I don't want my computer to
overheat and shutdown.

I don't want to become
groggy and less effective
because of this cold.

WANTED

I want to have an incredibly
productive day and have great
results from my efforts.

I want to experience unforeseen
and unexpected income.

I want today to work smoothly
and to be able to accomplish my
objectives free from distractions.

I want my computer to work
effectively and efficiently.

I want to feel vibrant and
energetic today

Do this next step for yourself now in your Back Forty Freedom Fliers Journal. Use the information from your what's Not Wanted list to reveal what to put on your Wanted poster.

Now how does that feel?

Though a seemingly simple process, it's amazing how many of us go into our days and weeks without taking such easy steps toward productive attraction and instead merely get more of what's already in our default, gripe-focused sights. And, beyond simply using this method as a way to refocus your day, you can use it to refocus your week, month, year or general life disposition.

The Not Wanted criminals and Wanted heroes come in all shapes and sizes. Depending on the breadth of your poster, as a final touch and given that a picture is worth a thousand words, try adding uplifting, heroic

> *A constant, graphical reminder of where to focus your attention steers your mind in the direction of more hope, lightness and joy and, thus, more availability to A Presence.*

images to the Wanted side. You can even blow the graphic up onto a poster-board and drop the Not Wanted side altogether, because it will have already served its purpose to get you focused on what you want to attract.

Hang your Wanted Poster in plain sight, and spend time contemplating it. A constant, graphical reminder of where to focus your attention steers your mind in the direction of more hope, lightness and joy and, thus, more availability to A Presence.

Affirmations

The Not Wanted/Wanted Posters exercise directs your focus to the hero and away from the outlaw, who's been stealing your attention. To supercharge your attraction of what's Wanted even further, to Be Cause and collaborate with A Presence, create statements *in the present tense* that reflect your *having already received* what is Wanted. This process of declaring your crystal-clear intentions as present-tense receptions is called affirmation; and the statements, affirmations.

Right thinking begins with the words we say to ourselves.
—*James Allen*

When expressed as positive, affirmative statements of fact, my desires as identified above in my Wanted day would become short, present-tense declarations of my intentions.

- My day is productive and yields wonderful results.
- I enjoy the freedom of earning unexpected and unforeseen income today.

- I am clear and focused on my goals today, and the Universe supports their attainment.
- I am blessed with smoothly functioning technology today, including my computer.
- I am enlivened, empowered and vibrantly energetic.

These, then, become my Affirmations for the day ahead. I'm affirming and focusing my attention away from what is Not Wanted and toward what is Wanted. What's Not Wanted is no longer even in the picture, because I've now declared that what is Wanted is already present.

Notice the shift in feeling tone, simply by my stating affirmatively what I want *and expect* from my day versus allowing what I don't want to reside under the rug in my mind. I'm speaking in the present tense, *already* acknowledging and appreciating with gratitude the experience of my intended day.

I'm allowing myself to *declare and feel* the feeling *now* as opposed to at some point in the future. I'm *coming from* the feeling and experience of what is wanted rather than *trying to get to* the feeling and experience. Accordingly, not only do I feel more uplifted now inside my affirmations but also, according to the age-old Law of Attraction, I'll better magnetically draw to myself situations and circumstances that match that feeling because I am aligning myself with A Presence, with all that is.

Embrace 7—Homeplay Alignment Practice 4
Forming Affirmations

Now, in your Back Forty Freedom Fliers Journal, take your clearly defined statements from your Wanted list and mold them into your own present-tense, affirmative intentions for your day today. You will open yourself up to more of what you want with these uplifting and magnetic affirmations.

Affirmations are most powerful when you regularly plant them in your mind throughout the day. That doesn't mean you need to become a repetition robot, but your default habit of focusing on your Not Wanted criminals doesn't end immediately after stating an affirmation once. A negative-leaning habit can be old and deeply rooted from beliefs planted over a lifetime and even simply part of the culture in which we live. Psychologists call it a "negativity bias." So, it's prudent Back Forty farming to plant, plant and plant new empowering beliefs as much as you can, so they eventually overtake the old weeds of habitual, pessimistic thinking. Focus on tending to, watering and nurturing the new seeds while paying less attention to the old weeds. Eventually, you'll have a whole new Back Forty Core Beliefs Garden to run around in.

Remember, behind everything that you don't want is something that you do want. So, you can apply this same Not Wanted-to-Wanted technique to a meeting you're about to have, a health prognosis you're about to receive, a relationship you want to impact and any other situation in life. You can apply it not only to your day but also your week, month, year ahead. Basically, affirmations can be used to strengthen any budding belief that you want to increase in awareness. They are a tool for conscious Back Forty gardening.

> **Basically, affirmations can be used to strengthen any budding belief that you want to increase in awareness. They are a tool for conscious Back Forty gardening.**

You can use affirmations to further establish in your belief system various elements you discovered in your Embraces. Insert them into your internal dialogue to shape and guide that barely noticeable or extremely loud voice always running inside your head. By constructing statements which affirm the realizations you've made through your Discovery & Expression analyses, your gifts and values surveys, your rejoices and pledges as well as what you've begun to see in terms of your Purposeful Practice, you empower and make them more real, tangible and vibrant in your everyday awareness.

Darrell's Puzzle Pieces Affirmations

Pulling from my own Self Expression Directives, gifts and values, as compiled in Appendix C, these are some affirmations I might construct:

- I am in the process of accepting, loving and having compassion for myself.
- I am growing to trust myself to make good decisions.
- I do my best, and my best is good enough.
- I express my authentic Self.
- I am resilient. I grow and go forward. . .and never give up.
- I see and extract the greatness in others.
- I am in the process of becoming disciplined and focused.
- I am recognized and appreciated as an inspirational public speaker.
- I am viewed as a great coach and guide.
- I offer people an inspiring positive outlook.
- I am centered in serenity, wisdom and worthiness in every action I take.
- I release authentic Self-expression and wild creativity as a way of life.
- I am in the process of growing a strong, deep and abiding relationship with my son.
- I allow and accept travel as an ever-growing aspect of my work and life.

Practicing affirmations regularly keeps you trued up, whether the affirmations are specific for the day ahead or broader pointed toward your radically playful, passionate and purposeful second half.

Be sure to always have your affirmations *believable in the present* or else your logical mind will discount them or write them off entirely, leaving you planting unproductive seeds. The attraction element of the affirmation doesn't work when you're cynical about the affirmation itself or think you may be pipe dreaming. When you want to become or do something that you don't feel you're completely capable of embodying yet, you can still benefit from the power of affirmations. You just don't want to blow out your BS detector with a statement that you clearly don't believe. Adding a qualifier such as "I am in the process of. . ." simply affirms your growth in the direction you want to go, even if you're not there yet. It makes the statement always true for you, no matter where you are in the process.

You'll notice that a few of my affirmations above could have been written with more conviction than they were, but I wouldn't have believed them. For example: instead of "I am in the process of accepting, loving and having compassion for myself," I could have written the affirmation, derived from the first of my Self Expression Directives, more definitively as "I accept, love and have compassion for myself." However, when originally compiling these affirmations, the soil of my Core Beliefs Garden was not in such a condition yet that it would allow that particular seed to germinate and take root. My garden still had some hard, rigid dirt along with weeds of past unfavorable self-opinion blocking a successful planting of that seed. In other words, if I were to repeat that affirmation aloud, my internal voice would respond with "bullshit!" So, without diminishing its long-run impact, the affirmation was qualified somewhat by adding the phrase "I am in the process of. . ."

Wording and speaking affirmations this way tills the soil of your consciousness. Affirmations allow fresh, new, hopeful seeds to impregnate previously rigid ground and to bypass obstructive, deeply established weeds to land in the vibrant soil of your inspired psyche. Those new thoughts can then, at the very least, begin to take root and grow. Later, you can switch to the stronger versions of those affirmations when the new roots have become established enough to withstand and overcome the bullying of old weed encroachment (i.e., any remaining disbelief).

In areas where there are no internal obstructions to an affirmation, I need no qualifiers. Also, in areas where I'm simply reporting on the observations of others—whether my internal BS detector believes them or not—the statement is simply of the facts. For example, from my Back Forty Information Campaign Incite Matrix (Appendix C), what others said about me is simply the way it is *for them*; and, therefore, I can declare and claim it as such.

- I am recognized and appreciated as an inspirational public speaker.
- I am viewed as a great coach and guide.
- I offer people an inspiring positive outlook.

With these few guidelines in the development of affirmations, it's possible for you to plant productive and spirited seeds in your Back Forty Core Beliefs Garden. Then, your job is to continually water and nurture their growth, by holding them in mind. In this way, your cultivated Back Forty beliefs begin to establish the ground upon which you stand and your new Self begins to preside over your old self. A new substratum forms.

> *In this way, your cultivated Back Forty beliefs begin to establish the ground upon which you stand, and your new Self begins to preside over your old self. A new substratum forms.*

This will not happen by memory or habit. It can't unless you are already an affirmations guru. Even then, it's smart to set up or schedule support systems and accountability to ensure that you continually mind your Beliefs Garden. This can be done in various ways:

- Place post-it notes of your affirmations where you'll see them: the bathroom mirror, the car's dashboard, the fridge, your computer as a screensaver, your coffee mug, your lover's forehead. . .
- Set a recurring and soothing music alarm to go off on your phone every couple of hours with an affirmative text popping up for you to read.

- Record your affirmations in your own voice and listen to them while running or working out.
- Build affirmations into your regular morning, evening or other daily practices of opening up to A Presence.
- Partner with a friend to confirm that you've each completed your Back Forty gardening for the day without necessarily sharing your affirmations with them unless you choose to.

Those are just some of the ways you can consistently remind yourself to put your focus on your Wanted-poster second-half life through tending to your new Core Beliefs Garden.

One last point: whenever possible, be sure to state your affirmations aloud. Beyond the point of only *reading* them, which is about thinking, actually *hearing* them has these new thoughts open up a new ear for you to listen through in your Collaborative Creatorship with A Presence.

> **When you've transformed your becauses and own your life and direction and now place your attention on what is Wanted, you're more available to receive it.**

How does this practice of affirmations relate to an expanded relationship with A Presence? Think about it: when you've transformed your becauses and own your life and direction and now place your attention on what is Wanted, you're more available to receive it. You've heard the old saying, "God helps those who help themselves." This is simply a tool for one of the parts you play in the Collaborative Creatorship with A Presence: to design and Be Cause your future.

Embrace 7—Homeplay Alignment Practice 5
From Puzzle Pieces to Affirmations

With all of the data, gleaned from your discoveries in earlier chapters and calibrated into your Purpose-Feeling Compass, you have the makings for literally hundreds, if not thousands, of affirmations.

Pull out the compilation of your Puzzle Pieces of Purpose—your Self Expression Directives, your gifts and talents, your values and rejoices/pledges—those elements that speak to your most radical and purposeful Back Forty ahead and construct affirmative declarations to keep those ideas in the forefront of your awareness. In your Back Forty Freedom Fliers Journal, give yourself some time to write out 20 to 30 affirmations that recognize and represent your fully expressed Self,

> *With all of the data, gleaned from your discoveries in earlier chapters and calibrated into your Purpose-Feeling Compass, you have the makings for literally hundreds, if not thousands, of affirmations.*

your sweetest gifts, your most deeply-held values, and your juiciest directions of Purposeful Practice.

Affirmative Prayer

Now with an understanding that you can regularly affirm what it is that you want, it's just a short jump to *Affirmative Prayer*, which is *to speak from the perspective that what is being prayed "for" is in fact already given and received.*

That's saying a lot, yes. Yet, all of these Back Forty practices of Collaborative Creatorship with A Presence are cutting-edge (Be Cause) compared to the less-empowering and default Front Forty belief systems, where we had less say in the matter of our lives (because).

In affirmative prayer, rather than attempting to beseech, persuade or cajole some seemingly capricious and unpredictable Intelligence greater than us into forking over the goods that we've asked for, we affirm that we're already in possession of our Good right now.

Whatsoever things ye desire when ye pray, believe that you receive them and ye shall have them. —*Mark 11:24*

Though this concept seems easy enough to grasp at first, even if hard to accept as a reality, it requires some fundamental shifts in perception that will inherently impact its success. Each shift will empower you in best utilizing the tool of affirmative prayer to cultivate greater access and availability to A Presence.

You don't get what you pray for, you get where you pray from.
—Michael Beckwith

Shift in Perception #1: "I know what's best for me."
One critical shift is to move away from the oft-held opinion that we know what is best for us, for those we love or for the flow of life itself. If we hold *ourselves* as being *the* Infinite Intelligence of the Universe, affirmative prayer will fall flat every time because it's not about being able to magically conjure up that new car, perfect soul-mate, million-dollar bank account or trim figure through the force of our single, egoic, know-it-all willpower.

The practice of affirmative prayer requires a willingness to surrender into an Intelligence greater than your conscious mind while *at the same time* affirming the qualities or feeling tones of the things or directions you seek even as you may outline specifics. For example, including your availability for "divine right transportation" and "harmonizing prosperity" inside of an affirmative prayer are going to click more into A Presence than *only* affirming the hottest new brand-name, hybrid, fully-loaded, leather-interior sports car of your choice.

Affirmative prayer can definitely impact the attraction of specific desired outcomes but not when used as an infantile will-to-power/get-whatever-I-want manipulation tool. A practice of affirmative prayer is not about immediately and indulgently pacifying your specifics. Rather, it supports the attraction of specifics by claiming and owning the generalized and interconnected qualities that lie behind those specifics. Focusing on the universal qualities of Abundance, Prosperity, Joy, Wholeness (of the planet) as well as the values of Beauty, Elegance, Style, etc., will put you in the right vibration to allow for a possible experience of driving that wondrous machine. . .or one of a similar nature.

A Presence (It) generally knows a lot better than your conscious self what it is that you truly want and need! Deep below your surface ego-based drives and reactionary ways of living exists a "soulular" direction and plan for which you came. You collaborate in that plan, though perhaps unknowingly, in your Front Forty R & D and then more consciously in your tapped-in, proactively designed Back Forty. That plan is not necessarily helped and may be hindered when shiny and often momentary egoic "wants" are the main focus. Burning desire is a great thing to help us move forward; yet, after affirmatively staking our claim, trusting that our Highest Self, in collaboration with A Presence, will bring about what's *truly* wanted and needed is a faith-filled second-half step we can take.

> *Deep below your surface ego-based drives and reactionary ways of living exists a "soulular" direction and plan for which you came.*

Many wise individuals have spoken of this idea:

> **Some luck lies in not getting what you thought you wanted but getting what you have, which once you have got it you may be smart enough to see is what you would have wanted had you known.**
>
> ✿
>
> GARRISON KEILLOR

> **I have lived to thank God that all my prayers have not been answered.**
>
> JEAN INGELOW

> **Success is getting what you want; happiness is wanting what you get.**
>
>
>
> INGRID BERGMAN

> **Need nothing. Desire everything. Choose what shows up.**
>
> NEALE DONALD WALSH

With all of the Back Forty exploration that you've accomplished, hopefully you can now relate to the idea that your apparent having what you want or not at any particular moment in time is NOT the truest indicator of your own best good being fulfilled!

Look at that huge and wonderful amalgam of experimental learning opportunities from your Front Forty! You didn't necessarily get what you would have chosen or wanted from those experiences. . .not on a conscious level, at least. But, from a Be Cause perspective, you definitely got what you *needed* to now get to where you really always wanted to go: who you came here to be and what you came here to do.

> **Remember that not getting what you want is sometimes a wonderful stroke of luck.**
>
>
>
> DALAI LAMA

> **You may not realize it when it happens,**
> **but a kick in the teeth may be the**
> **best thing in the world for you.**
>
> WALT DISNEY

There are *all kinds of ways* an Intelligence greater than your small s self in collaboration with your Higher Self might put things together to produce the results you want, or even results *beyond* what you want. So, although you can *define the direction* of your passions and interests in affirmative prayer, it's *important not to decide or dictate how* that ultimate direction is to be achieved. Your Big S Self in cahoots with A Presence may have something better in Mind.

You always want to allow room for *true* Infinite Intelligence, that collaborative confluence of the greater You and It, to determine the best ways and means by which the universal qualities you seek are actually experienced by your conscious self. Get clear, affirm both specifically and generally, and then let go of the result. A good rule of spiritual thumb is "if not this, something better."

For instance, what if you didn't need to earn a bunch of money to buy that sports car, but you won one in a contest? Or, let's say you want to live on the beach in Hawaii. Rather than needing to be rich enough to buy a resort condo, what if your desire were met by a wealthy friend who asked you to housesit for several years while he or she travelled? That's not to say that desiring more personal prosperity isn't a worthwhile focus of prayer. It just may come in different ways and means when an Infinite Intelligence collaborating with You *beyond* your conscious intelligence is at play.

> *Although you can define the direction of your passions and interests in affirmative prayer,* it's important not to decide or dictate how *that ultimate direction is to be achieved.*

As another example, the ultimate highest and greatest good for all concerned *may not be* that ninety-eight-year-old Grandma gets out of the hospital again. . .at least alive. It's all dependent on the quality of life she's currently able to experience. Though we love her and enjoy her presence, it may be time for her to move on to her next appointment and for her family to get on with the evolution of life after Grandma in physical form. Accordingly, we might not pray for Grandma to be home today. Rather, we could pray to know Healing, Divine Right Action, Wholeness, Peace of Mind, All Needs Met and Perfect Order for and around Grandma, her current situation and her entire family.

Shift in Perception #2: "I know everything about what 'It' is and how 'It' operates."
Another shift required for affirmative prayer to be most effective is to create an open, conscious environment freed up from past views (and, often, non-thought programming) as to what A Presence is and how It works. Know upfront that this suggested shift may tip more sacred cows. Yet, I offer this inquiry as simply part of the multitude of new thoughts to consider in expanding awareness beyond the Front Forty "wisdom" (i.e., prison) you may have built around life.

Remember, as stated earlier, the first step in a Core Beliefs Inventory is to begin to question why you believe the things you do. Then, the next step is to start playfully challenging those beliefs, which, in some cases, may turn out to be superstitions. This second huge shift in perception may for some be new, and it involves opening up the very idea of "A Presence" to whom/which we pray.

Whether or not a particular new concept of A Presence or praying to A Presence in new ways resonates with you, it's always a good Back Forty practice to stretch yourself and give a workout to your own personalized version of the Incredible Shrinking World, which we examined in Embrace 6: Your Purpose. In other words, it pays to ongoingly explore where your perceptions may show you more of what you've already decided is "the way it is" simply because you've already decided that's "the way it is." Belief shapes perception. Perception confirms belief. The spiral is in the direction of a smaller and smaller world of being "right" and won't lead you "up and out."

In yet other words, it's worthwhile to notice what plants may have been growing in your Core Beliefs Garden for so long that you've never even questioned their presence.

Create an open, conscious environment freed up from past views (and, often, non-thought programming) as to what A Presence is and how It works.

Whether or not a new-idea shoe fits you personally, by at least trying it on and considering it, you gain more openness and availability to A Presence, which, in the end, includes ALL of life. You may not choose to include that shoe as part of your own Back Forty collection, but it doesn't negate the other new-idea shoes that may fit. So, don't throw the Back Forty baby out with the bathwater if you don't connect with one particular new idea or not.

All that said, here's a Back Forty new-idea shoe to try on about "It/ A Presence."

Depending on our religious or other cultural upbringing, many of us had embedded within us at an early age the image of an anthropomorphic Being to whom we speak our prayers, a Being to whom we ascribe not only a human form but a human personality with human tendencies.

Whether or not a new-idea shoe fits you personally, by at least trying it on and considering it, you gain more openness and availability to A Presence, which, in the end, includes ALL of life.

Sometimes It is seen as a Santa Claus-like male, perched in the clouds, peering down and meticulously keeping track of who is naughty or nice. Other times, perhaps It is perceived as an elderly, stern judge, robed and sitting high upon a judicial bench, carefully weighing all the evidence of our worthiness to receive what we want, while showing no emotion whatsoever. Or, further still, It can even be regarded as capricious and unpredictable, subjective and erratic, maybe in a good enough mood to help us out or maybe not. Therefore, we may traditionally approach prayer with the mindset that:

1. We need to ask for what we want, because apparently It, this supposedly All-Seeing, All-Knowing, All-Powerful and All-Present Being doesn't already know. We, therefore, give It our laundry list of wants, pleas and to-dos.

2. We need to persuade and beseech It for what we want because, unless a good enough case or enough repetitions of our plea can be made, this "high court" may deliver a no-go verdict.

3. A go-between is required, an intermediary or emissary of some type, to represent our case before this high court and then channel down to us the decisions (or penalties) thus rendered.

4. We need to have been "good" or bargain for being "good" in the future in order to warrant It even taking the time to hear our case, lest we be found summarily guilty and thrown out of court or receive a bag of coal or switches instead of the goodies we want.

5. We may or may not get what we asked for because, after all, It has moods and feelings and good days and bad days just like the rest of us. Plus, "It" reserves the right to withhold and parcel out goods based on a unique and unknowable decision-making algorithm that we'll never understand. Also, depending on our past infractions and the thickness of our court records, we may need to do some hard labor or penitentiary time before we will be worthy of having our goodies released.

6. There's a tight schedule during which prayers can be heard and the amount of goods that can be delivered because there's just no way It can handle all of everyone's needs at the same time. Plus, we need to bundle all of our prayer requests into a certain

form of presentation at a specific time of day, which is our "appointment time" in Its calendar, given that It is also being called upon by so many others.

Yes, I'm being majorly and playfully facetious. And I'm sure many sacred cows are snorting.

Still, many of us hold A Presence inside a very narrow, Front Forty-defined box that may limit our ability to experience connectedness to It in a more empowered, second-half/best-half way. Perhaps our default way of relating to It comes from a viewpoint that there's a Being "out there" that we are trying to have notice us and what we need "over here." And, if we can only get this Being to notice us and our needs, then we will be able to receive what It has over there over here. Also, many times these pleadings only occur when the heat is on, sort of a FedEx® model of expectancy: "when it absolutely, positively has to be there overnight."

If all of that sounds in any way familiar, a new, consciously designed laboratory experiment of inquiring into It might be fun for you to implement. For example, though perhaps playfully shocking to consider. . .

1. What if this Being isn't a Him but a Her? Or what if this Being isn't a Him or a Her, but something beyond the duality of human sexuality—an "It," as we've been referring to A Presence? Or, even better yet, what if this Being isn't a Him or a Her or an It, but an Intelligence? Or, best yet, what if this Being isn't a Him or a Her or an It or an Intelligence or even a Being but A Presence that simply can't be described in words or concepts?

2. What if A Presence isn't something outside of us but rather something inside of us? What if we don't really need to go traipsing around looking for handouts from those on the well-to-do side of town (Heaven) but can find all that we need here within us, at home? What if it were true, like Dorothy's realization at the end of *The Wizard of Oz*, that if I ever go looking

for my heart's desire again, I won't look any further than my own backyard.

3. What if we don't need to go through any middleman, envoy or arbitrator to connect to or engage with A Presence, but rather can communicate and interface with A Presence directly on our own? What if, as Dorothy was informed, we don't need Glenda (The Good Witch) or our particular version of the same as our ticket to get back home and we've been able to get there all along?

4. What if we don't need to tell A Presence anything because if we really believe that this Presence is All Powerful, All Knowing, All Seeing, and All Present everywhere at all times simultaneously (within us too!), how could we tell A Presence anything It doesn't already know?

5. What if A Presence doesn't need persuading, negotiating or repeated pleas from us at all but instead is always ready and willing for us to have whatever it is that we desire, no questions asked? What if A Presence is simply complete and unabashed givingness, responding to every thought, desire and feeling with the statement "As you wish!"

6. Matter of fact, what if our Good is already given and no prayer request is even necessary except perhaps as a request from our Big S Self to our small s self for us to be willing to allow the receipt of it? What if the only convincing to be done to receive our desires is convincing our self on behalf of our Self? What if the only one questioning my worthiness to receive is just little, old who-I've-always-considered-myself-to-be me?

7. What if A Presence, in collaboration with the highest aspect of our Self, truly knows better than our small self, as mentioned above, what it is that we truly need and desire, wants that for us and gives it willingly?

8. What if A Presence doesn't suffer the moods, personalities, scarcity-mindedness or judgmentalism of humans and is completely unbiased and partial to no one, regardless of socio-economic, racial, religious, national or gender characteristics or affiliation and joyfully gives freely to the "saint" and to the "sinner" based on their respective relationship with A Presence? What if we are never imprisoned for our past deeds except in our own mind? What if A Presence holds us guiltless and deserving of all the Good we desire and gives to the extent that our inner worthiness will allow us to receive right now, in the present?

9. What if A Presence is always "on," 24/7, never sleeping, eating, checking out or unavailable because someone else is on the line but rather here and now available to commune with us every moment of our day? Or, better yet, what if A Presence doesn't operate by our time structure and, therefore, the term "24/7" is meaningless because A Presence is timeless and eternal? What if we don't need specific appointment times and can experience conscious communion with A Presence at any time we choose, to re-Mind ourselves of Who we are, of the One Mind we are part of and of the Collaborative Creator that partners alongside and within us?

There's a reason it's called The Presence. It's because it's never absent. It doesn't come and go. It doesn't ebb or flow. It's always right here, right now in Its fullness. —*Michael Bernard Beckwith*

I just posed a lot of "what ifs," with some perhaps a bit difficult for ANY Front Forty-carved brain to quickly comprehend. That's okay. Even though "what ifs" are an absolute necessity in creating a radical second half of play, passion and purpose, they are simply "what ifs." I don't purport that these ideas are "the truth," just as much as I can't deem all the ideas that I've been handed down over a lifetime are "the truth" either. However, one of the perks that comes with the invitation into a radical Back Forty is the license to inquire: the right to ask plenty of "what ifs" in the face of a long-ago-planted and possibly overgrown-with-weeds Core Beliefs Garden. Besides, as you may recall: the value, power and goodies of inquiry come from getting immersed in the questions themselves, not in finding an "answer."

> **"What ifs" are an absolute necessity in causing a radical second half of play, passion and purpose.**

Simply entertaining these "what ifs" might have your prayer practice show up differently. I believe it's safe to say that, at a minimum, these possible interpretations of A Presence offer a more free-flowing, easy, accepting and loving energy around "It" than some of the ones most of us inherited. Yes, it requires tremendous courage to inquire into areas you think you've always already known and that are fixed in your world. For a radical second half, however, those kinds of across-the-board inquiries can become a source of new freedom and power. In the end, if you can feel that you're in a more friendly relationship with A Presence, and It occurs as more openly available to you, then you'll probably experience It all the more.

If you knew Who walks beside you on the way that you have chosen, fear would be impossible. —A Course in Miracles

The ultimate "what if" question is this: what if It can become a mystery to you in The Back Forty instead of all that you've "known" It to be in your Front Forty?

Just how would that particular shift support affirmative prayer? By letting go of the way you *know* It is and how It operates, you begin to short-circuit many of the old pathways you used to travel to ask for and receive your Good. You begin to practice *knowing* something is already yours by convincing yourself to see it and receive it from your Self rather than *seeking* its existence by beseeching something outside of you. You transform from a *seeker* to a *finder* of A Presence within you.

After all, if A Presence is in and as all things everywhere at all times, then It is right here at home within you. And, if It is the Source of all Good things, then you have access to all the Good It's got. And, maybe you or your old Front Forty beliefs are the only thing between you and your Good?

Affirmative prayer really works on your own mind to accept that the Universe is always giving and has already given. It works your muscles of Collaborative Creatorship, empow-

> *The ultimate "what if" question is this: what if It can become a mystery to you in The Back Forty instead of all that you've "known" It to be in your Front Forty?*

ering you to see that which you desire *now* rather than at some point in the future. When you believe more in what you don't see (what you want) than what you do see (what you don't want), you'll begin to see more of what you didn't see (what you want) and see less of what you did see (what you didn't want). In other words, when you believe it, you'll see it.

When you pray for your day ahead or various aspects of your life or the lives of those you love or your community or the world as a whole, consider praying *affirmatively*, acknowledging the existence of certain qualities that reflect the nature of Good. *Knowing with conviction* that these qualities exist *now*—Abundance, Wholeness, Perfect Order, Divine Right Relationship, Peace, Joy, Harmony, All Needs Met, Love, Acceptance, Guidance—opens the door for the more detailed specifics of what you desire to come to you in whatever forms they may initially or ultimately take.

> *By letting go of the way you know It is and how It operates, you begin to short-circuit many of the old pathways you used to travel to ask for and receive your Good.*

If you can conceive of anything, that means that *whatever* you've conceived now exists already in *potential*, though perhaps not yet in visible form. The role, then, of affirmative prayer is to open a pathway such that what is currently invisible can become visible. For that reason, though you may allude to certain specifics of what you're praying for, it's best to focus mostly on the qualities and spiritual environment in which those specifics can arise, opening the door so that they can be seen.

It's valuable to couch your affirmative prayers inside of the recognition that you are not separate from A Presence or from your Good, but rather, you're already One with It. You want to close the seeming gap between yourself (the small sense of who you are) and the Source that provides those aspects of Good that you're affirming. This will allow Good to flow more quickly and freely through your Self (the larger truth of who you are) because you're not waiting for a response, an approval or a verdict from something outside of you.

> *When you believe more in what you don't see than what you do see, you'll begin to see more of what you didn't see and see less of what you did see. In other words, when you believe it, you'll see it.*

Also, it's wise to conclude your prayer with gratitude and acknowledgement for already receiving that for which you pray—basically recognizing that it is already here in potential and coming into form. Then, the final step is to just let go and allow it.

RURTR

A helpful acronym to remember in practicing affirmative prayer is RURTR, which outlines the five-stage process that forms a well-rounded affirmative prayer. These steps are: Recognition, Unification, Realization, Thanksgiving, and Release. The acronym can be playfully and easily remembered as "R U Ready To Receive?"

Recognition *(It is):* Simply acknowledging that A Presence beyond your everyday senses exists, whatever you may call It, and that It has only the highest and greatest good in Mind for you.

Unification *(I am)*: Aligning your Self with A Presence, allowing your Self to feel One with It, acknowledging that It is within you and that you are not separate or removed from It. This alignment also goes for those with whom or for whom you pray. They are One with It too.

Realization *(I realize, know, accept)*: Stating with faith and conviction the presence of that which you desire as already present. Affirming the qualities, situations, events and desires of the heart as here and now occurring in right timing and right order.

Thanksgiving *(I give thanks)*: Expressing gratitude *now* and feeling the joy *now* of receiving that for which you pray, allowing your Self to believe and affirm that you are *already* in possession of it.

Release *(And so it is)*: Being willing to let go and allow it to unfold in perfect order. Accepting that you've done your part to realize and call forth your desires, you now rest in faith that A Presence that knows all, is in all places and is all powerful has indeed provided.

Remember our ninety-eight-year-old grandma in the hospital? Let's see what an affirmative prayer for her might look like.

Recognition: I pray now, recognizing A Presence that is everywhere in everything, an Intelligence that knows, guides and allows for the highest and greatest good of all concerned at all times.

Unification: I accept and believe that this Presence is not separate from me but is right here with me and in me as well as in all of life. So, I affirm that It is also here with and in Grandma. I let myself feel and know that I am One with the Intelligence of the Universe and, therefore, I align with the weight and authority of that Intelligence in this prayer I speak.

Realization: I pray knowing that all is well in the infinite Universe in which Grandma resides. I know that Perfect Order is taking place and that Divine Healing and Wholeness are happening right now. I accept that the Highest and Greatest Good of all concerned is assured and know that only Love, Peace, and Harmony surround Grandma and her entire family. I declare ease and grace as her experience in body, mind and spirit and allow the release of all concerns. I see perfection in every organ and function of her being and make room for her highest and greatest good to unfold both here in this world and in that which lies beyond. I accept Divine Right Timing as shaping all that occurs.

Thanksgiving: I give thanks for the opportunity to know this prayer I speak is already being realized in form. I am grateful to know that, even before being spoken, prayer is always answered by this Infinite Intelligence behind the All Good of the Universe which demonstrates in and as each and every life.

Release: I release this prayer, accepting that it is already done. All is well, and I need do nothing more than allow the unfoldment and perfect manifestation of the path of life and spirit known as Grandma. Amen.

Here's another example, this time of what an affirmative prayer for the unfoldment of one's purpose could be. Of course, you would speak your affirmative prayer in your own words whether or not you choose to use this outline.

Recognition: I recognize A Presence beyond this human mind and human condition that also encompasses this human mind and human condition. I accept and believe that A Presence beyond what I see is at the Source of all life. I recognize It as here and now present in all things.

Unification: I therefore recognize that this Presence is within me, not separate or removed from me, not something I need strive toward or beseech. This Intelligence actually shows up in this world as me, right here and right now, as an individualized expression of Itself. I accept that I am One with this Infinite Intelligence.

Realization: Therefore, I speak this prayer acknowledging the absolute and undeniable fulfillment of the unique and individualized purpose and expression for my life. I have a particular purpose spawned in co-creative collaboration with A Presence, which I am here to fulfill. I claim Divine Right Action, Clarity and Joy in the unfoldment of that purpose; and I allow A Presence to inform me at all times on what I am to do, where I am to go, what I am to say, to whom I am to say it, the thoughts I am to think and the words I am to give the world. I affirm and allow within me an increasingly greater ability to hear the voice of A Presence and to distinguish it easily and with greater acuity from the voice of ego. I claim the courage to follow that voice. I relish my Purposeful Practice, knowing that I add value as I move forward with Ease, Grace, and with All Needs Met in the fulfillment of the unique Self-expression I came to be and the unique purpose I came to fulfill.

Thanksgiving: I am so grateful to know that my speaking says nothing new to A Presence, for It already knows all of it. Yet, I speak this word of thanksgiving to accept this truth within and for myself and to know that my being and doing in the world is infinitely guided and informed by an Intelligence that intends my highest and greatest good and the highest and greatest good of all.

Release: I release this prayer, knowing it is done. I simply and lovingly allow it to be. And, so it is. Amen.

Practicing affirmative prayer consistently in ways like this allows you to know and affirm your purposeful direction for the week, the day, the

hour or the moment. Along with practicing your shorter affirmations, praying affirmatively positions you inside a constant flow of good energy (your
Being) surrounding your efforts and activities (your Doing). You become
more consciously aware of your active collaboration with A Presence.

Tangible Supports for Affirmative Prayer

Here are some tools that can enhance and elevate your experience of affirmative prayer:

> **Creation Box (a.k.a. God Box)**: A simple box can serve as a visual
> reminder that you've given your desires over to A Presence and
> can empower you to operate in the faith that "*It is Done! The prayer
> is answered!*" Find a nice box that will sit in a special place where
> you see it quite often. Place some 3" x 5" index cards and a pen
> beside it. You might stick a label on the box that says "Creation
> Box: Everything in this box IS!" Then, every time you pray or sim-
> ply desire something to come about, write it out onto a card fol-
> lowed by the affirmation "It is DONE!" Then, drop the card into
> the box and absolutely forget your concern, trusting that it is han-
> dled. This action solidifies and ritualizes the belief that Infinite
> Intelligence (the collaborative creation of your Higher Self and
> A Presence) has "heard" and "understands" your desires and will
> always answer in terms of your highest and greatest good.

> **Gratitude Journal**: Because affirmations and affirmative prayer
> both focus on accepting what is desired as already present in this
> moment, not separate from us and to possibly be received down
> the road, the practice of giving thanks proactively for those as-yet
> unseen-by-the-eye desires creates an energy of attracting those
> desires to us. You might call it "pre-gratitude," as it primes us
> into the feeling place of gratefully receiving what we desire. The
> best way to get a feel for how this works is to take pen in hand
> and start your own dual gratitude list.

Embrace 7—Homeplay Alignment Practice 6
Affirmative Gratitude

Take out your Back Forty Freedom Fliers Journal and follow the steps below.

- Turn to two facing clean pages.
- Title the left page of the journal, "Gratitude for Things Seen."
- List on that page the things that you can physically see or have experienced for which you are thankful (e.g., your family, your relationship, your job, your home, a kindness offered). This gets you into an acknowledging spirit. List at least 10 things you are grateful for that you can already perceive in your life today.
- Then, on the right-hand page, write "Gratitude for Things Known."
- On this page list out all of those desires still in the unseen that you want to bring forth. Write in the present tense, "I am thankful for. . .," completing the sentence with something you want to have or be, thus affirming in advance its existence just waiting to be perceived as present by you. List at least 10 such affirmative statements of gratitude.

It is not only okay but desirable for you to repeatedly list the same things on your "Gratitude for Things Known" list as long as they remain desired and invisible to you. Make this dual gratitude list a daily practice. Keep up your knowing to support manifestations growing. (You might even get a a nice, blank journal that represents your style and label it "Gratitude Journal" to support you in daily gratitude for all that is seen and currently unseen.)

Daily Plan for the Growth Operations Director: You can bring clarity about the actions that are in your power to take today and which actions can be handed over to A Presence (your Growth Operations Director) to handle for you. This isn't an abdication of your responsibility, yet many of us get overwhelmed with all that we have to do, organize or create in order for our goals and desires to be fulfilled. Learning to distinguish what is rationally in your power to accomplish *today* while, at the same time, giving the bigger, I-don't-know-how-to-make-this-happen stuff over to a Higher Intelligence builds within you a faith in guidance. It also loosens up your receptivity to allow out-of-the-blue occurrences and relationships to simply appear.

The Growth Operations Director's Daily Plan can also be laid out as two facing pages in a notebook or a single page with a line drawn down the center. On the left side, write the title "For Me To Do Today." In that column, you might soberly list what steps you can take today to move your purposes forward (e.g., write five pages, meet with marketing consultant, conduct client coaching session, etc.). On the right-hand side, the column could be entitled "For My Growth Operations Director to Do Today." In this column, you might list the bigger tasks outside of your knowledge or wheelhouse (e.g., guide me to a perfect publisher, attract to me coachable clients and abundant partners, connect me with Oprah). The Daily Plan is not a pixie-dust solution, but a process of easing the mind from having to figure it all out while opening your Self up for A Presence to step in and work some wonders. It being a daily plan places this practice in the camp of affirmative prayer.

Trust and allow and don't ask how. —*Burge Smith-Lyons*

Embrace 7—Homeplay Alignment Practice 7
Growth Operations Director Daily Plan

Using the design described above, make a plan for tomorrow (or the rest of today if it's still early). List at least three things in each page/column—things for you to do and things for a Higher Intelligence to take care of.

Visualization

With a grasp of affirmative prayer and its associated tools, it's easy to extrapolate a basic understanding of visualization. Similar to your practice of affirmations and affirmative prayer, visualization involves knowing the reality of something and *seeing it first in your mind's eye before* that reality is seen by your human eye. This practice, which is often disregarded, can be the most valuable, intentional investment you can make in bringing about anything, whether it be a good meeting, a good performance, a good bank balance or a good night's sleep.

> **Whatever the mind of man can conceive and believe, it can achieve.**
> **—*Napoleon Hill***

We tend to operate as human *doings* rather than human *beings*. To counter that, visualization directly impacts who we're being more than what we're doing. It's all about getting yourself into a place of feeling the feelings *right now* that you would feel *then*, after a particular event or situation that you'd like to have happen has visibly occurred. As in affirmative prayer, by tapping into the feeling of gratitude and joy *now*, you allow yourself to proactively realize and give thanks for the desire being fulfilled. Pre-emptive capturing of desired feelings actually attracts the situations that can produce them!

For example, if you notice a weed in your Core Beliefs Garden rooted in the idea that you live in a challenging or hostile world of competition and you must struggle to get ahead, a regular visualization practice might entail simply seeing the day before you moving smoothly with good favor and lucky breaks coming your way, unexpected and unforeseen goodies showing up and helpful and friendly people all around you conspiring for your greatest welfare. In that visualization, you would *focus on how you would feel* in such an environment.

> *Similar to your practice of affirmations and affirmative prayer, visualization involves knowing the reality of something and seeing it first in your mind's eye before that reality is seen by your human eye.*

Specifically, taking five to fifteen minutes at the beginning of each day to preemptively walk through the hours ahead, seeing your planned activities moving with ease and your Self surrounded by "Can't Touch This" good fortune, you'll start to notice that your days do, in fact, tend to go smoother with cool, little "God shots" peppering your experience. (The term "God shot" refers to random acts of goodness or direction coming your way.) Because you are *being* a welcome vessel for good experiences to occur rather than being stuck in your old struggle-oriented mindset, which has become a self-fulfilling prophesy, you'll actually *experience* good turns of events, coincidences and fortuitous circumstances beginning to happen in real time. Internal vision becomes external experience. It's a fun way to play and live!

> *Pre-emptive capturing of desired feelings actually attracts the situations that can produce them!*

Visualization can also propel specific projects and initiatives in the current moment. Taking a few minutes before any particular endeavor to tap into the feelings and mood you'd like to experience *after* that endeavor has been completed, were it to go ideally in a couldn't-have-been-planned-better way, preemptively launches you into the event from a completely different mindset than were you trying to force a result to occur. You enter the situation from a space of *allowing* rather than a solitary focus on *doing*.

In even broader ways, visualization can support your overall life direction. Projecting your vision out days, weeks and months ahead, you'll notice that through imagining ideal events and relationships occurring and through *feeling* the feelings those perfect circumstances would evoke will begin to attract the right people and conditions to bring your ideas into fruition in a way that trying to figure out how to *make them* happen never will. The key is to *feel* without doubt the exhilaration of what you desire occurring *right now*, even though you don't know how it will actually come about.

Imagination is more important than knowledge. For knowledge is limited, whereas imagination embraces the entire world, stimulating progress. —*Albert Einstein*

Evidence shows that the mind can't distinguish between what's going on in the imagination and what's actually being experienced by the body. The world of sports psychology has shown that the mind can be utilized in creative ways to influence a future event. Many Olympians and other cutting-edge athletes use "visual motor rehearsal," what is now popularly referred to as "imagery," to plan out, play out and project the ideal turn of events in a performance or competition. This mental practice creates internal imagery that impacts the psyche and trains muscles to fire at appropriate times. Once an athlete has experienced the "win" so many times internally, it's more accepted in their beingness to experience it externally during performance.

You and I can utilize visualization in the same way in our everyday lives. Got an important meeting or date coming up? Invest some internal time into seeing it go swimmingly well. Feel right now the way you'd like to feel afterwards and let go of the concern about how to "make it happen."

Wondering how the bank balance will look at the end of the month? Take a few moments daily to experience the feelings of Abundance and All Needs Met. See yourself viewing credits to your account, processing transactions, receiving online payments and opening checks in the mail.

Rest assured, this isn't some magic-wand, woo-woo way to have desires materialize out of thin air. Yet, your receptivity and openness to A Presence working through you is enhanced when you build faith that an Intelligence collaboratively creates with you behind the scenes even while you're taking necessary steps in the world of action.

An old African proverb says, "When you pray, move your feet." Through visualization, affirmative prayer, affirmations and all the other tools offered here, you're ensuring that you have the prayer component (being) humming alongside of your persistent and responsible moving of feet (doing). Call it smart insurance for your doingness; you have nothing to lose and everything to gain by taking out a basic, visualization policy.

Related to, but distinct from, the active practice of creative visualization, a more receptive form of visualization can also add to your awareness and effectiveness. A less structured and more "listening" type of visualization occurs when you come into a meditative state and simply open up an internal inquiry into an area of interest or desire.

> *Through visualization, affirmative prayer, affirmations and all the other tools offered here, you're ensuring that you have the prayer component (being) humming alongside of your persistent and responsible moving of feet (doing).*

This visualization practice is one in which you allow yourself to be impressed upon with images or ideas that you aren't actually thinking up yourself. You're merely making yourself available to pick up whatever It would have you see, sense or understand about a situation. You might get words. You may see pictures. You could even simply sense colors or feeling tones.

Such receptive visualization is best achieved in an easy, relaxed, nowhere-to-get-to and nothing-to-achieve state of mind. In that state, you open your Self up to hear from It. This is visioning in the grandest sense because you're not limiting your Self to what you already think and "know" but letting a Higher Intelligence within you point the way and support your awareness in that area of interest or desire. You can incorporate this type of visioning as part of or a separate session of your regular meditation practice.

Tangible Supports for Visualization

Dream Board: To create a Dream Board, paste images from magazines that represent your desires onto a poster or bulletin board and keep it somewhere you will see it at least several times a day, preferably more if your life allows. Alternatively, pull images from online sources and construct a digital version using a graphics software or even Word. You might use the graphic representation of your vision as a screensaver on your computer, as the welcome image on your phone or even displayed in your social media.

Dream boards can depict different areas of life (e.g., career, relationship, prosperity) or life as a whole. Creating a dream collage is a prayer and the dream board collage itself is a constant reminder of that prayer when you see your board, whether consciously or peripherally.

Viewing the board trains the mind and reticular activating system—that part of the brain that acts as a filter—to allow you to notice more of what you desire in your everyday world, what matters most to you.

For that reason, it's a good idea to set aside a few minutes to consciously scan the images on the board on a regular basis. But, simply having boards on the walls around you—in your office, bedroom, living room, even your car—impacts your subconscious mind even when you're not actively looking at them. The brain processes over 400 million bits of information per second, though you're only aware of about two thousand. The brain registers those dream board images and becomes ever more calibrated to pick up similar images and ideas out in the world, whether you're conscious of it or not. In effect, having dream boards around you sets up internal alerts for your Self to notice more keenly that which brings you closer to your desires.

Dream Binder/Pocket Boards: Sometimes it's not possible to have a dream board up on display wherever we go, such as in corporate office settings, while traveling or on a job site. For those times, it's helpful to have a smaller version of your dream board images on 8½ x 11" sheets inside of a binder, which can easily be packed into a backpack or briefcase, or even miniature dream boards the size of index cards that can fit in a shirt or pants pocket on a construction site, in a medical facility or restaurant worksite. Anything that visually depicts the desires you hold dear can serve as a Dream Board/Binder/Card. Just remember, it needs to be *out and in front of you* (i.e., viewed) on a regular basis.

Treasure Finds: Along the same line as dream boards, binders and cards, is setting up Treasure Finds throughout your home, office or other areas you frequent. This fun game, which will remind you of what you are attracting into your life, involves making multiple copies of those same inspiring images or varied representations of them—such as a picture of your ideal car, ideal mate, ideal body type—and peppering those images throughout your drawers, inside your cabinets, tucked into your glove compartment, or even inside your pockets. You'll soon forget that you planted them. Then, you'll get to revel in the delight of a visual reminder every time you happen across one of them while living your everyday life.

Customized Displays: A more specific and focused use of the dream board principle is to create Customized Displays of the world as you would have it be by taking current-world media and interjecting yourself into it. For example, a fun way to keep your mind vibrating in the direction of your desires is to take a recent front page of a newspaper, magazine or highly-trafficked internet news page and paste onto it a picture of yourself with a caption that describes your new book, new business or other news about your achievements. Or, perhaps you print out the New York Times best-seller list and simply put your own name and book title over #1! Don't forget, you're engaging the reticular activation system, so make sure the displays are big enough to see and vividly notice-able on the walls of the environments you frequent.

As mentioned midway through this chapter, I don't profess to be the all-knowing expert on every tool you can use to tap into A Presence. I personally continue to explore and experiment. What works for me may not work for you, and vice versa. Yet, outlined above are some of what I consider to be the foundational pillars for The Back Forty practice of establishing conscious communion with A Presence. Simply starting with these, I believe, anyone can find a path to discovering more personalized guidance and direction. But, here are a few more to play with.

Additional Tools for Tapping into It

Below are some additional tools I've personally found helpful to both *be present* as well as *tap into* A Presence. Though I'll be lighter on the details, perhaps these mentions will at least point you toward other practices that would be a good fit for you.

Work/Hobbies You Love: An entire book could be written on this element alone, and "Embrace 3: Your Gifts" and "Embrace 6: Your Purpose" touch on this point. When you're engaged in Activities You Most Enjoy Doing That Give You JUICE, you step outside of the egoic structures of personal identity and tune in to something greater. As described in Embrace 3, JUICE is an acronym for Joyful Unification: Individual Communing with Eternal. I believe that when an activity detaches us from time, it connects us with the timeless from which we touch the Infinite. Our JUICE taps us into the bigger Self, that "zone" feeling when time stands still, and puts us in touch with the Eternal Being (Oneness) that we actually were before it broke up into seemingly separate bodies and identities with different names and stories: you and me.

Nature: What can be said about nature and its impact on your soul? Volumes, for sure, but I'll only briefly touch on this idea here. It's likely that you've experienced the connected feeling that comes when communing with nature or you've at least heard of that possibility. The Back Forty invitation is to invest in your Self with the time and attention necessary to feed your soul. To that end, nature can provide a major meal ticket. Many of us forget to unplug into the naked, untouched and un-teched Intelligence of the Universe to feel the renewal it offers. Time outside, around or in anything not manmade, is restorative and allows us to tap into something larger than ourselves. Also, taking your body and mind away from the activity of daily life gives you an opportunity to have inner peace shape your beingness. It also supports receptivity to insight, cutting through your attempts to figure things out. Lastly, nature gets you outside of your square boxes—the TV, the computer, the phone, the house—so that you can *be present*.

Yoga: A flexible body invites a flexible mind. "As above, so below, as within, so without, as the universe, so the soul," said Hermes. That quote tells us that anything we do to relax the outer will relax the inner and vice versa.

The Western world has a fitness emphasis to cut and mold the perfect, hard physique. Of course, huge mental discipline is required to accomplish that. Eastern philosophies offer us the value of both physical and mental looseness, limberness and agility through the various forms of yoga.

A Back Forty of flexibility to new ideas, concepts of our Self, perceptions of the world and what's possible for us in it is supported by practices that make our physical instrument (the body) more flexibly receptive to A Presence.

Automatic Writing: You'd be surprised at what your Self can offer your self if you only give it a chance. If you can get beyond the initial weirdness, it's fascinating to discover all that your higher-level consciousness can tell you above and beyond your day-to-day human experience.

Use a blank journal and simply practice. The next time you're faced with a question, issue or conundrum, write out your question or issue and ask for guidance. Then, allow your human mind to go blank and just begin to write below the question.

With practice, you'll be able to set aside your smaller mind and notice that a greater Mind can come through with ideas and direction beyond anything you'd have ever conjured up by yourself.

This tool may take a bit of time to flow naturally, as our judgmental and critical mind wants to dismiss it as "it's just me doing the writing." At first, it may be. But, over time with a playful easing of the barriers to entry, glimpses of Infinite Intelligence will start to appear and have you become the biggest fan of your Self.

Psych-K: One of the aims of our "because to Be Cause" 7-Step Discovery & Expression Method is to become consciously aware of, own and even appreciate the impact of our Front Forty victim-oriented experiences. It allows us to recontextualize our past as something we specifically designed to point us toward who we came here to be and what we came here to do by producing Self Expression Directives.

Psych-K is a technique which utilizes applied kinesiology or "muscle testing" to tap into core beliefs residing *under the surface* of our conscious awareness. Its aim is to shift those beliefs on a subconscious and even epigenetic level. Dr. Bruce Lipton, cellular biologist and author of *The Biology of Belief*, endorses this method as a viable avenue for inner beliefs rewiring. For Back Forty Freedom Fliers, this could be useful in identifying and bringing to the surface weeds *subconsciously* sown in our Core Beliefs Garden so long ago that they are difficult to perceive and uncover.

Hotline Messenger: Another tool that can be developed over time is the ability to bypass the logical mind of "best thinking" altogether to establish a personal and immediate communication channel with A Presence. This is a practice only you can validate for yourself. You'll never be able to prove it or make anyone else believe it. You must develop the trust in your Self alone to take these leaps of faith. Yet, if cultivated well, a direct hotline to A Presence can, of course, serve you enormously.

Here's an example. Let's say I'm having a hard time making a decision that has as many pros as cons. I could continue to attempt to resolve my dilemma rationally, digging further to uncover any remaining logical points to make the case one way or another. However, at some point, the logical mind becomes exhausted.

If I were to discuss with A Presence in whatever way I'd do that (e.g., meditation, prayer) that my small s self can't figure it out and I need guidance, I might utilize a pendulum process (a type of muscle testing technique) to arrive at my direction in a guided way. I would simply stand, place my hands over my heart, and make the statement "If I'm to choose [X], let me naturally lean forward and, if I'm to choose [Y], let me naturally lean back."

Like automatic writing, this tool requires a trusting relationship with your Self, nurtured over time. The logical, thought-centered mind has a hard time yielding to the intuitive, Big S Self world of unseen Intelligence. However, if you're playing a big Back Forty game and are willing to go outside the fixed Front Forty concepts of who YOU are and whence your immediate direction can arise, it's a fun way to collaboratively play.

Environmental Upgrades: We're each surrounded by a number of environments that shape our experience of living. These include basic physical, relationship, financial and technology environments as well as more obscure spiritual, self, and memetic (idea) environments. Our environments either remind us of and move us toward who we're becoming or remind us of and hold us back inside of who we've been.

Given your Back Forty imperative is toward becoming more of who you came here to be and doing more of what you came here to do, it pays to be conscious of your environments and upgrade them to reflect who you're becoming rather than who you've been.

A perfect example of this concept is your physical environment. In it is likely things reminding you of your past (e.g., old pictures, clutter, unfinished projects, broken items) while at the same time it lacks things that prompt you to think of who you want to become (e.g., customized displays, affirmations, dream boards, treasure finds). Similarly, certain individuals in your relationship environment keep you tethered to who you've been, while you could use more folks who'll draw you toward who you're becoming. Understanding and consciously upgrading your environments can assist in your Collaborative Creatorship with A Presence.

Volunteering/Tithing/Giving:

> **The meaning of life is to find your gift. The purpose of life is to give it away. —*Pablo Picasso***

As the quotation above expresses, this tool of giving and even living to be of service isn't anything new; and yet, it can be grossly underutilized. Some of us had a Front Forty rampant with scarcity thinking in our Core Beliefs Garden or somehow incorporated an accounting mindset telling us to make sure we got as much as we gave. . .or even a bit more.

Beginning to experiment in The Back Forty with random acts of generosity opens us up to an age-old principle that defies description or logic, yet proves itself time and again: you can't out-give the Infinite Abundance of the Universe.

Learning to play inside a mindset of generosity through service and giving always opens you up more to receive. You can't widen the channel in one direction without widening it in the other. You may receive in forms completely different than those in which you've given; but good energy always returns, one way or another.

Regardless of whether it comes back to you (the old accounting mindset), a uniquely special kind of life and relationship with A Presence is available when you feel aligned with the givers versus the takers.

I don't know what your destiny will be, but one thing I know: the only ones among you who will be really happy are those who have sought and found how to serve.

—Albert Schweitzer

Services and Programs: Many tools covered in this chapter are based on a more inward focus, which is good because that's where we begin to cultivate a new Back Forty relationship with A Presence. However, getting out among others is always an opportunity to open up to A Presence, which can reveal Itself in new relationships, intriguing ideas, novel insights and growth-provoking experiences.

Perhaps a true Back Forty way of attending worship services is not necessarily the one(s) of your well-patterned past, but rather opening your Self up beyond your current levels of understanding. Perhaps, as a Christian, it would open you up to attend services at a synagogue. Perhaps as a Jew, it would open you up to attend services at a Catholic church. Mosques, temples, churches or even 12-Step meetings or other spiritually based personal development programs of one kind or another are ripe for individual expansion.

The point is this: stretching your level of understanding and getting outside of your Front Forty comfort zone can enable you to see A Presence in ways you may have never conceived and to recognize a Oneness in all of It.

Community: Though this tool is embedded inside many of the others listed, it's important to have at least *some place* in which your Back Forty awareness and possibility can be watered and take root, grow and thrive. An essential element of true Back Forty community is accountability. Unless you're supported to get outside of your Front Forty comfort zones and take bold steps while engaging in cutting-edge, second-half thinking, you'll fall prey to your old Front Forty ways and your entrenched Incredible Shrinking World.

That natural, revert-to-old-self tendency doesn't mean that you're not interested in what's possible for you. It's just that you've worn into the ground some very deep and fixed ways of thinking and acting, which can't help but continue to dictate your path if you're left to your own devices. It takes effort to lift oneself out of the deep ruts of habit, carve new playful paths, chart innovative and unimagined courses and live radically.

Therefore, a first-and-foremost expression of dedication to your radical second half of life as well as establishing an insurance policy that your Back Forty design will be realized is to join a community of individuals for whom these ideas are not simply Pollyanna, good-for-the-moment inspirations but a Back Forty Flying Manifesto. You can't do The Back Forty alone. That's all there is to it. There is and never will be any self-made Back Forty man or woman. There'll be plenty of Self-made Back Forty men and women when we've all joined together to cause that future.[19]

---

19 Visit TheBackForty.com/book for opportunities to participate in this like-minded community.

Your membership in the Royal Order of The Back Forty Freedom Fliers is not for yourself, but for your Self.

Just as the wave cannot exist for itself, but is ever a part of the heaving surface of the ocean, so must I never live my life for itself, but always in the experience which is going on around me. —*Albert Schweitzer*

> *There'll be plenty of Self-made Back Forty men and women when we've all joined together to cause that future.*

I look forward to learning which of these "Tapping Into It" tools you find most beneficial as well as hearing about those you'll discover from your own experience of moving into a radically playful, passionate, and purposeful Back Forty. Though many of the above tools can be pulled out of your saddlebags on a moment's notice, defining and establishing a time of day for *consistent embrace of A Presence* will support the establishment of new Be Cause habits. A new, radical second half requires new habits. So consider putting into place some morning and/or evening practices, employing these tools or others you may find that move you toward newly or increasingly embracing A Presence.

> *A new, radical second half requires new habits.*

THE TAKEAWAY

The main message to get from Embrace 7: A Presence is that A Presence is not a *thing*, it is a *practice*. To embrace A Presence does not require holding onto an image of something greater than you, but rather, holding onto practices that put you in touch consistently with an *experience* of *Something* greater than your small s self and then allowing that *Something* to co-create with you. Embracing A Presence is about nurturing and maintaining a conscious communion with It such that now in your Back Forty you have the ability and privilege to be guided in your Self Expression Directives, Gifts,

Values and Purposeful Practices to best fulfill on that for which you came. Your entire life has been a uniquely powerful laboratory for the discovery and expression of *Something*, in your own individual and irreplaceable way.

You can now create consciously as you tune into your Collaborative Creatorship with A Presence. Embracing A Presence has you becoming useful (i.e., being used within) and living up to the unique functions on the planet you're capable of because you've put aside all that has kept you small—your victimized past, any current at-effect conditions and disempowering core beliefs. Your purposeful Back Forty is not something that can be defined in the last chapter of a book. It is, rather, something defined only by your living in a transformed way with transformed eyes and ears into the next chapter of your life.

> *Your entire life has been a uniquely powerful laboratory for the discovery and expression of* Something, *in your own individual and irreplaceable way.*

Your next chapter, based on your own unique Puzzle Pieces of Purpose—your Self Expression Directives, Gifts and Values and Purposeful Practice—will be very different from mine because we all have our own unique Self-expression plays to call and difference to make. We can, however, know and affirm through our individual, distinct Collaborative Creatorships with A Presence, combined with the supportive brotherhood/sisterhood of the Royal Order of The Back Forty Freedom Fliers that *Something* truly special now has the possibility of being fulfilled with us, through us and as us.

FINAL SEPTENARY ACKNOWLEDGMENT

I both acknowledge you and thank you for taking "the road less travelled" with me into The Back Forty.

Typical are those who'll never hear of this message and possibility. We can simply rest in the old adage that says, "When the student is ready, the teacher will appear."

Extraordinary are those of us—you and me—who've made it HERE to the launch of our own Back Forty of play, passion and purpose. You've not only engaged, endured and (ideally) enjoyed your way through the 7 Embraces but you're now also willing to manifest the possibility of a radical, Back Forty of life for you to enjoy and for all to see and be inspired by. As, yes, radical as it may seem, you are *now* only at the *beginning* of who and what your Self came here to be and to do. That's what makes you extraordinary.

I'm moved by what you stand for and I look forward to being inspired in fellowship with you. I have given these ideas to you so that you'll give them back to me when I most need to hear them. Together, supporting one another to live in this ever-expanding possibility, who knows what will get created, designed or fulfilled that wasn't "just going to happen anyway"?

> **All it takes to make a difference is the courage to stop proving I was right in being unable to make a difference, to stop assigning cause for my inability to the circumstances outside of myself, to be willing to have been that way, and to see that the fear of being a failure is a lot less important than the unique opportunity I have to make a difference.**
>
> **—*Werner Erhard***

See you in the Back Forty!

AFTERWORD

In everyone's life, at some time, our inner fire goes out. It is then burst into flame by an encounter with another human being. We should all be thankful for those people who rekindle the inner spirit.

ALBERT SCHWEITZER

These few remaining words complete a twenty-year quest to bring the initial "download" of a freeing and inspiring idea/message/philosophy into book form. From the moment this liberating thought was conceived—that my entire life has been a uniquely powerful laboratory for the discovery and expression of *Something*—this particular life has never been the same.

Since then, I haven't wallowed in a victim mindset for long. Sure, I'm as human as anyone and I'll initially go there when a seemingly unexpected or unforeseen situation or event occurs outside of my liking. However, I can no longer, for any appreciable amount of time, allow myself to moan and complain without doing some Self-discovery around whatever is at hand. . .to discover *my hand* in what's at hand. Therefore, I've rendered myself incapable of "because-ing" for long. You could say I'm ruined for playing the ruined card.

Altogether, I'm blessed with a new pattern of giving my Self a hand (applause) for having a hand in the matter (BE CAUSE) of my life. I've learned to applause my Be Cause. Through practicing this contrarian way of thinking, a newfound trust has emerged: in myself, my Self, and the Universe.

With a deeper grasp of how my situations and experiences of the moment are not limited to that particular moment, I've adopted a longer-term view of life as a developmental curriculum, so to speak. The ability to distinguish seemingly untoward occurrences happening in my present as an opportunity to requalify some patterned belief from my past gives me a never-ending personal development workshop of life, which is also supported by newly uncovered Self Expression Directives from a Front Forty of laboratory experiments, which are never fully mined. Add to this even more directives arising from my now conscious and proactive experimentation, and you have a bevy of ongoing insight, direction and growth.

This requires diligence. For some, what I describe might appear to be an existence of constant, laborious thinking. It is thinking, for sure; but for me it's not laborious. It's fascinating, illuminating and (I can't seem to say it enough) freeing. We each pick our paths of mind travel in life, and this path serves me. I'll take thinking over unconscious, default "thoughting" any day.

As stated in the very beginning of our adventure together, this book was written through me and for me for the immediate and, now I see, long-term healing of me. It was necessary for my own living of a second half/best half of life. In that regard, it's gotten its job done.

My hope is that this message has also given you a new starting point and new mindset that wherever you are is exactly where you're supposed to be to fulfill on what lies ahead of you: who and what you came here to be and do.

Be well. Enjoy the discovery. Revel in the Self expression.

Let's collaboratively design the *sunrise* we're headed into.

Founder and Back Forty Freedom Flier
TheBackForty.com

DISCOVERY AND EXPRESSION EXAMPLES

FROM "EMBRACE 1: YOUR PAST"

Change your story, change your life.

This appendix is comprised of eight Serious and Significant Events or Influences—"becauses"—that Alexandra, several participants in our 3-Day Back Forty INFUSE Programs and I let rule our Front Forty lives until we embraced our past and applied the Back Forty Discovery & Expression Method to recontextualize the events and transform their meaning to us.

The examples from participants in our program are from midlife, solid, successful professionals, and all these insights occurred on the first day of the workshop. While the Discovery & Expression Method supports everyone, individuals from all walks of life or states of affairs, the sample participants were chosen to underscore that even supposedly "got it together" folks can uncover and shake off many hidden or unexamined limitations.

A few things to consider. First, as you review these very personal "because to Be Cause" transformations, remember the story is being told in full victim mode as it was experienced at the time it occurred. If you are tempted to ask "would you like some cheese with that whine?" remember that the telling of the story is only one step of a seven-step transformative process.

Second, you may see each of us talking to ourselves in our analyses, as you'll be similarly dialoging with your own Higher causal Self when conducting your own analyses. The analysis takes place through this Self dialogue. This is a creative, Self-discovery process, and each example demonstrates the analysis of certain events while imagining what the Inner Mad Scientist had in mind when he or she put these laboratory experiments together.

You'll also find a naturally subjective slant to this process, despite its being based on a pseudo-scientific model. So, if you see me or others promoting certain angles in our findings—perhaps persuading toward a certain point of view—we're promoting them to ourselves. Any seeming "case" that we appear to be proving, we're proving it to ourselves. In the end, if this entire process simply allows each of us to argue, for ourselves, a positively slanted case for the perfection of our lives, then its purpose is fulfilled. We don't need to prove anything to anyone else.

Third, in reviewing these Discovery & Expression analyses, keep in mind that I've personally percolated in this process for years in elaborately outlining my "because to Be Cause" explorations. Therefore, my own analyses may appear more detailed than those of the INFUSE Program participants. Plus, I'm just a verbose kind of guy. One's personal style in using the 7-Step Discovery & Expression Method doesn't matter. Some people think more in bullet-points and short sentences. Others may write even more than I do. And, though I recommend finding at least ten blessings, the number of blessings participants extract will vary. This is a malleable process with the only goal being the gaining of freedom from one's past and creating a new story.

Lastly, what's impactful for each of us will differ, given our varied life experiences. My serious and significant events or influences and those of others you'll read here may seem inconsequential, or even trivial, compared to yours. You may even think that we somehow got off easier than you in life. Keep in mind that comparisons yield nothing. The process is individual to oneself.

In the Back Forty community, we don't discount the validity of each other's stories or the impact they had on the tellers. Instead, we greatly applaud any and all demonstrations of individuals turning their becauses into Be Causes and flying into a second half/best half of life while leaving victimhood behind.

As a refresher, here are the seven steps.

7-STEP DISCOVERY & EXPRESSION HOMEPLAY METHOD
because to Be Cause

1. Choose and name a serious and significant event or influence.
2. Tell your story in full (as it occurred then), victim form.
3. Identify the phenomena (blessings) from the event or influence.
4. Determine the possible hypothetical research questions you were experimenting for in the laboratory.
5. Assume your ownership of the laboratory and its design: how you picked the perfect lab assistants and ideal lab environments.
6. Determine the possible findings from your experimentation.
7. Determine or simply postulate your Self Expression Directives from the event or influence.

And now, getting back into the spirit of play. . .

MuuuuuuuAAAAAAAAAHaaaaHaaaaHaaaa!
MuuuuuuuAAAAAAAAAHaaaaHaaaaHaaaa!
MuuuuuuuAAAAAAAAAHaaaaHaaaaHaaaa!

Discovery & Expression Analysis
Alexandra's Experiment: Leaving Russia Alone

Step 1: Serious and Significant Event or Influence

"Leaving Russia Alone."

Step 2: Victim Story

I am nineteen years old, the sheltered only child of doting Jewish parents. I'm on an airplane, alone, scared, alone, trying to stay strong, alone, not allowing myself to cry.

Our family has been trying unsuccessfully to leave Russia for thirteen years—the government has not allowed us to leave. My grandparents left eight years ago. And just a few months earlier I was allowed to leave, while my parents had to stay.

At the emigration agency, the agent looks at me, then at my mother, and says, "You're a brave woman—you may never see your daughter again."

To their friends, my parents say, "If you were in prison and your child had a chance to get out, you would make them get out."

I grow up in a day. I take charge. I am head of household—the only nineteen-year-old girl among middle-aged fathers of families and a couple of older women getting ready to board this plane leaving Russia.

I am at the airport, watching my friends and family as they stand behind a fence. I'm saying goodbye, maybe forever, to my mom and dad. I'm going through customs, being told that I have something that is not allowed—and delighted to be able to take it back to my parents and see them just one more time. I'm free to leave. I'm getting the freedom that my family always dreamed of. It doesn't feel like freedom. It feels sickening, devastating, and lonely. Freedom is scary.

Then, I am on the plane. Alone in the world, really. I don't cry. I can't cry, because I have to stay strong to take care of myself. There are families all around me, people with husbands, children, and siblings. . .and they cry. Why are they crying! Their family is with them!

A very nice woman in the seat behind me is crying nonstop. Her husband and kids are next to her, comforting her. I find out that she is crying because she is leaving her cat. How weird! I decide then people are weird and I'm different and I'm all alone in the world, and I have to be strong. And then, I can't help but to cry. . .through the longest two hours in my life.

At nineteen, I decide that I never again want to experience loneliness or being alone, and never have I in twenty-seven years of my adult life lived alone. As much as I crave some "alone" time as an introvert, as soon as I experience my "alone" time as really "being alone," it feels uneasy, uncomfortable, and scary.

It took me eight years to leave a first unhappy marriage because I was afraid of being alone and I left only when I knew I wouldn't be alone—I'd be with my current husband. But I've been chicken shit for three years (so far), scared to leave a now fourteen-year second marriage that has become unhappy and unhealthy.

Step 3: Blessings Derived

1. I learned that if I really set my mind to it, I could do and handle anything. I developed an "I can handle anything" attitude.
2. It was a chance to get away from a loving, yet controlling, mother, make my own decisions and learn to be independent.
3. I was learning the ropes here in the U.S. on my own, instead of being directed/guided/sheltered by my parents. I myself made choices about work, education, dating, etc.
4. I learned to be responsible for myself.
5. I learned how really strong I am. And no matter what self-doubts and insecurities I ever had, since I was nineteen, I have never doubted that I am a very strong woman.

6. I learned that I can be very sad and go through with what needs to be done anyway.

7. This started me on the path of finding power and guidance within versus looking to others for power and fulfillment.

8. Even though my parents came here six months after me, the fact that I left alone gave me more independence and confidence to not be (as) controlled by my mother after they came to the U.S.

9. My parents developed a different level of respect for me— I became their guide and support.

10. I developed respect for myself—for being able to go through this experience powerfully.

Step 4: Hypothetical Research Questions

A. Can someone who a) has never "experienced" freedom in life; and b) is afraid of being free, actually learn to be free and to powerfully experience freedom as a way of being?

B. Can someone who decided that her survival depends on always being strong allow herself to be vulnerable with people?

C. Can someone be powerful and vulnerable at the same time?

D. Can someone who has an ongoing internal conflict between being controlled and being alone learn to reconcile the two and have it not be either/or (either controlled or alone)?

Step 5: Owning the Lab Design

MY LAB ASSISTANTS

1. Parents in Russia
2. Grandparents in Los Angeles
3. Friends and boyfriend in Russia
4. Immigration agent

MY LAB ENVIRONMENT

1. Communist Russia
2. Being an only child
3. Living as dissidents and not being allowed to leave Russia for thirteen years

Step 6: Findings

A. *Question:* Can someone who a) has never "experienced" freedom in life; and b) is afraid of being free, actually learn to be free and to powerfully experience freedom as a way of being?

   Findings: I don't have the answer to that. I have been on that journey for the last few years. I have made major progress, and I am not yet there. Inconclusive.

B. *Question:* Can someone who decided that survival depends on always being strong allow herself to be vulnerable with people?

   Findings: I am not sure about this one as well. I still have challenges with being vulnerable with people I do not know. Inconclusive.

C. *Question:* Can someone be powerful and vulnerable at the same time?

   Findings: Maybe, to some degree. I think I am always at least somewhat guarded.

D. *Question:* Can someone who has an ongoing internal conflict between being controlled and being alone learn to reconcile the two and have it not be either/or (either controlled or alone)?

   Findings: I don't have the answer to that, either. I'm still on the discovery path here.

Step 7: Self-Expression Directives

- **Freedom as a way of being**
- **Being powerful versus being strong**
- **Vulnerability**

Discovery & Expression Analysis

E.V.'s Experiment: Nurtureless

Step 1: Serious and Significant Event or Influence

"Nurtureless"

Step 2: Victim Story

I was four when my mother gave birth to my sister. She was premature and, coupled with my mother's age (forty at the time), the stage was set for my sister to be coddled, protected and nurtured. I have very spotty childhood recollections but clearly remember the first time I saw my mother holding my baby sister through the glass window of the hospital room. Little did I know that I would feel as if I was on the outside looking in from that moment on.

Step 3: Blessings Derived

1. Resourcefulness.
2. A self-starter with a high degree of independence.
3. Made me strong—served me well in 2011 (breast cancer).
4. Created the drive to achieve and succeed with little direction.

Step 4: Hypothetical Research Questions

A. Can someone lacking nurturing learn to nurture/be capable of providing it to others?
B. Can self-expression be learned when absent for many years?

C. Can someone love and accept herself when not being fully self-expressed?

Step 5: Owning the Lab Design

LAB ASSISTANTS & LAB ENVIRONMENT

My mother was the perfect lab assistant. One of three sisters born of older parents in Cuba, she came to the U.S. and struggled with the challenges of a new country, language and culture. She and her sisters became teachers in Cuba in spite of a very humble upbringing. She was fiercely independent and outspoken for her time.

Having come to the U.S. in her thirties, my mother did not really understand things like after-school activities—sports, cheerleading, etc.—and, as an older parent (thirty-six when she had me), she was over-protective and cautious. Much of what my American friends were doing was not necessarily okay and a "no" was not uncommon. I learned to not ask for fear of or in avoidance of "no." My self-expression became stifled.

Her relationship with my father was challenged by their significantly divergent needs—him, the outgoing, social "butterfly;" her, the antithesis of that. My father, my second lab assistant, was the nurturing party that I should have gravitated to but his need for socializing resulted in absences that eventually turned to resentments as his and my mother's relationship soured.

Step 6: Findings

A. *Question:* Can someone lacking nurturing learn to nurture/be capable of providing it to others?

Findings: Yes! Although I decided to not have children very early on (likely a self-conscious assumption that I would be unable to provide nurturing), I was able to prove this is possible when I took in my niece for a couple of years. This also created a shift in my perception of parenting and a newfound respect for my parents, my sister and others whom I might have previously misjudged.

B. *Question*: Can self-expression be learned when it has been absent for many years?

Findings: This was not an easy one for me and is something I remain committed to. But the work I have done over the last fifteen-plus years has opened me up to the possibility of asking for what I need and expressing myself authentically. It is a work in progress, but achievable, nonetheless.

C. *Question:* Can someone love and accept herself when not being fully self-expressed?

Findings: Again, this has not always been an easy journey, but it is one well worth the effort and discomfort. When I feel uncomfortable with expressing myself in my relationships, I know that it is an opportunity to push past the fear and take the leap of faith that has me asking for and receiving what I want and need.

Step 7: Self-Expression Directives

- **Self-express**
- **Ask and be willing to receive**

Discovery & Expression Analysis
Darrell's Experiment: Brother's Psychological Abuse

Step 1: Serious and Significant Event or Influence

"Brother's Psychological Abuse"

Step 2: Victim Story

Another shaping impact of my overly critical father story was a series of events taking place in the third grade that set the stage for this particular serious and significant event or influence story.

I was always the class clown in school and developed a quick wit and sharp sense of humor early in life. I craved and grabbed attention in every way I could. In the early days, it was in a negative way, as a prankster and disrupter of the class. Later in high school, it expressed itself more positively, becoming the Straight-A-Student-Council-Vice-President-Star-of-the-High-School-Play. Either way, I was a sponge for attention.

In third grade, unbeknownst to me, my teacher told my parents that I should see a child psychologist because of my unruly and mischievous behavior.

First, it's important to realize that in 1970 Southeast Texas, at least in my household, anything that smacked of psychology implied that something was seriously wrong. I don't know for sure, because I was only a child; but I'll bet that seeing a psychologist back then in my community was as indelibly fixed on a person as the big "D" of "Divorced." In those days and in those parts of the world, it was a completely different environment around relationships and matters of the mind than exists today.

Dutifully following instructions, as caring parents, my mom and dad arranged for me to see a psychologist on a weekly basis for four weeks. I was driven by my father to the appointment in a town thirty minutes away. This was the bomb for me!

It wasn't the private meetings with some unknown, portly and balding man behind a desk, who asked me to look at ink-blots or figure out equations in my head, that excited me. It was the private meetings with this unknown man behind the steering wheel driving me there that gave me a unique thrill.

Me! Alone with him, my father! The man who related so well to my brother (but not to me) was now spending time with only me! In the truck! For thirty minutes each way! Once a week! Wow! I had my dad all to myself!

As mentioned in an earlier story of mine (Experiment: Overly Critical Dad) from Embrace 1, my father and I had many sensibility differences. It was rare for me to get his full attention rather than its going to my brother, who was more cut from my father's cloth. Needless to say, I relished those drives.

I don't remember what we spoke about. But I have a feeling, as I look back, he may have been harboring the thought that "something is wrong with Darrell," and therefore was probably uncharacteristically mild, loving and sweet with me. Perhaps his demeanor reflected how you'd drastically shift your interactions and mood with someone in your life once you found out they were going to die tomorrow.

The drives made me happy inside, and I did whatever I had to do with the unknown, portly, bald man behind the desk just to keep those drives going.

When I was twenty years old and home from college for a weekend, I learned from my mother, based on her recollection of events long afterward, that on the fifth week my parents went to see the unknown, portly, bald man behind the desk for his assessment of me. What she described to me, so many years later, shocked me.

She said the man told them, "You have a very bright, intelligent and creative son. He just needs more attention from his father." An astute observation from the unknown, portly, bald man behind the desk. BULLSEYE!

According to my mother, that same weekend, we visited our cabin by the lake in East Texas, where we generally traveled once a month. She described a scene in which we were fishing in the boat and I wanted to learn how to drive it.

She said she watched in amazement as my father sat patiently, giving me time and attention while gently showing me how to drive the boat. She described thinking to herself, "Who is this? I don't recognize this man!" as she watched my father. According to her, I was grinning from ear to ear, completely overjoyed and happy.

Unfortunately, on that same night when going to bed in the cabin, she said my father told her, "To hell with it! I can't do it," thereby ending his short Give-Darrell-Some-Specialized-Attention experiment.

Of course, this alone was hugely significant in my early, life-shaping influences. However, at the time, being unaware of all this behind-the-scenes activity, I only retained fond memories of those weeks spent going to see the unknown, portly, bald man behind the desk. So, the focus of this particular Discovery & Expression analysis is only on the aftermath of those events.

My brother and I had already divided into our respective camps by my third-grade year. Starting off as being close (so I'm told), by third grade we were in separate rooms and modeling the same dynamics as our parents' relationship: living within the same house and family, yet hugely different people—and argumentative as hell about it.

On a physical level, I lost fistfights with my brother. He was only twenty months older, so size wasn't really a factor. I guess he gained confidence from being cut from the same cloth as our father, who attended his sports practices and games and coached his teams.

I believe this gave him a psychological advantage over me because, as mentioned in my earlier analysis of Experiment: Overly Critical Dad, my father only came to my more creative events (e.g., band concerts) under duress from my mom. I was softer and sensitive like Mom; my brother was rougher and dominating like Dad.

A seeming mistake my parents made when I began to visit the unknown, portly, bald man behind the desk was to pull my brother aside privately and tell him, "Don't say anything about it, but your brother is going to see a psychologist." Then, they instructed him, "Be nice to Darrell."

Okay then! How is THAT for loading up the armory with enough ammunition for an entire childhood and adolescence of sibling rivalry? My brother was supplied with enough deadly tear gas to wrest control of each and every conflict in which we'd find ourselves for the next eight years. From then on, at some point within any argument or fight between us, this would be his arrow striking my Achilles heel: "Why don't you go see your psychologist, Little Psychologist Boy?"

Boy, did it work! Combined with inattention from my father and the stigma surrounding mental health professionals in that world, throwing out this simple ten-word line rendered me powerless and in tears. Over the next eight years, with my brother's consistent and affirmative support, I became thoroughly convinced that there was "something seriously wrong" with me. I carried this conviction into adult life.

Step 3: Blessings Derived

1. I became acquainted with and developed an appreciation for the domain of psychology much faster in my life than I would have. Having seen a psychologist for only four weeks at nine years of age would have probably been long-forgotten had it not been for my brother's continual reminder of being the "Little Psychologist Boy."

2. My consequential resistance to my brother pushed me away from more shallow, rough and tumble, dominant, hard-ass male personalities and toward deeper, intellectual, creative and spiritual males.

3. Trained me first-hand in how self-hatred arises, along with its dynamics and, therefore, how I might help myself and others overcome it.

4. Acquainted me with my internal world, where I would retreat emotionally. Even though it was a world of self-judgment, it nonetheless opened the door to an internal world.

5. Established within me a very sensitive and heart-centered aspect to my personality, one that I am even now becoming more authentically connected with.

6. Taught me the nature of psychological domination.

7. Gave me the ability to self-analyze. It was unhealthy and critical self-analysis at the time, but self-analysis nonetheless. At least the beginning of a window to Self.

8. Had me go out in search of my own empowering ways, peoples and environments in life because I wasn't getting the acceptance, encouragement and love I needed from my family of origin.

9. Gave me an internal check system, to keep me modest, humble and very present to my weaknesses.

10. Had me begin to learn how people are influenced in ways other than physical, brute force and bullying. The power of the mind. The power of inspiration.

Step 4: Research Questions

Possible research questions I was experimenting for in my life laboratory.

A. Can an individual trained in self-condemnation during self-concept-formative years ever heal through the power of the mind? Can the fields of psychology, ontology or any other "ology" successfully implant a love of Self?

B. Can an internal world historically planted with weeds and sticker bushes ever be cultivated into a beautiful floral or even Zen garden?

C. Can negative self-analysis ever be replaced with positive Self-analysis? Can one's ingrained nature in this regard ever be permanently shifted?

D. Can a cultivated, internal, check system that keeps someone modest (i.e., an internal critic to prevent standing out or getting too loud) ever be converted to an internal "what-the-heck" system to risk being magnificent? Can the voice that wants to keep a person small be replaced by one that supports standing tall?

E. Can someone shift an ingrained belief that "something's inherently wrong" with them to a new belief that "something's inherently right" with them?

F. Can the drive to go find empowering ways, peoples and environments be redirected to go within and find my own empowering ways, voices and mental and spiritual environments?

Step 5: Owning the Lab Design

MY LAB ASSISTANTS

Here's how I picked the perfect lab assistants to test my questions. My lead assistant, the star hire for this lab work, was, of course, my brother. What better way to staff a lab for experimenting on the above questions than to arm a ten-year-old boy, who's grabbing at any morsels for his own self-esteem, with ammunition like knowing that his little brother was going to do something his parents considered weird?

Having already staffed the environment with the father that I did, my brother was no less affected by the lack of positive strokes around our household. He needed his too and got some from the sports-oriented support of our father. But, of course, as would any adolescent, he naturally did whatever he could to feel "better" than the next kid. Watch kids. Heck, watch adults! Often, the way people feel good about themselves and deal with their own insecurities is to put someone else down. That somehow makes them feel "better." But whether or not as adults we mature beyond that tendency, kids are notorious for it.

So, I hired a kid just as thirsty for self-esteem-building acknowledgment as I was to play the role of delivering the nasty message. Without ingesting the nasty message, I could not have tested my hypotheses. My brother was just doing his job, and he did a bang-up performance! Heck, let's give that guy a performance bonus!

MY LAB ENVIRONMENT

I hired a couple supporting assistants for this experiment (lead lab assistants in other experiments, but supporting ones here)— my parents. In this experiment, these two VERY different people created the environment. To this day, they have proven that the old values of keeping a marriage together no matter what can succeed. However, three, five, or ten years into their marriage, when my brother and I were about those ages (in our Southern culture, you had kids immediately upon marriage), they fought like cats and dogs.

They were obviously working out their differences. Yet, from the perspective of my brother and me, disagreement, discord and domination comprised the ways two people interacted in close quarters; and we simply modeled that relationship. In modeling after them, for as far back as I can remember, we bickered in the same way our parents did; and I apparently chose the weaker, dominated side. How else could I test my hypotheses?

Also, I've mentioned that the home, family, cultural and societal environment in which I grew up did not put a lot of stock in things of a mental or internal nature. Therefore, anything that smacked of psychology or counseling, anything that pointed to an internal world, any sensitivities or sensibilities beyond the gregarious and swaggering "Texan" way of being was simply considered "crazy." What a perfect surrounding in which to choose to conduct my experiment.

My Mad Scientist deserves an Oscar for Casting and Set Design because the talent and location scouting was epic!

Step 6: Findings

A. *Question:* Can an individual trained in self-condemnation during self-concept formative years ever heal through the power of the mind? Can the fields of psychology, ontology, or any other "ology" successfully implant a love of Self?

   Findings: I believe so; and that really says it all, because "belief" (i.e., faith, knowing, conviction) is the one essential power of the mind that determines anything and everything that is possible. My job is to keep building the muscle of belief, for example, believing that I am free from any patterns from the past, believing that I am unlimited in what I can accomplish, believing that a full sense of internal love and acceptance is possible for me.

B. *Question:* Can an internal world historically planted with weeds and sticker bushes ever be cultivated into a beautiful floral or even Zen garden?

   Findings: Great question, isn't it? I must acknowledge my Mad Scientist for even coming up with such a great question to experiment with. Again, as in the findings of question A above, I believe so. The practice is to diligently keep planting new seeds while tending the garden. Left unattended for any amount of time, the weeds and stickers dominate again.

C. *Question:* Can negative self-analysis ever be replaced with positive Self-analysis? Can one's ingrained nature in this regard ever be permanently shifted?

Findings: This whole permanent-shifting-of-ingrained-nature question is bigger than my experiment has so far explored. I'm obviously still conducting that experiment, so I don't have conclusive results yet. But I get the sense, as in the findings of question B above, that with diligent and continuous practice, new, positive patterns can be developed and, perhaps over time, a permanent shift can occur. Until permanent, if ever, surely temporary and perhaps longer bouts of the positivity can emerge. The big and crucial factor to accept here is the need to pay continual attention to the tendency toward the negative, lest the garden become overgrown quickly.

D. *Question:* Can a cultivated, internal, check system that keeps someone modest (i.e., an internal critic to prevent standing out or getting too loud) ever be converted to an internal "what-the-heck" system to risk being magnificent? Can the voice that wants to keep a person small be replaced by one that supports standing tall?

Findings: All of these findings seem to be yielding the same conclusions. Yes, with continual and diligent cultivation of the tall-making voice while blessing the small-making voice, I have experienced that new, freeing patterns can come about.

I say blessing the small-making voice because attempting to do battle with or eliminate it only meets with resistance. This small-making voice arose initially to keep me safe. It was developed to help me protect whatever amount of self-esteem or self-love I had and to shield me from more outside criticism and judgment. So, that voice is not my enemy. It is simply uneducated at this point. It has failed to mature along with the rest of my mind, body and soul. It still thinks that holding on to me tightly in an attempt to keep me "safe" is the best option. But, like the character Lennie in *Of Mice and Men,* who gripped the mouse he loved too strongly, the small-making voice continuing to ignorantly hold on so firmly could eventually kill me and my true spirit. So, I can choose to bless that small-making voice and appreciate that it helped me survive early on. Rather than resist or reprimand it now, I can ask it to simply be willing to join me in following the tall-making voice to see what it can show us.

The small-making voice can be educated and matured. Like encouraging my young son to join me on a theme park ride that he is initially scared of, I can gently and playfully nudge that small-making voice to come along and see the bigger games to play that the tall-making voice is revealing.

E. *Question:* Can someone shift an ingrained belief that "something's inherently wrong" with them to a new belief that "something's inherently right" with them?

Findings: Same findings here: Yes, *if* I'm vigilant to affirm the latter to myself and to notice, watch and acknowledge all instances in which that truth is revealed. With that, I have a good chance of believing that "something's inherently right" about me." If I don't actively look for and make note of what's inherently right on a daily basis, I will default to my old programming of seeing what I perceive to be those things inherently wrong. The Law of Attraction states that we get more of whatever we focus on. So, by shifting my focus on a daily basis, I will see more of what I want to see and less of what I don't want to see, thereby creating the chance for a new pattern to take root.

F. *Question:* Can the drive to go out and find empowering ways, peoples, and environments be redirected to go within and find my own empowering ways, voices and mental and spiritual environments?

Findings: Yes, and I'm continuing that process here in this whole Back Forty adventure. As mentioned before, I've searched externally through multitudes of spiritual, personal development and enlightenment communities and have always been one to look for an "answer" in some new program. I don't discount or question at all the value of having done that. It has aligned me with some of the greatest minds and uplifting communities on the planet. Yet, virtually all of these empowering programs and communities have taught the same message: All That I Need is Within Me. I believe that's the sign of a truly empowering outside influence versus a dominating or controlling one—it directs each of us to our own truth within.

So, though I'll likely continue to expand myself with even newer discoveries of what's "out there" in consciousness, at the same time I'll continue highly regarded expansion of the new discoveries of what's "in here" to play with and for.

Step 7: Self-Expression Directives

Possible Self-Expression Directives from "Brother's Psychological Abuse."

- **The Power of Belief, specifically, Belief that Change is Possible**
- **Self-esteem Renewal (at any age)**
- **Accentuate the Positive**

- Bold Self-expression
- Self-reliance

Discovery & Expression Analysis
Alexandra's Experiment: Brain Scan

Step 1: Serious and Significant Event or Influence

"Brain Scan"

Step 2: Victim Story

I am in some medical room, very cold and bare, with scary looking equipment everywhere. My mom and dad are there and they are telling me I will have to sleep there for the night, without them. I am three or four or five—I don't remember how old. I'm petrified. Then I am in a chair and someone is shaving bits of hair off my head. Locks of hair fall on the floor as if pieces of me are torn out of me. Tears of terror are running down my face, but my parents tell me that everything will be okay. I don't think it will be okay.

Then I am on a hospital bed, and someone is gluing things to my head that are connected to a machine. I'm helpless and I can't move. My parents tell me that there is something wrong with me and my head and that I need to get this medical test done. All this feels cruel and scary. I cry and plead to no avail. They kiss me goodbye and leave.

They are not allowed to stay with me, and I need to spend the night with my head connected to the scary machines. This is scary. . .life is scary. . .world is scary.

I am scared and alone, and I'm helpless. There is nothing I can do about it. Lab machines are big and powerful. I am small and powerless. I decide that if my parents, the two people who know me best and love me most think that there is something wrong with me, then there really *is* something *wrong* with me. And

I go through life with a deep-seated belief that there is something wrong with me, that I'm really messed up, fucked up, not okay. Not smart, not beautiful, not interesting. . .not much at all.

For over forty years, I go through life saying that I don't have any talents or special gifts. I'm still not clear if I have any, really.

Step 3: Blessings Derived

1. I developed a well-put-together, outer persona. As my coach friend Peter said, "Only someone really screwed up could look so perfectly well put together on the outside."
2. I may have learned deeply that, no matter what happens, I will be okay, given that, as scary as that was, I survived and my parents picked me up in the morning.
3. I learned modesty, humility and to not be full of myself.
4. I may have learned to trust my parents because they did what they said they would do.
5. I learned to be likeable and agreeable.
6. Because of my belief that I am not naturally talented, I learned to work hard for what I wanted, as things were not going to just come to me.
7. I learned to be content with what I have, as I never thought of myself as being extraordinarily deserving of more.
8. I developed appreciation for my life, my family, and my daughters—as I have said repeatedly for years, I'm amazed I ended up with a normal life, as a wife and a mother, instead of ending up in some mental institution.
9. I don't like going to doctors.
10. I learned to be accepting of other people, their idiosyncrasies, their strangeness and their messed-up ness.

Step 4: Research Questions

A. Can someone who thinks there is something wrong with her learn to stand up for herself and for what she believes in and learn to be fully self-expressed?

B. Can someone who's view of herself is that she is screwed up develop a voice that is to be heard, an inner voice to be listened to, and learn to trust herself, her judgment and her intuition?

C. Can someone who has believed there is something wrong with her accept herself as Divine's perfect creation?

D. Can trusting yourself be learned in The Back Forty?

E. Can someone who sees the world as inherently scary and herself as helpless learn to not only be safe and heard, but also to stand up for herself?

F. Can someone who is used to seeing herself as small accept her own bigness?

Step 5: Owning the Lab Design

MY LAB ASSISTANTS

1. Mom and Dad (loving yet firm in leaving me there).
2. Unfriendly medical assistants, who operate from a there's-many-of-you-and-one-of-me mentality; so don't expect warmth and compassion.

MY LAB ENVIRONMENT

1. Sterile, cold, impersonal lab room.
2. Scary lab equipment: machines are big; I'm small.

Step 6: Findings

Findings: Yes, to all of the hypothetical research questions. Yet again, requiring personal work, self-digging, and being what I say I am instead of what I feel like. Learning to see myself with the eyes of the Divine.

Step 7: Self-Expression Directives

- **Be Divine Creation**
- **Trust my intuition**
- **Be big in the world**
- **Self-expression**

- **Be heard**
- **Be safe**
- **Stand up for myself**
- **Self-trust**

Discovery & Expression Analysis

Darrell's Experiment: Losing Luggage in Newark

Step 1: Serious and Significant Event or Influence

"Losing Luggage in Newark"

Step 2: Victim Story

Having my luggage stolen is a seemingly inconsequential event in the bigger picture of adult life, but it created a very significant shift and disconnect in my sense of belonging at the time.

As a twenty-two-year-old college grad, I left the U.S. for a year abroad in Europe. I was part of a student exchange program enabling me to work in London for a year after six-weeks of vagabonding throughout mainland Europe. I had never been overseas and had only been out of the country once during a high school band trip to Mexico. I felt like a fifteenth-century explorer traveling to distant lands. Other than my father and an uncle who had joined the Navy, I was the first young person in my extended Southern family to go abroad.

During my college years, I was a five-hour drive from my hometown. The distance made it easier to create the personal identity I wanted, rather than the one I'd inherited from childhood.

Now, in planning to be abroad for over a year, I decided to take everything with me that was near and dear to that new identity. Needless to say, it turned out to be way too much luggage!

My two huge, stretchable, vinyl suitcases were loaded with everything that reminded me of who I was. I packed awards, journals, various college pictures, spiritual materials, favorite books, clothes, etc. I had to sit on the bags to zip them up! They were packed so tightly that, in today's TSA/hyper-security-alert airports, they would be considered tantamount to bomb-laden cases. Also, given they were probably 150 lbs. each, it would cost a small fortune today to take them on a plane.

My plan was to leave the two bags in London while I traveled and to keep with me a backpack, which was also stuffed tight with everything I would need for six weeks of vagabonding through Europe before beginning the job in London.

Completing the first leg of my flight, arriving in Newark from Houston early in the morning, I didn't retrieve any bags at baggage claim. I had organized a full day of seeing New York City for the first time before continuing my trip later that evening. I planned to claim the bags and move them to the other airline at that time.

The day in New York was fabulous—as much as you can see in eight hours. But, upon arriving back at the terminal, my plan fell apart—my large bags were gone, only my backpack remained.

Eastern Airlines' policy was to lock up unclaimed baggage with a long cable passing through the baggage handles. Unfortunately, that day little attention was paid to the cable being securely fastened. Also, unknown by me was the fact that Newark International Airport was then notoriously famous for stolen luggage because they didn't check baggage claim tickets when people left the terminal, as was the general practice in other airports at that time.

Headed to Europe—the biggest departure from everything I knew in my small, simple world—I had now lost everything that reminded me of who I was. The missing bags held my identity. Getting out into the world for the first time, this was more of a rude awakening than I had bargained for.

I spent the night in a Newark hotel while the airline confirmed, for certain, that I had neither any bags nor baggage insurance. I talked for hours on the phone with my parents and girlfriend, seriously and significantly questioning whether this was a "sign" that I should stay home. I cried a good bit and made an inventory from memory of the contents in the bags including my recently earned graduation ring. *Why wear it while vagabonding?* I had thought when putting it in the bag.

After much wailing and gnashing of teeth, I proceeded with the trip, catching a plane to London the next evening. This time, however, I was leaving home a different person because now I had nothing to tell me who I was. Dramatic? Yes, I thought so. And that's the point of telling the story.

Step 3: Blessings Derived

A. Losing my "bagged" identity, I became more open and impressionable, more available to be impacted by the new worlds I explored, rather than having a boxed-in perspective represented by old stuff. I was more raw and engaged than I would have been just as an identity-provisioned tourist/observer.

B. This violent uprooting had me more quickly complete a previously begun developmental phase of my life (the college years transition away from my familial roots) and move more rapidly into the next phase of bigger-picture, less parochial thinking. Though going to Austin for college was a big step outside of my small-town upbringing, even that cultural environment, when coupled with a strong Texan mentality, could severely limit a greater world view.

C. Without my usual stuff to tell me who and what I was, I adapted to and adopted other ways of living, dressing, and conducting my life.

D. This young adult lesson of giving up stuff from the past (physical/tangible, mental and emotional) served as a first training ground and warm-up to many more opportunities to un-stuff later in life.

E. This instant immersion into a bigger world served me well in accelerating my growth. It gave me both an experience and a particular confidence arising from that experience, which still allows me to instantly immerse myself into new environments with general ease when the need arises.

Step 4: Research Questions

A. Can a security blanket-carrying small-town guy be catapulted into big world culture shock virtually overnight without breaking?

B. Can someone who previously identified with his stuff get to know and identify with who he is under the stuff?

C. Can one learn to let go of the trappings of the past and be available and open to the present moment and the world of possibilities available in it?

D. Can a person grow where he's planted, regardless of where he came from?

Step 5: Owning the Lab Design

MY LAB ASSISTANTS

By far, the lead Lab Assistant in this experiment was the person I hired to steal my bags. See how this works? I *hired* someone to do a job for me without ever even meeting them on the conscious level!

Interestingly, when I stand in a place of responsibility for having put together this whole experiment myself, I can get even more pointed in my depiction of what happened: I didn't hire him or her to *steal* my bags; I hired him or her to *take away my bags* or to *relieve me of my bags.*

When I look at the goodies I got out of being "relieved" of these bags, it's obvious that they were a burden that I wasn't consciously aware of. It's clear now that they were a block to my greater growth and ability to perceive a bigger world, which I was only beginning to open up to. So, I can now say, "Bully good job, Unknown Person, who did what you were hired to do!"

MY LAB ENVIRONMENT

I've pondered this event a great deal since it occurred. I picked an airport with obviously sloppy security and a reputation of having bags stolen, which I only found out later. Here's the fascinating point: those big airports that used to check your claim ticket then don't do that anymore and I've *never had another bag stolen in over thirty years!* That's counting times when I haven't claimed my bags immediately for whatever reason and includes golf clubs, skis, and other obvious items of value. I clearly chose the perfect environment that I needed at the time—Newark International—to accomplish my experimental objectives!

Step 6: Findings

A. *Question:* Can a security-blanket-carrying small-town guy be catapulted into big world culture shock virtually overnight without breaking?

Findings: Obviously, the answer is yes because I kept breathing (amid tears) and kept moving forward instead of retreating.

B. *Question:* Can someone who previously identified with his stuff get to know and identify with who he is under the stuff?

Findings: Interesting that this was my first opportunity to go "understuff" (akin to undercover) to know who I was. I've had similar opportunities presented to me over the course of my Back Forty initiation, when circumstances of the moment removed houses, cars and savings from my world of possessions. I now *know* that real power lies in identifying with the true Self under the stuff. I am, however, still actively "in the lab" on this one.

C. *Question:* Can one learn to let go of the trappings of the past and be available and open to the present moment and the world of possibilities available in it?

Findings: Yes, I did it back then for sure, as I tapped into fresh moments ahead of me after being freed up from physical ties to the past. As with the findings of question B above, however, this is an ongoing work-in-progress as I learn to let go of more mature trappings of stuff (e.g., mental, emotional, physical).

D. *Question:* Can a person grow where he's planted, regardless of where he came from?

Findings: Yes. Fact is, I realize that we either grow or die. Our job is simply to grow. To grow *anyway*. To grow despite how the "gardens" we land in don't fit the *Better Homes & Gardens* pictures in our heads even as we unconsciously choose exactly them. Have you ever noticed that plants and weeds can grow right through concrete? I see this all the time when running. I'll notice the smallest crack, where it's completely unimaginable that any light could have crept in, and there will be a shoot coming through that crack in the road, be it asphalt or concrete.

So, yes, as proven by plants, it's possible to grow wherever we land and in whatever conditions we find ourselves. Or, just die. No in between.

Step 7: Self-Expression Directives

- **Grow and Go Forward**
- **Know Thy "Understuff" Self**
- **Be Here Now**
- **Resilience**
- **Find the Light. . .In Any Darkness**

Discovery & Expression Analysis

G.A.'s Experiment: Psycho-Mom

Step 1: Serious and Significant Event or Influence

"Psycho-Mom"

Step 2: Victim Story

Happened on numerous occasions, from being a young girl of eight to when my mother died when I was fifty-four. I would be sitting quietly on my bed, reading or watching TV, and my mom would come in and start ranting, "Get up! There's a lot of work to do! What, do you think, a maid lives here?" Or, I would be sleeping on Sunday morning and she would come in and start vacuuming at 7:00 a.m. and start yelling at me and my sister to get up.

As a little kid, it left me feeling confused and with a belief that I always had to be in motion. And I think it resulted in a form of PTSD and caused a lot of anxiety in just waiting to see what she would do next.

To this day, I feel a lot of anxiety. For example, if a client calls with a request that is urgent, I get anxious and start stressing out even if the request only takes a few minutes to address.

Step 3: Blessings Derived

1. I could have gotten stuck in some very self-defeating patterns but was able to rise above it all and see the truth.
2. Became a very productive, hard-working person who has accomplished a lot more than I ever thought I would as a kid.
3. Learned to move beyond limitations imposed as a kid with a drive to succeed and do even more.
4. Helped me understand people better and treat them with more kindness and empathy than what I was raised with. Helped me learn to respect people.
5. Taught me to manage myself around adversity and anxiety.
6. Had me decide it was okay to have fun, and maybe even play first.
7. Helped me learn to deal with different people.
8. Gave me an entrepreneurial spirit to move beyond limitations.
9. Gained a blessing of discipline by growing up with two parents teaching it in their own way.

Step 4: Research Questions

A. Can an anxious, self-critical gal get past this busyness, having to stay busy, and really stop and have some fun?
B. Can a person who has been taught to work like the dickens ever kick back and have some fun, balancing work and play?

Step 5: Owning the Lab Design

LAB ASSISTANTS

Psycho-Mom was old-school Greek with a hard-work-ALL-the-time ethic. She grew up on an island in Greece during World War II. What formed her personality was that she was very poor and lived through World War II occupation by the Germans.

LAB ENVIRONMENT

In the 1960s and 1970s, this was how things were done.

Step 6: Findings

A. *Question:* Can an anxious, self-critical gal get past this busyness, having to stay busy, and really stop and have some fun?

Findings: Yes! Take what I learned and move forward. Yes!

B. *Question:* Can a person who's been taught to work like the dickens ever kick back and have fun, balancing work and play?

Findings: Yes!

Step 7: Self-Expression Directives

- Have fun
- Play and experiment
- Change is good

Discovery & Expression Analysis

G.A.'s Experiment: Company Collapse

Step 1: Serious and Significant Event or Influence

"Company Collapse"

Step 2: Victim Story

Issue happened between 2012 and 2013. Cruising along working for a company. It was a high-growth and profitable start-up. Manufacturing issue was discovered that almost took the company down. So, managing a high-growth company turned into managing cash by the minute.

I thought by 2013 that I would have cashed out and been rich. Instead, I was struggling to keep the doors of the company open. Ended up with pay cuts, layoffs, loss of confidence of the Board of Directors, and they brought in a part-time CFO.

Ended up feeling demoted and demoralized by the experience after putting my heart and soul into the job. Also felt old and stale because now I was fifty-three or fifty-four and considered an older worker. I had been with this company for seven years. I was lost and, for the first time, realized it might be hard to get a job.

Step 3: Blessings Derived

1. Decided to leave the job and, two years earlier than planned, start my own consulting business, realizing a dream I had wanted to pursue.
2. Met Darrell, went through career transition program, got branding and started networking.
3. Got up to date on technology tools used in accounting and finance, cloud tools.
4. Started looking for a new job, brand new spiffy resume with Darrell.
5. Realized I was more than this job and started taking care of myself.
6. Learned to manage cash in crisis situations, a skill that has come in handy in working with start-ups and small companies.
7. Recognized I had a lot of marketable skills in finance.
8. Much better prepared to work with start-ups and deal with the typical start-up issues with a sense of calm and experience. Cash flow is the number one issue.
9. Learned to handle crisis and negotiate with vendors, banks and Boards of Directors.

Step 4: Research Questions

A. Is it possible to make BIG career moves and play BIG after fifty?

B. Can someone over fifty start their own business and have marketable skills they can sell?

Step 5: Owning the Lab Design

LAB ASSISTANTS

Big cast of characters:

1. CEO
2. Board of Directors
3. Vendors
4. Bank
5. Staff at the company

LAB ENVIRONMENT

Startup, turned into growing company, turned into manufacturing mess. The perfect laboratory.

Step 6: Findings

A. *Question:* Is it possible to make BIG career moves and play BIG after fifty?

   Findings: Yes!

B. *Question:* Can someone over fifty start their own business and have marketable skills they can sell?

   Findings: Yes!

Step 7: Self-Expression Directives

- **Motivated**
- **Self-trust**

- Faith in Self
- Fun
- Confidence in Self

Discovery & Expression Analysis

Darrell's Experiment: Breakup with Sandra

Step 1: Serious and Significant Event or Influence

"Breakup with Sandra"

Step 2: Victim Story

For a guy who has been married and had many other long-term relationships, why would one breakup at the age of twenty-three stand out?

Because what happened then shaped every other relationship from that point forward.

While in college, I had lots of girlfriends; however, I met Sandra while working for the Texas State Senate during my first five months after graduation. I was in the process of setting up my upcoming year overseas and, out of left field and for the first time, I experienced falling in love. We met four months before I was to leave and fell youthfully, sticky sweet for each other. We planned for her to focus on graduating during my year abroad, but to visit me in London during the year-end holidays. Upon returning to the U.S., I would go to law school, we would get married and do the romantic house + 2.5 kids + dog + SUV dream.

To maintain connection during my travels, she gave me forty-five individual love-notes and cards to carry with me in my backpack while vagabonding. (International calls were outrageously expensive then and personal cell phones were virtually non-existent.) I opened one letter per day while traveling until I settled in London. My heart was captured.

After the backpacking tour, I began a work-exchange program in London with what was then considered a "Big 8" accounting firm. I spent the first four weeks of my lunch hours at the travel store on the corner, planning a holiday trip with Sandra. I booked us on a train to the Italian Alps for Christmas. I sent her pictures from brochures of sleigh rides and skiing, keeping the destination a surprise. I planned what would surely be a Big Screen-worthy, love story getaway.

Despite the cost, I thought I'd surprise Sandra with a call on Thanksgiving Day back in the States. So, at about 4:00 p.m. London time, I called to hopefully wake her up in Texas with an unexpected "Happy Thanksgiving!"

I made the call and I said it, but her reaction didn't match my intention behind the "happy" and "thanks." Sandra quickly told me she'd met someone while she was back in school, was happy with him, and apologized for not telling me sooner. So, rather than an expatriate experiencing hometown Thanksgiving energy, it quickly became a typically dank British day.

Granted, we had only fallen in love some ten months earlier and had only spent six of those in proximity to each other, but it still came hard. Maybe this was because I was, in fact, in love; or perhaps she was just my last foothold on a former identity that was now fully stripped away. Regardless, I felt devastated. The months of strategizing our reunion, the excitement of romantically whisking her off to the Italian Alps all came crashing down in minutes.

I recall leaving home that evening bound for somewhere on the London underground. An hour later, I found myself in an unknown park in the middle of a torrential rainstorm, sitting under my "brolly" (umbrella) at a picnic table. I was sober, but drunk with sorrow. I even begged and bargained with God on what I'd do if I got through this. Highly dramatic. I felt destroyed.

In looking back, I sense that I unconsciously decided that I never wanted to experience that level of pain again. I believe that survival-based, subconscious resolution resulted in a pattern of head-based and logical, rather than heart-based and emotionally intimate, relationships from that point forward. I was never going to feel that out of control ever again.

Step 3: Blessings Derived

1. Freed me up from more baggage and ties to my past and the security-blanket therein.
2. Opened me up to more introspective, personal time while out in the bigger world.
3. Made me available to relationships, activities and interactions I would not have otherwise engaged in without the additional time and freedom.
4. Left me raw and more impacted by the people and environments around me because I had no remaining lock on my identity.
5. Allowed for a completely different future to unfold from what had been previously planned and agreed upon. I was to go back to Texas from London, get married and go to law school. An entirely other-than-that future took place.
6. Got me off the straight and narrow path to law school. With the intensity I lived from in those days, I'm sure as a lawyer I would have experienced a heart attack by age thirty.
7. Got my first jolt of the importance of a self-identity independent of relationship.
8. Was the final straw in breaking from my parochial Texan past and a corresponding catapult into the world of Self-discovery and personal development.
9. Provided a lesson in relationship integrity, given I had slept with a British girl only a month before Sandra broke up with

me. Coincidence, or lesson? I've always looked back at that incident when tempted to cheat in a relationship, and it has kept me straight.

10. Had my first, surrendered, giving-up-to-a-Higher Power spiritual experience in the wake of the breakup, as I was truly distraught.

Step 4: Research Questions

A. Can a person be stripped of the major identity foundations upon which he stands and still remain open to the world around him?

B. What does openness allow for that rootedness and stability do not?

C. How does one develop trust that a better plan than your own will take you where you're supposed to be?

D. When emotional foundations are removed, how fragile can one become before breaking?

E. What is the value of fragility for spurring on growth and change?

F. Is who I am dependent upon who I am in relationship with?

G. Do my small, seemingly invisible breaches of integrity really impact my life?

Step 5: Owning the Lab Design

MY LAB ASSISTANTS

The lead Lab Assistant was obviously Sandra. I hired someone who fit my need to uplift and inspire. I had a pattern at the time of getting into relationship with women who were down in some way and building them back up. It was a penchant for training/developing/helping in intimate relationships that I only learned to let go of many years later.

Sandra had dropped out of college when I met her and, in our few months together before leaving, I encouraged her to go back and finish her degree while I was abroad. It was in one of her classes that she met her new guy.

She was enough of a perfect combination of gorgeous and Texas-feminine (a distinction all its own) to warrant my putting everything on hold. I remember that I was so incredibly faithful while traveling six weeks through Europe that when beautiful, topless French women smiled at me on the beach in Nice I kept on reading my pre-packaged card for the day. I didn't even talk to them.

My Supporting Lab Assistant would be the British girl whom I did sleep with a month before the breakup. Though she played a minor role, her participation gave me experience in relationship integrity, which I still reflect on even to this day.

MY LAB ENVIRONMENT

Obviously, the best way to strip someone of all foundations of identity is to take them completely out of their surroundings and sever all ties with those who know them as they are. With both luggage and relationship "baggage" now lost, I was fresh and raw.

Sure, I had my family back home; but as described in earlier analyses, those ties did not affirm who I wanted to be. They weren't critical to the stability of my identity. Going into a new culture and losing a major emotional tie on my heart and my sense of self created the best laboratory conditions for the testing of my hypotheses.

Also, to support the lab test on relationship integrity, no better environment exists than the allure and attraction of exoticism. From a small-town Texas boy's perspective, this British gal's accent and foreign culture made for exotic allure and high turn-on. Funny that I resisted in France but succumbed in England.

Step 6: Findings

A. *Question:* Can a person be stripped of the major identity foundations upon which he stands and still remain open to the world around him?

Findings: Yes, and unless you stay driven in a futile attempt to reclaim the fallen foundations, no other choice exists than to remain open to the world around you. The former path keeps you closed and insular.

Thank God some things in life are taken away without *any* possibility of reclamation. Otherwise, for sure, I would have wasted huge efforts in attempting to get my losses back. My lost luggage could absolutely not be found, no matter how much I fretted. Similarly, even were I to have spent a fortune on phone calls or dropped everything and returned prematurely to the States, any attempt to reclaim Sandra from the more immediate arms of someone in her backyard would have, no doubt, proven futile.

B. *Question:* What does openness allow for that rootedness and stability do not?

Findings: New paths, new adventures, new connections, new relationships, new awareness. Jesus said, "In my Father's house there are many mansions." If we stay solely focused on our own particular door to our own particular house, our own particular furniture laid out the way we know it and our own particular stuff organized within that house the way we've organized it, we can never see nor explore what lies through other doorways beyond our own lone world.

Mental health professionals, as well as life, teach us that a certain amount of rootedness is necessary for our human mind and nature to feel safe. A sense of "home" is a basic stability structure we rely on. It's a foundation which, when in place, allows us to better aspire to greater levels of personal development and Self-expression. However, my answer to the hypothetical question, from my own laboratory of experience, is that rootedness and stability at too great a level can impede openness to other doorways and mansions available to us. Therefore, in short, my lesson is to pray for uprootedness.

C. *Question:* How does one develop trust that a better plan than your own will take you where you're supposed to be?

Findings: Two ways: First, allowing your plans to be changed (ideally without kicking and screaming all the while) gives you real, first-hand experience in seeing a better plan unfold. Second, analyzing every changed plan for the unique Discovery & Expression goodies it contains provides the proof in the pudding. Confidence that a better plan than your own can take you where you're supposed to be is developed by building the muscle of trust. That trust grows when you make it a self-fulfilling prophecy that ANY plan that unfolds (your own, or another) is PERFECT by analyzing the Be Cause perfection in it.

D. *Questions:* When emotional foundations are removed, how fragile can one become before breaking?

Findings: Obviously, I didn't break, so I don't know the answer to that one, nor am I consciously interested in finding out. But it does bring up the question of exactly what "breaking" refers to. What is it to "break"? To become completely non-functional is not useful, and that may be the first impression that occurs when we consider "breaking." Yet, to be *broken* free and thereby released from old concepts or false emotional foundations can definitely serve a purpose.

Often what may appear to be a "nervous breakdown" is simply a high-momentum release from old foundations we're not meant to continue building upon. Metaphorically speaking, going back to rebuild those structures after a storm, as opposed to finding new land upon which to build, may be the worst use of one's energy. Nonetheless, rebuilding is how the mind wants to deal with a "break," so as to avoid or shorten the period of non-functioning. It wants to go fix what was versus moving on to what's next.

I've heard it said, "don't avoid the void." So, perhaps allowing for a certain amount of non-functional time for lessons to sink in is a wise move. The void may offer some valuable real estate advice about new land upon which to build.

E. *Question:* What is the value of fragility for spurring on growth and change?

Findings: The fear most associated with fragility is becoming non-functional. As stated above, complete and ongoing non-functionality does nobody any good. Yet, being forced to a point of fragility that precedes "breaking" can serve a valuable purpose to elicit growth and change.

Let's face it: We don't change when things are moving along well. Growth and change only occur when we're outside of our comfort zones. Therefore, the question, which I continue to explore, becomes how much change must come about through unplanned (i.e., unconsciously planned) pain and discomfort versus by way of consciously planned pain and discomfort? Perhaps this is a strange concept to consider: planned pain and discomfort. Yet, it's a very real tactic I've learned to employ.

It's been said that pain pushes until vision pulls. When you consider pain, what is it other than the discomfort experienced when something is not easy? A good example is the pain of exercise or working out in the gym to build tone and muscle. Muscle mass is only grown by the constant tearing down of what already exists to rebuild something stronger. Yet, such pre-planned pain and discomfort are much more tolerable than the pain from the alternatives of ill health, low energy or weak muscles.

In the same way, I've learned that creating visions out ahead of me—things, circumstances or conditions beyond what I'm experiencing now—definitely creates pain and discomfort because I must face who I am to be and what I am to do to fulfill that vision. Yet, the pre-planned pain and discomfort of visioning is much more tolerable, and even enjoyable, in forwarding my life than the alternative of having unplanned pain and discomfort direct the show. My spirit wants me to grow; so, I can either take a proactive hand in designing visionary, outside-my-comfort-zone experiments to accomplish that, or I can blindly rely on the Mad Scientist to simply do it all himself.

Some high-performing individuals demonstrate an interesting, next-level development of the visioning idea: when *true* visioning actually results in absolutely painless advancement. Growth without the push of pain! That higher-level possibility has me continuing my experiments in the lab.

F. *Question:* Is who I am dependent upon who I am in relationship with?

Findings: It used to be. I used to depend on the other person knowing my greatness and loving me as support for my ability to love myself. I lived on second-hand self-love. I say second-hand because, as we dig deeper into the whole responsibility question (the choice to see ourselves as the total and complete CAUSE of everything we experience), we *realize* that we've hired all of the lead and supporting lab assistants in every aspect of our lives. If I hired someone to know my greatness and love me, then I was really wanting that outside vehicle to give me back what I already must have known at some deeper level about myself: that I am great and worthy of being loved.

The rub is that I'm still hiring individuals to fulfill this function as lab assistants for me (while I fulfill it for them) and still very much enjoy and appreciate their service!

At least, now I have an awareness that who I AM is independent of any of the love-and-greatness-affirming assistants I've hired. I'm now aware, as the Mad Scientist of my domain, that I have infinite ability and capacity to re-staff my lab at any point. Therefore, I'm not dependent on any particular assistant for WHO I AM.

G. *Question:* Do my small, seemingly invisible, breaches of integrity really impact my life?

Findings: Of course, I could tell myself that Sandra was already in the process of breaking up with me a month before I called her, since she must have met and started dating this other guy long before then. However, how do I really know that my tryst with the British girl around this time didn't impact something in the Universe to bring about the breakup?

It all comes down to whatever meaning I'm going to attach to the event. As humans, we possess meaning-making machinery. We manufacture and choose the meanings we wish to ascribe to anything and everything in life, whether we're conscious of it or not. Some will choose an empowering meaning out of the same event/situation/circumstance that another person would choose to see as devastating.

My goal is to choose meanings that empower me. Therefore, I've chosen to answer this hypothetical question with yes. I've continued to experiment with this question for most of my adult life. It's sometimes hard to believe that the little, even invisible (to others) things I do that don't support my long-term advancement and fulfillment can truly impact my results; but, in ongoing experimentation, I find that they do.

It's a darn good thing I had Sandra break up with me! I obviously opened up to learn so much more through her having done so!

Step 7: Self-Expression Directives

- Begin Again (. . .and again. . .and again)
- Stay Open and Flexible (no matter how solid things appear)
- Trust a Bigger Plan than My Own
- Milk the Void
- Pre-Plan My Pain. . . or Just Vision
- Know My Self Firsthand
- Integrity is Everything

My three stories above, along with "Experiment: Overly Critical Dad," shared in "Embrace: Your Past," and another I will share later in Embrace 5 make up my Top 5 Serious and Significant "becauses" from the past when beginning my own Back Forty explorations. The process—this 7-Step Discovery & Expression Method—has taken me a long way towards being the Be Cause of my life, with no one to blame, nothing to forgive and nothing needing closure. Best of all, it has helped me ignite my wasn't-just-going-to-happen-anyway future from the Formulas of Unique Self Expression (FUSEs) found in the Self-Expression Directives that emerged from my Discovery & Expression investigations.

DARRELL'S LIFE E-VALUATION RESULTS

FROM "EMBRACE 4: YOUR VALUES"

Here I'll lay out my own personal responses and insights from several years ago to the various surveys included in "Embrace 4: Your Values." You'll see how I ranked the list of values and my answers to the corresponding questions for each survey.

Remember, of course, that my answers are mine and yours are yours. We are each simply unfolding our own discerning roadmaps for our respective Back Forties. Don't limit yourself in any extent based on my own insights or extent of writing. Explore and write down everything that seems relevant to you. This is your map.

Darrell's Survey Responses
Feeling & Experiencing Values
Ranked in order of importance, with 1 being highest in value and 20 being lowest.

1. __1__ Achievement—success and contribution
2. __2__ Worthiness—value and self-esteem
3. __3__ Wisdom—deep knowledge and insight
4. __4__ Spirituality—sensing a bigger plan or direction
5. __5__ Serenity—inner calm and peacefulness
6. __6__ Affluence—prosperity and material comforts
7. __7__ Thrill—excitement and adventure
8. __8__ Autonomy—independence
9. __9__ Wellbeing—physical, mental and emotional health and vitality
10. __10__ Approval—appreciation, acknowledgement and recognition
11. __11__ Intimacy—primary relationship, romance and deep love
12. __12__ Camaraderie—fellowship and friendship
13. __13__ Fun—joy and playfulness
14. __14__ Family—proximity and bonding of close relations
15. __15__ Legacy—having an impact
16. __16__ Fairness—equality for all
17. __17__ Global welfare—world peace and brotherhood
18. __18__ Beauty—aesthetics of nature and the arts
19. __19__ Security—safety and certainty
20. __20__ Style—flair and fashion

You'll notice that my ranking is in the same order as in the survey list itself.

My Insights about My Feeling & Experiencing Values

1. *What do you notice from ranking your list?*

   I notice that I rank more long-range, lasting-impact and age-less Feeling & Experiencing values higher. That's not to say my lower-ranking values can't be perceived as long-range as well.

I just see achievement, worthiness, wisdom and spirituality as more personally important and longer lasting than concern over my security or expression of style.

Yet it's interesting that legacy falls in the lower half for me, and what I see out of the overall flow of my rankings is that I'm more concerned with the fullest expression of life here and now than any concern for what comes afterward.

I also see an emphasis on wanting to experience, express and fulfill on the potential of my own life as being higher than concern for others close to me: intimacy, camaraderie, and family. (Remember: we make no judgments of ourselves in how our rankings fall out—it's all for insight.)

Even though this could be interpreted as selfish or self-centered, it's not like loved ones don't matter to me. But, as in an airplane, you have to put on your own oxygen mask before you can be of any service to someone else, even your kid. So, I see that I am intent on fulfilling my fullest Self-expression first, hopefully enabling me to then better provide for and/or model this priority for those closest to me. We have to BE an idea first in order to represent any possibility of it for others.

This reminds me of a story about a father trying to work while his young son kept interrupting him, wanting him to play. To hopefully distract the boy and keep him busy, the father found a large picture of the earth on a page in a magazine. He ripped it out and tore the page into many tiny pieces. He gave all the pieces to his son saying, "Here buddy, here's a jigsaw puzzle for you to work on. See if you can tape all of these together to make a picture of the earth."

The man thought this would buy him some quality work time as his son figured out how to put it all together. However, in only a minute or two, his son returned with the completed page of the earth, taped together in perfect order. Chagrined, the father asked his son how he was able to assemble it so fast. His son flipped over the page, revealing a picture of a man's face and replied, "I saw this man on the other side and easily put him together. I guess when you have the man together, the world comes together too."

2. *Did you experience resistance or confusion? If so, why do you believe you did?*

Only when initially judging my first-blush rankings, thinking that a "better" person would have ranked family, intimacy, legacy, global welfare and even fun a lot higher than I did. However, as you see in my insights from the prior question, I remembered that, for the sake of our truest Self-expression, these surveys must remain a judgement-free zone.

3. *What items ranked higher than you would have expected?*

None of the higher ranked elements surprised me, for who I am now.

4. *What items ranked lower than you would have expected?*

I'm a bit surprised that approval and fairness ranked so low. Given my history, I would have thought they'd rank higher.

5. *Have these values changed over time? If so, why do you believe that is?*

On a first-blush scan, the overall feel for this list is probably close to what it would have been twenty to thirty years ago, save for a few shifts in position. I believe worthiness and approval would have nearly swapped places because, at that time, I was much more focused on the need for outside versus internal validation. It took many years into adulthood to realize the depth of worthiness issues within me.

Also, affluence and intimacy would have each ranked respectively higher because of my earlier belief that amassing wealth was the key focus of life, together with my then-belief in a naive concept of unconditional, romantic love. At the time, those both seemed to be the solvers-of-all-issues; but, though still important, they are no longer the be-all and end-all pillars upon which my life stands.

Lastly, serenity ranks higher than I believe it used to and, perhaps accordingly, affluence is lower. Again, from my teens up through college and into my thirties, I was very outwardly focused on money and getting rich. Back then, I don't think I even knew the word serenity, whereas now it is of higher importance than a lot of other elements that previously outranked it. For me, perhaps serenity and affluence have had an inverse relationship.

6. *How might you express your highest current values in bigger and better ways?*

Again, I notice what seem to be timeless Feeling & Experiencing values more often ranking higher than more ephemeral values with, as mentioned, a focus on having my world in order so as to spill over to a bigger world in order. I see that I want to play fully *now* rather than place a lot of concern on what comes afterward. Lastly, though I have attempted in the past to have fun and leisure be my main focus, I'm wired to feel a certain amount of fulfillment through effort and accomplishment and, therefore, rank work before play.

Overall, since it's been said that we should teach what we want to learn, to express my highest-ranking values in a greater way would be to promote and share them.

Darrell's Responses

Being & Interaction Values

Ranked in order of importance, with 1 being highest in value and 20 being lowest.

1. __4__ Competent—skilled and capable
2. __2__ Authentic—truthful and genuine
3. __8__ Self-Sufficient—autonomous and free
4. __1__ Self-Expressed—sharing gifts and ideas
5. __3__ Creative—inspired and inventive
6. __12__ Accountable—where the buck stops
7. __16__ Determined—driven and ambitious
8. __6__ Brave—daring and heroic
9. __7__ Trustworthy—honest and steadfast
10. __11__ Dependable—reliable and responsible
11. __13__ Supportive—encouraging and compassionate
12. __9__ Smart—intelligent and quick
13. __14__ Friendly—gracious and affable
14. __20__ Reasonable—sensible and practical
15. __5__ Progressive—embracing change, progress and improvement
16. __10__ Tolerant—open-minded and forgiving
17. __17__ Reverent—respectful and honoring
18. __19__ Graceful—refined and elegant
19. __15__ Patient—enduring and accommodating
20. __18__ Orderly—neat and tidy

My insights about My Being and Interaction Values

1. *What do you notice from ranking your list?*

   In Being & Interaction values, I see that I won't sell out for niceties over the solid truth of who I am and expressing that in creative ways. I obviously have little regard for reasonableness or respect for either the past or proper protocol. It looks like bold truth comes first, then value structures supporting that truth (self-sufficient, accountable) and only then the niceties and manners around delivery (supportive, friendly). It seems I'd rather others understand who I am, what I believe and anything I have to offer in the most integrous way than to put much stock in style, form or propriety.

2. *Did you experience resistance or confusion? If so, why do you believe you did?*

   Not so much resistance as a challenging time of evaluating each one over the others. I truly had to pick #1 and then ask myself, "If I could only have one of the remaining values, which would it be?" It worked. Often, however, I experienced a pull to go with what would be the good and seemingly "right" next value instead of how I really felt. I had to remember that I'm only doing this for myself, not to justify or prove myself to anyone.

3. *What items ranked higher than you would have expected?*

   None ranked higher than I would have expected.

4. *What items ranked lower than you would have expected?*

   Supportive and friendly ranked lower than I would have expected given my current self-concept. Yet, considering the choices, they obviously aren't as important as other key values. Also, determined is a value that I used to covet much more than I do now. Blind or driven ambition doesn't do it for me anymore.

5. *Have these values changed over time? If so, why do you believe that is?*

   I think the fact that self-expressed and authentic show up on top, while graceful and reverent pull up the rear shows that I now have much less regard for appearances and doing what's "right" versus a solid, what-you-see-is-what-you-get, earnest offering of my Self. Also, I now have a deep respect for structures like accountability holding me in line, as opposed to the ball-and-chain I may have previously perceived it to be. I've learned how easily I can stray.

6. *How might you express your highest current values in bigger and better ways?*

Many of my highest-ranking Being & Interaction Values harken back to some Self Expression Directives found in the Discovery & Expression analyses of serious and significant events or influences of my past. Therefore, one surefire way to express these values in a greater way is to truly live by those Directives— those pointers toward my Back Forty Future, which are Bold (Brave) Self-expression, Authenticity, Self-trust (trustworthy to my own Self, and then to others).

Also, developing increasingly more competence in my bold, authentic and creative Self-expression is what this whole experiment called The Back Forty is about for me, so I'll keep plowing that field.

Darrell's Responses
Orientation & Focus Values

Ranked in order of importance, with 1 being highest in value and 16 being lowest.

1. __7__ Freedom—operating independently without many constrictions
2. __10__ Influence—impacting people, situations and organizations
3. __16__ Stability—grounded, conventional and preferring what is foreseeable

4. __5__ Spirituality—awareness of a greater power or presence
5. __4__ People—interacting with others in community, friendships and close relationships
6. __1__ Growth—pursuing ongoing education, training and personal development
7. __14__ Winning—driven to overcome obstacles and come out ahead
8. __11__ Service—selflessly helping others or contributing to a cause
9. __3__ Adventure—seeking to explore, see and do new things
10. __2__ Creativity—original and inventive from a unique vision
11. __15__ Directing—calling the shots and responsible for results
12. __8__ Balance—blending all aspects of life into a unified whole
13. __13__ Riches—amassing large amounts of money, property or other assets
14. __9__ Proficiency—being the best at what you do, the expert in an area
15. __12__ Family—focused on the welfare and primary relationships of home
16. __6__ Joy—doing what is joyful and fulfilling in the moment

My Insights about My Orientation & Focus Values

1. What do you notice from ranking your list?

First, I noticed how extremely difficult this Orientation & Focus Values list was to rank! Though on the other lists I've successfully used a method of finding my #1 and then asking "If I could only have one of the remaining values, which would it be?" this list was more challenging. Therefore, after completing the ranking for the first time, I used a check system of going back and comparing each higher ranking item to the one just below it, asking "Would I choose to have #1 before #2? Would I choose to have #2 before #3?" working my way down the list again. Turns out I stuck with my first, gut choices, but they were very tough. Yet, I see that, by forcing myself to choose, I gained some valuable insights.

2. *Did you experience resistance or confusion? If so, why do you believe you did?*

Not resistance and not true confusion, but challenging choices.

3. *What items ranked higher than you would have expected?*

None are necessarily higher than I would have expected, given my current self-concept.

4. *What items ranked lower than you would have expected?*

Spirituality, service and family all ranked lower than I would have thought in the grand scheme of these choices. Also, I see that I'm less committed to freedom, directing and winning than I might have thought. It looks like I'd be willing to give up a sense of being "in charge" and winning for the sake of connecting to my growing Self, to people and to a zest for living.

5. *Have your values changed over time? If so, why do you believe that is?*

Balance is higher than it would have been many years ago, as I now have an appreciation for that critical element in my life. On the other hand, influence is lower than it was previously because I now possess a more operative radar for anything that smacks of my ego running the show. Making a difference is important, for sure. Yet, influence for influence's sake or to prove my worth is not how I'm currently wired.

6. *How might you express your highest current values in bigger and better ways?*

Were I to even operate with only my top six to eight Orientation
& Focus Values at the forefront of my mind and spirit, modeling and demonstrating them to my Self, I can only imagine that
a radical Back Forty Future couldn't help but unfold. Of course,
service ranked lower than I would have expected. Yet, I would
imagine that just by living and Being my top Orientation &
Focus Values, I would be providing a great service to humanity.

Darrell's Responses

Work Values/Elements

Scored independently in terms of importance on a scale of 1 to 3, with 1
being a higher priority and 3 being lower.

1. __2__ Teamwork—solving problems or addressing issues
   through group efforts
2. __2__ Stability—permanence of a job and assurance
   of income
3. __2__ Risk—going into unchartered waters of a situation,
   idea or industry
4. __1__ Wealth—in a position to receive a great deal of money
   and amass assets
5. __2__ Precision—dealing with meticulous and strict matters
   or materials
6. __2__ Challenge—dealing regularly with tough issues and
   problems to be solved
7. __1__ Learning—engrossed in topics involving higher
   knowledge or development
8. __3__ Pressure—intense involvements where time and
   performance are critical
9. __2__ Beauty—focus on areas involving aesthetics and
   the emotions
10. __3__ Management—directing the efforts and results of others

11. __1__ Solitude—working primarily alone with little interaction with others

12. __1__ Flexibility—opportunity to manage work responsibilities around own schedule

13. __1__ Stimulation—finding enthusiasm and joy in the work

14. __1__ Exposure—on the front line and working with the outside world

15. __3__ Competition—going head to head with others or outside entities to win

16. __1__ Artistic—engaging with materials and projects of a creative nature

17. __2__ Diversity—work that involves continually changing duties and roles

18. __3__ Association—known as belonging to an organization or enterprise

19. __2__ Authority—definitive decider of directions and actions to be taken by others

20. __1__ Acknowledgement—noticed and appreciated for the work

21. __1__ Wide Impact—affecting community or society as a whole

22. __1__ Freedom—calling my own shots and determining my way

23. __1__ Camaraderie—growing deeper connections with others and coworkers

24. __1__ Ethical—abiding by a code of principles important to me

25. __1__ Helping—being of direct assistance to individuals in need

26. __1__ Smart—the most astute on a subject

27. __1__ Originality—designing new ideas or approaches to old problems

28. __2__ Constancy—a steady and predictable focus of attention and workflow

29. __1__ Impact—able to affect overall courses of direction or groups of people

30. __3__ Volume—a large amount of issues or items to be dealt with

My Insights about My Work Values and Elements

1. *What do you notice from scoring each element?*

    I notice that certain values that I rated as 2 are those I don't feel I absolutely *need* and yet are not elements I would necessarily avoid either. For the most part, the 1s were very clear, except for wealth, as I don't want to operate from the need of it. Yet, with the inclusion of the idea "in a position to receive. . ." I felt comfortable rating it as a 1 because I am wholeheartedly willing to attract wealth as well as take all the actions I'm joyfully inspired to take to allow and receive it.

    Beauty was a little challenging in that, although I'm all about emotions, I haven't necessarily been one to exert a hugely critical eye toward aesthetics.

    I find it interesting that I can clearly rate both solitude and exposure as 1, likely due to my wide range of sensibilities as both an introverted writer/thinker and an extroverted teacher.

    The lack of need to compete with anyone other than myself nor the desire to attach to anyone's coattails for gaining esteem by association had me rate both association and competition a 3. *I do* wonder if I'm fooling myself a bit.

    Seemingly very similar ideas rated differently, probably due to conscious and/or subconscious associations with the terms. For example, I rated teamwork a 2 because, again, I don't *need* it so much when I'm in my creative/artistic mode, and yet I rated camaraderie a 1 because a close sense of relationship with those with whom I work is important.

    I'm an overall honest guy, sure, and yet ethical got a 1 only because I'm not interested in some pre-ordained or even societally-sanctioned proclamation of ethics. I value thinking for myself.

Though bearing no significance, I notice that I had only 5 values rated at 3 with 9 at 2, and the majority, 16, at 1. It's a good thing I am self-employed, as that might be a tall order for any outside employer to fill!

2. *Did you experience resistance or confusion? If so, why do you believe you did?*

No. This flowed easily, and I only reviewed it once afterwards to confirm my first-blush, gut-reaction rankings, changing none.

3. *What items scored higher than you would have expected?*

Despite all the explanations offered in Question 1 above, none scored higher than expected.

4. *What items scored lower than you would have expected?*

For all the explanations offered in Question 1 above, none scored lower than expected.

5. *Have these values changed over time? If so, why do you believe that is?*

I believe many of the values I rated as 3 were probably more important when I was younger because of the general, societally-accepted expectations that I adopted from business school (valid or not), which included these as key elements of success: climbing the corporate ladder toward management; a desire and the chops to engage in risk and competition; the ability to endure pressure; and the power of association. Again, I'm not immune to some of these now, and yet I've become attuned to my own sensibilities in contrast to those enculturated by a capital-based educational system needing to keep the corporate machines turning and offices filled.

6. *How might you express your highest current values in bigger and better ways?*

Given my answer to Question 5, perhaps a continued or turbo-boosted commitment to independent, original and creative living—following the beat of my own drum—will allow my greatest Self-expression to continue to unfold.

Darrell's Responses

Workplace Environment Values

Scored independently in terms of importance on a scale of 1 to 5 (1 = absolutely required; 2 = highly desired; 3 = desired; 4 = unimportant; 5 = avoid completely).

1. __1__ Balance—valuing the holistic individual including family and personal life
2. __3__ Independence—offering work involving little interaction with others
3. __3__ Communication—front-line contact with people in or outside my organization
4. __3__ Management—presenting opportunities to direct and supervise the efforts of others
5. __4__ Velocity—emphasis on a rapid pace and volume of activity
6. __3__ Low Stress—offering consistent, reliable and frustration-free work
7. __2__ Adventure—supporting bold actions or risky endeavors
8. __2__ Affiliation—where development of close personal relationships can be expected
9. __5__ Exacting—involving clear-cut, rigid or meticulous processes or standards
10. __1__ Freedom—autonomy and control over schedule and direction of involvements
11. __5__ High Pressure—involvements and settings of an intense and time-critical nature

12. __2__ Artistic—emphasis on projects involving artistic media

13. __1__ Significance—centering on matters of extreme import and magnitude

14. __3__ Appreciation—where individual contributions are noticed and recognized

15. __2__ Leadership—encouraging authentic influence rather than chain of command

16. __3__ Teamwork—stressing group engagement and accomplishment

17. __3__ Loyalty—mutual high regard between individuals, management and organization

18. __2__ Status—involved in high-profile work or with an organization of popular regard

19. __1__ Equal Opportunity—valuing and rewarding all individual contributors

20. __3__ Beneficence—generosity of the organization in terms of benefits and perks

21. __1__ Portability—offering moves throughout the organization, country or planet

22. __2__ Challenging—pushing the personal envelope in terms of overcoming and growth

23. __4__ Physical—engaged in work of bodily skill or strength

24. __5__ Hierarchy—structured around conservative lines of control and decision making

25. __1__ Enthusiasm—work of an exciting nature or involving invigorating elements

26. __1__ Fulfillment—affording opportunity and structures to reach one's highest potential

27. __2__ Diversity—involving people and ideas from varied cultures and backgrounds

28. __2__ Like-mindedness—alignment with organizational values, ethics and goals

29. __2__ Expansion—where one can anticipate upward growth
and development

30. __1__ Mobility—incorporating a high degree of travel

31. __1__ Contribution—priority on serving humanity and the
world as a whole

32. __2__ Liberal—unstructured and flexible in terms of goals
and direction

33. __2__ Variety—including diverse and constantly shifting
areas of involvement

34. __1__ Intelligence—high regard for knowledge, expertise and
professional development

35. __2__ Community—located within an area that fulfills
personal and family needs

36. __2__ Stability—a structure that ensures continuity of work
and reliability of income

37. __1__ Profits—enabling highest personal earnings and
asset development

38. __1__ Creativity—involved in designing new ideas
or approaches

39. __5__ Competitive—emphasizing challenge among
co-workers and/or other organizations

40. __3__ Environment—workspaces which enhance social,
creative, and ergonomic comfort

My Insights about My Workplace Environment Values

1. *What do you notice from scoring each element?*

I notice that it may be somewhat difficult, as a self-employed
person, to answer many of these, which relate more to large
organizations with corporate structures. That was the design of
the survey, yet it doesn't relate to me as much. I answered from
the point of view of my job as a writer, coach, and head of a

small business with co-workers/staff, clients, partners, affiliates and locations of virtual and live program operation.

Interesting to note that I scored both diversity and like-mindedness as highly desired.

I could write a paragraph for every score I gave; let it suffice to say that I see that I am all for egalitarian and democratic independence of structure and thought to inspire creativity and individual contribution with acknowledgment for that contribution. It's apparent that I want to be involved in something that will shake up the world and make a difference for humanity and that I am not a fit for more rigid, stable, steady-as-she-goes issues or pressurized work schedule, though stability of income does rank high. Creativity- and ingenuity-promoting environments seem to score highest.

2. *Did you experience resistance or confusion? If so, why do you believe you did?*

No. Again, the only slight rethinking was to see what I do in my "job" as an independent business owner and to think of how all of these elements show up outside of an employer-employee structure.

3. *What items scored higher than you would have expected?*

I suppose, being honest with myself, stability scored a bit higher than I would have expected. Despite my desire for free-wheeling creativity and autonomy, I am nonetheless able to best capitalize on that creativity when the foundational structures of steady and reliable income are present.

4. *What items scored lower than you would have expected?*

Management scored lower than I would have expected. Yet, it's true that I'm happiest when co-workers/staff are self-driven and self-initiating. I like it when others can do their jobs with no need for interference, much less understanding, from me.

5. *Have these values changed over time? If so, why do you believe that is?*

In line with the insights from the earlier survey on Work Values/ Elements, I believe discovering for my Self—through my Front Forty of R & D—that I'm not the corporate-climbing, business magnate I thought I went to business school to become, I have settled into a more flexible, liberal and creative relationship with my Self, my work and the corresponding work environments.

6. *How might you express your highest current values in bigger and better ways?*

Continued growth in developing a business with models that facilitate the sharing and incorporating of *best ideas and practices* while also supporting freedom, flexibility, creativity and mobility seems to be the path to go. Virtual and online programs and product development are likely to become greater routes to pursue.

And now an additional summary question:

7. *Drawing from the five values surveys taken thus far, what are your greatest insights about what's important for you to express now? E-Valuate yourself and journal on your three greatest insights about where you are now and the directions you see that you want to move in life, in work, in your overall Self-expression.*

So much insight and awareness from these various lists! To encapsulate my three greatest insights:

First, I see that I am a very different person than I was twenty to thirty years ago and correspondingly E-Valuate life quite differently. I'm not one for the youthfully encouraged path of safety and integration into established structures, but rather, more of a pursuer of a road less traveled. Perhaps I'm simply rationalizing why none of those structures worked for me—the corporate job, the home in the suburbs—and yet, in keeping with the philosophy of The Back Forty, all the R & D put into experimenting with the externally offered and encouraged path netted great awareness of my true, internal wiring and sensibilities. In other words, what I've seen and experienced has shown me what I don't want.

Second, I perceive myself as a sort of soldier for creative and independent thought, for Self-discovery, for equality of opportunity and contribution, for growth and expansion beyond prescribed or perceived limits, for freedom to express and excel on a battleground of centered and balanced compassion and inner fortitude. No doubt whatsoever exists of the tie between this ingrained mission and all of the formative serious and significant events or influences of my past. These values surveys drive home the point even further that "your entire life has been a uniquely powerful laboratory for the discovery and expression of something," whether we know what it is or not. The Front Forty has carved out a second-half values system, which I appreciate being able to see so clearly.

Third, it's time to run with my own values. I can truly say I own these Back Forty values because they were forged and strengthened by my own experience and experiments. This is what an examined life affords: the ability to think versus regurgitate or replicate or, worse, live from non-thought/ default value systems altogether.

The unexamined life is not worth living. —*Socrates*

DARRELL'S PUZZLE PIECES OF PURPOSE

DARRELL'S SELF EXPRESSION DIRECTIVES FROM *PAST* SERIOUS AND SIGNIFICANT EVENTS OR INFLUENCES

Includes Directives from Embrace 1, Embrace 5 and Appendix A

Self-love	Accentuate the Positive	Begin Again (. . .and again. . . and again)	Do Your Best
Self-acceptance	Bold Self Expression	Stay Open and Flexible (no matter how solid things appear)	Wake Up and Listen to the Universe
Self-compassion	Self-reliance	Trust a Bigger Plan than My Own	Get Real
Self-trust	Grow. . .and Go Forward	Milk the Void	Humility

Authenticity	Know Thy Under-Stuff Self	Pre-Plan My Pain or Just Vision	Authenticity
The Power of Belief	Be Here Now	Know Myself First-hand	
Belief that Change is Possible	Resilience	Integrity is Everything	
Self-esteem Renewal (at any age)	Find the Light amid Any Darkness	Never Give Up! Never Give Up! Never Give Up!	

DARRELL'S SELF EXPRESSION DIRECTIVES FROM *PRESENT* SERIOUS AND SIGNIFICANT EVENTS OR INFLUENCES ANALYSES[20]

BE Happy (special emphasis on the BE)	Spiritualizing ALL of Life	Forthcoming-ness	Express My Self NOW!
BE Peace (vs. right)	Patience	Authenticity	Be of Service with My Gifts NOW!
Centered Allowance for the Labs of Others	Acceptance	Stability	Align My Activities with My Authentic Self NOW!
Empowered Non-attachment (to things and ego)	Gratitude	Peace	Make Self Expression Time a Sacred Investment

---

20 Includes directives from analyses shared in this book (Embrace 2) and from other analyses of then-present serious and significant events or influences when writing the first draft of the manuscript.

Don't "Sweat" That Small Stuff	Non-Judgment	Trust in the Highest and Greatest Good for All	Know and Extract Others' Greatness

DARRELL'S GIFTS AND TALENTS SELF-SURVEYS

From Embrace 3: Your Gifts

THINGS I DO BETTER THAN THE AVERAGE JOE	ACTIVITIES I ENJOY DOING THAT GIVE ME JUICE	THE ELEMENTS BEHIND THE SURVEY RESULTS	SPECIALIZED SKILLS, KNOWLEDGE, EXPERIENCE, EDUCATION, TRAINING, AND RESOURCES
Communicate and express ideas	Writing and wordsmithing	Fascination with language	Ability to convey ideas
Friendly comfort with all kinds of people	Expressing humor and wit	Quick wit	Speaking and teaching
Humor and quick wit	Performing	Quest for positive attention	Developing workshops and trainings
Technically adept	Interviewing notable people	Inquisitiveness	Conducting teleseminars
Disciplined	Traveling	Social butterfly	Coaching
Focused	Coaching	Fascination with human nature	"Backdoor" job search
Some understanding of human nature	Getting outdoors	Discipline	Recruiting/ headhunting skills

Lover	Meeting people	Helpfulness	Spiritual counseling/ prayer treatment
Affirmative prayer	Engaging in philosophies	Playfulness	Network marketing skills
Conversationalist	Physical fitness	Driven-ness	Internet advertising
Public speaking	Learning golf	Logical thinker	Home business setup
Counseling and coaching	Attending seminars and workshops	Spiritually-oriented	Book writing, editing, publishing, and promotion
Discipline-oriented parenting	Long drives	Boldness	Acting and performing
Singing	Flying	Creative	Enrollment
Daredevil/high adventure	Playing video games with son		Custody and single-parenting issues
Drawing/ artwork	Growing as a marketer		An inspiring transformational community of which I am an official spiritual counselor
Physical Fitness	Reading		1° to 2° connected to many top players in speaking, inspirational and career counseling arenas

Reader and assimilator of ideas	*Meditating and visualizing*		*Positioned at top income levels in a couple personal development-oriented network marketing organizations*
Inspiring leadership	*Making a sale*		*SEP-IRA savings*
Risk-taking			

DARRELL'S GIFTS AND TALENTS BACK FORTY INFORMATION CAMPAIGN INCITE MATRIX
Includes evaluations by family, friends, and associates from Embrace 3

Remember, as mentioned in Embrace 3, I share with you the full, detailed and "incite-ful" feedback from my Back Forty Information Campaign in a free downloadable document at TheBackForty.com/book. I share those replies not because of the particular details but to demonstrate for you the wondrous opportunity this courageous survey affords to gain insight on yourself that you'd never gain otherwise.

What you see on the next page is a matrix I created from those responses in order to assimilate all of the responses in a way that would offer me a big-picture view. It's a compilation of all responses, not a linear representation of responses related to each responder (i.e., entries on a single row are not from the same respondent). The numbers in parentheses (e.g., (4)) represent the number of times that exact/almost-exact same response occurred within a category (column). Tags such as * or ^ or • have been added to show responses of a very similar energy or nature also occurring within a single category (e.g., all entries in a vertical column with an asterisk (*) are similar).

STRENGTHS/ STRONG SUITS	GIFTS, TALENTS, ASSETS, ABILITIES	AREAS TO EXCEL/HAPPY AND FULFILL- ING ROLES	AREAS FOR IMPROVEMENT/ WEAK SUITS	AREAS TO AVOID	OTHER IDEAS TO BE ON PURPOSE
Determined (4)	Ability to speak to anyone; Relating; Meet new people; Good people skills; People person; Being with people (7)	Public/ Motivational speaker (8)	Too much explaining or nagging (2)	Something boring and unfulfilling that pays bills but doesn't lift spirit and leader within; Mundane tasks; Ditchdigger (3)	Permission to be incorrect
Relating to all people; Make friends wherever; Talk to anyone (3) (*)	Speaking/ Oration (5)	Coach (7)	Keep alternatives in mind when coaching job seekers; Challenges with back-door approach (2)	Doggedness; Hanging on when it's time to move on; Doing things same way even if not working (2)	Direct efforts toward gifts
Engaged, dedi-cated, invested, devoted dad (3)	Communicator (4) (*)	Writing/Writer/ Author (6)	Being on time/ Punctuality (2)	Intellectualizing	Think of entire US as a market; Mass media
Taking actions consistent with commitments (3)	Always looking to improve, expand horizons, knowledge and personal growth (4)	Minister/ Pastor/Priest/ Spiritual guide (4) (*)	Need for validation (*)	Focus on people, not numbers	Price according to impact of my approach & lead-ership's impact on bottom line

Inspiring (3)	Ability to motivate/inspire others to greatness/refocus in positive direction (3)	Trainer (4)	Need to belong to a larger group may sacrifice forward progress (*)	Cut down pay-by-hour and one-on-one focus on seminars/groups/TV/print	Ambition clouding true vision and purposeful living (*)
Positive outlook/orientation; Upbeat (3)	Writing; Convey complex issues simply (3)	Teacher/Professor (4)	Designing my life using others' models (*)	Coattails	Allow life to show my purpose rather than ego seeking purpose (*)
Confidence/belief in Self (3)	Listening (2)	Leader; Leading groups/seminars (4)	Depending on others' structures to provide my approval (*)	Pie-in-the-Sky	Self-acceptance and self-appreciation without attachment to ego (*)
Great sense of humor; Quick-witted; Funny and fun (3)	Commitment to contribute (2)	Husband (3)(^)	Stop listening to others selling their own package (*)	Avoid Stress	Find ways to maximize self-expression while earning money
Ability to empathize (2)	Inclusiveness/making people feel welcome and a part of (2)	Father (3)	Distance (^)	Working within a large corporation	Find a new hook

STRENGTHS/ STRONG SUITS	GIFTS, TALENTS, ASSETS, ABILITIES	AREAS TO EXCEL/HAPPY AND FULFILLING ROLES	AREAS FOR IMPROVEMENT/ WEAK SUITS	AREAS TO AVOID	OTHER IDEAS TO BE ON PURPOSE
Natural leader (2)	Sense of humor (2)	Tour/travel guide, with perhaps a spiritual/self-help tone (3)	More openness with others (^)	Avoid certain network marketing companies	Get out of own way
Motivator (2) (^)	Organizational skills/well organized (2)	Counselor (2)	Follow through on meeting team members at events (^)	Technical jobs (*)	Go for "The Leading Expert" based on hard work
Speaking (2)	Focus on personal success AND success of others (2)	Cheerleader (2) (*)	Allay the need for recognition and "outstanding-ness," or ego (°)	Avoid going back to same well of clients	Figure out how to support others in "The Follow Up" (^)
Want to help folks; Want people to be happy, fulfilled and successful (2)	Create community	Career counseling; Guru/Coach (2)	Let go of ego in terms of not knowing how; Have faith and trust (°)	Avoid areas requiring quick sensitivity to a situation	Keep pursuing spiritual until clear I am being spoken to directly (°)

Acknowledge persistence and commitment in setting bar high	Acknowledge continually overcoming limitations, fears, and doubts	Acknowledge honesty and willingness to put myself out there	More concern for others thinking I'm successful than knowing it internally (*)	Know that I'm walking the path I came here for and trusting God's plan (°)
Any role not involved at the top	Roles involving focus on analysis (*)	Quick-profit ideas	Surrender and come to terms with my maker	Anywhere being punctual is critical
Attention to detail with new associates getting started (•)	Providing information for beginners to avoid duplication of effort (•)	Seeing the "Emperor's New Clothes" versus inner wisdom/voice	Network more with others "making it" in areas of similar pursuits	Give and own what you "have"— e.g., experience, knowledge, expertise, passion
Advisor (2)	Lawyer (2)	Transformational work/personal development (2)	Driving people to achieve goals/reach for success (2) (*)	Community builder
Grounded as a man	Safe for women	Dedicated to transformation	Communicating larger concepts/ideas to groups (*)	Natural leader
Perseverance (2)	Focused (2)	Grounded	Loyal	Intelligent

STRENGTHS/ STRONG SUITS	GIFTS, TALENTS, ASSETS, ABILITIES	AREAS TO EXCEL/HAPPY AND FULFILL-ING ROLES	AREAS FOR IMPROVEMENT/ WEAK SUITS	AREAS TO AVOID	OTHER IDEAS TO BE ON PURPOSE
Contemplative	Seeker	Fully actualized intimate relationship (^)	"Iffy" on project follow through	Making-it-happen determination can push things away	More relaxed, smile more, happy
Competitive	Bridge-builder	Directing	Find passion/ purpose that overrides financially driven purpose	Customer service	Be same person regardless of where I am, what I have, who I am, how things are going (*)
"Barnabas"	Drive point home with purpose	Politics	Authenticity	Teaching	Natural leader; Embrace it and expand
Encourager (^)	Curiosity	Human resources	Read more	Day trader; Wall Street; Fast-paced, frantic environments	Be 100% involved in success of team members and upfront about what it takes to succeed (^)

Give strength and courage (^)	Sincere desire to see people succeed	Outplacement firm head	My fresh ideas are mingled with other people's ideas		Don't listen to too many people —the answer is inside of me (°)
Willingness to pursue an approach beyond perceived payoff	Setting and keeping goals	Placement firm head (°)	Generosity		
Ambition	Leading by example	Contract labor services manager (°)	Smart worker versus hard worker		
Guidance	Outreach	Manage groups of doctors, lawyers, engineers to be best in niche	Bull in a china shop		
Sharing/ Conveying life experience for others' benefit	Loyalty	Sharing passion	Ask upfront questions others wouldn't ask		
Will to keep going	Networking	Coordinating	Awareness of possibly hurting others while focused on my gifts and talents		

STRENGTHS/ STRONG SUITS	GIFTS, TALENTS, ASSETS, ABILITIES	AREAS TO EXCEL/HAPPY AND FULFILL- ING ROLES	AREAS FOR IMPROVEMENT/ WEAK SUITS	AREAS TO AVOID	OTHER IDEAS TO BE ON PURPOSE
Good people skills (*)	Focus on being pleasing to others	Running own operation	Do I really want to help or something in return?		
Tactful and professional	Branding process	Settings where I can shine	Does it always have to be my way?		
Attentive to details	Asking insightful questions	Webcasts	Accepting others fully even if I disagree with what they're doing		
Useful insights	Fresh ways of think- ing about things	Inspiring and empowering others (*)	Need elevator pitch covering last 5 years of activities—show relevance		
Ability to bounce back and refocus	Getting people to understand even if contrary to thinking	Network marketing leader	More structure and dedication to running groups		
Willingness to work hard	Discipline to study and learn	Coaching and motivation programs for schoolkids	Let go of the past		

Gift of gab (*)	Debate	Being on stage	Better listener/less interruption
Great Smile	Admit when wrong	Being out there	Impatient about time
Can be very businesslike	Connecting deeply with people	Providing for my family	Comparing to others
Direct (•)	Running seminars	Praying	Need to be busy
Asking for help	Energy and enthusiasm in voice	Meditating	Taking carefree time for self and partner without feeling guilty
Owning up to mistakes	Interest in people's lives	Fighting for a cause	Patience
Great message	Planner	Dealing directly with people/straight conversations (*)	Standing in another's perspective
Goal-oriented	Intellect (^)	Working with people (*)	Heal what's not working with throat
Generous	Sharp mind (^)	Non-profit CEO	Give people I'm leading freedom to choose topics while having a plan B

STRENGTHS/ STRONG SUITS	GIFTS, TALENTS, ASSETS, ABILITIES	AREAS TO EXCEL/HAPPY AND FULFILLING ROLES	AREAS FOR IMPROVEMENT/ WEAK SUITS	AREAS TO AVOID	OTHER IDEAS TO BE ON PURPOSE
Spiritual	Direct and honest communication		Too nice—can be construed as passive		
Warm-hearted	Positive		Too willing to concede		
Ability to build people up (^)	Focused		Be more assertive but maintain integrity/ diplomacy		
Good listener	Explaining concepts/tools to others				
Sincerity; No nonsense; Direct/ forthright (•)	Confidence				
Good mentor	Responsibility				
Identifying strengths and success factors	Ability to keep moving forward toward dreams				

Taking care of body

Romantic

Loving

Understanding

Compassion

Seeing many sides of an issue/subject

Tactful coach without stepping over anything

Humility

Kindness while leading

Ability to digest info/ what's being said

Comprehensive methodology

Resume styles

Outgoing personality (*)

Communication skills

Exercise skills

Workaholic; Fill every minute

Love to be productive

Willingness to play big

Focus on short-term goals

Passionate

STRENGTHS/ STRONG SUITS	GIFTS, TALENTS, ASSETS, ABILITIES	AREAS TO EXCEL/HAPPY AND FULFILL- ING ROLES	AREAS FOR IMPROVEMENT/ WEAK SUITS	AREAS TO AVOID	OTHER IDEAS TO BE ON PURPOSE
Have a high listening for people					
Supportive					
Honesty					
Capacity to follow up with teammates					
Can stay calm and in control					
Patience					
Understanding					

DARRELL'S BEST JOBS IN THE WORLD AND WHY

From Embrace 3: Your Gifts

1. Charlie Rose: paid to do research, to educate himself and then to sit down in a collegial way with influential and intelligent individuals, touted as the experts in their fields, and glean their wisdom in a major media format.

2. Oprah Winfrey: all of the above with the additional role of being a *thought leader,* leading people into areas of thought that she deems to be forward moving for the planet.

3. Tony Robbins, T. Harv Eker and other motivators and workshop leaders: ability to have their life "scheduled" by their teams, so they can then show up and motivate.

4. The late Dr. Wayne Dyer: the ability to inspire and operate like a traveling, lecturing mystic—a devout and almost monkish researcher, writer and spiritual statesman/professor doing the lecture circuit.

5. Esther and the late Jerry Hicks: open recipients of life-altering information, which they then disseminate, benefiting personally from the teachings received while getting the message out to interested and waiting ears.

6. Travel Channel or other "tour guides": getting paid to explore while they take you somewhere else, to a physical place or into a new body of knowledge.

DARRELL'S E-VALUATION SURVEYS

From Embrace 4: Your Values

It's important to know where all of the respective values ranked in the various surveys taken, and yet we might choose to keep our minds focused only on those rising to the top, so I have listed here my top 5 from each ranking survey and all that I scored as having #1 importance to me in the score-based surveys.

Of course, choose for yourself how many of your own responses to include in your own compilation of your Puzzle Pieces of Purpose. Here are mine:

Feeling and Experiencing Values (top 5)

1. Achievement—success and contribution
2. Worthiness—value and self-esteem
3. Wisdom—deep knowledge and insight
4. Spirituality—sensing a bigger plan or direction
5. Serenity—inner calm and peacefulness

Being and Interaction Values (top 5)

1. Self-Expressed—sharing gifts and ideas
2. Authentic—truthful and genuine
3. Creative—inspired and inventive
4. Competent—skilled and capable
5. Progressive—embracing change, progress and improvement

Orientation & Focus Values (top 5)

1. Growth—pursuing ongoing education, training and personal development
2. Creativity—original and inventive from a unique vision
3. Adventure—seeking to explore, see and do new things
4. People—interacting with others in community, friendships and close relationships
5. Spirituality—awareness of a greater power or presence

Work Values/Elements (#1 importance, no specific order)

1. Wealth—in a position to receive a great deal of money and amass assets
2. Learning—engrossed in topics involving higher knowledge or development
3. Solitude—working primarily alone with little interaction with others
4. Flexibility—able to manage work responsibilities around own schedule
5. Stimulation—finding enthusiasm and joy in the work
6. Exposure—on the front line and working with the outside world
7. Artistic—engaging with materials and projects of a creative nature
8. Acknowledgement—noticed and appreciated for the work
9. Wide Impact—affecting community or society as a whole
10. Freedom—calling my own shots and determining my way
11. Camaraderie—growing deeper connections with others and coworkers
12. Ethical—abiding by a code of principles important to me
13. Helping—being of direct assistance to individuals in need
14. Smart—the most astute on a subject
15. Originality—designing new ideas or approaches to old problems
16. Impact—able to affect overall courses of direction or groups of people

Workplace Environment Values (#1 importance, no specific order)

1. Balance—valuing the holistic individual, including family and personal life
2. Freedom—autonomy and control over schedule and direction of involvements

3. Significance—centering on matters of extreme import and magnitude

4. Equal Opportunity—valuing and rewarding all individual contributors

5. Portability—offering moves throughout the organization, country or globe

6. Enthusiasm—work of an exciting nature or involving invigorating elements

7. Fulfillment—affording opportunity and structures to reach one's highest potential

8. Mobility—incorporating a high degree of travel

9. Contribution—priority on serving humanity and the world as a whole

10. Intelligence—high regard for knowledge, expertise and professional development

11. Profits—enabling highest personal earnings and asset development

12. Creativity—involved in designing new ideas or approaches

DARRELL'S TOP 10 REJOICES/1,095-DAY PLEDGES

From Embrace 4: Your Values

Rejoice 1: I'll transform and develop my relationship with my son.

Rejoice 2: I'll transform my relationship with "success," redefining it so that it's not some ending place with a certain amount of money, notoriety and security, but rather a way of living and being.

Rejoice 3: I'll put performance back into my life (e.g., Karaoke, plays).

Rejoice 4: Damn it! I'll finish this book, The Back Forty, an idea I've nursed for over ten years.

Rejoice 5: I'll find my soulmate before I head back to soul.

Rejoice 6: I'll believe that a life of travel is still possible for me.

Rejoice 7: I'll begin reading the great and classic books that I've amassed and fantasized over.

Rejoice 8: I'll dust off, revamp and fulfill my "101 Things to Do Before I Die" list.

Rejoice 9: I'll achieve "success" in my own eyes.

Rejoice 10: I'll adopt and create a 1,095-day game around the motto "Be kinder than necessary. Everyone is facing some kind of battle."

The above collection of my initial Self Expression Directives, Gifts and Values made up my Purpose Puzzle Pieces when I first worked with the Embraces. I let them inform my flight map for being who I came to be and doing what I came to do.

If you have not now done so, gather *your* Puzzle Pieces from the first five Embraces and put them together in a single document for you to use as you move forward in your Back Forty adventure.

ACKNOWLEDGMENTS

It's beyond comprehension to sufficiently acknowledge all of the people, places and programs that have made up the amalgam of my life thus far, which has in turn resulted in this book. As soon as I've listed all the serious and significant events or influences that brought me to the point of completing the book, I will, no doubt, remember yet another direction in which to point gratitude for formative support. Yet, I can only play forward from here and attempt to cast the most comprehensive acknowledgment net as possible.

First, in the most general terms and to catch right off the bat all those complicit in my life and times—more than half a century of laboratory experience—I'd like to thank everyone serving as "laboratory assistants" in my lifelong growth and development. A core message of the Back Forty philosophy is that *everyone* in our lives is a "lab assistant" supporting us in the quest for our own Formula of Unique Self Expression (**FUSE**). Of course, there are too many of those valuable assistants in my life to name individually, yet I will offer this: if you and I have travelled together along life's pathways in any capacity, be it through blood relationship, human relationship, fellows along the road to greater understanding or even seeming foes avoiding awkward glances, to one degree or another, you and I have performed as foundational spear carriers in each other's operas. Without you, I wouldn't have experienced the labs necessary for becoming my ever-evolving, greater-yet-to-be expression of Self.

Neale Donald Walsh's *The Little Soul and The Sun: A Children's Parable*[21] is a kid's book written for adults. It's about a little soul who wants to leave the All-Knowing Oneness of God ("heaven") and come to earth so as to actually *experience* life versus just knowing and being All That There Is. That little soul is offered help by another little soul who agrees to come at the same time to facilitate the first soul's growth in awareness by doing some "thing."

The second little soul tells the first little soul that she will join him on earth to do that "thing" necessary for the him to achieve the awareness he wants to gain. However, the second soul advises the first that, when in the midst of the second soul acting in an apparently dark way, the first soul should not forget *who they really are*, because, after all, the "thing" was only being done to assist.

What's the moral of the story? Ideally what you've already surmised or will surmise through reading *The Back Forty*: that you and I are only ever surrounded by partners and blessings in our own co-created laboratories to become who we came here to be and do what we came here to do and that there's never anyone to forgive and only everyone to thank. . .profusely.

And so, to my family of origin, my love relationships including my first wife, our son and all others who've graciously participated in my lifetime of laboratory experiments thus far, I thank you on the present-day, earthly level *for every single thing* and on the higher-level of our Oneness for this group dance of Becoming.

To now turn these acknowledgements specific, I'll begin with blood first. My mother gets credit for my interest in words and emotional and intellectual pursuits. From an early age, she nudged me to speak grammatically correctly, even when the rest of my environment wasn't concerned. She also encouraged

---

21 *Hampton Roads, 1998.*

me early in high school to pursue excellence in grades. She wanted a lawyer second son. From that point forward, I achieved nearly straight As. Though I didn't become a lawyer, due to her, my love of words and matters of the mind has always been central. Thank you, Mom, for giving me a foundation for the softer side, which I'm only now rediscovering in the second half of life.

I thank my father and brother, the other significant contributors and laboratory assistants in my family of origin. Both my father and brother were and are significant blessings in who I came to be and what I came to do. Both great men, they are powerfully devoted to family and demonstrate solid, Southern male stability. My father showed us that, no matter what, his commitment to family was paramount and he would go wherever and do whatever to ensure his family was taken care of. I am eternally grateful for his and my brother's partnership and environmental-design collaboration, helping me grow in my first gymnasium-of-Becoming. I couldn't be who I now choose to be without their soulular support. Thank you, Larry and Larry.

I want to particularly thank my son, as well as his mother, because the laboratories co-created with them on a higher plane have been the greatest ones of Self-discovery thus far. I thank my son's mother for assisting in the Front Forty dance of discovery of my Self. And I'm so gratefully looking forward to the possibility of radical, pro-active experiments and further discovery and expression together with my son in The Back Forty.

It takes a village to raise a spirit, and I've been fortunate to have several main spirit-raisers, all of whom offered a conscious or an unknowing hand of support in the cultivation of this message. First and foremost is my enduring and long-blessing wife, Alexandra Levin. This Back Forty philosophy proved itself in spades as she came into my life, first as a friend, then as a volunteer manuscript reader, and eventually as my life partner and co-Freedom Flier in designing The Back Forty. The Back Forty message transformed her then-situation in life; and she, in turn, transformed me. Luckily, because she is a sapiophile and loves possibility-oriented discourse, my words and never-ending state of inquiry have kept her around. If I do what works and know what's good for me, I'll stay in such an inquiry.

Alexandra gets sole credit for bringing the possibility of *activating* this Back Forty philosophy into our lives. Otherwise, without the love, intelligence, incite-ability, fun, adventure, stability and structure within which she has encased me, this whole ideology may have been only a novel and passing inspiration. It was simply a skeletal manuscript and forming idea until her partnership brought it, and me, to life in a unique and distinctly Back Forty way. Thank you, babe, for turning the key to start up the ride of our life together.

My second main spirit-raiser is my prayer partner and confidant for many years, Rev. Margaret Shepherd. Throughout the years of her powerful and affirmative prayer support and ever-present prosperous optimism, she had helped build within me a foundation upon which this life-begins-after-40 Back Forty message could be built. She even co-conspired the entrance of my life partner, Alexandra, into my world. Thank you, Margaret.

Third is my friend, stabilizer and personal Yoda, Allen Zadoff. Besides his generous spirit constantly and steadfastly providing his experience, strength and hope in our mutual quest to live right-sized lives, I also appreciate and honor the sense of true brotherly relationship I've rarely experienced in adult life. For his being the centering sounding board, the wise writing-world guide and humility-centered reminder that control is an illusion, I'm forever grateful.

I must also thank the spirit-raising impact of a newly forming family by marriage and reclamation over the last several years: my son, Hunter Gurney and our adult-ish, authentic and grounded relationship; his wonderful partner, Emily Moser; my new and best-ever-mother-in-law, Yelena Levin; my astounding step-daughters, Bella Lerner and Emily Lerner; and their father, Ilia Lerner. Joining with all of you in designing a Back Forty future of family gives me excitement and joy.

As to other influential laboratory environments, I must acknowledge the world of personal development as a whole. Of course, any interest in human potential always starts within: an interest in one's own potential. I'm nowhere near my fullest potential and that thrills me. Thank God there's always someone yet to BE and something yet to DO to move me aspiration-ally forward. I'm grateful for the generations upon generations of seekers, finders and sharers of new thinkings and new teachings of ancient wisdom that make up the world of modern-day self-development.

The number of individuals and organizations to thank on the personal development front is long and varied. I'd like to acknowledge the impacts and lifelong inquiries given me by Werner Erhard, Jerome Downes and the staff and assistants of Landmark Education. Of all the arenas of personal growth I've enjoyed, I always come back to Landmark because there's just no summiting those mountains of ontological understanding and possibility. Thank you to Tovah Love for initially enrolling me in possibility *as a possi-bility* and to all those who've served and whose saws I helped sharpen by providing the rough edges of my own evolvement.

Thank you to Justin Sterling, The Sterling Institute of Relationships, and "the men" for helping integrate a missing piece in my adult life: powerful male relationships. I'm also blessed to have basked in the spiritual aware-nesses of Michael Beckwith and The Agape International Spiritual Center and of Dr. Mark Vierra and Rev. Marc Laponce and The North Hollywood Church of Religious Science. Thanks to Marianne Williamson for alerting us to "our deepest fear" and for a lifetime of conscious impact; Coach Dave Buck for Coachville.com, a play-focused model of growth, and for his tire-lessly playful spirit; Jerry and Esther Hicks for *The Teachings of Abraham* and *The Law of Attraction*; T. Harv Eker for his demonstration of wealth while making a difference; Wayne Dyer for his inspiration and embodiment of a spiritual-leadership role model; Neale Donald Walsh for his *Conversations With God* series; Julia Cameron for her paving of *The Artist's Way;* and Berny Dohrmann (a.k.a. "Dad") of CEO Space International for teaching win-win Oneness in business.

As for those assisting directly with the evolvement of the book itself, I want to thank Jubal Raffety for listening and providing encouraging feedback on the first musings around *The Back Forty* so many years ago; Shauna Markey, Richard Cornfield, Bryan Winter, Janice Long, Rick Hoppe and Craig Greager II of my Landmark group for their accountability support while writing the full first draft; Wendy Taylor for editing the first stages of the beginning manuscript; Elizabeth Estrada for reviewing the initial message and assigning the word "radical" to it; for all of those who joined in the reading and review groups to offer feedback, including Spryte Loriano, Burge Smith-Lyons, Allen Zadoff, Jackie Lapin, Trish Carr, Bud Williams, Liz Raci, Connie Hall, Kathleen Jaap, Diana Zwein and Graciela Schneider; and to the earliest adopters of this book, the Groundbreaker pre-order purchasers, Alesia Jackson, Brian Baird, Glenn Ackerman, Pat Finn, Spryte Loriano, Stacey Bevill, Brian Germain, David Thomas, Donna Blevins, Eugene Mitchell, Lloyd Stone, Maria Mizzi, "JB" John Brown, Liz Apodaca and Troy Hoffman.

Thank you to Alicia Hinkle, who served as my executive assistant when we first began broadcasting The Back Forty possibility some five years ago. Thank you to my "accountability buddy," Eugene Mitchell, who supports me to stay on track with this and many other concurrent projects. And a special thank you goes out to those participating in our first live Back Forty 3-Day INFUSE Programs, trusting us with this process of recontextualizing your lives thus far so as to distinguish the absolute perfection of them for who and what you're here to be and do.

I offer a special shout-out to Joel Roberts, media coach extraordinaire and former prime-time KABC radio talk-show host in the #2 radio market in the world, Los Angeles. It was in a media workshop with Joel, when I was bringing out my first book, that I heard him use the phrase, "Your entire life has been a uniquely powerful laboratory for the discovery and expression of something." That phrase stuck with me and is a through-line in the philosophical makeup of *The Back Forty*.

As we live our lives exposed to a multitude of ideas, philosophies and mindsets, they form a unique amalgam inside each of our emotional, mental and spiritual bodies. It's been said that there's not a new idea on the face of the earth, but only former ideas presented in new ways. I don't doubt that. Yet I also don't doubt that a plethora of ideas from various teachers, when mixed together inside a unique being with his or her own particular sensibilities and perceptions, can emerge in a unique way with a unique voice even though speaking age-old wisdom. I make extreme efforts to attribute everyone I can remember who has influenced me with any particular pearl of such wisdom, and yet the unique string of pearls that became *The Back Forty* formed inside the shell of my own unique experience. I can't comprehensively cite the origins of my particular string but hope that my sharing of it encourages the reader to crack open and expose the beauty of their own unique string of pearls.

I offer thanks to those assisting in the final production of the book. First, thanks to my God-send of an editor, Kay Derochie. After cultivating and nurturing this message and manuscript for many years, I behaved like a doting grandmother, extremely cautious and picky as to who I'd entrust my favored child to. Putting your baby under the knife, even if you know surgery is necessary, is a big decision; and I was no less protective of the manuscript than Gollum over "my precious." Kay was the perfect midwife, surgeon and nursemaid to care for this baby, and her thumbprint of expertise in the areas of self-help, spirituality and recovery are evident in the final version.

I also want to thank my book cover designer, Liana Moisescu, for capturing the multi-faceted makeup of this Back Forty idea inside of one simple image. Who doesn't want to see themselves at midlife (when small-self questions abound as to what one has to "show" for themselves and their accumulated years on the planet) as being mighty and strong? Also, who doesn't want to see themselves at a ripening or ripe age just as young, vital and strapping as any sprig just starting out? The reflection on the cover, accordingly, goes both ways. That's what The Back Forty is all about: *starting out* from wherever we currently are as the *perfect* place from which to be and do what we came for and knowing that inside of that small s self is a mighty and strong Big S Self just waiting to reflect back upon Itself.

For the book's interior, I want to thank Tamara Dever and Marisa Jackson for also assuming midwife and nursemaid roles in birthing the message's textual design. Many authors and readers are unaware of the incredible complexity involved in creating an inviting read. With the multiple levels of headings, lists, exercises, quotes, surveys and graphs involved in this comprehensive midlife-makeover book, Marisa's abilities to invite the reader into the book as warmly as to any cuddle-up novel has been priceless.

Lastly, I want to thank those of you who over the last twenty years ever heard me ask, "What if the first half of life was only R & D, research and development, for who you came here to be and what you came here to do? What if your biggest game is yet to come?" and responded with a smile, a laugh, an easing of the brow or even a momentary illumination of possibility in the corner of your eye. It was that consistent and reliably positive response that propelled me, through my own ongoing research and development, to pursue the vision that would become this book.

I once had a friend who decided to get married for the first time in his mid-40s. I asked him, "So, it took you this long to find the right one?" He answered, "No, it took me this long to become the right one." Whether it took me twenty years or twenty lifetimes, I thank everyone who has helped me finally become the right one to birth *The Back Forty*.

ABOUT THE AUTHOR

DARRELL W. GURNEY has thirty years' experience as an executive, business and career advisor; speaker; workshop facilitator, author and licensed spiritual counselor. He presents to professional, trade and community groups as well as MBA programs and university alumni organizations nationwide.

Darrell is a known leader when it comes to creating and living your best life. Drawing on his business expertise and his own personal development experience, he supports individuals in designing fulfilling careers and prosperous businesses and in expanding their personal lives.

After graduating summa cum laude from the University of Texas at Austin and obtaining degrees in finance and international business from the honors program of The Red McCombs School of Business and gaining experience with Arthur Young (now Ernst & Young), one of the then "Big 8" accounting firms, Darrell moved to the world of entertainment with MGM/United Artists. His career thereafter has been primarily devoted to coaching individuals seeking greater expression in their work lives and in the pursuit of purpose. He offers both live and online programs and workshops to provide the conscious nudge individuals need to become the best version of themselves.

His first two books, *Headhunters Revealed: Career Secrets for Choosing and Using Professional Recruiters* and *Never Apply for a Job Again: Break the Rules, Cut the Line, Beat the Rest,* teach professionals how to ensure that time spent in their work, one-third to one-half of their lives, is thoroughly rewarding.

Darrell lives with his wife and fellow Back Forty Flier and Co-Founder, Alexandra Levin, in Long Beach, California. They enjoy being sandwiched between their octogenarian parents and adult children, as they create their second halves of life as their best halves.

More information and availability for interviews, presentations and programs can be found at TheBackForty.com and CareerGuy.com and in the Support and Solutions listing on the following pages.

INDEX

SUPPORT AND SOLUTIONS FROM THE BACK FORTY

THE BACK FORTY™ PLAYGAME COACHING

Expand yourSelf as a committed player in your Back Forty of infinite growth potential, all inside a model of coaching that emphasizes play, mastery and becoming. Produce the results you really want for a second half/best half of life while having fun doing it. You worked your way to results in the first half. From now on, play your way forward.

WORKSHOPS AND SEMINARS
Online and Live—For Individuals and Groups

Our workshops and seminars, including The Back Forty™ INFUSE Program (**I**gniting a **N**ew **F**ormula of **U**nique **S**elf-**E**xpression) and The Back Forty™ Re-NEW-ALL Program, are designed to immerse you in the mindset and community necessary to design your second half of life as your best half.

THE BACK FORTY™ BUSINESS AND CAREER COACHING

If retirement ("drawing back") is not as appealing as playing your way forward in your career or business life, know that you have infinite growth potential still to be cultivated. You're never too old to do what you came here to do. Explore and build your future using our proven career-transition and business-building methods.

KEYNOTES AND PRESENTATIONS

Invite Darrell and Alexandra to speak for your group, company or professional organization. With their combined professional backgrounds in coaching, consulting, human resources, leadership development and organizational design and their passion for consciousness/personal/spiritual growth and development, they bring a lively and inspired joyful awareness to your audience to create mindful and motivated teams.

THE BACK FORTY™ MIDLIFE FLIERS & ACCOUNTABILITY ALLIANCE

Support and expand your Back Forty second half by participating in a thriving and engaged Facebook© group, accountability groups or one of our social media venues.

To learn more about The Back Forty™ and support offerings:
Call: 732-663-9463 (SECOND WIND) · Email: Engage@TheBackForty.com
Visit: www.TheBackForty.com/book

ALSO AVAILABLE

FROM THE BACK FORTY TEAM

The Back Forty™ IMBUE Journal
Inspiring Massive Beauty Uniquely Expressed

Treat yourself to a gift that will support tender loving care of your self-esteem around body, mind and spirit. Written by The Back Forty co-founder Alexandra Levin for those who've ever had the thought that anything about them was less than perfect.

Available on Amazon Now

Made in the USA
Middletown, DE
22 July 2022

69671397R00328